To Richard

with best regards

Tom

July 2000

The British Brass Band

THE BRITISH BRASS BAND

A Musical and Social History

Edited by Trevor Herbert

OXFORD

UNIVERSITY PRESS

OXFORD
UNIVERSITY PRESS

Great Clarendon Street, Oxford OX2 6DP

Oxford University Press is a department of the University of Oxford
It furthers the University's objective of excellence in research, scholarship,
and education by publishing woldwide in

Oxford New York

Athens Auckland Bangkok Bogotá Buenos Aires Calcutta
Cape Town Chennai Dar es Salaam Delhi Florence Hong Kong Istanbul
Karachi Kuala Lumpur Madrid Melbourne Mexico City Mumbai
Nairobi Paris São Paulo Singapore Taipei Tokyo Toronto Warsaw
and associated companies in Berlin Ibadan

Oxford is a registered trade mark of Oxford University Press
in the UK and certain other countries

Published in the United States
by Oxford University Press Inc., New York

British Library Cataloguing in Publication Data

Data available

Library of Congress Cataloging in Publication Data
The British brass band : a musical and social history / edited by Trevor Herbert.
p. cm.
Rev. and enl. ed. of: Bands : the brass band movement in the 19th and 20th centuries. 1991.
Includes discography, bibliographical references, and index.
1. Brass bands—Great Britain. I. Herbert, Trevor. II. Title: Bands.
ML1331.1.B75   2000   784.9'0941—dc21   99–057637
ISBN 0–19–816698–2

1 3 5 7 9 10 8 6 4 2

Typeset by Graphicraft Ltd., Hong Kong
Printed in Great Britain
on acid-free paper by
Biddles Ltd
Guildford & Kings Lynn

PREFACE

—◦—

This book is based on another which was published in 1991. It had the title
Bands: The Brass Band Movement in the Nineteenth and Twentieth Centuries,
and was a volume in the Open University Press series, 'Popular Music in
Britain'. The opportunity to reissue the book in a greatly revised and extended
form with Oxford University Press was greeted with enthusiasm by myself and
my fellow contributors.

The present volume is considerably different from the book published in
1991, though evidence of the earlier book will be apparent to anyone who
knows it. Four chapters from the original volume (Chapters 1, 2, 3, and 6) are
retained in this one, but they are all revised, and in some cases extensively
rewritten. Chapter 4 was a technical appendix in the 1991 book, but it is now,
more properly I think, brought into the main body of the book. Two chapters
which appeared in the 1991 book are not published here, but much of their
subject-matter has been retained in other chapters.

Three chapters in this volume are entirely new. I felt that Salvation Army
bands received inadequate coverage in the 1991 volume, and that matter is put
to rights here with an entire chapter devoted to the subject. Chapters 7 and 8,
which deal respectively with repertoire and performance practice, provide the
book with a more musical focus, another element which was lacking in the
earlier volume. There are other features of this volume which are entirely new:
the introduction, most of the appendices, the bibliography, and further end-
matter, as well as several new illustrations and tables.

As more than half of the book is either new or entirely revised, I decided that
it would be misleading to allow it to be published with the same title as the
1991 volume. The original volume came about through the visionary idea of a
series which would provide a critical history of British popular music. I and the
other contributors to *Bands* are proud to have been a part of that series, and,
for my part, I lament the fact that the series was not more extensive and more
widely disseminated. The series acted as something of a catalyst for the study
of the history of British popular music, and I am extremely grateful to the
series editors, Richard Middleton and Dave Harker, as well as to the original
publishers, for the part which they played in stimulating the work which has
resulted in the present volume.

Acknowledgements

∞

I wish to acknowledge my gratitude to those who have given permission to reproduce pictures and quotations in this book. The details of such permissions are given below.

I wish to thank staff of the Library of The Open University for services which they provided when this volume was in preparation, and also to other librarians and archivists too numerous to mention by name.

I am especially grateful to Bruce Philips at Oxford University Press, who enthusiastically encouraged the preparation of this volume and also Helen Foster, who steered it through the production process. The index was prepared promptly and expertly by Annette Musker.

I owe an incalculable debt to Dr Helen Barlow, who assisted me in my own researches, prepared the bibliography, and copy-edited the book before its submission. My contributors and I have much to thank her for.

Individual contributors have acknowledged debts of gratitude in notes to their chapters. From my point of view, my greatest debt is to them, the contributors, who cooperated fully and amicably in the preparation of the book. I hope that the final product does justice to their endeavours.

T.H.

Cardiff
August 1998

Permissions

ᴇᴏ·

Acknowledgement for kind permission to reproduce illustrations, music examples, and other material is due to the following:

Fig. 2.5*a*–*b*: Hulton Getty Images.

Fig. 3.1: By courtesy of the Sussex Archaeological Society.

Fig. 3.2: Trevor Herbert.

Fig. 3.3: Lewes Town Council. Photography: Richard Carter.

Fig. 4.1: Cyfarthfa Castle Museum, Merthyr Tydfil, and John Webb, Esq., Padbrook, Wiltshire respectively. Photography: Antonia Reeve, Edinburgh.

Figs. 4.2, 4.3, 4.8, 4.10, 4.11: The Edinburgh University Collection of Historic Musical Instruments. Photography: Antonia Reeve, Edinburgh.

Fig. 4.4: Frank Tomes, Esq., Merton Park. Photography: Antonia Reeve, Edinburgh.

Fig. 4.5: The Edinburgh University Collection of Historic Musical Instruments and Arnold Myers, Esq., Edinburgh, respectively. Photography: Antonia Reeve, Edinburgh.

Fig. 4.6: The Edinburgh University Collection of Historic Musical Instruments and Christopher Baines, Esq., Burford, respectively. Photography: Antonia Reeve, Edinburgh.

Fig. 4.7: The Stalybridge Band. Photography: Antonia Reeve, Edinburgh.

Fig. 4.9: Cyfarthfa Castle Museum, Merthyr Tydfil, and the Edinburgh University Collection of Historic Musical Instruments, respectively. Photography: Antonia Reeve, Edinburgh.

Fig. 8.1: Bradford and Bingley Building Society.

Fig. 8.4: Margaret Mortimer.

Ex. 4*a*–*d*, 5, 6*a*–*b*, 8, Novello & Co. Ltd.

Ex. 7*a*–*b* © Boosey & Hawkes Music Publishers Ltd.

Appendix 3: National Brass Band Championships of Great Britain, 1989, Boosey & Hawkes plc.

Contents

Notes on the Contributors   xi

List of Illustrations   xiii

List of Tables   xv

List of Music Examples   xvi

Note Pitches   xvii

Introduction   1

1   Nineteenth-Century Bands: Making a Movement   10
Trevor Herbert

2   'What's Wrong with Brass Bands?': Cultural Change and the
Band Movement, 1918–*c.*1964   68
Dave Russell

3   The Musical Revolution of the Mid-Nineteenth Century:
From 'Repeat and Twiddle' to 'Precision and Snap'   122
Vic and Sheila Gammon

4   Instruments and Instrumentation of British Brass Bands   155
Arnold Myers

5   God's Perfect Minstrels: The Bands of the Salvation Army   187
Trevor Herbert

6   The Brass Band in the Antipodes: The Transplantation of
British Popular Culture   217
Duncan Bythell

7   Building a Repertoire: Original Compositions for
the British Brass Band, 1913–1998   245
Paul Hindmarsh

8   Aspects of Performance Practices: The Brass Band and
its Influence on Other Brass-Playing Styles   278
Trevor Herbert and John Wallace

Contents

Appendix 1. Prices of Brass Band Instruments   306
Appendix 2. The Salvation Army   312
Appendix 3. Contest Rules   317
Appendix 4. Enderby Jackson's Crystal Palace Contests   327
Appendix 5. Open and National Championship Results   328

A Note on Discographies and Recordings   354
Select Bibliography   356
Index   369

Notes on the Contributors

—◦—

TREVOR HERBERT is Professor of Music at The Open University. He was born in Cwmparc, Wales, and was introduced to music through the Treorchy Youth Brass Band. He played modern and early trombone with many leading London orchestras, and chamber and early music groups, before joining the staff of The Open University in 1976. He continues to play, with, amongst others, the Wallace Collection. He is a frequent broadcaster, and has published numerous important books and articles in international journals relating to brass instruments. With John Wallace, he has edited *The Cambridge Companion to Brass Instruments* (published by Cambridge University Press in 1997).

DUNCAN BYTHELL has recently retired after teaching history at the University of Durham since 1965. He has been a Visiting Fellow in the Research School of Social Sciences at the Australian National University on three occasions. Since 1985, he has been resident conductor of the Muker Silver Band in Swaledale, North Yorkshire.

VIC GAMMON studied history at the University of Sussex, where he completed a doctoral thesis on popular music in nineteenth-century rural society. He performs traditional music and composes electronic music particularly for drama. He was formerly the Head of Music at Downlands School, Hassocks, West Sussex and is now Lecturer in Music Education in the School of Education at the University of Leeds.

SHEILA GAMMON has a long-standing interest in music and social history. Her previous work has included teaching and looking after an ancient monument. She is now a relief teacher for a special school in Kirklees.

PAUL HINDMARSH is a Senior Music Producer for BBC Radio, based in Manchester. He was introduced to music through the brass bands of the Salvation Army. He has produced a wide range of music programmes for BBC Radio 3, including several series devoted to areas of special musical interest, British music of the twentieth century, and brass band performance. He is the author of *The Music of Frank Bridge*, and has edited many works of Bridge and Benjamin Britten for publication. He was the Musical Director of the Besses o' th' Barn Band from 1990 to 1993, and is much in demand as a brass band conductor and producer.

ARNOLD MYERS is the Director and Curator of the Edinburgh University Collection of Historic Musical Instruments, and is editing a catalogue of the Collection, which has been in course of publication since 1990. He completed his doctorate at the University of Edinburgh with research into acoustically based techniques for taxonomic classification of brass instruments. He carried out much of the research and planning of the touring exhibition Brass Roots: 150 Years of Brass Bands (1989–90), and researched and wrote the introduction to the facsimile edition of Algernon Rose's *Talks with Bandsmen*.

DAVE RUSSELL is Reader in the History of Popular Culture at the University of Central Lancashire. He is the author of *Popular Music in England, 1840–1914: A Social History*, *Football and the English*, and a number of articles and essays on nineteenth- and twentieth-century popular culture.

JOHN WALLACE is one of the world's leading trumpet virtuosi, and Head of Brass at the Royal Academy of Music. He began playing the cornet when aged 7 with the Tullis Russell Mills Band, Markinch, Fife, Scotland. He has been principal trumpet of the Philharmonia Orchestra and the London Sinfonietta, and many leading composers have written concerti for him. His group, the Wallace Collection, has an eclectic repertoire which includes performance of nineteenth-century virtuoso music on period instruments. With Trevor Herbert, he has edited *The Cambridge Companion to Brass Instruments*.

LIST OF ILLUSTRATIONS

1.1. Cyfarthfa Band, *c*.1855   20
1.2. Thomas Harper, Jr.   23
1.3. Principle of the operation of valves   29
1.4. Shopfront of the firm of Joseph Higham in 1892   30
1.5. Band of the 4th Lancashire Rifle Volunteers in October 1865   41
1.6. Bradford Brass Band Contest Regulations, 1860   50
1.7. Poster for a contest in Sheffield, 1859   51
1.8. Entrance form for the 1861 Crystal Palace Contest   52
1.9. Enderby Jackson's *Yorkshire Waltzes*, 1856   60
1.10. The cornet player, Beatrice Pettit   66
2.1*a*, *b*, *c*. The Treorchy Youth Brass Band   78–9
2.2. Brass band competing at the 1952 Belle Vue Contest   90
2.3. Programme of the 1938 National Band Festival   91
2.4. The One Thousand Guinea Trophy   92
2.5*a*, *b*. Two images of the 1937 National contest   114
3.1. Unnamed brass players, East Sussex, *c*.1860s or 1870s   139
3.2. *The Village Choir*   141
3.3. Detail from *Arrival of William IV and Queen Adelaide at 'The Friars', Lewes*   142
4.1. Keyed bugles, *c*.1840   159
4.2 Contrabass saxhorn, *c*.1865, and ophicleide, *c*.1840   160
4.3. Cornopean, *c*.1845   162
4.4. Clavicor, *c*.1840   163
4.5. Narrow bore trombone, *c*.1895, and wide bore trombone, *c*.1980   165
4.6. Tenor and contralto saxhorns, *c*.1845   166
4.7. Cornet presented to Alexander Owen in 1874   167
4.8. Tenor tuba, *c*.1855   175
4.9. Tenor and bass trombones, *c*.1845   178
4.10. Euphonium with four valves, 1911   181
4.11. BB♭ bass, 1900   186
5.1. Application form for prospective bandsmen or songsters in the Salvation Army   195
5.2. The Bandmaster's and Band Member's Bond   196
5.3. The instrument factory of the Salvation Army   201
5.4. The Household Troops Band   202
5.5. The International Staff Band   203

5.6. Salvation Army War Chariot, USA   216
6.1*a*, *b*. Australian rotundas for outdoor brass band performances   220
6.2. The Christchurch Bicycle Band   227
8.1. The Black Dyke Mills Band, 1998   279
8.2. *The Bandmaster* Journal, 1872   281
8.3. *Distin's Brass Band Journal*, 1869   282
8.4. Jack Mackintosh and Harry Mortimer   297

LIST OF TABLES

Table 1. The Instrumentation of Salvation Army Brass Bands,
  Musical Salvationist, 1896   198
Table 2. Salvation Army Bands with a Composition of 10–20
  Instruments, Minus Drums, 1940s   211
Table 3. Salvation Army Bands with a Composition of 21–36
  Instruments, 1940s   212
Table 4. Statistics of Salvation Army Bandsmen, 1878–1998   313–15

LIST OF MUSIC EXAMPLES

Ex. 1. Note pitches	xvii
Ex. 2. Harmonic series on D	26
Ex. 3. Harmonic series on C	26
Ex. 4a–d. Percy Fletcher, *Labour and Love*	248
Ex. 5. Henry Geehl, *Normandy*	251–2
Ex. 6a and b. Eric Ball, *Resurgam*	259
Ex. 7a and b. Wilfred Heaton, *Contest Music*	268
Ex. 8. John McCabe, *Cloudcatcher Fells*	271
Ex. 9. Ophicleide part of an arrangement of 'The Rhine Daughters'	286
Ex. 10. 'Keel Row'	289
Ex. 11. 'Jenny Jones'	290
Ex. 12. Jack Mackintosh's 'cowboy' cadenzas	298
Ex. 13. Basil Windsor, *Alpine Echoes*	299
Ex. 14. Grand March from *Aida*, Verdi	299

NOTE PITCHES

∽

Throughout this book we have used the American Standard system to describe note pitches. In this system, middle C is called C_4, and $A_4 = 440$Hz. The octave C_0 to B_0 includes the lowest pitches that are audible to humans, and C_9 to B_9 the highest notes ever written in Western music.

Ex. 1

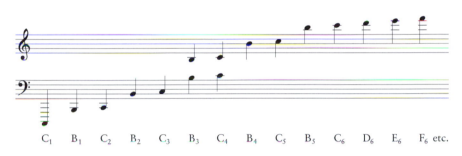

$C_1 \quad B_1 \quad C_2 \quad B_2 \quad C_3 \quad B_3 \quad C_4 \quad B_4 \quad C_5 \quad B_5 \quad C_6 \quad D_6 \quad E_6 \quad F_6$ etc.

Introduction

Every so often, an aspect of British popular culture becomes the focus of attention for movie makers, and is temporarily forced into the foreground of a wider consciousness. Such was the case with the film *Brassed Off*, released in 1996.[1] It is a study of the way that a brass band in the north of England copes with adversity and social change. The band in question is a colliery band, and the colliery faces closure. The community in which the band exists hangs in a state of gloomy equivocation. The band's conductor is sick, and the social coherence which has bound the band together for so long is cracking. The plot centres on the band's capacity to win a vaguely defined 'national contest', and it makes a point (rather crudely, some thought) about working-class attitudes to Thatcherite reforms. The band, of course, triumphs in the contest. It does so as the conductor conquers apparently serious illness. Its efforts are aided by the arrival of a new and talented player—one whose roots lie in the locality, and who is (as is often the case with brass bands) a member of a dynasty of band players. This new player contradicts the common stereotype on two counts: it is not a coal miner who plays so inspirationally, but a quantity surveyor, employed by the reductionist pit management. *And*—the player is a woman.

Parts of the brass band community reacted angrily to what was seen as another misrepresentation of its great movement, and it is easy to understand why. Aspects of the film were appallingly inauthentic; anyone with a passing knowledge of brass bands and their practices will have cringed at the inaccuracies. But, of course, it was not a documentary; it was a fictional account of a place and a moment. The place was the community of a brass band, and the moment was—symbolically—a time when history and tradition confront modernity. And, as is often the case with fiction, it told us something about the tone and meaning of that confrontation which the starker facts of reality often obscure.

Brassed Off was one of the most successful films of the decade. Its popularity was truly international. One of the most fascinating of many questions

[1] Mark Herman (dir.), Channel Four Films & Miramax Films.

raised by the movie is whether or not the essential message of the film—the triumph of a traditional community pastime over the effects of social change and deprivation—would have been weaker if it had been focused on some other activity, such as a football team or an amateur dramatic group. In my view, it would have been, because in the brass band the producers had chosen a good example—perhaps the best—for focusing the minds of their audience on two associated issues: the British working-class experience on the one hand, and the tension between continuity and change on the other. These issues were evident not just in the plot which was acted out, but also in the sound world of the band, which audiences throughout the world found impressive and moving. Indeed many critics commented on the most moving scene in the film, which came when the band played the *Londonderry Air* outside the conductor's hospital window. The homogeneous sonorities captured much of the essence of the brass band idiom, and in so doing conjured in the viewer's mind—unconsciously perhaps—resonances of place, class, and time. Such associations have been utilized by many image makers, and they are easily drawn because of the distinctiveness of the brass band sound and the very real way in which brass bands, musically and socially, show evidence of their nineteenth-century origins.

The influence of the Victorian inheritance of brass bands is all-pervasive. The widely peddled stereotype of brass bands as exclusively northern and working-class is not entirely authentic. Their geographical distribution is much wider than that and always was so, and in the modern era, bank managers, doctors, brokers, and computer programmers are commonplace in the ranks of band players. Furthermore, while the associations of brass bands with the male gender are still strong, very few of them do not now include women among their players. There are many other changes to the practices which were so apparent in the Victorian era when the brass band movement was established. The instruments that are played are as likely to be made in the USA or Japan as in Britain, and the music which is arranged or transcribed for bands to play, which in the nineteenth century was operatic, is now just as likely to originate as film or television soundtracks.

Despite such changes, however, for anyone who takes more than a glance at it, the compelling vision of the brass band is one of consistency and continuity. The standard instrumentation has remained more or less intact for a century, and many of the core musical and organizational practices for just as long. They are sustained by the buoyant exuberance of band players, who, as individuals, take delight in being part of a brass band sound, and who hold the confident knowledge that their enthusiasm for the world of the brass band is shared by many of like mind and spirit. The brass band movement has survived so well for so long because of the nourishment which brass band players draw from each other, because in many different ways, brass banding is at heart a communal activity.

The term 'brass band' is used throughout the world to describe many different types of ensemble. In almost all cases outside Britain, the concept of a brass band is a loose one, and even in those countries which lay claim to having a brass band tradition, the instrumentation and repertoire conform only approximately to set parameters of style and instrumentation. It is common, for example, for brass bands outside Britain to include wind instruments which are not strictly members of the brass instrument class. The country which probably has most brass bands is India, where it has been claimed there may be as many as 800,000 band players, but here the bands are collections of miscellaneous wind and percussion instruments, and the repertoire is partly remembered and partly improvised, rather than played from written music.[2]

Many European and South American countries have brass bands, and they are also prevalent in Africa, the Pacific countries, and throughout Asia. Typically, they play light music outdoors. But though such bands have discernible and distinctive styles, they are not based, as the British species is, on consistent, defined, and imitated performance practices. The United States has a rich tradition of brass band playing, which became especially distinctive and important at the time of the Civil War. But while the contribution of American brass playing to idiomatic brass performance values throughout the world has been as strong as any other force, the term 'brass band' has not acquired the precision of meaning there that it has in the UK.[3] Indeed, in the nineteenth century, many mixed woodwind and brass instrument bands were called brass bands, even though they conformed to the type of formulation which is now called 'brass and wind band' or (more often in the UK) 'military band'. Such bands were given a sure place in American music history through the impact of exemplary professional ensembles in the late nineteenth century, most notable among them being Patrick Gilmore's band and the yet more famous bands of John Philip Sousa.[4] However, they developed in a different way to British brass bands, and their inheritance should be seen in appropriately different terms.

The British brass band is unique in several respects. Its musical formats exist in other parts of the world only where the British model is purposely imitated.[5]

[2] See Rob Boonzajer Flaes, liner notes, *Frozen Brass Anthology of Brass Band Music*, i: *Asia*, Pan, 2020CD. See also Trevor Herbert and Margaret Sarkissian, 'Victorian Bands and their Dissemination in the Colonies', *Popular Music*, 16/2 (1997), 165–79.

[3] It is important to stress that the fact that US brass bands have not become formularized, in the same way as their British counterparts, does not reflect a tradition that is less rich or one that has been less influential in wider spheres of musical life. For excellent overviews of brass banding in America, see R. Camus, *Military Music of the American Revolution* (Westerville, OH: Integrity Press, 1975), and M. H. Hazen and R. M. Hazen, *The Music Men: An Illustrated History of Brass Bands in America, 1800–1920* (Washington, DC: Smithsonian Institution Press, 1987).

[4] On Sousa, see J. Newsom (ed.), *Perspectives on John Philip Sousa* (Washington, DC: Library of Congress, 1983); also P. E. Bierley, *John Philip Sousa, American Phenomenon* (New York, 1973), and *John Philip Sousa: A Descriptive Catalog of his Works* (Urbana, 1973).

[5] See e.g. Ch. 6 by Duncan Bythell in this volume, and Newcomb, *Challenging Brass: 100 Years of Brass Band Contests in New Zealand 1880–1980* (Takapuna: Powerbrass Music Co. Ltd, 1980).

It is marked by two important features: the consistency of its musical practices, which have prevailed from the mid-nineteenth century until the present day; and the formal infrastructures which are usually associated with individual bands and contests, national and regional associations, and so on. Brass banding in Britain has been almost entirely an amateur movement, and is based on a series of organizational and musical features which are described throughout this book. The instrumentation for contesting bands became formalized, then fixed, in the late nineteenth century: soprano cornet in E♭, eight or nine cornets in B♭, one flugel horn in B♭, three tenor horns in E♭, two euphoniums and two baritones in B♭, two tenor trombones and one bass trombone, two basses in E♭, and two basses in B♭. Percussion is also used. The distinctive sound of this combination comes from the preponderance of instruments of conical bore (only the trombones are made of primarily cylindrical tubing). Though some bands may not have all of these instruments, the repertoire is published for this combination, and even smaller, less ambitious and accomplished bands imitate the performance styles followed by standard contesting bands, because it is the performances of these bands which are most widely disseminated through recordings and broadcasts.

Brass bands occupy a terrain in British music culture somewhere between art music and popular, light music. The best bands are virtuoso, and they contribute to art-music culture in important ways. They supply all branches of the music industry with most of their brass players, and one suspects also that stylistic influences permeate through this route. Bands also serve communities, institutions, and agencies as entertainers, and by marking important traditions and rituals such as civic events and trade-union marches. But despite the proximity of bands to the people who constitute their audiences, the brass band world is, as Ruth Finnegan has pointed out, 'a self-conscious, separate world' in which there are shared practices and values.[6] Those outside the brass band world regard its workings with an air of incredulity, but, as with the case of *Brassed Off*, when it comes before the public consciousness as a musical phenomenon, it seldom fails to make a notable impression. Many writers have characterized the British brass band as one of the great achievements of the working class. This is indeed the case, but the really interesting features of its story are found in the complex details of the relationship between bands, their communities, the developing popular music industry, and other musical and social traditions with which brass bands have engaged.

The outline history of the brass band movement is easy to draw. It can be said to have started in the 1840s or 1850s. Brass bands of sorts existed earlier than this, as did most of the instruments which are now typically found in brass bands, but it was not until the middle of the century that brass banding

---

[6] R. Finnegan, *The Hidden Musicians: Music Making in an English Town* (Cambridge: Cambridge University Press, 1989).

4

became a mass activity in which working-class people engaged as players and audiences. These developments came about because new technologies produced instruments which were easier to play than had previously been the case. The most important factor was the invention of efficient piston valve instruments. These instruments lent themselves to mass production techniques, and because of this and the relative cheapness and abundance of raw materials, they were produced in large quantities and sold comparatively cheaply. To such particular factors can be added some which were more commonly shared by other popular music forms and practices. The more general development of commercial popular music was based on new patterns of production and consumerism. These patterns were themselves aided by certain demographic trends, especially the simultaneous growth of the British population, and the increasing proportion of it which was urban. As more easily accessible modes of communication developed, those who wished to sell the idea of brass bands were able to address a single mass market. These same forces also allowed those who were perceived as making up that market to nurture ambitions which—as the progress of the brass band movement showed—were entirely realizable.

The speed of growth of the brass band movement in Britain in the mid-Victorian period was especially striking, and this growth had much to do with the efficiency of the industrial infrastructure which supplied instruments, music, and other necessary accoutrements to brass bands. It was also aided by other factors, such as the common perception that music making among the lower orders was to be encouraged as an 'improving' activity. But having taken into account these background features, the key factor which caused brass bands to capture the public imagination and become a vital part of the new Victorian leisure industry was the advent of the brass band contest.

Contesting is central to the brass band movement. It is, of course, not the sole public activity in which brass bands are, and have been, engaged, and many brass bands never compete. But the shape and character of the brass band movement has been defined by processes, rules, values, spheres of influence, power structures, and performance practices which emanate from contesting. Since the middle of the nineteenth century, there have been local and 'national' contests which have acted as a focus and a spur for the brass band movement. The contest has made the British brass band a species which can be described in terms which are unambiguous and generic.

The origin and growth of the brass band contest should be seen in terms of the wider development of Victorian mass leisure practices. In this story, no one is more important than Enderby Jackson, a candle maker's son from Hull, who was a musician and composer of sorts, but who came to prominence because he possessed an apparently inexhaustible entrepreneurial flair. He also has something to answer for in terms of the way that the history of brass bands has sometimes been written. In 1896, Jackson published a series of articles in the *Musical Opinion and Musical Trades Review* under the title of 'Origin and Promotion of Brass Band Contests'.[7] These articles are an important source for anyone interested in the subject. In them, Jackson gave his version of the history of the brass band movement and the development of contests. In this story, Jackson's personal contribution is given considerable emphasis. Most writers have swallowed Jackson's account in a single gulp, and passed over what seems to me to be the obvious truth that, despite the undoubted importance of his own contribution to contesting, Jackson—by now an elderly man—was airing his own considerable prejudices, and inventing a history of which he had not been an observer, and on aspects of which he was not especially expert. Among the most spurious aspects of Jackson's account are his claims concerning the earliest origins of brass bands, and these are discussed in Chapter 1, but it is nevertheless fair to say that Jackson's influence on the development of the brass band contest was pivotal.

In his unpublished autobiography he claims that he conceived of the idea of brass band contests when he observed the popularity of agricultural competitions. He describes a brass band contest held at Burton Constable near Hull in 1844, at the home of Sir Clifford and Lady Constable. According to his detailed account, the event demonstrated some of the features which became common in later brass band contests. In 1856 he ran a contest at Hull which may well have been the prototype for all his later major contests, and though he was not the only entrepreneur to run such events, he was the most important. He was also (he claims) the first to perceive the potential for the brass band contest to profit from new facilities such as railway excursions. He claimed to have invented the concept of the cheap day excursion; a similar facility was available for the 1851 Great Exhibition, but his negotiations with railway companies in the late 1850s have all the flavour of it being an entirely new idea, and it may be fair to say that through him, the practice became more widespread.

Arthur Taylor has put forward the credible argument that two other contest organizers, and collaborators with Jackson, deserve more credit than posterity has afforded them for the development of the contest.[8] These were James Melling and John Jennison, who instigated the Belle Vue Gardens contests in Manchester in 1853. But it seems that Jackson's contests, and the rules and regulations which he put in place to run them, formed the basis of all contests which were to follow. Each band had to submit an entrance form for a contest. The players' names had to be declared, as well as the instruments and their pitch,[9] and every player also had to declare his occupation. By soliciting this

---

[7] E. Jackson, 'Origin and Promotion of Brass Band Contests', *Musical Opinion and Music Trade Review* (1896: serialized).

[8] See A. Taylor, *Brass Bands* (St Albans and London: Granada Publishing, 1979), ch. 3.

[9] Some of the information on instruments was needed so that arrangements could be put in place for a massed brass band concert, which was held after the contest.

latter piece of information, Jackson's intention was to ensure that brass band contests were for amateur players. A selection of contest rules and regulations is given in Appendix 3. From these, it can be seen that the successive tendency has been to develop rules which make bands compete in increasingly standardized ways. By the twentieth century, bands were expected to conform to a standard instrumentation, and a number of other details became enshrined into the regulatory framework which helped to create and sustain a common orthodoxy of brass banding.

Contests were held throughout the country, but in the nineteenth century, two contests assumed the status of 'national' events. The first of these was the aforesaid Belle Vue Manchester 'Open' contest held annually from 1853.[10] The other was the contest held from 1860 at the Crystal Palace, following its move from Hyde Park to Sydenham. The Crystal Palace Company commissioned Jackson to organize a contest which would help popularize the new Crystal Palace site at Sydenham. Two contests were run over two days: the 'Great National Contest' and the 'Sydenham Amateur Contest'. (Appendix 4 lists the prize-winning bands.) The Crystal Palace event gave the brass band movement its first really conspicuous exposure in the south of England, but though it was successful and drew audiences of thousands, it was only held for four consecutive years.

The Belle Vue contest (as the British Open Championship) has run continuously, but it was not until 1900 that John Henry Iles, a businessman totally infatuated with the sound of the brass band, reinstigated the National Contest at the Crystal Palace. In 1936, following the destruction of the Crystal Palace by fire, the National Contest moved to Alexandra Palace, then, after the Second World War, to the Royal Albert Hall. The Open and the National contests have a shared status in the brass band movement as being the most prestigious. They have both attracted a variety of sponsors and been run by imaginative and far-thinking organizers, and they have always attracted the best brass bands. International contests have also had some success. A glance at the list of winners at the National and Open contests, and the music played by them (see Appendix 5) provides an interesting profile of the movement.

The basic organization of the brass band contest is straightforward. Bands enter through a process of registration, and on the day of the contest they draw for the order in which they have to play. The adjudicators are encased in a tent, behind screens, or in a cubicle (known as a box) for the entire contest, and they ascribe a score and a brief critique of the performance to each contesting band. Because the judges are not privy to the order of the draw, they are oblivious of which band is playing at any one time. The adjudicators signal their readiness to hear a band by blowing a whistle or ringing a bell. When all bands have been

---

[10] The 1859 contest was cancelled because few bands entered. It became known as the British Open Brass Band Championship.

heard they announce the winner by the number in the playing order at which that band performed.

Further sophistications were introduced to contesting in the twentieth century. In 1900, the idea of classes or sections of bands was introduced to the National Championship,[11] and a further three sections were introduced in 1902. This system survives: each band is placed in a division according to its playing standard, the highest being called 'championship section' and the lowest the fourth section. Bands can be relegated and promoted, but the intention is that they compete against others of a more or less similar standard. The works which bands are expected to play in competition are intended to be appropriate for the technical competences typically found in such sections. From 1946, a national Register of Bandsmen has been in place. There are regional qualifying contests for the National Championship.

Though there are march contests and solo contests, by far the most important form of contest is where full bands, usually sitting indoors, play one work of about ten minutes in length. They may be required to play one of two types of piece: a set 'test piece' (a work declared some weeks before the contest, which has to be performed by each band) or an 'own selection' (usually a well-known test piece of each band's own choice). In the nineteenth century, brass bands played arrangements made by their own conductor or bandmaster. In the twentieth century, because the instrumentation was standardized, it became possible for all bands to play a standard test-piece arrangement or an original composition for brass band. The growth of the idiomatic brass band repertoire is almost exclusively a twentieth-century phenomenon, and because test pieces are so important, almost every brass band work of any significance started life as a championship-section test piece.

The significance of the contest in the world of brass bands will become obvious in the chapters which follow, and it is clear that it is this feature of the movement—the idea that bands contest against each other to be judged best or worst, according to commonly understood criteria—which has produced almost all its idiomatic characteristics. But despite this apparently all-consuming feature, there is more to brass banding than contesting, and what might be taken to be the introspection of brass bands should not obscure the fact that the movement has not only been influenced by external forces but has also exerted an influence. This book, hopefully, provides such a balanced profile.

The first two chapters deal, respectively, with the origins and development of brass bands in the Victorian period and with the place of bands in the twentieth century. The latter chapter does not deal explicitly or at length with brass bands after the mid-1960s, but more modern aspects of brass banding are picked up in later chapters, particularly in Chapters 7 and 8. Both Chapters 1 and 2 explore a number of themes and topics, and show how brass bands

[11] The Scottish Amateur Brass Band Championship had two sections in 1895.

have engaged with broader spheres of music culture and society. Though these chapters are not presented either individually or collectively as a comprehensive history of the brass band movement, it is intended that they should provide the essential context for the remainder of the book. The subsequent chapters deal with topics and themes which seem too important to deal with briefly. Chapter 3 offers a context for the origins of brass bands in the nineteenth century, and raises important issues about the nature of amateur music making at that time. Chapter 4 provides further contextualization of the music making of brass bands with a detailed analysis of the development of the musical instruments of the brass band. The bands of the Salvation Army, which, since their foundation, have been separate from other brass bands, are discussed in Chapter 5. Chapter 6 provides a case study of brass bands in Australasia, the region where the British model has been most carefully imitated. Chapter 7 provides a detailed study of the repertoire of brass bands in the twentieth century; and the final chapter discusses the performance practices and influence of brass band players.

As editor, I have been less concerned with avoiding overlap and repetition than with ensuring that each chapter sustains its individual sense and integrity. Some cross-references have been made, but it will be evident that I have regarded this book, as I did the volume upon which it is based, as a collection of complementary essays which is not reliant upon any one key essay for its rationale. Hopefully the whole will provide a contribution to the study of this subject which is at least equal to the sum of its parts.

Nineteenth-Century Bands:
Making a Movement

TREVOR HERBERT

The growth of brass bands in Victorian Britain can be viewed as something of a watershed. It represents an important manifestation of change in popular music culture, and even though it is but one aspect of the wider phenomena underlying the rise of popular music, it possesses features which make it special. It provides a prime example of the fusion of commercial and philan-thropic interests and attitudes; of art music and vernacular musical practices; of technology and 'art'; and of dominant and emergent ideologies. It could also be regarded as one of the more important aspects of British art music in the nineteenth century, and certainly an element which impacted in a lasting manner on the broad infrastructure of British music: its industry, institutions, and even styles. One of the achievements of the brass band movement is that it created what was probably the first mass engagement of working-class people in instrumental art music, not just in Britain, but possibly anywhere. But even while this process was taking place, as early as the 1880s, there were sure signs of the reassertion of traditional social divisions forcing brass bands into the uneasy, ambiguous middle ground between art and popular culture. In the first edition of Grove's dictionary, J. A. Kappey, an army bandmaster

I am grateful to the librarians and archivists who have assisted me during my research for this chapter, and to Dave Russell, Richard Middleton, Mike Lomas, and Arnold Myers, for reading the earliest draft and making valuable suggestions; also to William Boag; to Alma Sanders for material relating to the Besses o' th' Barn Band; to the custodians of the Black Dyke Mills Band library; to the Curator and staff of the Cyfarthfa Castle Museum; to Julia Williams, who typed the original manuscript, and Jill Grey who typed this revised version. Also, I owe a special debt of gratitude to Dr Helen Barlow.

and self-styled musicologist, who, through various enterprises, had made no small profit from brass bands, declared that 'many bands had reached a high state of excellence', but, 'of course, looked upon as high art culture, brass bands are of no account'.[1] Given the status that *Grove* was to assume, Kappey's short article may have sown the seeds of a schism between bands and élite art culture which many in the movement would argue has existed ever since.

It is possible to see the development of the brass band movement in the nineteenth century as falling into three, perhaps four, overlapping periods in which critical developmental stages are evident, and in which such developments are explained by the presence of vitally important social, musical, cultural, and economic trends. Also significant are particular events, such as the invention of valves, which gave brass instruments fully chromatic facilities, and the parallel careers of groups of key individuals such as Distin, Sax, and Jullien, or Swift, Gladney, and Owen, names that figure prominently later in this chapter.

These periods condition the structure of this chapter. The first occupies the opening years of the nineteenth century, and ends at about the time when Victoria came to the throne. Although most writers have linked the wind bands of the early nineteenth century to the brass band movement,[2] I see these relationships, even though they are plentiful enough, as more circumstantial than causal. The second period, beginning around 1840, is one in which a number of potent forces combine, explaining why brass bands, as opposed to any other type of amateur ensemble group, gained popular ascendancy. The third of my periods starts around 1860. From this time, the growth of the movement accelerates most strongly. The number of bands multiplies, and their prominence in working-class life, as well as their function in the common territory *between* classes, is evident. In the last twenty or thirty years of the century, about half-way through this 'third period', it is possible to distinguish two subtle but major structural changes taking place. The first concerns what may be described as the 'standardization' of musical identity. While it is reasonable to regard this as one of the most important features of the period, it is worth exercising some caution, for, even though many vital musical identifiers which eventually defined the brass band idiom were consolidated at this time, the majority of bands still did not conform to the 'standard' line-up of instruments. The second change is in some ways more interesting. Whereas brass banding had previously been led either by commerce or by socially superior classes, from this time the working classes were vital participants in what was, at the very least, a consensual partnership between organized working people and entrepreneurs. Also, brass bands became largely decoupled from patronage and paternalism, elements which were in any case not always

[1] G. Grove (ed.), *A Dictionary of Music and Musicians* (London: Macmillan, 1879–90), s.v. 'Wind-band'.

[2] See e.g. D. H. Van Ess, 'Band Music', in N. Temperley (ed.), *Music in Britain: The Romantic Age 1800–1914* (London: Athlone Press, 1981), 138.

clear.[3] It is in this period, interestingly enough, that brass band people start referring to themselves as a 'movement'.[4]

Brass Instruments in Britain before the Nineteenth Century

Prior to the nineteenth century, there had not been a widespread tradition of amateur brass playing in Britain. There were comparatively few professional brass players, and these were based in London and the main provincial centres. Furthermore, only three types of brass instrument existed before the nineteenth century—the trombone, the trumpet, and the horn. The trombone has remained largely unchanged since its invention in the fifteenth century. The horn and trumpet were of relatively simple construction, giving their players the facility to produce a single harmonic series from each fixed tube length. Trombones were introduced into England at the beginning of the Tudor dynasty. Indeed, their importation was part of the cultural expansion that was intended to assert that dynasty. The players were all foreign; the most important were Venetians, many of them clandestine Jews, who established a highly skilled dynasty of trombonists at the Tudor court.[5] From the early sixteenth century until the Commonwealth period, the importance of trombonists in the royal musical establishment was reflected in the consistency of their employment and the size of their fees. Trombones were used to play gentle chamber music, dance music, probably (although none survives) declamatory processional music, and, from the closing decades of the sixteenth century, to support sacred music, even the music of the liturgy itself.[6]

The chief provincial employers of trombonists were the civic authorities who still employed waits. Waits, who had been part of civic foundations since the Middle Ages, performed at ceremonial functions, and in earlier times were, it seems, employed to keep and sound the watch. Although the waits were regulated by local authorities and were required to conduct themselves under strict disciplinary regulations, evidence shows that they also freelanced independently of these authorities—either collectively or as individuals.[7]

---

[3] In *Work, Society and Politics: The Culture of the Factory in Later Victorian England* (London: Methuen, 1982), P. Joyce has argued that processes such as this reflect the changing nature of business and the shift to limited liability companies.

[4] By the end of the century, it seems to have been usual to refer to 'the brass band movement'. It is impossible to say when this first occurred, but a report on the Crystal Palace Contest in *The Times* of 11 July 1860 mentions the term.

[5] R. Prior, 'Jewish Musicians at the Tudor Court', *Musical Quarterly*, 69/2 (1983), 253–65.

[6] See T. Herbert, 'The Trombone in Britain before 1800' (Ph.D. thesis, Open University, 1984), 361–76.

[7] Ibid. 37 ff. and 427 ff. The first record of a trombonist being employed as a wait is found in the Repertory of the Court of Aldermen for the City of London in 1526 (Guildhall Library, London, R7.f.137).

The other main provincial employers were cathedrals, many of which accommodated trombonists in their statutes. It is probable that in some cities the cathedral players were waits who were freelancing; it is certainly true that cathedrals without trombone players on their statutes made *ex gratia* payments to trombonists for special services.[8]

Before the last few decades of the seventeenth century, trombonists played with any combination of quiet and loud instruments. The most frequent treble partner for the trombone was the 'cornett' (It., *cornetto*; Ger., *Zink*). This is *not* the nineteenth-century cornet, but an entirely different instrument made from wood, having a finger-hole system similar to that found on the recorder, and a cup-shaped mouthpiece similar to those used on brass instruments.

For most of this period the trumpet and horn had little special and individual significance in art music in Britain. Trumpets were maintained at court and in other places, but they were primarily declamatory ceremonial instruments. Horns, too, were exclusively functional, and were associated with the hunt. But towards the end of the seventeenth century and through the eighteenth century, fundamental changes took place in the musical role and status of brass instruments. These changes form an important context in which the development of brass bands should be seen.

The trombone (unlike the trumpet and horn) was entirely chromatic across its entire pitch range—a player could produce every note between the highest and lowest point of the instrument's compass. But by the end of the seventeenth century, it was obsolete in Britain. It began to fall out of fashion in the later years of the reign of Charles II, and by the opening years of the eighteenth century, few in England knew what a trombone (or *sackbut*, to give it its old English name) was. There are several reason for this, but the primary one is that tastes current in art music in England during the mid-Baroque period favoured homogeneous sonorities of the type produced by balanced string and wind groups. British tastes in art music have always been fairly uniform and centrally determined, and for this reason the trend was national. There is abundant evidence of trombones being discarded and players switching to other instruments. It is not unusual to find records such as that in the Canterbury Cathedral Inventory of 1752, which refers to a chest containing 'only two brass Sackbuts not us'd for a grete number of years past'.[9]

On the other hand, just as the popularity of the trombone was declining, the trumpet had entered a period of ascendancy. A school of exceptional London-based trumpeters was contemporary with composers such as Henry and Daniel Purcell, Jeremiah Clarke, and John Blow, and there emanated from this coincidence a rich virtuoso repertoire, the musical characteristics of which

---

[8] Canterbury Cathedral included trombonists on its statutes in the 16th cent. See Herbert, 'Trombone in Britain', 83.

[9] Ibid. 293.

were to define the idiom of the trumpet in Britain for more than a century. This musical idiom was strengthened and underlined by the high and jealously protected social status with which trumpet playing, and, to a lesser extent, horn playing, were endowed. The most overt and powerful device that established trumpet playing as a professional, centralized, and in many other ways hierarchical activity, was the office of 'sergeant trumpeter'. This office was first instituted in the sixteenth century, but in the seventeenth and eighteenth centuries all trumpeters had to submit themselves to the sergeant trumpeter (a royal appointment) to be licensed. This system of licensing may well have been in direct imitation of the Imperial Guild of Trumpeters and Kettledrummers, formed in 1623, and operated throughout the Holy Roman Empire under sanction of Ferdinand II.[10]

The regulatory systems for trumpeters were less strongly enforced in the later eighteenth century, but it is possible that this thinly disguised freemasonry continued to condition some attitudes to professional trumpet playing—except, perhaps, in the military, which had its own regulations. The office of sergeant trumpeter continued to exist until the early twentieth century, but its function was titular by that time.

The trombone was reintroduced into Britain in 1784 for the celebrations at Westminster Abbey and the Pantheon in commemoration of the birth of Handel. The music historian Charles Burney wrote that players of the 'SACBUT, OR DOUBLE TRUMPET' were sought, 'but so many years had elapsed since it had been used in this kingdom, that, neither the instrument, nor a performer upon it, could easily be found'.[11] Some were found, however—seemingly all foreigners (almost certainly Austrian or German) who had recently moved to England. In the late eighteenth century, the trombone was effectively a new instrument as far as the British were concerned, and for more than a hundred years before the nineteenth century there is not a shred of evidence to suggest that there was a single native-born trombone player working in Britain. Indeed, one observer at the Handel celebrations was so confused by these novel instruments that he jotted on his programme against the word 'TROMBONES', 'Are something like Bassoons, with an end like a large speaking trumpet'.[12]

The waits were finally and formally made defunct in the early 1830s under the terms of the various municipal and parliamentary Reform Acts. The changing administrative infrastructure, together with the expediencies caused by financial pressures that local and civic authorities faced, removed the last mechanism that supported them. Some writers have given this date and

[10] S. Sadie (ed.), *The New Grove Dictionary of Music and Musicians* (London: Macmillan, 1980), s.v. 'Trumpet I'.

[11] Herbert, 'Trombone in Britain', 471.

[12] Trevor Herbert, 'The Sackbut in England in the Seventeenth and Eighteenth Centuries', *Early Music*, 18/4 (Nov. 1990), 614.

these events undue significance.[13] In fact, the waits had been an anachronism for more than half a century. The link which some have erroneously drawn between the waits and Victorian brass bands, and which Arthur Taylor,[14] for example, has treated with appropriate scepticism, is based on the fact that two members of the York waits (whatever they were in the 1830s) were subsequently members of a brass band. By the nineteenth century, the waits had no general characteristics which make it appropriate for them to be regarded as the embryonic form of the brass band movement.

EARLY MILITARY AND CHURCH BANDS

The early nineteenth-century bands that are relevant to the development of mid-nineteenth-century brass bands were those of the army and the auxiliary forces, village bands, and church bands. Full-time military bands of sorts can be traced back to the seventeenth century, but most have their origins in the late eighteenth century. In the early nineteenth century most regimental bands were restricted to ten players, and all were the private bands of the commanding officers concerned.[15] A standing order issued by letter in 1803 instructed that 'not more than *one* Private soldier of each troop or company shall be permitted to act as musicians'.[16] This order was largely ignored, and eighteen years later, letters were still being dispatched instructing commanding officers to restrict the number of musicians in each troop or company.

Regular army bands (or their prototypes) were but one feature, however, of 'military music' in Britain in the late eighteenth and nineteenth centuries. Many bands were associated with the militia which had been revived in 1757 and the volunteer corps which emerged in the 1790s. They were widely dispersed, and were funded primarily by subscriptions, as well as (unwittingly) by government funding, and by the direct patronage of officers. They normally numbered between six and twelve players, and were usually amateur, though many contained professional players. As well as percussion, the most common instruments were trumpets, clarinets, fifes, and flutes on treble parts, with horns, bassoons, serpents, and (much less usually) trombones on the lower parts.[17]

---

[13] This link is mentioned in *New Grove* (s.v. 'Brass Bands'); it is also given some emphasis in J. F. Russell and J. H. Elliot, *The Brass Band Movement* (London: J. M. Dent & Sons, 1936), ch. 1.

[14] A. Taylor, *Brass Bands* (St Albans and London: Granada Publishing, 1979), 23.

[15] See H. G. Farmer, *The Rise and Development of Military Music* (London: W. M. Reeves, 1912; revised edn., 1970).

[16] University of Glasgow Library, Farmer MS.115. (Letter dated 5 Aug. 1803 from Harry Calvert, Adjutant General of the Forces.)

[17] See E. Croft-Murray, 'The Wind Band in England', in T. C. Mitchell (ed.), *Music and Civilization* (British Museum Yearbook, 4; London: British Museum Publications Ltd., 1980), 135–63. See also M. J. Lomas, 'Militia and Volunteer Wind Bands in Southern England in the Late Eighteenth and Early Nineteenth Centuries', *Journal of the Society for Army Historical Research*, 67/271 (Autumn 1989), 154–66.

Such bands played a mixed repertory. Concert programmes included titles of national and patriotic melodies, as well as arrangements of popular art music. There was also a minor publishing industry centring on military bands. Many bands had marches 'dedicated' to them by publishers, and issued in parts and score with a keyboard reduction. The music was not technically demanding, but functional and entertaining. As well as the published copies, manuscript sources survive. Probably the most eminent composer to contribute to this repertoire was Joseph Haydn, who, during his stay in London in the 1790s, wrote a *March for the Prince of Wales* and two *Marches for the Derbyshire Cavalry Regiment*.

Some of the players in the early military bands were to have an influence on brass bands later in the century. John Distin, for example, started his career as a bandboy in the South Devon Militia,[18] while John Gladney, widely referred to at the time of his death as 'the father of the brass band movement', was the son of the bandmaster of the 30th East Lancashire Regiment,[19] and William Rimmer, one of the most eminent late nineteenth-century conductors, was the son of a militia bandsman.[20] The Godfrey family, which included the composer, Dan Godfrey, and the conductor, Charles, could trace its association with the Coldstream Guards Band back to the late eighteenth century.

The church bands of rural Britain, particularly England, also provided a tradition of amateur instrumental ensemble music making. Such bands were common throughout the country. The survival of a large written repertory of church band music indicates widespread musical literacy among players in these types of ensemble. It is doubtful, however, whether the repertoire of such musicians was confined to what is revealed in the surviving manuscript sources, or to the music of the church, or, indeed, to any written music. As Vic and Sheila Gammon point out later in this book, there existed alongside the text-based practices of the church and village bands a vernacular, instrumental 'plebeian tradition', which was well developed, improvised, and 'popular'.[21]

Evidence of the extent of instrumental performance in English churches is abundant. McDermott[22] cites dozens in Sussex alone. Galpin[23] has drawn a similar picture in Dorset. William Millington, in his *Sketches of Local Musicians and Musical Societies*,[24] describes a network of bands in the north

---

[18] J. L. Scott, 'The Evolution of the Brass Band and its Repertoire in Northern England' (Ph.D., University of Sheffield, 1970), 441.

[19] R. A. Marr, *Music for the People* (Edinburgh and Glasgow: John Menzies, 1889), 120.

[20] Southport Public Library, Sp. 920. RIM (William Rimmer Documents).

[21] See also V. Gammon, 'Babylonian Performances: The Rise and Suppression of Popular Church Music, 1660–1870', in E. Yeo and S. Yeo (eds.), *Popular Culture and Class Conflict 1590–1914* (Brighton: Harvester, 1981), 62–88.

[22] K. H. McDermott, *Sussex Church Music in the Past* (Chichester: Moore and Wingham, 1923).

[23] F. W. Galpin, 'Notes on the Old Church Bands and Village Choirs of the Past Century', *The Antiquary*, 42 (1906), 101–6.

[24] W. Millington, *Sketches of Local Musicians and Musical Societies* (Pendlebury, 1884).

of England; and even on the island of Anglesey in North Wales, where the Anglican religion cohabited with the Welsh language, there are sources for instrumental church music.[25] One of the main functions of church bands was to double and support sung parts. It is undoubtedly true, however, that the bands were important and even focal agencies in church communities, in a way suggestive of the social significance which Nonconformist hymn singing acquired in Wales later in the century. The social function of bands may, in some cases, have been born of necessity, because though some parish priests encouraged church bands, others were absenteeist.[26] According to J. A. La Trobe, many left it to the church community to 'regulate and inspirit [sic] the music of the church. In most places, the choir are left to their own fitful struggles, without any offer of clerical assistance.'[27]

Brass instruments did not figure prominently in church bands. Nicholas Temperley's summary of the instrumentation of church bands in the first thirty years of the nineteenth century cites no brass instruments,[28] but other sources occasionally do. McDermott's investigation of Sussex church bands revealed eight trombones, four serpents, and a bass horn.[29] Unfortunately, McDermott's energy in research was not equalled by the detail in which he cited his findings, and the dates when these instruments were found are not known. It is extremely doubtful if the trombones, for example, were in use very early in the century. The most common instrumentation for early nineteenth-century church bands was strings with woodwind. Bassoons and cellos were the most common bass instruments. Treble parts were generally played on violin, flute, clarinet, or oboe.

Church bands were most common between about 1780 and 1830;[30] the militia and volunteer bands were at their strongest somewhat earlier. But it is important to stress that such ensembles did not die out early in the century. Church bands existed in some parts of the country even at the end of the nineteenth century, and military bands, particularly those of the regular army, were a constant musical feature of the Victorian period.

Numerous accounts exist from the second and third decades of the century, which show that bands were featured in local functions such as fêtes, fairs, and seasonal festivals. The bands are seldom named, but they seem to have been well established in the tapestry of community life. Arthur Taylor has cited numerous examples of bands existing in the years previous to Victoria's reign,[31]

[25] A clarinet and syrinx from this period survive at the Old Church of Llaneilian, Anglesey. I am grateful to H. E. Griffiths, rector of Amlwch, for providing me with this information.

[26] See Gammon, 'Babylonian Performances', 71 ff.

[27] J. A. La Trobe, *The Music of the Church Considered* . . . (Thames Ditton, 1831), 72.

[28] In N. Temperley, *The Music of the English Parish Church* (Cambridge: Cambridge University Press, 1979), 197.

[29] Ibid. 198.   [30] Ibid. 197.   [31] Taylor, *Brass Bands*, 17–21.

and there is evidence of similar bands being formed in Scotland[32] and southern England[33] in the same period.

Many sources can be drawn on to link early village, church, and military bands with distinguished brass bands,[34] but while such examples may show how a particular band originated, they do not illustrate or explain the origins of the brass band *movement*. The zest with which some modern bands have adopted a strictly linear approach to this history in order to establish a distant, unbroken pedigree has created some important distortions in this respect. The early military, church, and village bands did, however, provide an important legacy for the eventual development of the brass band movement. These early bands were the first to create a tradition of literate instrumental ensemble music making outside the professional, middle- and upper-class enclaves in which such activity had previously been centred. Their activities established an infrastructure that was to be sustained and developed through the century. That infrastructure was rooted in five critical conditions underlying the commercial, economic, and social factors which in turn fuelled the rapid growth of bands: (1) evidence of amateur instrumental performance; (2) a performance convention that was primarily literate and text-based, as opposed to aural and improvisatory (though aurality was to remain fundamentally important); (3) the witness of that activity by 'audiences' who were the peer groups of the performers; (4) some evidence of supporting services for music (shops, instrument repairers, teachers, and arrangers); and (5) some evidence of cultural crossover between art/middle-class music and the lower orders. The evidence of the latter condition is found in the repertory that these bands played, which was primarily but not exclusively the repertory of the military bands.[35]

THE EARLIEST BRASS BANDS

It is perhaps worth mentioning the question of the 'first brass band', an issue which has been debated widely since the 1880s. Several publications cite the first brass band as the one formed near Blaina, Monmouthshire, at the Brown Brothers Iron Mill in the village of Pontybederyn in 1832. The first author to proclaim this was Enderby Jackson, in his 'Origin and Promotion of Brass Band Contests' (1896). At the time of writing, Jackson was 65 years old, and was confidently referring to matters which occurred during the year of his

[32] See 'The History of the Brass Movement', University of Glasgow, Farmer Manuscripts 99/2, a 2p. typescript article by H. G. Farmer referring to the researches of Mr George Thompson of Airdrie, and listing a number of early Scottish wind bands.

[33] W. Alberry, 'Old Sussex Amateur Bands', *Sussex County Magazine*, 18/12 (1944), 314–20.

[34] e.g. see Taylor, *Brass Bands*, chs. 1 and 2, *passim*.

[35] e.g. Millington (*Sketches*, 11 ff.) writes of parish instrumentalists and choirs meeting 'for the practice of vocal and instrumental music, principally oratorios of Handel, Haydn and other eminent composers'. See also R. Elbourne, *Music and Tradition in Early Industrial Lancashire 1780–1840* (Woodbridge: Brewer, 1980), 115–33.

birth, an event which took place in Hull, a town hundreds of miles from Blaina. He did not say how he had acquired this information, but this was not untypical of Jackson. All this would be of no significance were it not for the fact that almost every text (including *Grove 6*) in which the history of brass bands has been addressed has quoted this 'fact' without discrimination. It matters comparatively little which band was the 'first brass band', compared to the need to understand the sequence of events which established brass bands as a form of mass recreation and entertainment. The present writer does not know which was the first brass band—nor does he especially care; but suffice it to say that his best efforts in the archives of South Wales, and his scrutiny of all the major relevant topographical works, have failed to establish the existence of a place called Pontybederyn (or even variants of this spelling), or of Brown Brother's Iron Mill, or a morsel of evidence to support Jackson's claim. There was indeed an ironworks in Blaina in the 1830s, and one of its directors was a man called Brown (hardly an uncommon name), but there were no brothers, and the works was not known as 'Brown Brothers'.

Though the early bands provide evidence of an 'infrastructure', the real and immediate prehistory of the brass band movement is found in the period between the late 1830s and the middle of the century. In this period, there was a sudden increase in the popularity of brass instruments. Though it was common for bands to describe themselves as amateur, 'brass band' playing was neither exclusively amateur nor working class. Bands made up entirely of brass instruments existed from the 1830s.[36] In 1838, the Preston United Independent Harmonic Brass Band petitioned Mr Thomas Clifton, of Lytham Hall, Lancashire:

Sir, by the desire of a Fue Respectable Friends of yours in Preston has caused hus to write to you with a Petition as a Solisitation for a job of Playing at your Dinnering Day as they told hus is taking place on Tuesday the 10th of March Inst. at Lytham which if you are having a Band of Music at Dinner we shall be very glad to be ingadged for your on that Day it is one of the first Bands in the country. Our Band consists of 10 in number it is a Brass Band and the Name of the Band is the United Independent Harmonic Brass band Preston which our charge is not so much considering the Band the charge or Pay for hus for one Day is 8/6 each man for the number of 10 comes to £4–5–0 and Meat and Drink as soon as we get their and all the time we stay their, if so hapen we have to come if you make up your Mind for hus to come to Play for dinner on that Day we shall please no doubt.

N.B. if writing for hus you must Direct to our leader Edwd. Kirkby Leader of the United Independent Harmonic Brass Band at No. 31 Alfred Street, Preston. We can come either in uniform or not according to the weather.
From your Humble Servants
   The Band[37]

---

[36] There are several claims as to what was the first all-brass band. (See Taylor, *Brass Bands*, ch. 1.)
[37] Lancashire County Records Office, DDC1 1187/18 (Clifton of Lytham Muniments).

Figure 1.1. The Cyfarthfa Band, *c*.1855. Founded in 1838 by the iron baron, Robert Thompson Crawshay, at Merthyr Tydfil, S. Wales, this is probably the earliest known photograph of a brass band. The photographer was probably Crawshay himself.

There is no other surviving information concerning Preston Harmonic Band; it was a *brass* band, and this was deemed worthy of emphasis. The fee, by the standards of the time, was fairly substantial, certainly compatible with the players being professional or semi-professional. The day on which work was being sought was a Tuesday, suggesting that the players were earning a living either solely or partly from playing. If they were semi-professional, it follows that they were self-employed or had jobs in which they had a modicum of control over their working hours.

   An example of a different type of origin for a band is illustrated by the story of the Cyfarthfa Band, founded in Merthyr Tydfil, South Wales, in 1838, by the industrialist Robert Thompson Crawshay.[38] (See Fig. 1.1, the earliest picture of the band.) By the 1830s, Merthyr was by far the biggest industrial town in Wales, and one of the greatest centres for iron smelting in the world.

---

   [38] See T. Herbert, 'The Virtuosi of Merthyr', *Llafur: The Journal of Welsh Labour History*, 5/1 (1988), 60–7.

The scale of immigration into the town was unprecedented. Crawshay started the band from scratch. He enlisted some local talent, but appointed to critical positions players who were already established as professionals. These included a distinguished family of musicians from Bradford, London theatre players, and travelling musicians such as those who visited the town with Wombwell's Circus and Menagerie.[39] Although the function and status of the band changed over the remaining years of the century, it was founded as a private band. The players were given jobs in Crawshay's ironworks and probably some help with housing. Whether they received payment for performing is difficult to establish, but it is probable that fees for engagements were distributed among members.

Sources relating to the Crawshay band are more extensive and wide-ranging than those for any other band of this period, but the practice of a well-to-do landed gentleman supporting a brass band, primarily for his private use, was not unique to Cyfarthfa. There are, of course, many precedents for aristocratic patronage of musicians. In England, the strongest immediate precedent is found earlier in the century, in the support given to volunteer and militia bands by landed gentry who were the commanding officers of auxiliary force corps. There are, however, other examples. Thomas Lee, one of the earliest conductors of Besses o' th' Barn Band, was responsible for the formation of a private band for Lord Francis Edgerton at Worsley (Edgerton later became 1st Earl of Ellesmere). Lee was also associated with the Duke of Lancaster's Own Yeoman Cavalry Band, which was a brass band.[40] References are made in Chapter 3 to the private band of Sir Walter W. Burrell, a wealthy Sussex landowner and Member of Parliament; and a private band was also formed in the 1840s by the son of the mill owner, W. L. Marriner, at Keighley in Yorkshire. Like the Cyfarthfa Band, Marriner's Band took part in early contests. It is also worth noting that Queen Victoria formed a private band in 1837 which consisted of seventeen players. Apart from a percussionist, all of them were brass or woodwind players and 'master of more than one instrument'.[41] This private band eventually merged with the state band, by which time it was, in effect, a small, multi-functional orchestra, but in the middle of the century it was primarily a brass/wind band, playing arrangements of works by Spohr, Meyerbeer, Weber, and Beethoven, a repertory similar to that which was being performed by the Cyfarthfa Band.[42] Such patronage of private bands may

[39] Wombwell's was in Merthyr in 1846 (*Cardiff and Merthyr Guardian*, 1 Aug. 1846); it is probable that it made an annual visit to the town.

[40] B. Rogerson, 'A Touch of Local Brass', *Eccles and District History Society Lectures* (1977–8), 4.1–4.4.

[41] J. Harley, 'Music at the English Court in the Eighteenth and Nineteenth Centuries', *Music and Letters*, 50 (1969), 334–6.

[42] See T. Herbert, 'The Repertory of a Victorian Provincial Brass Band', *Popular Music*, 9/1 (1990), 117–31.

well have been a model for some of the industrial meritocracy a decade later, many of whom took great pride in having their works band play at garden parties and other social gatherings for their well-heeled friends and associates.

OTHER PROFESSIONAL ENSEMBLES AND SOLOISTS

Many of the players in private bands were drawn from travelling show bands. Circuses and travelling shows are important in the history of British popular music, because they are one of the first types of well organized, commercial entertainment which sought to attract audiences from different classes, and which—because of their itinerant nature—were among the first agencies for spreading similar or identical tastes in popular music and comedy across wide areas of the country. In this respect, such shows, which eventually became important stages for American entertainers, can be said to be prototypes of the thoroughly commercial and sophisticated professional entertainments that manifest themselves as music hall. These travelling shows almost always had bands which were featured in their advertisements. Although Wombwell's Circus and Menagerie was the most famous and perhaps the best, it was not the only itinerant troupe to have a distinguished band. Others included Batty's Menagerie Band, and Howe's Great London Circus. As early as 1833, the *Yorkshire Gazette* was praising the skill of four trombonists from Cooke's Equestrian Circus who had agreed to perform in the 24th Annual Yorkshire Amateur Musical Meeting. 'It is a pity', the paper lamented, 'they are not placed in a situation where their acquirements would be more conspicuously displayed.'[43]

Some of the brass players in these entertainment troupes were conspicuously displayed. Around 1839, Tournaire's Circus featured 'Herr Popowitz', a musical clown who amazed audiences with masterly performances on brass instruments. His performances, according to the recollections of Enderby Jackson, included 'operatic solos, national melodies and airs with brilliant variations in a style unknown before his advent'.[44] There were other brass virtuosi who gained national respect and fame among middle-class audiences. The most celebrated was the trumpeter, Thomas Harper. He was born in Worcester in 1786, and was sent to London to study with Eley, the Duke of York's military bandmaster. At the age of 10 he played in Eley's East India Brigade Band and various London theatre orchestras. Both he and his son, Thomas John Harper, taught at the Royal Academy of Music, and also performed regularly in the provinces.[45]

[43] *Yorkshire Gazette* (5 Jan. 1883).
[44] E. Jackson, 'Origin and Promotion of Brass Band Contests', *Musical Opinion and Music Trades Review* (1896: serialized).
[45] Sadie, *New Grove*, s.v. 'Harper, Thomas'. See also S. Sorenson and J. Webb, 'The Harpers and the Trumpet', *Galpin Society Journal*, 39 (Sept. 1986), 35–57.

Figure 1.2. Thomas Harper, Jr., Professor of Trumpet at the Royal Academy of Music, and the greatest exponent of the slide trumpet, in the uniform of Trumpeter to Her Majesty Queen Victoria.

Another great force was the popular (not to say populist) conductor, Louis Jullien. In his London concerts, which began in 1840, and in the provincial tours he undertook every year, brass instruments were prominently featured. No individual players in Jullien's orchestra were afforded a higher profile than the cornet player, Koenig (whose *Post Horn Gallop* became something of a classic), and the ophicleide player, Prospère (Jean Prospère Guivier). Many other great brass players were either permanently or temporarily associated with Jullien, including Thomas Harper, though Harper—who became Sergeant Trumpeter—was generally involved with more élite sectors of the profession.

It is easy to cast scorn on Jullien's unashamed extravagance and excess, and many have been reluctant to afford him his proper place in nineteenth-century

British music history.[46] It cannot be denied, however, that his impact on audiences was immense. His brass players possessed genuine virtuosity, and no matter how excessive it may seem to twentieth-century tastes, the sound of 'Suona le Tromba' from Bellini's *I Puritani*, played on twenty cornets, twenty trumpets, twenty trombones, twenty ophicleides, and twenty serpents[47] must have been not only astonishing but also influential at a time when all-brass bands were trying to gain a foothold in British musical life.

In December 1844, Jullien featured the Distin family at one of his London concerts. They played saxhorns which they had recently acquired from the inventor, Adolphe Sax, while on a visit to Paris.[48] The Distins already had a distinguished reputation as performers on brass instruments. They were playing as a family quintet in 1835,[49] and gave performances throughout the country, but it was not until they converted to saxhorns and took out the British agency for the instruments that they had their most significant effect.[50] They toured widely, performing mostly in music and concert halls, and their main contribution to the development of brass bands (apart from the interest that they aroused through their own virtuosity) lay in their popularization of the Sax instruments. They were also involved from the early 1850s with a highly successful publishing enterprise which was responsible for a large number of widely distributed journals and score arrangements.

Jullien and the Distins had a great influence in the 1840s, but it is doubtful how many of their concerts were attended by the people, or indeed the *class* of people, who would be the members of brass bands in the decades that followed. Although it is impossible to be certain, it seems that the audiences for the Distins' concerts and for Jullien's extravaganzas were often middle-class. *Punch* provided a lucid description of those attending one of Jullien's concerts:

Amid the merry, but decorous throng, we notice several families of professional gentlemen and tradesmen, as well as persons of higher rank; and many men, who we personally knew, had brought their sisters . . . Many of the young men wore plain black suits and white ties, and though some of these youths, thanks to the early closing movement, may have been linen-drapers' assistants, a greater proportion evidently were of the aristocracy, and not a few, who abstained from actually dancing, had all the appearance of curates. A bishop occupied a private box among the spectators . . .

---

[46] See e.g. R. Nettel, 'The Influence of the Industrial Revolution on English Music', *Proceedings of the Royal Musical Association*, 77 (1946), 33.

[47] A. Carse, *The Life of Jullien* (Cambridge: Heffer, 1951), 53–4.

[48] Ibid. 52. See also W. Horwood, *Adolphe Sax 1814–1894: His Life and Legacy* (Baldock: Egon, 1983), ch. 4, *passim*. The instruments were not announced as saxhorns at Jullien's concert. According to Distin, the organizers had refused to give this title to them because their launch a few weeks earlier had been a failure.

[49] See the *Scotsman* (11 July 1835 and 13 Apr. 1836).

[50] The Distins performed primarily on horns, slide trumpet, and trombone before the famous meeting with Sax. However, Enderby Jackson, 'Origin', states that they were playing valve instruments made by the London firm, Pace, before 1844.

The general tone of the assembly was that of perfect ease, and perfect propriety; the unrestrained and correct expression of amiability and animal spirits.[51]

THE NEW TECHNOLOGY

The invention of the piston valve system and its application to brass instruments is described as the principal reason why a large, working-class, brass band movement came into existence. The various developments in brass instrument technology are detailed later in this book by Arnold Myers. However, it is worth mentioning at this point the fundamental advances that took place and the manner in which those advances affected mass working-class music culture. It is also worth emphasizing that, while these technical advances were fundamental to the brass band movement, they were also momentous in the entire field of instrumental music. It took some time for the changed idiom of brass instruments to find expression in the work of major composers—Brahms, for example, wrote little for the trumpet which could not be played on valveless instruments—but these technologies were to have an irrevocable effect on art music. However, it is in many ways interesting that the exploitation of these new instruments, and the techniques which were associated with them, was most radical among brass bands and other vernacular or working-class music makers.

From the late eighteenth century onwards, experiments were being conducted independently in different parts of Europe which were aimed at the invention of a system which would enable brass players to play the entire chromatic spectrum on instruments of various sizes and pitches. It is perhaps worth explaining why, apart from the trombone, brass instruments of the time lacked such a facility. The pitch of a note played on a brass instrument is determined by the speed at which the player's lips vibrate. This depends on the control of the player's embouchure muscles, and is strongly influenced by the resonance frequencies of the air column in the tube of the instrument. On an instrument which has a fixed length of tubing—such as a bugle—a player can obtain a series of notes. The frequencies of vibration of the player's lips when playing the natural notes of a brass instrument approximate to a harmonic series. The natural notes of an instrument in 7ft D (such as many natural trumpets) would be as shown in Ex. 2. A player with an instrument made from a longer length of tubing would be able to play a lower series of notes, but with

---

[51] *Punch*, 27 (1854), 255, quoted in Carse, *Life of Jullien*, 49–50. Some impressionistic evidence loosely links working-class audiences with Jullien's concerts. Manuscripts relating to Marriner's Band at Keighley refer to some members of the band walking from Keighley to Bradford to see Jullien; it is not known, though, what social status these players had. Enderby Jackson, 'Origin', somewhat floridly describes 'foundries and workshops . . . [being] crowded with disputants on the music marvels Jullien brought to their district'.

Ex. 2. Harmonic series on D

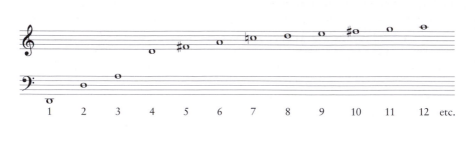

Ex. 3. Harmonic series on C

the same musical intervals between the notes. The natural notes of an instrument in 8ft C would be as shown in Ex. 3.

At the lower end of the series the notes are widely spaced; at the top end, the notes are closer together. The technical problem as it stood at this time was that it is extremely difficult to play these very high notes (this is why Bach's trumpet parts, in, for example, the Mass in B minor, could be played by only a few very skilled professionals), while at the other end of the range, the notes have so many gaps between them that the possibilities for playing tuneful melodies are extremely limited. What brass players needed was what most other instrumentalists had, the facility to play every adjacent note in the range of the instrument. The trombone had such a facility: the telescopic, U-shaped, slide mechanism of the trombone gives that instrument complete chromaticism, because every time the slide is extended or retrieved, the tubing through which the player is blowing becomes (respectively) longer or shorter. In the late eighteenth century, this principle was successfully applied to much shorter lengths of tubing than those used on trombones, by the English inventor John Hyde, and the resulting instrument was used by some professional players as a 'slide trumpet'.

A more widely used invention was the keyed bugle. Keys (larger in size than those on a clarinet, but similar in design) were applied to bugles, and the instruments were widely manufactured. The most celebrated early English key system was that patented by Joseph Halliday in 1810.[52] It was similar to eighteenth-century Austrian inventions for the keyed trumpet or *Klappen-trompete* (it was for such an instrument that Haydn's Trumpet Concerto was written), but no evidence exists to show a direct link between Halliday and other inventors. Valve systems eventually superseded the other designs, but it is important to exercise some caution in attributing the development of brass playing in Britain in the nineteenth century exclusively to the invention and distribution of valved brass systems.

Perfectly serviceable valved instruments were invented by the end of the 1820s, but the complete range of saxhorn instruments was not easily available in Britain until the mid-1840s. Before that time, valved instruments were no more common in brass bands than keyed instruments. The early development of bands was primarily the development of keyed instruments in combination with other types of instrument. The publications of brass music were aimed as much at keyed brass players as at valve instrumentalists. Thomas Harper published his *Airs* for keyed bugle in about 1825, and Tully's *Tutor for Keyed Bugle* was published in 1831 as part of Robert Cocks & Company's Series of Modern Tutors. In 1836, Cocks also published McFarlane's *Eight Popular Airs for Brass Band*, which is regarded as the first British publication specifically for brass bands of sorts. MacFarlane's instrumentation calls for three keyed bugles on the *primo* treble parts, as opposed to cornopeans (the early name for the cornet), but of course the same music could be played on either instrument.[53] In 1836, Blackman and Pace published *The Cornopean Companion of Scales . . .* and it is evident from publications and surviving records of the instrumentation of bands that cornopeans were used throughout the country, but it is equally obvious that early valve systems did not usurp the popularity of keyed instruments. The London firm of Pace was advertising cornopeans in the late 1830s, and, according to Enderby Jackson, the Distins possessed Pace piston instruments before their famous Paris encounter with Adolphe Sax in 1844. However, the Distin family had made their reputation using slide trumpets, french horns, keyed bugles, and trombone, and it was keyed instruments that Robert Crawshay bought from Pace in 1840.[54] The fact should not be overlooked that most of the best British brass players of the first forty years of the nineteenth century played keyed or slide instruments; valve skills were not especially widespread until well into the 1840s.

The other proof of the continuance of older, key-based technology is the dogged survival of the ophicleide until quite late in the century. The ophicleide

---

[52] A. Baines, *Brass Instruments: Their History and Development* (London: Faber, 1976), 194–5.

[53] See Scott, 'Evolution of the Brass Band', 124–9 and 194–6. D'Almaine published a collection under the title *The Brass Band* in 1837; the arrangements were by J. Parry, formerly bandmaster of the Denbigh Militia.

[54] National Library of Wales, Cyfarthfa Papers, Box XIV (Invoice from Pace to Crawshay 21/3/1840).

was eventually replaced by the euphonium—manufacturers encouraged the change by offering euphoniums as prizes for the best ophicleide players at contests—but mid-century reports of the death of the ophicleide were greatly exaggerated. Ophicleides were much in evidence at the Crystal Palace contest in the 1860s, and Sam Hughes, who, with the possible exception of Prospère, was the greatest ophicleide player of the nineteenth century, never, as far as is known, played a valved instrument. It was as a specialist on the ophicleide that he was appointed to a professorship at the Military (later the Royal Military) School of Music at Kneller Hall in 1859, and at the Guildhall School of Music in 1880. Indeed, Kneller Hall appointed Alfred Phasey as euphonium professor at the same time as it appointed Hughes.[55]

A yet more vivid example of the way in which the older technology overlapped with the new was the persistent faith of Thomas Harper in the future of the slide trumpet. He played it all his life, and his *Instructions for the Trumpet*[56] is almost entirely devoted to the slide trumpet. His son, though a brilliant valve instrument player, continued to teach the slide trumpet at the Royal Academy of Music, and, while he was the author of *Harper's School for the Cornet-à-pistons* (undated), in the mid-1870s he also published *Harper's School for the [Slide] Trumpet*.[57] Even at the very end of the century, trumpet players at the Royal Opera House were wrestling with the demands of the Italian opera repertory on slide instruments. One of the Royal Opera House players, W. Wyatt, invented a double-slide instrument in 1890.

A related point here concerns the idea that technical progress goes hand-in-hand with musical, cultural, or artistic improvement, and it is worth rebutting the absurd notion that virtuosity on brass instruments is exclusively related to valved instruments. Since the 1970s, a number of professional trumpet players have learnt the techniques of keyed brass instruments, and have demonstrated a technical facility on keyed brass just as on valved instruments. Primary sources in the form of manuscript music for keyed instruments bear out the same point.[58]

The Distins gave the Sax designs a powerful endorsement which stimulated more instrument manufacturers, music publishers, and others to recognize that a market had come into being which had not existed previously. That market was easily identified as constituting the inhabitants of the

[55] See Lieutenant Colonel P. L. Binns, *A Hundred Years of Military Music* (Gillingham, Dorset: The Blackmore Press, 1959).

[56] T. Harper, *Instructions for the Trumpet* (facsimile of the 1837 edn., with commentary on the life of Harper by John Webb and Scott Sorenson; foreword by John Webb (Homer, NY: Spring Tree Enterprises, 1988)).

[57] Sadie, *New Grove*, s.v. 'Harper, Thomas'. See also Sorenson and Webb, 'The Harpers'.

[58] See T. Herbert, 'The Reconstruction of Nineteenth-Century Band Repertory: Towards a Protocol', in S. Carter (ed.), *Perspectives in Brass Scholarship: Proceedings of the International Historic Brass Symposium* (Stuyvesant, NY: Pendragon Press, 1997), 185–213; R. T. Dudgeon, *The Keyed Bugle* (Metuchen, NJ, and London: 1993).

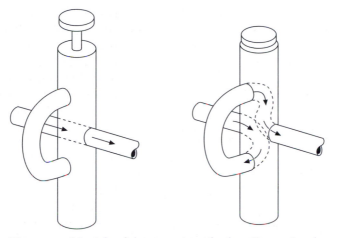

Figure 1.3. Principle of the operation of valves. Depressing the valve lengthens the air column by introducing an extra length of tubing.

comparatively new industrial communities, and especially the more 'affluent' members of the working class. Valved instruments possessed qualities that rendered them particularly suitable to be produced and marketed in large quantities. The musical virtues of the newly designed instruments were self-evident. When a valve was depressed, it instantly changed the length of tubing through which the player was blowing (see Fig. 1.3). The instruments were, therefore, fully chromatic, and reasonably in tune across their entire range, and furthermore, the valve principle could be applied to *any* voice of instrument from the highest cornet to the lowest bass or bombardon. This was a critical advantage of the valve over key-system instruments, for in the latter, only bugles and ophicleides were successful enough to be commonly used.

Valved brass instruments had other features that were equally important. Their production required a less exacting process of manufacture than key-system instruments. After the initial 'tooling' was completed, they could, at least in part, be manufactured by mass-production methods. The older designs, and other instruments such as keyed, woodwind and string instruments, continued to rely on traditional craft skills.[59] Each valve instrument was played with just the three most dextrous fingers of the right hand. To a right-handed player, the initial experience of holding a brass instrument in its playing position is instantly comfortable and natural; this is much less the case with a violin or flute, for instance. Consequently, brass instruments could be learnt easily, and a common fingering technique could be applied to each voice of instrument. The instruments were durable, they used easily available raw

[59] See R. Barclay, *The Art of the Trumpet-maker* (Oxford: Clarendon Press, 1992).

Figure 1.4. Shopfront of the firm of Joseph Higham at 27 Strangeways Manchester in 1892, showing the proprietor, Mr Peter Robinson with most of his seventy-strong staff.

materials, and the manufacturing process employed variants of many existing processes of metal fashioning used for a plethora of domestic and commercial machines and utensils.

From the middle of the century, the number of manufacturers and re-tailers of brass instruments increased dramatically. Some companies were just importing foreign instruments and engraving them with their own names, but many started manufacturing their own models. By 1852, the Manchester firm of Joseph Higham, formed in 1842, was advertising itself as 'Makers to the Army'. The Distins set up a manufacturing business in the early 1850s, and some of the longer established firms eventually diversified into brass instrument manufacture.[60] Scott[61] has cited eighty-six British patents relating to brass instruments registered at the London Patent Office between 1853 and the end of the century, and between 1845 and 1862 twenty-nine specifications for improvements to brass instruments were registered under the terms of the 1843 Design Act.[62] Interest in the newest designs of brass instruments was

[60] W. Waterhouse, *The New Langwill Index: A Dictionary of Musical Wind-Instrument Makers and Inventors* (London: Tony Bingham, 1993).

[61] Scott, 'Evolution of the Brass Band', 424–30.

[62] J. Webb, 'Designs for Brass in the Public Records Office', *Galpin Society Journal*, 38 (Apr. 1985), 48–54.

intensified by the appearance of many at the 1851 Great Exhibition. The most successful exhibitor was Sax, who won a 'Council Medal', but two British designers won 'Prize Medals': George MacFarlane for his 'Improved cornet-à-piston', and John Köhler for his 'Slide Trombone and for the application of his patent valves to other metal wind instruments'.[63]

The widespread adoption of valve instruments, mainly the Sax designs, occurred at a time when the impact of entrepreneurialism on the music industry was at its strongest, and ran parallel to what Cyril Ehrlich has called 'the flood' of activity that occurred in the music profession in mid-nineteenth-century Britain.[64] Between 1841 and 1851, the number of professional musicians and music teachers active in England and Wales rose from 6,600 to 11,200. In the next decade, the numbers were to rise again to 15,000,[65] and though there was a steady increase over the remainder of the century (to 38,600 in 1891), it is in the 1840s and 1850s that the real origins of the musical buoyancy of the late Victorian period are found. The growth of the music profession in Britain is important to the development of bands, because it corresponded with an increase in the entire range of services and activities that supported music, and this phenomenon was not confined to London and a few provincial centres. Concert-going became a more common activity, and, perhaps more importantly as far as the story of brass bands is concerned, the franchise for listening to 'serious' music widened beyond the middle classes. It was not the first time that this had happened, but in the second half of the century it was on an altogether unprecedented scale. One wonders, indeed, how prominent the middle classes were in concert audiences. A report in the *Sheffield Independent* in 1858 noted that 'with the exception of the gallery' (which was, presumably, occupied by the less well-off), 'the house was not more than half filled'.[66]

During the nineteenth century, the population of Britain doubled, but the number of people who made their living from music increased sevenfold.[67] An important element of this development was the increase in music education at all levels. Many private teachers of music—most, apparently, with a lust for the acquisition of diplomas and certificates—set up shop as 'Professors of Music'. These teachers were of critical importance to the development of brass bands. Conductors listed for the 1860 and 1861 Crystal Palace contests included the evocatively named Thomas Tallis Trimnell, Professor of Music, who conducted the 6th Chesterfield Volunteer Band; James Melling, Professor of Music (Stalybridge Old Band); Isaac Dewhurst, Professor of Music (4th West York R. V. Halifax); W. Froggitt, Professor of Cornet (Deptford Pier

---

[63] P. Mactaggart and A. Mactaggart, *Musical Instruments in the 1851 Exhibition* (Welwyn: Mac & Me, 1986), 104–6.

[64] C. Ehrlich, *The Music Profession in Britain since the Eighteenth Century: A Social History* (Oxford: Clarendon, 1988), ch. 5.

[65] Ibid. 236.   [66] *Sheffield Independent* (22 May 1858).

[67] See Ehrlich, *Music Profession*.

Saxhorn Band); and A. Scoll, Professor of Music (Scoll's Operatic). Many more bands throughout the country were trained by men who probably knew little or nothing about brass instruments, but considered themselves qualified to teach virtually anything musical. Such teachers were aided in their endeavours by the existence of 'primers': instruction books which gave the most basic information about playing brass instruments.

THE SOCIAL CONTEXT

Another factor which was helpful to the development of banding was the belief, widely prevalent in the Victorian period, that music, and, in particular, art music, represented a force for the moral elevation of working people. The performance, and, indeed, the reception of music, was a 'rational recreation', a panacea for the many ills to which the working class were believed to be susceptible. Evidence of these views abounds, ranging from the bizarre postulations of the Reverend H. R. Haweis (whose *Music and Morals* (1871)[68] cheerfully proclaimed that certain types of melody could induce virtue, and was reprinted twenty-one times between 1871 and 1906), to the equally enthusiastic, but more measured, testimonies of George Hogarth. In 1846, Hogarth had written in his short-lived weekly newspaper, the *Musical Herald*:

The tendency of music is to soften and purify the mind . . . the cultivation of musical taste furnishes for the rich a refined and intellectual pursuit . . . [and for the working classes] a relaxation from toil more attractive than the haunts of intemperance [and in] densely populated manufacturing districts of Yorkshire, Lancashire and Derbyshire, music is cultivated among the working classes to an extent unparalleled in any other part of the kingdom . . .[69]

Brass bands were often held up as exemplars of the potential of the working man. This is evident from an article entitled 'Music in Humble Life', which Hogarth wrote with W. H. Wills for Charles Dickens's journal, *Household Words*:

Another set of harmonious blacksmiths awaken the echoes of the remotest Welsh mountains. The correspondent of a London paper, while visiting Merthyr, was exceedingly puzzled by hearing boys in the Cyfarthfa works whistling airs rarely heard except in the fashionable ball-room, opera-house, or drawing room. He afterwards discovered that the proprietor of the works, Mr Robert Crawshay, had established among his men a brass band which practises once a week through the year. They have the good fortune to be led by a man (one of the 'roll-turners') who must have had somewhere a superior musical education. I had the pleasure of hearing them play, and was astonished at their proficiency. They number sixteen instruments. I heard them perform the Overture to *Zampa*, *The Caliph of Bagdad*, and *Fra Diavolo*, *Vivi tu*, some concerted music from

[68] H. R. Haweis, *Music and Morals* (London: Strahan & Co., 1871).

[69] *Musical Herald* (4 July 1846), 24. This article contains materials from Hogarth's *Musical History: Biography and Criticism* (London: John W. Parker, 1835).

Roberto, *Don Giovanni*, and *Lucia*, with a quantity of Waltzes, Polkas, and dance music. The bandmaster had them under excellent control; he everywhere took the time well, and the instruments preserved it, each taking up his lead with spirit and accuracy; in short, I have seldom heard a regimental band more perfect than this handful of workmen, located (far from any place where they might command the benefit of hearing other bands) in the mountains of Wales. The great body of men at these works are extremely proud of their musical performance, and like to boast of them. I have been told it cost Mr Crawshay great pains and expense to bring this band to its present excellent condition. If so, he now has his reward. Besides this, he has shown what the intellectual capacity of the workman is equal to, and, above all, he has provided a rational and refined amusement for classes whose leisure time would have been less creditably spent than in learning or listening to music.

The habits and manners of these men appear to have been decidedly improved by these softening influences . . .[70]

There are a number of views as to how and why music was perceived to be operating in this way. Mackerness has argued that any act of collective endeavour, such as banding, which by definition required cooperation among working people, was seen as being good.[71] Another explanation concerns the 'goodness' that many believed was inherent in high art music. Association with it through performance was, therefore, association with virtue. A less complex, but equally compelling reason why playing in a brass band was regarded as a 'rational recreation', was that many working-class men quickly acquired and lucidly demonstrated deft skills as instrumentalists. These skills could be immediately recognized and appreciated by their social superiors, because they could be easily assessed according to a long-established scale of middle-class values. There was another related reason as to why, initially at least, the impetus for the formation of working-class brass bands in the valve era was encouraged by a socially superior sector of society. The higher classes, witnessing the growth of a self-conscious working-class identity, perceived it to be a potential problem. Whether that problem was real or imagined is of little consequence to us here. The important point is that the more enlightened members of the middle classes sought to engage working-class people on a cultural middle ground where certain activities, pastimes, and pursuits were commonly shared across class boundaries.[72] Ultimately, the parameters of that middle ground, and, indeed, its internal identity, were determined from above rather than below, but the point of contact is unambiguously revealed in the repertoire that the bands played, because that repertoire consisted primarily of light, middle-class, and art music.

[70] 'Music in Humble Life', *Household Words* (11 May 1850), 161–4. The authorship of the article is identified in A. Lohrli, *Household Words: A Weekly Journal 1850–1859* (Toronto: Toronto University Press, 1973), 60.

[71] E. D. Mackerness, *A Social History of Music* (London: Routledge and Kegan Paul, 1964), 164.

[72] H. Cunningham, 'Class and Leisure in Mid-Victorian Britain', in B. Waites, T. Bennet, and G. Martin, *Popular Culture Past and Present* (London: Croom Helm, 1982), 69–70.

SETTING UP BANDS

The availability of relatively cheap instruments that were comparatively easy to play, the existence of a network of educated music 'professors' of one sort or another, the new social environment in which working people found themselves, and the commonly held belief among the most influential in society that music was a path to rectitude, combined to provide the context which nurtured the mid-century development of brass banding. It is impossible to measure the number of bands with any accuracy. At the end of the century, brass band magazines tried to calculate the number of bands in existence; their estimates were almost certainly exaggerated. For the period between the 1840s and 1880s, one can only draw on impressions of the number of bands that were active in Britain; these impressions have to be gained from those reports that merited press attention or are mentioned in concert advertisements. Several sources mention the proliferation of bands. Enderby Jackson reflected that in the middle of the century, after cheap valve instruments became generally available, 'almost every village and group of mills in the north of England had its own band. It mattered not to them how the bands were constituted, or of what classification of instruments was in use.'[73]

The 1850s were a particularly important period of growth for banding. Many of the most important developments which generated a widely based, brass band movement, primarily involving working-class people, date from that decade. There was no standard pattern for the origins (or transformation) and sustenance of brass bands, but from the middle of the century, and leaving aside private bands, there appear to be three major types of band. First, there were those which were linked to a single workplace, or which were the beneficiaries of some form of paternalism or direct and sustained patronage from a single, wealthy, benevolent source. The second type were subscription bands which relied for their origin and development on support from a wider community, perhaps through other institutions such as mechanics institutes or temperance societies. These two categories are often difficult to distinguish from each other, because works bands were often subscription bands. The fact that a band carried the name of a mill or factory did not necessarily mean that it owed its origins to the owner of that mill or factory. Indeed, as I discuss below, while it is commonly presumed that Victorian brass bands received direct philanthropic sponsorship—for example, from mill, factory, or mine owners—such patronage probably accounted for only a small percentage of the bands that were formed. The wealthy industrial middle classes were indeed important, however, because subscription bands, while taking money from anywhere they could get it, relied heavily in their early days on such people as major subscribers. The third category consists of those bands which originated

---

[73] Jackson, 'Origin'.

with or were adopted by the 1859 volunteer movement. Some volunteer bands received funds through subscription, others through some form of middle-class patronage. But the funding of volunteer bands is sufficiently complex and interesting to warrant special attention, and this is given below.

This is not to say that there was no direct industrial patronage; such patrons existed from at least the 1840s. The cotton manufacturers, George and Joseph Strutt of Belper, formed a musical society, and 'whatever time [was] consumed in their musical studies [was] recovered in their working hours'. They were often heard to be 'blasting on the ophicleide and trombone'.[74] Another industrialist, Titus Salt, was sufficiently ambitious for his Saltaire Band to promise it a bonus of £50 if it won the 1860 Crystal Palace Contest.[75]

Of the bands that originated through direct industrial patronage in the 1850s, none is more famous than the one formed in the village of Queensbury in the West Riding of Yorkshire. There had been a band of sorts associated with the village since 1816; it appears to have been run by a local publican called Peter Wharton. The village grew rapidly in the first half of the century due to the successful enterprise of John Foster. Foster was the son of a yeoman farmer. He was initially involved in coal mining, but later he established a cotton mill on a piece of land known as 'Black Dike'. Queensbury, or 'Queenshead' as it was known at that time, was a typical example of a small community which existed around a single employing institution. In 1855, Foster, who is reported to have been an amateur french horn player earlier in the century, created a brass band, apparently from the barely smouldering embers of the old village band. The *Halifax Courier* noted that Foster had provided all the principal requisites: (valved) instruments, a room in which to practice, a band teacher, and uniforms.[76] The essential price for Foster's altruism was that the band should henceforth be known as the John Foster and Son Black Dyke Mills Band; it is doubtful whether he anticipated that, despite the high quality of his textiles, the mill would become more famous for its band.

The story of the Black Dyke Mills Band is exceptional because the band's achievements are so exceptional, but it offers a neat illustration of several features that were common to bands of its type. It was formed in a small community rather than a large conurbation. To Foster, its foundation was an act calculated to 'improve' his work people. Many more of the Foster family's gestures in the nineteenth century were aimed at expanding the cultural base of the community: the building of an Albert Memorial outside the mill gates within eighteen months of the Prince Consort's death, and the provision of a school, a library, and a modestly ornate 'Victorian Hall'. Indeed, the adoption at the same time of the name 'Queensbury' instead of Queenshead (the name of one of the local pubs) was a part of the same process. The origin of the 'Black

[74] *Musical Herald* (28 Aug. 1846), 40.   [75] Taylor, *Brass Bands*, 54.
[76] *Halifax Courier* (15 Sept. 1855), 1.

Dike' band provides a good illustration of the sharp difference between brass bands and their immediate predecessors, which casts doubt on theories of continuity in small-town music making during the nineteenth century. Though Wharton's band is known to have existed in 1816, and though there was some sort of musical activity in the village in the years immediately prior to 1855, there is little evidence of continuous musical activity through the first half of the century. Within a few years of its formation, the Black Dyke Mills Band was playing transcriptions of art music in major contests. To draw a causal relationship between the old village band and the 1855 band is analogous to claiming that the motor car was the direct descendant of the bicycle.

Subscription bands, which became more and more numerous as the century progressed, were often started from scratch. Notices were posted in the village of Lynn in Norfolk in November 1853, announcing 'a public meeting' at the Town Hall, 'precisely to take into consideration the propriety of forming a saxhorn band, when the attendance of all persons favourably disposed towards such an object amongst the working class of society is respectfully invited'.[77] By 1855, the Lynn Working Men's Band was firmly in existence, playing quadrilles in the town's 'commodious room' to collect money for 'coals for the poor'. In August 1853, 'A Grand Musical Fête' was held at the Pomona Gardens, Cornbrook, for the benefit of the City Royal Brass Band.[78] The Accrington Band was a subscription band which, as early as 1842, was successful in getting enough money from local gentry to buy instruments.[79] Most bands eventually became subscription bands, because as the century progressed, they relied less on direct patronage and more on homespun entrepreneurship.

THE 1859 VOLUNTEERS AND BANDS

The relationship between the volunteer movement and the brass band movement is complex and intriguing. Contest reports testify to the number of bands which, from as early as 1860, carry the names of volunteer corps. Many of these bands existed under different names before the formation of volunteer movements. By the 1850s, the perceived threat of invasion by a foreign force had grown to proportions that could not be ignored—this period has been termed 'the second scare'. Two factors sharpened concern. The first was the strength of the French armed forces. Franco-British tensions seldom subsided during the century, and were heightened by the foreign policy of Napoleon III. The second cause of concern was that, though the British armed forces were large, well equipped, and highly trained, at any one time a significant proportion of them were abroad, defending and enlarging the Empire. The militia was re-established by the Militia Act of 1852, but seven years later steps

[77] Lynn Museum, Norfolk.   [78] *Manchester Guardian* (20 Aug. 1853).
[79] Taylor, *Brass Bands*, 25.

were taken to constitute a widely dispersed home volunteer force. On 12 May 1859, Jonathan Peel, Secretary of State for War, sent a circular letter to the Lord Lieutenants of all counties instructing them to form a force of volunteers. The principal and most important provisions were that volunteers would 'be liable to be called out in case of actual invasion', and that while under arms they 'would be bound by military law'.[80] Thirteen days later, Peel circulated a second letter which was less earnest and more aware of the need to make the service attractive to potential recruits: 'The conditions of service should be such, while securing and enforcing the above necessary discipline, to induce those classes to come forward for service as volunteers who do not . . . enter into the regular army or militia . . . Drill and instruction for bodies of volunteers should not be such as to render the service unnecessarily irksome.'[81] There was no necessity for an Act of Parliament to establish the 1859 volunteers. The terms of the 1804 Yeomanry and Vounteers Consolidation Act were invoked. Volunteers were exempt from the militia ballot, but were required to receive military training and attend twenty-four drills a year.

From the beginning, bands were seen as a desirable and, to many, an essential part of the volunteer movement. They had a practical use at drills, and they afforded a sense of occasion to special events such as 'annual reviews'. In many respects, they authenticated, or at least gave an air of authenticity to, the activities of the volunteers as they strove for a serious military image with all the necessary resonances of imperialism and patriotism. They were also valuable in promoting good relations between volunteer corps and communities. No provision was made for the funding of bands by the government through the War Office. It is obvious, however, that moneys paid in the 'capitation grant', the official mechanism for government funding, were being appropriated to pay for bands, and soon the issue of volunteer banding became controversial. Within a year of the foundation of the first corps, a correspondent of *The Times* criticized the extravagance of the movement, which, he feared, would be 'the rock on which is it likely to split': 'The expenses of some corps are enormous 400 l or 500 l; being expended on their bands . . . Now, bands ought to be viewed as luxuries, and paid for, as is done in some cases, not out of the funds of the corps, but by a special subscription.'[82]

Many bands were formed by the volunteers from scratch, and, of these, most were probably funded in the proper way by private subscription. A popular way of raising money was to impose on officers an annual subscription over and above the normal corps subscription (as a rule, about 10 guineas a year), specifically for the band fund.[83] Concerts were also held to raise funds.

[80] C. S. Montefiore, *A History of the Volunteer Force: From Earliest Times to the Year 1860* (London, 1908), 403.

[81] Ibid.   [82] *The Times* (15 Aug. 1860), 5.

[83] I. F. W. Beckett, *Riflemen Form: A Study of the Rifle Volunteer Movement 1859–1908* (Aldershot: Ogilby Trusts, 1982), 41.

A graphic account of how bands were formed within the spirit of the standing orders was given by Charles E. Murray, Captain commanding the 16th Middlesex Rifles, in a response to *The Times* letter quoted above. 'Marching without a band', he said, 'would become a dismal business':

Out of some 30 applicants . . . I have formed a band of 17 performers . . . from a separate subscription I have furnished them with instruments and clothes and given them paid instruction.

    The terms on which they serve are

1 They are attested members of the corps.
2 On leaving, they are bound to resign their instruments, etc.
3 They agree (beside meetings for practice) to play once a week at 6pm at HQ.
4 If wanted for a whole day, for instance for the great review, then and only then to be paid for loss of time.[84]

Murray emphasized that the men were 'respectable', and, he added, 'As to position in life they are of the tradesmen and respectable artisan class'. He hoped that 'unpaid bands may become as general as they are possible'. However, many bands were engaged and paid *en bloc* by corps to perform the duties of volunteer bands. In 1874, the Penrith Volunteer Band was costing its corps £52 a year, and the Whitehaven Band £74 a year.[85] In the 1880s, the Dobcross Band was demanding £60 a year to wear the mantle of 'Band of the 34th West Yorkshire Volunteers'.[86]

    In 1861, at least ten of the entrants to the Crystal Palace Contest carried the name of a Rifle Volunteers Corps. The well-established band of W. L. Marriner from Keighley openly referred to themselves as 'W. L. Marriner's Band, also the Band of the 35th Rifle Volunteer Corps'. A year later, they were again calling themselves 'W. L. Marriner's Private Brass Band'. The 1st West Yorkshire Volunteer Fire Brigade Guards was the same band which a year earlier had entered as the Flush Mills Band from Heckmondwike.[87]

    The patriotic element of volunteering afforded it the status of a rational recreation; but the discipline of volunteer corps was variable. There was sustained and stout defence of volunteering in the establishment press, but there was much to defend—not only the behaviour, but also the incompetence of some corps in the exercise of operational duties. In 1861, volunteers at Exeter 'by some strange oversight . . . forgot to keep their sponge wet' and were 'horribly disfigured' by the resulting explosion.[88] There were regular report of volunteers being accidentally killed when 'on the march', and the *Volunteer Gazette*, in one of its regular reports of such incidents, mentioned

[84] *The Times* (22 Aug. 1860), 5.   [85] Beckett, *Riflemen Form*, 116.
[86] H. Livings, *That the Medals and the Baton be Put on View* (Newton Abbot: David & Charles, 1975), 15.
[87] Private collection of Mr Raymond Ainscoe of Kirkby Lonsdale, kindly conveyed by Arnold Myers.
[88] *The Rifleman* (23 May 1861).

the 'unfortunate occurrence' of a young boy being shot while the 3rd Cheshire Rifles were practising.[89]

Men who carried arms and attended a specific number of drills were termed 'effectives'. Bandsmen were not classed as effectives unless they had satisfied the relevant requirements. Some bands contained no effectives, because the means by which they were funded was deliberately disguised. This was especially the case when the band was no more than a civilian band which was contracted in by a discreet and dubious local arrangement. Despite the desirable qualities of these bands, they were a mixed blessing, as it was often impossible to impose military discipline on them. A correspondent of the *Volunteer Service Gazette* in 1868, who signed himself 'a commissioned officer of the volunteers', described bands as 'one of the main causes of the disgrace which has recently fallen on the volunteer force'. He had found at camp a volunteer band marching along with 'a train of boys and girls kicking up dust', and had later found the same men in a railway train, where they were using 'disgraceful language and were too drunk to stand'. Some had challenged a fellow passenger to a fight. He added: 'I think that this incident shows that it is from the bandsmen of some corps that the volunteers get into disrepute. They are notorious for straggling away from their corps and feeling themselves under no sort of constraint and acknowledging no authority whatsoever.'[90]

It is difficult to distinguish the motives of some bands which subscribed to the volunteer force, particularly in respect of their political or radical affiliations, but it seems that some were not always impartial. In August 1868, the Band of the 2nd Cambridgeshire RVC allegedly escorted the Liberal candidate at Wisbech, and in July 1873, the Band of the 5th Fife Artillery Volunteers illegally participated in a trade-union demonstration. The 1st Worcestershire AV Band gave a concert in aid of the Conservative Working Men's Association in Newport, Gwent, and in August 1883, a volunteer band at Renfrew allegedly took part in a procession of the Orange Grand Black Chapter in Glasgow.[91] A further incident took place on the outskirts of Liverpool in September 1883, when two volunteer units fought each other; the fight was apparently caused by a volunteer band deliberately playing a tune which inflamed an Irish mob.[92]

An 1862 Royal Commission on the volunteers[93] concluded that there was too much emphasis on the social activities, which seemed to be the real reason why many joined the corps. This social side can be traced back, at least in part, to the second of Peel's 1859 circular letters to Lord Lieutenants of counties, which strongly inferred that volunteers' duties should be enjoyable, and, in

---

[89] *Volunteer Service Gazette* (20 June 1861), 406.

[90] *Volunteer Service Gazette* (25 July 1868), 531.

[91] Beckett, *Rifleman Form*, 145.   [92] Ibid. 273.

[93] PP 1862 [*c.*3053] xxvii. 89, *Report of the Royal Commission of the Condition of the Volunteer Force*. See also A. Tucker, 'The Army in the 19th Century', in R. Higham (ed.), *A Guide to the Sources of British Military History* (London: Routledge & Kegan Paul, 1972).

the most desirable sense, 'recreational'. While the volunteer movement was regarded as serious and important—reports of volunteer activities were regularly featured in *The Times*, and usually focused on the formal functions of the movement—it is evident that the recreational aspect persisted. This ambiguity surrounding the image of the volunteer movement continued in the 1860s and 1870s, and the bands often acted as a focus for such controversies.

The relationship of the volunteer corps to the brass band movement in the nineteenth century is probably more important than is generally realized. Some proof of this is revealed in the 1878 Departmental Committee Report on the Volunteer Force of Great Britain, chaired by Lord Bury.[94] For the Bury Report, all volunteer corps in the country were circulated with a questionnaire that asked them to detail, under a number of separate headings, their average expenditure over the five-year period from 1873 to 1877. Though there was at this time no formal device to fund bands from volunteer finances, of the 278 of those who returned questionnaires, all but a handful admitted that they supported bands. It was in the interests of the respondents to understate their expenditure on bands, and it is certain that estimates under this heading were artificially low. However, many returns show that the support of a band was a major financial burden. Some officers who were called to give evidence to the Commission admitted to spending a large part of the capitation grant on bands. Lieutenant Colonel J. A. Thompson of the 1st Fifeshire Light Horse VC was challenged: 'Your band cost you 10s. a man: that is a heavy item to come out of the capitation grant: it was £62 last year for 119 men—that takes up the whole equipment fund . . . it runs away with your capitation money.'[95] To this, the officer replied: 'Yes, it does'. Captain and Adjutant Ball of the 1st Middlesex Engineer Volunteer Corps admitted to an average annual expenditure of £280 on the band. When asked for particulars of that expenditure, he replied:

. . . we pay a bandmaster. That expenditure will be lower in the future. We have a new system. We give the bandmaster £12 a year and he provides instruments, clothing and everything for the band. We enrol any men that he likes and we give him the capitation grant for those men. If he has 30 men he can draw the capitation allowance.[96]

Major Sloan of the 4th Lancashire RVC declared an expenditure of £105, and further pleaded that the band 'should be exempt from firing as the buglers are. Their attendance as bandsmen qualifies them for efficiency as far as drill is concerned'. He suggested no substitute duties: 'We have as good a band as we can get . . . but they look upon firing as a heavy task . . . to keep up a good band is one of our difficulties and a good band is necessary in order to get recruits.'[97]

[94] PP 1878/79 [c.2235] xv. 181, *Report of the Bury Departmental Committee.*
[95] Ibid. 1216 ff.   [96] Ibid. 2213.   [97] Ibid. 2550.

Figure 1.5. Band of the 4th Lancashire Rifle Volunteers, later Bacup Old Band, in October 1865. This was the pre-eminent brass band in the period 1862–71. Its instrumentation was typical for the period, though the use of alto trombone was old-fashioned.

The value of a good band to a corps was not disputed, but issues concerning their discipline and funding remained a subject of contention. Ralph H. Knox, deputy accountant general at the War Office, who was also a lieutenant in the 2nd Middlesex RVC, cited bands as one of the three principal causes for excess expenditure on volunteer corps (the other two were extra pay to permanent staff, and county associations). J. R. A. MacDonnal, editor of the *Volunteer Service Gazette*, suggested that the cost of bands should be exclusively borne by commanding officers. Bury concluded: 'No allowance for bands is made in the disembodied period for any branch of the auxiliary forces, any expense under this head being defrayed by private subscription. The Committee cannot advocate any allowance under this head.'[98] In 1887, the Harris Departmental Committee, being sympathetic to the problems of recruiting officers because of the costs required of them for 'balls, bands, refreshments and so on', and noting the recent changes in the funding of regular army bands, recommended that 7.5 per cent of the capitation grant be made for the funding of bands.[99] However, this recommendation was not acted on until the end of the century.

The repertoire of volunteer bands was not strikingly different from that of civilian, contesting bands. The music they were required to play at drills—primarily marches—was a standard feature of the non-volunteer band repertoire, and there is sufficient evidence of volunteers playing band contests and concerts to conclude that when volunteer bands were brass bands (as opposed to a combination of woodwind and brass instruments), as most probably were, their musical identity was barely distinguishable from that of their non-volunteer counterparts.

Notwithstanding the controversies that surrounded the behaviour and discipline of a proportion of bands, others probably benefited from the patriotic and respectable associations of volunteering. The material results of such associations manifested themselves most potently in the band funds. It was in the economics of banding in the nineteenth century that the volunteer force had its impact. It provided a ready source of financing for instruments and bandmasters; drill halls very often doubled as band rooms, and the provision of uniforms was an additional bonus.

Apart from those bands which owed their foundation to the volunteer movement, many were either saved or revived by it. The Bacup Band, after disintegration and amalgamation, were reconstituted to great effect in 1859 as the 4th Lancashire Rifle Volunteers.[100] The Oldham Band, formed in 1865, became Oldham Rifles in 1871, and was extremely successful under Alexander Owen. The volunteers were also responsible for stimulating interest in banding in areas of the country distant from the industrial north. In Sussex, for

---

[98] Bury Report, p. xviii.
[99] PP 1887 [c.4951] xvi. 271, *Report of the Volunteer Capitation Committee*.
[100] Taylor, *Brass Bands*, 50.

example, the Arundel Band was maintained for years as the 2nd Administrative Battalion Royal Sussex Rifle Volunteer Regiment, and there were similar stories at Rudgwick, East Grinstead, and Crawley.[101]

THE ECONOMICS OF BANDING

The volunteer movement sustained many brass bands and may even have saved some from extinction in the second half of the nineteenth century. This was a time when their number multiplied further, when popular interest in them was at its height, and when brass band contests were woven not just into the movement but into the entire fabric of popular music culture. The period has appropriately been called the 'Golden Age'. It was also a period when the commercial zeal of the brass instrument and sheet music industry was most impressive. The seductive pressures exerted by the forces of commerce were adequately matched by brass bands with organized, lucid, and entirely rational strategies for self-determination and economic independence.

From the late 1850s, the cost of musical instruments fell. This was due partly to the removal of protective tariffs through such measures as the 1860 Cobden-Chevalier Treaty, and partly to increased trade volume and a higher level of competition among domestic manufacturers and retailers. Cyril Ehrlich has shown how the prices of woodwind and string instruments fell in the second half of the nineteenth century;[102] a similar picture emerges for brass instruments. In 1839, D'Almaine was advertising cornopeans at prices between £5. 12s. 6d. and £8. 8s. od.; in 1840, Charles Pace was charging £8 and £10 for cornopeans. In about 1873, Boosey & Co., trading as Distin, were offering a 'new model cornet in B♭' for £3. 3s. od. Even in 1889, Joseph Higham was able to advertise new cornets at £3. 3s. od.[103] It is true that these prices were for the cheapest models, but even the more luxurious versions were not beyond the means of a reasonably successful, enterprising band. It is often difficult to determine the actual price of brass instruments in this period. Virtually every purchaser seems to have benefited from a Byzantine system of discounting. Cash, cheques, deferred payments, and any other means of payment, were discounted. There must also have been a huge market for second-hand instruments, for while many bands started up and flourished in the second half of the century, many folded after a few years. Given the durability of brass instruments—even the cheaper ones—it is possible that many of them continued to circulate.

There was no precedent for the quantity of instruments available. By 1895, Bessons employed 131 men in its London factory, making 100 brass instruments

---

[101] Alberry, 'Old Sussex Amateur Bands', 318–19.

[102] Ehrlich, *Music Profession*, 11 ff., gives an excellent succinct account of the economics of the music industry at this time.

[103] Price lists for most of the companies quoted here are reproduced in Appendix 1.

a week. Between 1862 and 1895, the firm produced 52,000 brass instruments. Joseph Higham employed 90 men who produced 60,000 instruments between 1842 and 1893.[104]

From the middle of the century, hire-purchase schemes were available. In 1855, the Bradford Brass Band was engaged in a hire-purchase agreement,[105] and as the century progressed many others entered into similar agreements. At the end of the century, Algernon Rose observed that 'the credit system has become the very basis of the brass band'.[106] Brass instrument manufacturers used several ploys to persuade people to buy brass instruments or exchange their current ones for newer 'improved' models. The award of new instruments as contest prizes for 'the best soloists of the day' was a calculated effort in this direction. Instruments were often advertised not just as new models but as entirely original systems and designs. New and improved valve systems were being introduced, each one claiming to be better than the others. As Arnold Myers explains later in this book, there was a genuine problem with the way some valve designs affected intonation, especially on larger instruments. Manufacturers frequently claimed to have found a definitive solution to the problem, and turned their endeavours to searching for appropriate superlatives to proclaim their availability. In the 1860s, Distins marketed instruments with names such as 'Distin's Celebrated Patent Light Valve Cornet' and the 'First-Class Equisonant Piston Cornet'. The advertising explosion was not confined to Britain. In the USA, Ernst Albert Couturier, a cornet virtuoso who had made a name for himself with Gilmore, employed autobiographical sketches to endorse instruments:

One night before I was to play solos with *Le Garde Republicaine* in Paris, I did five miles at a dog trot in driving rain. I had been practising for five hours daily on my European tour. The next night, as I stood before the audience, waiting for the conductor's nod, a question assailed me. 'Why is it', I thought, 'that, train as we may for breath control, and practice as we will for technical perfection, we brass players must remain at the mercy of an imperfect instrument?'[107]

Some manufacturers offered cash incentives to those who won contest prizes using their instruments. In the 1890s, Silvani and Smith were offering the first band to win a first prize at the Belle Vue Contest, Manchester, using 'a complete set of their instruments', a reward of £50 in cash. Manufacturers also set great store by the endorsement of leading army bands, and on the

---

[104] Scott, 'Evolution of the Brass Band', 103.

[105] D. C. Russell, 'The Popular Music Societies of the Yorkshire Textile District 1850–1914' (D.Phil. thesis, University of York, 1979), 38; see also pp. 138–45.

[106] A. Rose, *Talks with Bandsmen: A Popular Handbook for Brass Instrumentalists* (London: William Rider, 1895; facsimile with an introduction by Arnold Myers, London: Tony Bingham, 1995), 305.

[107] Quoted in G. D. Bridges, *Pioneers in Brass* (Detroit: Sherwood Publications, 1972), 38.

award of prizes at international inventions exhibitions. Besson's proud boast in 1888 was that it had won forty-two highest honours from international exhibitions, and thirty-nine medals of honour awarded to 'the Besson proto-type band instruments', including one award which was 'the ONLY medal ever awarded for TONE quality. Another proof of the incontestable superiority of the prototype instruments.'[108] Attempts were also made late in the century to seduce bands to the latest fashions. An example of this was the pressure put on bands by manufacturers to convert from a brass to a 'silver' band. This meant nothing more than that the brass instruments were subjected to a process of electro-silverplating (ESP). This process added considerably to the cost of instruments, and in 1892 the Pendleton Brass Band paid the high price of £339. 14*s.* for a set of twenty-four ESP instruments from Besson—they may well have discarded perfectly good brass instruments.[109]

There was a variety of ways in which bands met the costs of buying instruments and otherwise sustaining themselves. In 1893, a brass band was started at the Broadwood Piano Factory. In order to provide the workers with an adequate context for their endeavours, the official in charge, Algernon Rose, gave a series of lectures on the history of brass instruments. He subsequently appended a couple more discourses to his writings, and published these as a book which he called *Talks with Bandsmen* (1895). Rose had travelled widely in Britain and abroad—one of his compositions was in the Sousa repertoire. He was an urbane, apparently knowledgeable musician, whose relationship with Broadwood's was not smooth. His book is the most substantial of its type to survive from the nineteenth century, and is particularly valuable for the insights he had gained from visiting various manufacturers of brass instruments. The final chapter of the book, 'How to start a brass band', appears to be a combination of his personal reflections on the subject and an account of his observations of common practices. He advocates a procedure which aspiring bandsmen could use when approaching their employer for his support, supplying them with a model letter:

Dear Sirs,

We, the undersigned, being desirous of employing our leisure time in practising music, request permission to form a brass band in connection with this factory. We shall feel honoured if [you] will consent to become President of the Band. Unfortunately, we are unable at the beginning to defray the entire cost of the purchase of instruments. Messrs. [Bessons] are prepared to sell us the brass instruments required, provided that the firm, whose name we should like to take, will act as surety for the deferred payments.

We are, dear sirs, yours respectfully[110]

---

[108] *British Bandsman* (Dec. 1888).
[109] *Wright & Round's Brass Band Journal* (1 Jan. 1892).
[110] Rose, *Talks*, 303–4.

Rose was probably describing a practice that was well established, and one which was doubtless instigated by the purveyors of musical instruments. It is interesting that his advice was to procure guarantees, not sponsorship. As I said earlier, a number of bands were the recipients of direct patronage by industrial entrepreneurs, but it is doubtful if this type of practice was extensive. R. T. Crawshay, as far as we know, was not simply donating instruments and facilities to the members of his band. Though Crawshay's name was engraved on the bells of the instruments, his cash books contain indications of regular payments *to* him from the bandsmen 'for instruments', suggesting that they were repaying loans.[111] It was much more usual, particularly towards the end of the century, for bands to rely on entrepreneurial income and subscriptions. Subscriptions came from the members of the bands themselves; for example, as early as 1842, W. L. Marriner's Band was imposing monthly subscriptions on its members.[112] Special expenditures, such as the purchase of new instruments, caused bands to issue appeals for general subscriptions. In 1866, the Llanelly Band purchased a set of fifteen instruments at 'the lowest trade price of £75. 16. 3'. This amount was raised as follows:

Subscriptions at the start of the band	£36. 2. 6
Concert, November 1885	£ 7. 3. 2
Athletic Sports, June 1886	£13.16. 11[113]

The band also carried an amount of £14 made up from subscriptions from the members for 'current expenses'.

Income from concerts was very important in the economics of nineteenth-century banding. In 1885, the St George's Works Brass Band, Lancaster, operated on a monthly balance of about £4. This amount included total contributions of about 4s. to 7s. a week from members. But the collection or fee for a single concert would raise almost £4 in one evening.[114] Seaside bands at major resorts were often professional. They operated on much larger balances, up to about £500, but their funding was based on the same principles. For example, on Saturdays in August 1874, the Llandudno Promenade Band was collecting amounts between £25 and £27 a day.[115]

Apart from the cost of the upkeep of instruments and uniforms, and necessities such as heating, lighting, and sometimes hiring rehearsal rooms, the other regular items of expenditure were the fees to conductors. These often came to about 5s. a week; the top conductors may well have cost considerably

[111] See Herbert, 'Virtuosi of Merthyr'.
[112] University of Leeds Brotherton Library, W. L. Marriner's Caminando Band Minute Book.
[113] *Llanelly and County Guardian* (28 Oct. 1886). I am grateful to Dr David Evans of the University College of Wales, Bangor, for sources relating to the Llanelly Band.
[114] 'The Treasurer's Book for Members of the St. George's Works' Brass Band, Lancaster 1885–1886', Morecambe Library, Lancashire.
[115] Gwynedd Archive Service XM/3121/791 (private papers of Thomas Hughes).

more. Journal music was another regular expense. Journals varied in price, but bands spent between 1s. and 2s. per issue per month. In the 1880s, *Wright & Round's Journal* cost between 19s. and £1. 9s. 6d. a year.

Another important source of income for the major bands was prize money from contests. The more successful of them, such as Besses o' th' Barn and Black Dyke, measured their winnings in pounds, shillings, and pence. In the first thirty years of its contesting career, Besses o' th' Barn had won prizes to the total value of £3,359. 17s.[116] Prize money varied according to the status of the contest. Small contests, like the ones at Clitheroe, Middleton, and Rochdale, were worth between £5 and £7; larger ones were worth a lot more. Belle Vue paid about £35 plus benefits to the winners in the 1870s. For winning the 1887 contest, Kingston Mills Band received a cash prize of £30, and an euphonium valued at £30 [*sic*], and the individual band members won gold medals to the total value of £78. 15s.[117] Many bandsmen received fees for playing in concerts and contests. Even the smaller bands in the south-east of England charged 2s. or 3s. per player, plus a free dinner for their services.[118] There is little doubt that many brass band players supplemented their regular income by playing, and for larger contesting bands, winning contests brought income and an additional *gravitas* which secured further fees from concert engagements. It is likely that the unsavoury scenes that followed disputed results at contests in the latter part of the century were caused as much by injuries that the bandsmen felt to their wallets as to their pride.

RUNNING A BAND

Mid- and late Victorian bands were able to exercise strict and successful control of their finances, because most were constituted on fairly democratic lines and adhered to lucidly expressed sets of rules and regulations. Most of the surviving band constitutions exhibit prominent concern for the proper handling of money. Subscription rates were fixed and outgoings carefully policed. One senses a certain pride in the authorship of such documents; they are often self-consciously detailed, with little left to doubt or chance. Many bands engaged solicitors to draw up their deeds and constitutions. Even small enterprises such as the Maelor Brass Band League near Wrexham, whose sole purpose seems to have been to run an annual contest with a cup as a prize—a contest deemed to be properly constituted if just two bands entered—went to the trouble of engaging a leading local solicitor to draw up a lengthy trust deed which was attested by all of the proper deed and stamp duties.[119]

---

[116] J. N. Hampson, *Besses o' th' Barn Band: Its Origin, History and Achievements* (Northampton: Jos. Rogers, *c.*1893), 70.
[117] Ibid. 72 ff.   [118] See Alberry, 'Old Sussex Amateur Bands'.
[119] Clwyd Archive Service DD/WL/251.

The most remarkably forward-looking and entrepreneurial band of the nine-teenth century was the Besses o' th' Barn Band from Whitefield, Lancashire, which, in 1887, with all the necessary legal properties, formed itself into a limited company. It is generally assumed that the band had started as Clegg's Reed Band in or by 1818. John Clegg was a local cotton manufacturer and keyed bugle player. Privately owned documents relating to Besses o' th' Barn include a set of 'Articles' of the 'Stand Band', dated 1828. The leader is named as Thomas Lee, who is known from other sources to have been associated with the early years of the Besses o' th' Barn Band. The instrumentation of the Stand Band is not revealed in the Articles, but James Melling is named as a commit-tee member—probably the same man who wrote *Orynthia* and who collabor-ated with Jennison on the first Belle Vue contest. The remarkable thing about these Articles is their rigorous attention to detail, matching most documents of this type composed later in the century. Assuming that the Stand Band was Besses under an earlier name, it indicates a long history of self-government, discipline, and careful administration. The Band had been extremely success-ful, and 1887, the year of Victoria's Golden Jubilee, brought a flood of engage-ments and contest successes which gave it sufficient faith in its musical and entrepreneurial abilities to engage the Manchester solicitors, Alfred Grund and Son, to draw up and prove the necessary documentation. The company was called the 'Besses o' th' Barn Old Band Union Limited'. It had already bought a 'club' building which was the registered office. The object of the company was 'to establish and maintain a brass band . . . and to sell, improve, manage, develop and maintain the property of the band . . . to invest the monies of the band . . . and to do what else was required to further the objects'. The fourth article of the company concerned the income from contests and concerts: 'To enter and play at Brass Band Contests in Great Britain and Ireland; to acquire money by playing for remuneration in any other manner and to get up, conduct, and carry out any concert or other entertainment, or to join any other company, society or person in carrying out the aforesaid objects.'[120]

Because bands were fastidious over record-keeping, the sources that have survived and are available show that the practice of paying players was com-mon. Band account books often record the distribution between members of takings from contests and engagements. The records of W. L. Marriner's Band leave little doubt that players were being paid at a time when they were taking part in contests (contests usually outlawed professionalism), and a written agreement drawn up between the Idle and Thackley Band in 1898 and the trombonist Willie Hawker is entirely explicit: 'Willie Hawker does herby [*sic*] agree to give the whole of his services as solo Trombonist to the above band for 12 Calendar months at a sum of £5. 0. 0. And that he receives all engagement moneys when other members do . . .'[121] It is important to stress, however, that

---

[120] Hampson, *Besses o' th' Barn Band*, 42–3.   [121] Bradford District Archives 54D80/1/6.

band rule-books also show evidence of concerns which are wider than those pertaining to finances. They are laced with phrases that safeguard democratic processes, but at the same time, most delegate musical and disciplinary authority to the bandmaster or conductor. St George's Works Band delegated 'All power . . . to the bandmaster during practice',[122] and the Idle and Thackley Band allowed 'the Bandmaster for the time being . . . [to] have full control over all the members of the band and if any member or members disobey him, or otherwise misbehave himself shall be fined'.[123] Musical and social indiscipline was treated seriously. Idle and Thackley Band would 'expel any member for misconduct or for not being musically gifted enough to become a good player in the band'. Bands also legislated to promote the ethos of social harmony and cooperation that the rational recreationists held in such high regard. The rules of W. L. Marriner's Caminando Band, perhaps not surprisingly, provide a good example of this: 'As this brass band is formed for mutual amusement and instruction in music, and, as peace and harmony are essential to its welfare, it is highly requisite that no dispute or angry feeling should arise among its members, therefore for the prevention of any such occurance [*sic*], the following rules and regulations have been adopted.'[124] This sentiment was enforced by Rule 7 of the Band's regulations which threatened to impose upon its members 'for every oath or angry expression, [a] penalty of 3/-'.

Such bureaucracies and administrative structures were not, of course, uncommon among organized working-class groups. Trade unions, mechanics institutes, and even churches, provide abundant evidence of committees, rule-books, and schemes for democratic organization. But the primary reason why nineteenth-century bands were *so* well organized is that they had to be, in order to survive. From the moment a band entered into a hire-purchase agreement, it was bound to a debt that could only be repaid if it was organizationally and musically successful. Such pressures were intensified if the guarantor of the loan was the employer of most or all of the band's members.

Another factor which encouraged the formality of the business organization of bands was the rules and regulations that surrounded contests (see, for example, Fig. 1.6 and Appendix 3). Leaving aside the embryonic brass band contests which took place before about 1850, the earliest contests were entrepreneurial and primarily aimed at entertainment. The influence of Enderby Jackson was especially important in the birth and development of the brass band contest. Jackson was a brilliant businessman, with real entrepreneurial flair and not a hint of modesty. He claimed to have invented the brass band contest in its 'modern' form, and it is likely that he was right. He also claimed to have invented the idea of the cheap day railway excursion, in order to enable

---

[122] Morecambe Library, 'Treasurer's Book'.
[123] Bradford District Archives 54D80/1/5, 2.
[124] University of Leeds Brotherton Library, W. L. Marriner's Caminando Band Minute Book.

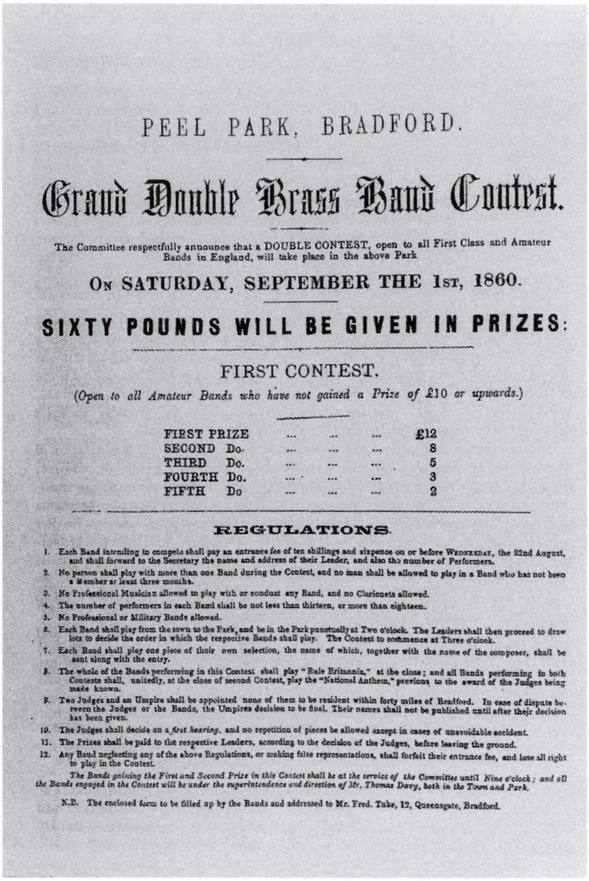

PEEL PARK, BRADFORD.

Grand Double Brass Band Contest.

The Committee respectfully announce that a DOUBLE CONTEST, open to all First Class and Amateur Bands in England, will take place in the above Park

ON SATURDAY, SEPTEMBER THE 1ST, 1860.

SIXTY POUNDS WILL BE GIVEN IN PRIZES:

FIRST CONTEST.

(Open to all Amateur Bands who have not gained a Prize of £10 or upwards.)

FIRST PRIZE	... ...	£12
SECOND Do.	... ...	8
THIRD Do.	... ...	5
FOURTH Do.	... ...	3
FIFTH Do	... ...	2

REGULATIONS.

1. Each Band intending to compete shall pay an entrance fee of ten shillings and sixpence on or before WEDNESDAY, the 22nd August, and shall forward to the Secretary the name and address of their Leader, and also the number of Performers.
2. No person shall play with more than one Band during the Contest, and no man shall be allowed to play in a Band who has not been a Member at least three months.
3. No Professional Musician allowed to play with or conduct any Band, and no Clarionets allowed.
4. The number of performers in each Band shall be not less than thirteen, or more than eighteen.
5. No Professional or Military Bands allowed.
6. Each Band shall play from the town to the Park, and be in the Park punctually at Two o'clock. The Leaders shall then proceed to draw lots to decide the order in which the respective Bands shall play. The Contest to commence at Three o'clock.
7. Each Band shall play one piece of their own selection, the name of which, together with the name of the composer, shall be sent along with the entry.
8. The whole of the Bands performing in this Contest shall play "Rule Britannia," at the close; and all Bands performing in both Contests shall, unitedly, at the close of second Contest, play the "National Anthem," previous to the award of the Judges being made known.
9. Two Judges and an Umpire shall be appointed none of them to be resident within forty miles of Bradford. In case of dispute between the Judges or the Bands, the Umpires decision to be final. Their names shall not be published until after their decision has been given.
10. The Judges shall decide on a *first hearing*, and no repetition of pieces be allowed except in cases of unavoidable accident.
11. The Prizes shall be paid to the respective Leaders, according to the decision of the Judges, before leaving the ground.
12. Any Band neglecting any of the above Regulations, or making false representations, shall forfeit their entrance fee, and lose all right to play in the Contest.

The Bands gaining the First and Second Prize in this Contest shall be at the service of the Committee until Nine o'clock; and all the Bands engaged in the Contest will be under the superintendence and direction of Mr. Thomas Davy, both in the Town and Park.

N.B. The enclosed form to be filled up by the Bands and addressed to Mr. Fred. Tuke, 12, Queensgate, Bradford.

Figure 1.6. Bradford Brass Band Contest Regulations, 1860. The rules for this contest are similar to many that are found in the same period. (Later contest regulations can be found in Appendix 3.)

bands and their supporters to travel to his contests. Notwithstanding the fact that such excursions were in place in order to allow people to travel to the 1851 Crystal Palace exhibition, it is likely that he was right in this respect too, for the correspondence between him and the railway companies, in which he proposed such an arrangement, shows them to have treated the proposal as novel.

Jackson claimed to have been inspired with the idea of brass band contests as a leisure spectacle (see Fig. 1.7) when he noticed the success of agricultural shows in which pigs and sheep were matched against each other, with every spectator trying to second-guess the judge. He organized contests in several parts of the country, but the most important were the Belle Vue contests which he ran from 1853, and the short-lived but influential National Contest at the Crystal Palace in Sydenham, which he presented for three years from 1860.

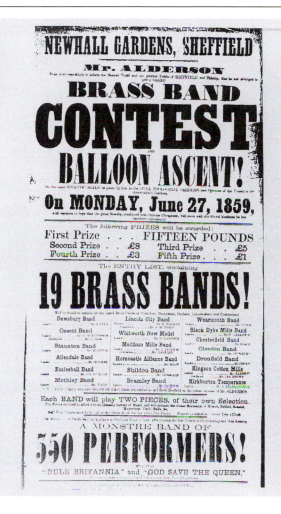

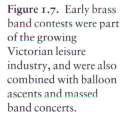

Figure 1.7. Early brass band contests were part of the growing Victorian leisure industry, and were also combined with balloon ascents and massed band concerts.

Jackson's contests became important and drew wide popular support. Soon the idea was imitated by others, and as the brass band movement gathered pace, the seriousness and fervour of the contestants had to be accommodated by careful regulations. It soon became necessary for each band to submit a detailed application form indicating the instruments that would be used, the uniform worn, and the occupations of the players (to guard against professionalism). For the 1860 Crystal Palace Contest, bands were also required to give the pitch for each instrument (so that a massed band concert could be organized), as well as to indicate the railway company they would use and the station at which they would board (so that Jackson could make the necessary arrangements for excursions) (see Fig. 1.8). Eventually, the now-familiar

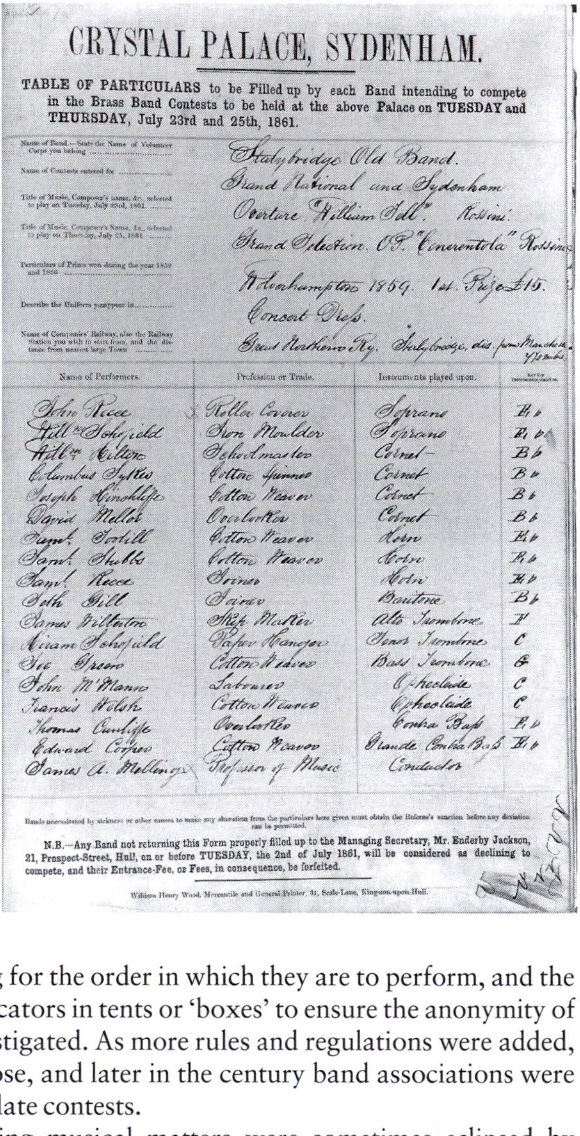

CRYSTAL PALACE, SYDENHAM.

TABLE OF PARTICULARS to be Filled up by each Band intending to compete in the Brass Band Contests to be held at the above Palace on **TUESDAY** and **THURSDAY**, July 23rd and 25th, 1861.

Name of Band.—State the Name of Volunteer Corps you belong .... Stalybridge Old Band.

Name of Contests entered for .... Grand National and Sydenham

Title of Music, Composer's name, &c. selected to play on Tuesday, July 23rd, 1861. .... Overture "William Tell". Rossini.

Title of Music, Composer's Name, &c., selected to play on Thursday, July 25, 1861 .... Grand Selection. O.P. "Cenerentola" Rossini

Particulars of Prizes won during the year 1859 and 1860 .... Wolverhampton 1859. 1st. Prize £15.

Describe the Uniform you appear in........ Concert Dress.

Name of Companies' Railway, also the Railway Station you wish to start from, and the distance from nearest large Town .... Great Northern Ry. Stalybridge, dis. from Manchester 7½ miles.

Name of Performers.	Profession or Trade.	Instruments played upon.	Key for Instruments played on.
John Reece	Roller Coverer	Soprano	E♭
Willm Schofield	Iron Moulder	Soprano	E♭
Willm Hilton	Schoolmaster	Cornet	B♭
Columbus Sykes	Cotton Spinner	Cornet	B♭
Joseph Hinchliffe	Cotton Weaver	Cornet	B♭
David Mellor	Overlooker	Cornet	B♭
Saml Tootill	Cotton Weaver	Horn	E♭
Saml Stubbs	Cotton Weaver	Horn	E♭
Saml Reece	Joiner	Horn	E♭
Seth Gill	Joiner	Baritone	B♭
James Wilkinson	Skep Maker	Alto Trombone	F
Hiram Schofield	Paper Hanger	Tenor Trombone	C
Geo Green	Cotton Weaver	Bass Trombone	G
John McMann	Labourer	Ophecleide	C
Francis Walsh	Cotton Weaver	Ophecleide	C
Thomas Cunliffe	Overlooker	Contra Bass	E♭
Edward Cooper	Cotton Weaver	Grande Contra Bass	E♭
James A. Melling	Professor of Music	Conductor	

Bands necessitated by sickness or other causes to make any alteration from the particulars here given must obtain the Referee's sanction before any deviation can be permitted.

N.B.—Any Band not returning this Form properly filled up to the Managing Secretary, Mr. Enderby Jackson, 21, Prospect-Street, Hull, on or before TUESDAY, the 2nd of July 1861, will be considered as declining to compete, and their Entrance-Fee, or Fees, in consequence, be forfeited.

William Henry Wood, Mercantile and General Printer, 31, Scale Lane, Kingston-upon-Hull.

Figure 1.8. The entrance form for the 1861 Crystal Palace Contest, submitted by the Stalybridge Old Band. The conductor, James Melling, was one of the founders of the Belle Vue Contest.

practice of bands drawing for the order in which they are to perform, and the system of encasing adjudicators in tents or 'boxes' to ensure the anonymity of competing bands were instigated. As more rules and regulations were added, so more controversies arose, and later in the century band associations were formed, primarily to regulate contests.

Controversies concerning musical matters were sometimes eclipsed by financial arguments, and there was tension between those who wished to develop genuine amateurism and the well-established contesting bands, whose members had grown used to having their incomes supplemented by share-outs or contest prizes. In 1893, Thomas Valentine, representing Besses o' th' Barn, Wyke Temperance, and Kingston Mills, three bands which had a lot to lose from the imposition of pure amateurism, wrote to the *Cornet* in response to 'The Proposed National Amateur Brass Band Association': 'It has been mentioned to me that several Contests are intended to be held next year on still stricter rules than at the recent Blackpool contest—that is to say, no paid players of any kind to compete, and as this affects more or less every band of note I HEREBY CALL A MEETING . . . [to take steps] to protect such bands.'[125]

In 1903, the issue of payment to contesting bandsmen was still prominent. The organizers of a new contest at Huddersfield felt that it was a matter that had to be settled before any progress could be made. The contest secretary frankly admitted: 'We cannot get a really big entry with the present system of shut playing bands (and their conductors) look upon it as an engagement & so it is, without any pay [*sic*]. They don't like the principle of it, this is what they kick against. I believe if we only gave 6*d*. to each bandsman we should have a bigger entry.'[126]

Contests offered material rewards and acted as focuses for the entire brass band movement. This was particularly important before the advent of specialist magazines, which, when they were introduced during the 1880s, served to intensify the interest in contests, underline their importance, and galvanize the orthodoxy which was to typify the movement as a whole. It would be grotesquely unfair, though, to characterize the significance of contests as uniquely or even primarily financial. The most important aspects of contesting were musical, and these matters are discussed below. At a more general level, contests engendered feelings of pride, not just among the members of bands, but among the people of the communities in which the bands resided. The most enduring impression of contesting bands in the late nineteenth century is of their earnestness and seriousness of resolve. The hackneyed image of a red-faced bandsman contentedly puffing at a B♭ bass in the upstairs room of a pub, while a pint of beer waits under his chair, is a hopeless misrepresentation of the truth. Contesting bands were single-minded and determined in their pursuit of excellence.

REPERTOIRE

There are three types of source that cast light upon brass band repertoire in the nineteenth century: the printed sources, the surviving manuscript music, and other, miscellaneous documentary sources, such as concert programmes. Examples of each of these types of source survive in archives and private collections throughout Britain, and it is likely that those which have been analysed by historians are but a small proportion of those which actually exist. The printed repertoire includes solos, quartets, brass and military band journals, and the printed so-called 'standard instrumentation' repertoire

---

[125] *Cornet* (15 Nov. 1893).
[126] Huddersfield Public Library S/HT.1 (Brass Band Minute Book, Huddersfield Band of Hope Union).

which appeared later in the century. These are important because they represent examples of the relationship between publishers and a wide social audience. The bands were no more than executants of this type of repertoire. Published music for early brass bands started to appear in the 1830s. MacFarlane's *Eight Popular Airs for Brass Band* was published in 1836. In 1837, D'Almaine published *The Brass Band*, a set of popular pieces arranged by J. Parry, a former militia bandmaster and music critic of the *Morning Post*.[127] Parry's *Brass Band* was the mainstay of the W. L. Marriner's Band in the early 1840s. From about 1840, publishers started producing brass band journals. The first regular subscription journal for brass band is probably the one published by Wessel & Co.[128] Brass band journals were musical publications; they contained little text other than musical text. Bands subscribed to them and received up to twelve publications each year. The instrumentation was flexible; alternative parts were provided for different instruments. Wessel's journals in the 1840s were for solo cornet-à-pistons, first and second cornet-à-pistons, two horns, three trombones, and ophicleide, with *ad libitum* parts for Db cornet-à-pistons or bugle, two horns, three trumpets, and kettle drums. The arrangements were workmanlike and functional. Brass bands were not the only ensembles to be served by journal music; concertina bands, military bands, string bands, and a plethora of other instrumental combinations were also catered for. The journals contained a mixture of light pieces and arrangements of art music. Several publishers brought out band journals. Smith's *Champion Brass Band Journal* was published in Hull from 1857; Chappell, Distin, Jullien, and Boosey all published journals. *Distin's Journal*, which was published by Boosey from 1869, was:

FOR A BAND OF TEN.—1st Cornet in B flat: 2nd ditto; 1st Cornet in E flat; 1st and 2nd Tenors in E flat; Euphonion; Bombardon; Side and Bass Drums. The Euphonion and Bombardon parts may be had in either the Treble or Bass Clef.

Subscription: Ten shillings and Sixpence per Annum for Ten Performers (Postage Free in the United Kingdom), payable in advance. Price to Non-Subscribers: One Shilling each Number.

This Journal is arranged to suit a Band of any size, and extra Parts may be had for the following Instruments: Repiano Cornet in B flat; Cornets, 3rd and 4th, in B flat; Solo Tenor in E flat; 2nd Baritone in B flat; 1st and 2nd Trombones in B flat (either in the Treble or Bass Clef); Bass Trombone; and Contra-Bass in B flat. Price of extra or duplicate Parts Twopence each, or to Subscribers Three Halfpence.[129]

There was also a considerable trade in the publication of solo and smaller ensemble pieces. In the mid-1840s, Boosey started publishing its *Repertory for*

[127] Scott, 'Evolution of the Brass Band', 194.

[128] There is some doubt as to when *Wessel's Brass Band Journal* was first published. Scott has dated it 1837. The British Library gives the date 1845 for books 10–14. This suggests that the first was issued in the early 1840s.

[129] *Distin's Journal* (London: Boosey, 1869–?).

Cornet and Piano. These publications were mainly arrangements of operatic arias; they cost 3*s*. each. In 1847, Distin published a *Selection of the most Favourite Swedish melodies* as *sung by Md. Jenny Lind* for cornet-à-pistons, saxhorn, or tuba with pianoforte accompaniment *ad lib*. Koenig's *Journal for Cornet-à-piston and Piano*, which was published by Chappell, eventually contained 140 items. Wessell also published *The Amateurs' Brass Band Quartets* (1852) for three cornet-à-pistons and ophicleide or valve trombone, and from about 1860, Robert Cocks & Co. started publishing their *Brass Band Magazine*, costing 2*s*. per arrangement, and apparently aimed at smaller bands of modest means and ability. By the early 1860s, journals were mainly devoted to arrangements of Italian opera. In 1875, Thomas Wright and Henry Round started publishing a brass band journal in Liverpool. Later publications by this firm were to be very influential.

Of the non-printed sources, manuscript part books are crucially import-ant to understanding the musical identity of bands. Whereas printed music indicates what a publisher saw fit to purvey, handwritten part books indicate what bands were actually playing. Among the major sources known to have survived are the Goose Eye band books at Keighley in Yorkshire, the Black Dyke Mills band books at Queensbury in Yorkshire, and—by far the most comprehensive and earliest complete run—the set at the Cyfarthfa Castle Museum in Merthyr Tydfil, South Wales.[130] The Black Dyke band books are incomplete—only eight books survive, dating from not long after the band was formed in 1855. They contain forty-three pieces. There is a mixture of dances (quadrilles, polkas, and waltzes), but also a significant proportion of pieces drawn from the art-music repertoire—especially opera transcriptions. The Goose Eye band music, dating from 1852, contains more than thirty pieces. The repertoire here is of an entirely different order: almost the entire collection is devoted to light music: dances and song arrangements, with a few arias and chorus arrangements. Five of the pieces—*Morning Star Polka, Bonnets of Blue, Rock Villa Polka, Lily Bell*, and *The Light Horseman*—are attributed to the Hull composer, arranger, and publisher, Richard Smith.[131]

Manuscript band parts dating from later in the century survive in band libraries and other private collections. Some sources are particularly interest-ing, because they contain the original interpretative annotations, and appear to survive with the entire set intact. Full scores are sometimes encountered, but such scores were not routinely written out. The Cyfarthfa conductor, for example, conducted from an annotated 'primo cornet' part-book.

Although there are clear differences, there are also a number of similarities between the repertoires of major bands. Most collections contain art music, popular pieces, and what can be loosely described as functional tunes such as

---

[130] See Ch. 8 for more detail on the handwritten part books of bands such as the Cyfarthfa Band.
[131] See Scott, 'Evolution of the Brass Band', 215.

national anthems, Christmas carols, and works which are idiosyncratic to particular localities. Original compositions for brass band constitute a tiny proportion of the repertoire. One is bound to ask what forces were at work to create such concordances. This question is best answered by looking not just at the manuscript music and printed parts, but also at the sources from which arrangements were made. I have already pointed to the increased availability of published music of all types from the middle of the nineteenth century onwards. Art music—particularly pot-pourris of foreign works—was popular among the middle-class consumers. Choral music such as oratorio, and major orchestral works, were also available at comparatively modest prices. Novello's publications, for example, were widely distributed. There was also a market for quadrilles, polkas, and waltzes in short score form produced for domestic pianists. Another type of music aimed, initially at least, at the middle-class market, was piano arrangements of opera extracts—Italian opera was the favourite. British publishers lost no time in making such extracts available to the wider public. Verdi's *Il Trovatore* was first performed in Rome on 13 January 1853. In February 1853, the *Music Publishers' Circular*, No. 2, carried a 'Musical Announcement' from Boosey & Sons: 'Verdi's new opera *Il Trovatore*. This opera has just been produced in Rome, with the most extraordinary success, the composer having been called before the curtain fifteen times during the performance—seven pieces now ready. The remainder of the opera is now in press.' It was probably from sources such as these that bandmasters and journal editors made their arrangements. James Smyth's brass band arrangement of the overture to Verdi's *La Forza del Destino*[132] was in circulation within a few months of the opera's first performance in St Petersburg in 1862.

Brass band journals, which also emphasized operatic transcriptions, were, ironically enough, the source for further arrangements and transcriptions. It is known that some bands had copies of journals, and also had manuscript arrangements of the pieces contained in those journals.[133] So it is likely that some band arrangements were fourth-hand, via the composer's original, the short score, the journal arrangement, and then the rearrangement by the bandmaster.

Although there is a great deal of similarity between the brass band repertoire and the middle-class musical tastes that ran parallel to it—art music, quadrilles, waltzes, and so on—there are certain types of popular Victorian music that seldom appear as arrangements for brass band. There were few arrangements of music hall songs, with the exception of minstrelsy tunes,

---

[132] Ainscoe Collection, shown at the 1989–90 *Brass Roots: 150 Years of Brass Bands* exhibition, University of Edinburgh Collection of Historic Musical Instruments.

[133] The Cyfarthfa Band, for example, won a set of journals in 1860, but continued to play from manuscript part books which contained many of the titles included in the journals.

and one seldom encounters arrangements of domestic song, even though this repertoire was hugely popular and widely available through the same distribution networks as operatic repertoire. However, some English music which had its origins as solo song did give rise to transcriptions; songs by Sir Henry Bishop seem to have been particularly popular, and Sullivan's 'The Lost Chord' is often found in sensitive arrangements for brass band.

There are obvious reasons why contests contributed to the standardization of the brass band repertoire. The cross-fertilization of ideas brought about by the congregation of many brass bands also had other effects. Such occasions provided opportunities for the creation of a common understanding of the musical idiom of the brass band, and of the instruments in it. Many of the brass band contest pieces that survive from the nineteenth century make extensive demands on players, not just in requiring technical agility and a command of wide dynamic and pitch ranges, but because they also assume that brass band musicians had considerable stamina. The players in the Cyfarthfa Band were required to play *complete* symphonies (all four movements) by Beethoven, Mozart, and Haydn. Besses o' th' Barn Band, under Alexander Owen, were tested with opera selections which lasted for thirty-five or forty minutes at a time.

In the last two decades of the century, the standard instrumentation that is still used for contests and by publishers of brass band music today—a mixture of cornets, saxhorn-type tenor and bass instruments, and trombones—was formulated. Publishers, perhaps most influentially the Liverpool-based Wright and Round, following the practices of some of the major northern bands—especially those which were conducted by the three greatest conductors of the period, John Gladney, Edwin Swift, and Alexander Owen—moved towards, and then established, a common system of instrumentation. Confirmation of the widespread acceptance by contesting bands of this standard ensemble is found in publications later in the century such as Lodge's *The Brass Band at a Glance*, which not only lists the instruments used, but also its clefs (treble for all instruments except trombones), transpositions, and ranges.[134]

It would be wholly misleading, however, to give the impression that brass bands became comprehensively uniform at this time. J. Ord Hume wrote in 1900 of 'the remote village band which is generally composed of an unlimited number, from ten upwards'. Such bands probably outnumbered the contesting bands which used the 'standard instrumentation'. 'Contesting', said Ord Hume, 'is in my opinion, the only way in which to raise the standard of moderate bands.' But many, even most, of these bands may never have competed. Their instrumentation varied as players left or joined. These bands were still playing from 'their favourite journals', and had enough of them to 'paper the

---

[134] E. A. Lodge, *The Brass Band at a Glance* (Huddersfield, 1895).

walls of their band rooms with music'.[135] The Cyfarthfa Band was still playing and adding to its manuscript band books in 1908, though it was not routinely entering contests. The music it added was as demanding as much of the rest of the repertoire, showing that, in some cases at least, contest success was not the only indicator of technical ability.

The mediators of musical tastes among brass band people by the late 1840s were the middle classes—as purveyors of printed music, or, in the case of private bands, as patrons. The repertoire played by the Distins and by Jullien's soloists usually, but not always, centred on dance music, particularly quadrilles, waltzes, and polkas, which were the most popular dances of the period. Pieces such as these were turned out in numbers by a buoyant music industry. Hundreds of institutions and topical events were honoured by having a polka or quadrille named after them, the Great Exhibition of 1851, and the Crystal Palace itself, proving to be popular sources of inspiration for works such as the *Quadrille of All Nations* (?c.1851) by W. Wilson, and *The Great International Exhibition Quadrille* (published in 1862) by J. Pridham. Another popular practice was to use operatic themes as the basis for dance music. Thus titles like *Lucrezia Quadrille* (based on a theme from *Lucrezia Borgia*) and *Lucia Polka* (based on a theme from *Lucia di Lammermoor*) abound.

Dance music found in brass band repertoires can be taken as having had two distinct functions, both of which reflect their origins in middle-class practices. First, the music was quite literally danced to. In Merthyr in the mid-nineteenth century, the wagon sheds of the Crawshay's ironworks were regularly decorated with flowers and transformed into sumptuous ballrooms where the dignitaries of South Wales and the West Country danced to the most popular music of the day, played by the Cyfarthfa Band.[136] It is likely that many of the very early 'brass' bands were, in effect, dance bands dedicated to this sort of purpose. However, some dance music was used in a non-functional way as instrumental music. Quadrilles, and more particularly, polkas, also formed the basis of instrumental virtuoso solos. In the same way that dance music metamorphosed into the first independent 'absolute' wind instrument music in the sixteenth century, by being subjected to decoration, embellishment, division, and other (initially) extemporized conventions, so polkas formed one of the first vehicles for cornet virtuosity through the application of the long-established but spectacular brass techniques of double and triple tonguing. It was to middle-class audiences, and anyone else lucky enough to be in earshot, that Koenig and the Distins performed such pieces, and, though they set a standard that amateur players could not at first match, they established an impression of what constituted virtuosity on brass instruments, and what type of technique was associated with it. It is probably a coincidence that the

---

[135] J. Ord Hume, *Chats on Amateur Bands* (London, 1900), ch. 1.
[136] These events are depicted in water-colours at the Cyfarthfa Castle Museum.

polka was introduced into London in 1844, the same year as Adolphe Sax's instruments, but it is less likely that the involvement of Jullien in the popularity of both the instrument and the dance had much to do with chance.

From the 1850s, when bands became much more prolific, the repertoire and musical tastes tended to be shaped by three main forces: the bandmasters, the music publishers, and, to a lesser extent, the organizers of contests. Because the only people who bought brass band music were the bands, there is little direct evidence for the popularity of particular pieces or types of music among audiences. Concert programmes provide some hints, but they do not help very much. Some pieces may have been performed frequently because bands liked playing them rather than because audiences liked hearing them, and few brass band concerts were reviewed by newspapers. Music which was fun to play may not have been such fun to listen to. However, the frequency with which certain types of music—Italian opera, for example—and particular works, such as selections from *Lucrezia Borgia*, occur in printed and manuscript sources makes it difficult to draw any other conclusion than that such pieces were well received by the people who heard them. Contest promoters influenced the music and even the techniques of brass bands, because they were the organizers of the events that gave bands their most conspicuous exposure. The music played at contests had to entertain and exhibit a particular *type* of virtuosity. Any brass player knows that one of the most difficult types of music to play is that which requires very slow movement across wide pitch intervals at a very quiet dynamic, but this type of virtuosity does not draw gasps of admiration. Spectacular runs over scalic passages are much more immediately impressive.

From the time that brass bands became a common and widespread movement, their membership was largely made up of people from the skilled working classes. From about the same time, these same classes produced their own musical leaders. Conductors at the Crystal Palace Contest of 1860 had to indicate their occupation on the contest forms. They included thirteen who entered their occupation variously as innkeeper, lead-ore smelter, warp dresser, heald knitter, woollen spinner, publican, manufacturer, tailor, schoolmaster, miner, cloth percher, blacksmith, carpet department [worker], joiner, cloth operative, and spade finisher.[137]

A number of highly distinguished and very influential brass band conductors emerged. Of the earlier conductors, James Melling, a Manchester-based 'music professor', enjoyed some prominence. He worked closely with the contest promoter, Enderby Jackson, on a number of projects. Melling was conductor of Stalybridge Old Band. He was reputed to be one of the main

[137] Ainscoe Collection, kindly conveyed by Arnold Myers. The surviving entrance forms for the 1861, 1862, and 1863 contests show a similar picture. The conductor of the 20th Shropshire Rifle Volunteer Corps Band, George Hudson, was a 'shoddy dealer'.

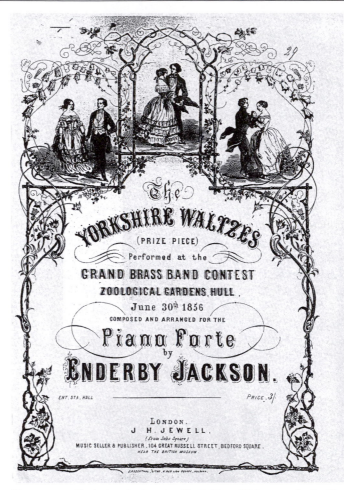

Figure 1.9. Enderby Jackson's *Yorkshire Waltzes*, 1856. The *Yorkshire Waltzes* was a brass band test piece, but the only surviving printed source is a piano arrangement. It is likely that Jackson's involvement finished with the completion of the piano part, and local bandmasters arranged the music for their bands. One such arrangement survives in fragmentary form in the first part books of the Black Dyke Mills Band.

suppliers of manuscript music to Yorkshire bands in the 1840s and 1850s.[138] He was also a composer: his *Orynthia* was the test piece for the 1855 Belle Vue contest. This was the first time that a common test piece was set, although no copy of it is known to have survived.

[138] Scott, 'Evolution of the Brass Band', 214.

The movement also produced composers and arrangers who came from a lower-class background. Enderby Jackson, who was the son of a candle maker, is best remembered as a promoter, but he was also a composer whose *Yorkshire Waltzes*, *Bristol Waltzes*, *Venetian Waltzes*, and *Volunteer Quadrilles* were specifically aimed at brass bands. A composer called J. Perry wrote marches for many Scottish contests in the nineteenth century, and in the Yorkshire textile district there were a number of prolific working-class composers of brass band music. These included Edward Newton, a textile worker who wrote and published over 300 marches; George Wadsworth, a monumental mason, whose works made up a large part of the catalogue of the Rochdale publisher, J. Frost & Son; and William Hesling, a weaver.[139] Joseph Parry, very much an establishment figure by the time he composed *The Tydfil Overture* for the Cyfarthfa Band in the late 1870s, was the son of an illiterate coal miner, and became the first Professor of Music at the University College of Wales.

Richard Smith, the publisher of the *Champion Brass Band Journal*, was a noted conductor. He was engaged by Titus Salt to train his Saltaire Band. By 1861, Smith was enough of a celebrity to earn a major profile in the *Illustrated News of the World*.[140] Another conductor who seems to have been particularly respected was George Ellis, who was associated with a number of bands, but particularly with Bacup Band between 1869 and 1871, when it won thirteen consecutive contests.[141]

However, the three most influential northern brass band conductors in the last quarter of the century were Alexander Owen, Edwin Swift, and John Gladney; between them they dominated contests for decades. Gladney was the only one of the three—as far as we know—who came from a musical family. He was born in 1839, the son of the bandmaster of the 30th East Lancashire Regiment. He started playing the flute at 8, and the violin at 9, saw a great deal of service abroad, and travelled with opera companies as a clarinet player. For some time he was the clarinet player and conductor of the Scarborough Spa Band.[142] He played the clarinet with the Hallé Orchestra in Manchester, and this was his professional base until the end of the century. He was associated with many of the top bands, and at the time of his death in 1911 was widely referred to as 'the father of brass band movement'.

The other two men had more humble origins. Alexander Owen was brought up in an orphanage in Swinton, and was taught to play the cornet at an early age by a military bandmaster.[143] Edwin Swift was born in Linthwaite in 1843. He left school at the age of 9 to become a shuttler, and he continued to work in mills until he was 32 years old. His first musical experience was in a drum and fife band; he then learnt the cornet. He played for the Linthwaite Band, and

---

[139] Russell, 'Popular Music Societies', 347 ff.
[140] Marr, *Music for the People*, 128.   [141] Ibid.   [142] Ibid.
[143] D. J. Lamora, 'Alexander Owen 1851–1920', typescript copy at Manchester City Library (F781 685 Owl). There is some doubt over the details of the early life of Owen.

was principal cornet and bandmaster at the age of 14. He led Linthwaite to victory over Gladney's Meltham Mills Band in 1874.[144]

Gladney, Swift, and Owen conducted and trained several bands. Other conductors spent their entire careers with just one. George Livesey, for example, conducted no band other than Cyfarthfa in the fifty years following his first association with it. Throughout the country, there were distinguished musicians of working-class origins who exercised great influence on the musical life of the communities in which they worked.

MANUFACTURERS AND MILITARY BANDMASTERS

Although local band trainers and conductors contributed significantly to the fashioning of the brass band movement, there were other influences which were less direct but equally potent. In the second half of the nineteenth century, music publishers exercised a defining influence on musical taste. Most were based in London, which was also the centre for almost all brass instrument manufacture. There were firms in the north of England, but the most successful had London attachments. Richard Smith, whose Hull-based *Champion Journal* was so successful, was himself resident in London from 1878,[145] and Joseph Higham, who had traded since the 1840s from Victoria Bridge, Manchester, eventually had a London address. The most important exception to the metropolitan strangle-hold on banding was the Liverpool firm of Wright and Round.

It has been argued that brass instrument manufacturing was based in London because London was the port of entry for raw materials. This argument is not convincing. Several manufacturing industries in the north of England relied on raw materials that had to be transported across country from distant ports of entry, a problem which, in any case, became considerably diminished with the development of the railway network. An alternative explanation as to why so much of the production of music and instruments for brass bands was based in London, when so many of the bands were in the north and west, is simply that the established London firms were successful in holding the market. A great deal of that success can be attributed to the close and not entirely ethical relationship between the publishing and manufacturing companies and the bandmasters of the regular army. Many of the regular army bandmasters were themselves involved in an uneasy relationship with their military employers. This unease emanated from two factors: first, there was concern over the number of foreign musicians who controlled army bands; and secondly there was significant disquiet about the extent to which the (civilian) army bandmasters were using their association with the military

---

[144] Anon., *Life and Career of the Late Mr Edwin Swift* (Milnsbridge, 1904).
[145] Russell and Elliot, *The Brass Band Movement*, 143.

in order to earn commissions from instrument manufacturers. The initiators of this corruption were the instrument manufacturers, who influenced the army appointment mechanisms by acting as agents between regiments and foreign bandmasters. The *Musical Times* was advertising Boosey's 'Register of Bandmasters' in 1854. Charles Boosey was prominent in these dealings. His position was made perfectly plain to a prospective bandmaster:

We have but one stipulation to make with you if you accept a situation through our influence. We do not ask for any remuneration but we do expect you to support our Firm exclusively, that is to say you will send us all orders for any instruments etc. that you require, for we need not remind you that Bandmasters have considerable influence with officers.[146]

It was eventually clear to the office of 'HRH, the Commander in Chief', that the high cost of maintaining bands was due to commanding officers leaving 'their dealings with the instrument makers chiefly in the hands of bandmasters', and a letter from the Adjutant General to Commanding Officers dated 24 February 1858 recommended that, in future, any bandmaster who, under any pretence whatever, received discount, fee, remuneration, or reward, should be subject to instant dismissal. The same letter suggested that instead of using instrument manufacturers as their agents for the hiring of bandmasters, 'they would do better by advertising in the public papers'.[147]

The foundation of what eventually became the Royal Military School of Music at Kneller Hall was stimulated by this need to train more native-born bandmasters, but these, too, were active and influential in the brass band movement. From its first issue in 1887, the *British Bandsman* pointed to army bands as the standard to which amateur bands should aspire. Many of the full-time army band conductors also received fees for being the conductors of volunteer bands. Others adjudicated at band contests or arranged music for brass band test pieces. Regular army men had intimate links with publishers. The majority of the London-based band publications were edited by them. Chappell's *Brass Band Journal* was arranged by W. Winterbottom of the Royal Marines; Fred Godfrey of the Coldstream Guards was also involved with Chappell's; Wessell's had J. R. Tutton of the Royal Horse Guards on its staff; D'Almaine used J. G. Jones of the 16th Lancers; and James Smyth of the Royal Artillery also put out arrangements. The Godfrey family was particularly prodigious. Charles Godfrey of the Royal Horse Guards Band was responsible for arranging the test pieces for the Belle Vue contests every year for more than twenty years. Bandmasters occupied musical and social positions which were considerably higher than those occupied by musicians in the north of England and in other parts of the country distant from London.

[146] Quoted in Binns, *A Hundred Years*, 27, 28. The letter is not dated.
[147] University of Glasgow, Farmer Papers, MS 115, 13–14.

They were familiar with styles, repertoires, and tastes recently imported from abroad and fashionable in London.

CLASS AND TASTE

Throughout this chapter, I have highlighted what I see as critically important influences on the brass band movement. Many of these influences originated with or were inspired by the middle classes. It is difficult to imagine how brass bands could have existed at all without the essentially capitalist-inspired motives of inventors, instrument manufacturers, and publishers. It is equally true that the music that was played by brass bands in Victorian Britain to a large extent mirrored middle-class tastes. Even the relationship between bands and the volunteer movement, a brief but important phase in band history, was primarily inspired by middle-class notions of patriotism.

It would be entirely wrong, though, to give the impression that the working classes were mere pawns in this story, or that individual and community working-class culture was passive. Indeed, one of the features of the brass band movement in Victorian Britain, a feature that makes it similar to other working-class leisure and cultural practices, was the extent to which it received this 'downward flow' of cultural products and made them its own, investing them with a new and lasting identity.

It is worth recalling that the brass band movement stimulated the first mass involvement by the working classes in performances of instrumental art music. This achievement (at least to this extent) was probably unequalled in any country where Western art culture had a stronghold. Brass bands had inspired the composition of no 'great' original works, but the fact that they played art music in transcription should not detract from, or devalue, this extraordinary accomplishment. In open-air concerts and contests, tens of thousands of working-class people had their first experience of 'serious' instrumental music through brass bands. The estimates given by newspapers for the number of people attending such contests need cautious treatment, but *The Times* estimated admissions of more than 22,000 for the second day of the 1860 Crystal Palace contest.[148] The 1864 Belle Vue contest is reported to have drawn an audience of 25,000.[149] The prices for such events were relatively low, certainly in the range common for other forms of popular mass entertainment.[150] Overwhelmingly, the repertoire consisted of arrangements of classical music. Audiences, irrespective of their individual wealth, sex, or literacy, had unequivocal access to high art music in this way.

[148] *The Times* (12 July 1860), 9.   [149] Taylor, *Brass Bands*, 61.
[150] The admission charge for the first day of the Crystal Palace contest in 1860 was 2s. 6d. (*The Times*, 10 July 1860). The second day cost only 1s. and 6d. for children. The 1s. entrance fee, with children at half price, was then held for several years. Promoters also negotiated concessionary rail excursions with the railway companies.

There were additional and more subtle relationships between brass bands and their audiences. Virtuoso performers were of the same social class, and often the same community, as their audiences. There emerged from the players in brass bands a number who possessed a special virtuosity. These players became musical heroes; they were often the focus of community pride, and exemplified working-class achievement and potential. From the 1880s, the band press started devoting space to profiles of such players, who thus gained national celebrity among bandsmen. In due course, brass band players would enter and eventually monopolize the principal positions in the leading professional orchestras of Britain. Though they carried with them the musical style of the brass band, they were technically comparable to the best professional players. As we discuss later in this book, these players were to have a defining influence on the idiom of brass instruments in British mainstream art music.

The symbolic association of brass instruments with the male gender seems to have held strong in the Victorian period. Certainly there is no evidence of women or girls playing in brass bands in Britain, though there is abundant evidence of female brass players in the USA in the same period.[151] Because banding was essentially a working-class activity, these instruments never made it into the bourgeois drawing room either. One piece of evidence suggests that such an initiative was tested. In the late nineteenth century, the London publisher John Alvey Turner brought out *Turner's Cornet Journal* at a cost of 1s. 6d., a price comparable to that charged for drawing-room ballads. The works included Koenig's famous *Post Horn Gallop* and a number of lyrical melodies. The distinctive feature of this publication is that it is dedicated to a female cornet player, Miss Beatrice Pettit. She is illustrated on the frontispiece as woman of beauty, grace, and taste (see Fig. 1.10). The publication is clearly aimed at a domestic rather than brass band market.[152]

By the late nineteenth century, brass bands had become a popular music tradition that, to a very large extent, was based on the performance of high art music. In the twentieth century, the idiomatic repertoire developed quickly, but the number of brass bands declined. One is bound to ask whether any part of the legacy of the nineteenth century contributed to this decline, and the subsequent residence of the brass band movement in a more or less self-contained cultural ghetto. A large part of this phenomenon can be attributed to the centrality of contesting in banding. Contests were the principal forum for brass bands. They raised standards of playing and contributed to the establishment of commonly held ideas about musical idioms and conventions. They were also primarily responsible for defining the purpose of bands—at least the more ambitious of them—as the pursuit of musical and technical excellence.

---

[151] See M. H. Hazen and R. M. Hazen, *The Music Men: An Illustrated History of Brass Bands in America, 1800–1920* (Washington, DC: Smithsonian Institution Press, 1987).

[152] *Turner's Cornet Journal No. 1*, compiled and arranged by A. Lemoine (London: John Alvey Turner, n.d.).

Figure 1.10. The cornet player, Beatrice Pettit. Women were seldom members of British brass bands in the 19th century, though this contrasts with practices in the USA, where there were a number of virtuoso players. This frontispiece, published in London in 1897, was clearly intended to promote cornet playing as an activity befitting well-bred young ladies. It appears not to have been successful.

There were, however, negative consequences which were hinted at as early as 1859 in the title of Charles Dickens's thinly veiled satire on brass band contests, 'A Musical Prize Fight'.[153] Contests, while encouraging virtuosity, encouraged a particular *type* of virtuosity, leading the style of brass bands to became a stereotype. They fashioned a strict and lasting orthodoxy—musical and social—which may well have contributed to the reluctance of the major composers to develop the genre. As other authors in the book point out, a number of major composers wrote a work for brass bands—but none wrote more than one. Also the notion of contesting as a *raison d'être* for brass bands, implying as it does a set of criteria that can be weighed up, measured, and scored, is anathema to the basic aesthetics of high art.

An even darker side to band contesting was seen in the frequent outbreaks of violence that accompanied the announcement of contest results. Such

---

[153] 'A Musical Prize Fight', *All the Year Round* (12 Nov. 1859), 65–8. The article is usually attributed to Dickens, who was the editor of the magazine, but it is not proven that he wrote it.

scenes caused anguish to many who genuinely and accurately recognized that they would undermine what, by the late nineteenth century, was seen as a musical and organizational achievement of the working classes. Sam Cope, founder of the *British Bandsman*, and a self-made musician who advocated forward-looking, benevolent, and educational schemes for bandsmen, and who saw 'No reason why Tom who plays the cornet, should be in a lower social or musical grade than Dick, who plays a violin',[154] lamented the 'jealous rivalry' of contests, and published numerous articles castigating the gratuitous indiscipline that often marked their conclusion.

While the prominence of contests may have been a self-inflicted constraint on the movement's wider development, there were other changes taking place at the end of the century which had broader class and cultural relevances. These changes were encouraged by the complex array of signals that emerged in the closing decades of the century, enabling certain types of activity to be seen as 'popular' and others as 'art'. These denominators were often synonymous with perceptions of 'working-classness' and 'middle-classness', and have been dealt with at length by cultural theorists and historians. This process of redefining the cultural status of certain activities owes much to what Eric Hobsbawm and others have called 'the invention of traditions'[155] that occurred from the 1870s onwards. In this process, brass bands became aligned with events such as May Day, trade-union demonstrations, and miners' galas, which epitomized working-class identity and behaviour. The categorization was further galvanized by the establishment of class-based musical developments such as subscription concerts, and a tendency of some musical institutions—the universities and some conservatories, for example—to keep brass bands at arm's length. This, in turn, gave orchestral playing a higher level of respectability than playing in a brass band. Consequently, by the turn of the century, playing in and listening to brass bands was one of the leisure pursuits that had, in a comparatively short space of time, acquired an identity sufficiently developed for it to be recognized as characteristic of the behaviour of the British working class.

---

[154] *British Bandsman* (28 Nov. 1908), 597.

[155] See e.g. E. Hobsbawm, 'Mass-Producing Traditions: Europe 1870–1914', in E. Hobsbawm and T. Ranger (eds.), *The Invention of Tradition* (Cambridge: Cambridge University Press, 1983). See also Dave Harker, *Fakesong: The Manufacture of British Folksong 1700 to the Present Day* (Milton Keynes: Open University Press, 1985).

2

'What is Wrong with Brass Bands?': Cultural Change and the Band Movement, 1918–*c*.1964

DAVE RUSSELL

In the course of the twentieth century, the brass band movement has followed two separate trajectories. On a purely artistic level, it has made enormous strides in terms of technical competence and of range and scope of repertoire. At the same time, it has ultimately lost the powerful—in some areas, central —position that it had held in popular musical culture. While this chapter is intended as a fairly wide-ranging discussion of bands in this period, its primary aim is to examine the second of these developments and to trace the process through which, by the 1950s and perhaps even earlier, the brass band had simply become yet another specialist pastime within an ever more variegated pattern of popular leisure.

What follows falls into four broad sections. The first investigates the structure of the movement in social, spatial, and organizational terms, the second its musical functions and repertoire. The third and largest component focuses on the processes challenging the position of the bands in musical life, while the final section attempts to locate their place within both the wider 'national' and the popular political cultures. The starting-point of 1918 is really one of convenience, for some of the key changes explored here originated in the early years of the twentieth century. The early 1960s, with pop music in rampant

I would like to thank Joe Pope for assistance with secondary sources at an early stage, Trevor Herbert for his appraisal of the first draft of this essay, and Richard Middleton and Dave Harker for helpful comments on the final draft.

ascendancy and the movement contemplating redemption through a new repertoire, seems a suitable stopping-point. The balance of the coverage is undoubtedly tilted towards the inter-war period. Although many of the conclusions here are intended to encompass the whole British experience, there is no denying the Englishness of the geographical coverage, with particular attention paid to bands of the Pennines and the industrial north-east. Detailed local studies will undoubtedly illustrate many subtle patterns of variation from the picture drawn here, and it is to be hoped that this preliminary survey will encourage such undertakings. Such research is especially needed on the period *c.*1914–56, which remains significantly under-studied by social historians and musicologists. This is a rich field and deserves investigation.

Brass Bands in the Twentieth Century

Historians must be able to count, but counting bands is a notoriously difficult procedure. Despite the development of an increasingly sophisticated organizational structure over the period, no definitive register of bands has ever existed, and enumeration has to be based largely on the estimates of contemporaries, on the reports of local correspondents in the band press, especially in the detailed *British Bandsman,* and on the sporadically published band directories. While these sources do not allow for exact measurement, they can form the basis for reasonable estimates of numbers at certain times, as well as illuminating some general trends.

Unfortunately, no half-way reliable estimate of the number of bands exists for the late Victorian or Edwardian eras as a context for the period under study. It is probable that the absolute numerical peak came in the 1890s and in the earliest years of the twentieth century, although it is impossible to say just how high it was. The band music publishers, Wright and Round, put forward the figure of 40,000 bands early in 1889, and 30,000 at the end of it.[1] It is not at all clear how these figures were arrived at. The great inconsistency between them hardly gives cause for confidence, and even the lower figure seems highly inflated, radiating a sense of commercial self-congratulation and aggrandizement. From about 1906, the band press does carry a definite, if anecdotal, body of evidence suggesting recruitment difficulty and a slightly higher rate of disbandment than in previous times.

It is easiest to deal with the issue of numbers and growth patterns from this point by considering in turn each of the sources mentioned above. The highest figures stemmed from individuals' estimates. In the inter-war period J. H. Elliot, who knew the movement well, put forward the figure of 5,000 on a number of occasions. In 1935, Arthur Bliss, a less experienced observer,

---

[1] *Wright and Round's Amateur Band Teachers' Guide* (Liverpool: Wright & Round, 1889); *Brass Band News* (Nov. 1889).

claimed 4,000 in 'the north' and perhaps 6,000 altogether. Few seemed willing to hazard a guess in the post-war period, although Peter Wilson, editor of the *British Bandsman*, suggested 2,000 as a figure for the early 1980s.[2]

Evidence from the second source, the *British Bandsman*, is worthy of very close attention. Particularly before 1939, it filled much of its space with the comments of local correspondents. What follows is a brief study based on two counties, Durham and Yorkshire, chosen because they both tended to receive particularly thorough coverage from their respective correspondents. Obviously, as is always the case with local studies, it is intended as a model for testing and not as a definitive statement.

In 1913 the *British Bandsman* recorded activity by some 230 bands in Yorkshire and 90 in Durham. These figures doubtless underestimate the total number of bands, the journal giving very little coverage to the village bands of east Yorkshire or of the more remote Pennine moorlands of both counties. They do at least give some indication of the size of the competitive movement, most of the bands being noted because they were involved in contests of one type or another. Although such exercises are perilous, it seems useful here to try and extrapolate a national figure from the local. These figures show for both counties the existence of one band for approximately every 15,500 people. If this is extended to the national population, it would suggest the existence of approximately 2,300 bands in England and Wales (2,600 if Scotland is also included). It must be repeated that these are minimum figures, but, if nothing else, they do illustrate the wildness of the claims made by *Wright and Round's* in 1889.

By 1920, the Yorkshire and Durham 'counts' had dropped to 156 and 54 respectively. To a large extent, this fall reflects a change in the nature of the source material, in that the *British Bandsman*'s local correspondents concentrated increasingly on a smaller number of bands. (Given this element of unreliability, national extrapolation does not seem appropriate.) However, there is more to this fall in numbers than the mere vagaries of sources, and it does seem likely that some bands did not recover from the disruption of the war, especially those which had been in a weakened condition before 1914. Here then, is a probable specific moment of decline.[3]

In the course of the inter-war period, numbers seemed to have remained reasonably steady, with only a slight decline. By 1938, the Yorkshire figure had fallen to 129, the Durham figure to 49. Significantly, however, most of the losses were concentrated in the period after late 1937. Broadening the geographical scope for a moment, it does appear that the late 1930s were a period of marked difficulty and quite rapid absolute numerical decline. In

---

[2] *Musical Times* (Oct. 1936); the *Listener* (4 Nov. 1935); A. Littlemoor (ed.), *The Rakeway Brass Band Yearbook* (Hollington: Rakeway Music, 1987), 43.
[3] See e.g. article on Almondbury Band, *British Bandsman* (9 Dec. 1922).

1938, the *British Bandsman* contained many anxious records of disbandings; the Lancashire correspondent claimed that some fifty local bands had folded in the course of the year, including some of considerable stature, notably Perfection Soap Works and Glazebury bands. Lancashire seems to have been particularly affected, but most regional correspondents listed a greater number of problems than normal. The fall in numbers was one reason behind the calling of a convention entitled 'What is Wrong with Brass Bands?' at the September Open in 1938.[4]

Although the Second World War caused massive disruption to bands, it does not appear to have added greatly to the overall fall in numbers. Analysis of the *British Bandsman* for 1954 gives figures for Yorkshire of 110, and for Durham of 40, a continuation of the downward trend, but not a particularly dramatic one. By the 1960s, the journal was devoting much more space to feature articles than to minute-book-like coverage of local bands, and it thus becomes impossible to carry out any sort of worthwhile enumeration. Impressionistic evidence, however, does suggest that the decline in numbers was virtually continuous throughout the period from the mid-1950s, and possibly faster than at any previous period since 1938. A note of depression was certainly evident in the band press, and, if the movement's collective memory is to be trusted, many bandsmen look back on the late 1950s and early 1960s as a bleak age.[5]

The final form of evidence is the directories, which are few in number and highly unreliable: they tend to be as much a measurement of the number of conscientious secretaries with access to a stationery account as anything else. The limited evidence they offer does, however, tend to reinforce some of the patterns suggested above. The first detailed listing of bands was probably Leo Croke's *The Standard Directory of Brass and Military Bands*, published in 1939, and essentially a guide to the band world for entertainment promoters. Croke admitted that the work was by no means definitive, and it is probable that only the better quality bands would have been contacted or would have responded. It records 1,242 bands in Great Britain as a whole, with the main body, some 1,100, in England and Wales. Two directories published in 1981 and 1987, both of them claiming to be thorough rather than definitive, record 710 and 670 bands respectively.[6]

Even from such a dense clutch of figures as this, the generalities are clear. First, without in any way seeking to deny the importance of the band movement, it is obvious that the number of bands in existence in the early years of the century was almost certainly a great deal more modest than many

---

[4] *British Bandsman* (31 Dec. and 17 Sept. 1938).

[5] A. Taylor, *Labour and Love: An Oral History of the Brass Band Movement* (London: Elm Tree, 1983), 17; Littlemoor, *Rakeway Yearbook*, 3.

[6] British Federation of Brass Bands, *Directory of British Brass Bands* (York: British Federation of Brass Bands, 1980–1), 51–63; Littlemoor, *Rakeway Yearbook*, 385–409.

have assumed. Throughout the period under study we are dealing with four-rather than five-figure numbers. Second, in terms of total numbers at any one moment, the estimates of informed insiders like Elliot and Wilson look sensible. Finally, the fall in the number of bands appears to have been continuous, with a probable acceleration around the end of the First World War, and a definite one in the late 1930s. It is almost certain that the late 1950s and 1960s saw another period of more rapid decline. Most of the above figures suggest that the number of bands has been more than halved over the period from 1913. Explanation, or attempts at it, will follow later.

The geography of banding can be delineated in a slightly less hesitant manner. In terms of settlement-type, the Victorian brass band was perhaps most often the product of small industrial villages and towns. This was almost universally the case with regard to contesting bands, and effectively remained so for the period to the 1960s.[7] With regard to geographical distribution, by the last quarter of the nineteenth century the brass band was a national phenomenon, in the sense that individual bands were established in virtually every part of Great Britain. The competitive movement, however, had a rather more narrow base, with the most active participants to be found in central Scotland, industrial North Wales, the industrial communities of South Wales, Cornwall, the Northamptonshire shoe towns, the textile and mining towns of the West Riding and Lancashire, and the coalfields of Leicestershire, Nottinghamshire, Durham, and Northumberland.

The absolute heartland of the pre-1914 movement was undoubtedly formed by the West Riding of Yorkshire, especially the textile district, and industrial Lancashire. Thirty-six of the eighty-one bands winning prizes at Belle Vue between 1853 and 1914, and fifteen of the twenty-seven at Crystal Palace between 1900 and 1914, came from these two areas.[8] It has been argued with some justification that to base élite status purely on lists of prizewinners is, to a degree, misleading. Research into band repertoires in other areas shows that there were bands which could play the most taxing music of the day, yet for whatever reasons—financial ones were probably the most common—chose not to contest.[9] Nevertheless, it would still be difficult to deny these two regions a privileged status in the band world.

Undoubtedly, the period from 1918 witnessed the increased presence of bands from areas not previously at the absolute core of banding. For example, in 1923, Luton Red Cross became the first southern band to win the National championship, while in 1927, Carlisle St Stephen's became the first Cumbrian

[7] D. Russell, *Popular Music in England, 1840–1914: A Social History*, 2nd edn. (Manchester: Manchester University Press, 1997), 205–11.

[8] All figures relating to contest success are based on an analysis of the contest results in A. Taylor, *Brass Bands* (St Albans and London: Granada Publishing, 1979), 258–99.

[9] T. Herbert, 'Victorian Brass Bands', lecture given at *Brass Roots* exhibition, Bradford, 1989.

victors.[10] Luton's victory was the prelude to the rise of a small but significant number of southern bands in the late 1920s and 1930s, most notably Callender's Cable Works from Belvedere in Kent, and Friary Brewery from Guildford. Aided by the spread of brass teaching in schools and by the reorganization of the National along regional lines in 1945, the profile of bands from outside the traditional strongholds continued to rise after the war.

However, in the final analysis, the traditional areas continued to dominate contesting and to produce a very high proportion of the leading players. While allowing for the limitations of contest results noted above, they still provide a good indication of the movement's spatial structure. Between 1919 and 1938, over half of the bands placed in the first six at the Belle Vue September Open came from Lancashire and Yorkshire, with some fourteen Lancashire bands taking forty-two of the possible 120 placings. Belle Vue results on their own would be a little misleading because the geographical proximity of Yorkshire and Lancashire bands to the venue gave them a huge advantage when trade depression made long-distance travel to contests less frequent. However, the National results over the same period show a broadly similar pattern, with the two counties taking one-third of the 114 top-six placings in the championship section. The slight decline in their position in comparison to the pre-1914 results stemmed largely from the much higher proportion of Durham and Northumberland bands contesting the National, with bands from these two counties taking just under one-fifth of the placings from 1919. It might have been expected that the introduction of eight regional heats into the National in 1945 would have led to a wider distribution of prizes. Certainly, there were individual years when bands from other regions did well, but in general, right up until the 1960s, Yorkshire and Lancashire bands dominated, taking some 40 per cent of the prizes.

At the same time, the established areas were still central to the production of soloists. 'In many cases it is the migration of Northern bandsmen which is responsible for a considerable amount of this improvement,' argued James Brier, editor of the *British Bandsman* in 1938, when discussing the rise of bands from the south and Midlands.[11] Certainly, the Luton band contained some outstanding local musicians, and was proud that ten of the 1923 band had joined as novices in 1918. However, the band's ambition and ultimate quality drew much from the appointment of northern bandmasters: J. T. Ogden from Kingston Mills as early as 1893, and Fred Mortimer from Hebden Bridge in 1912.[12]

Callender's progress in the 1920s was far more obviously based on northern talent. Shortly after the temporary closure of the St Hilda colliery in South Shields in August 1925, seven members of the colliery band, undoubtedly

[10] Enderby Jackson's short-lived (1860–3) Crystal Palace National 'contest' was won by Dorset-based Blandford Band in 1863.

[11] *British Bandsman* (Jan. 1938).

[12] *British Bandsman* (8 Mar. 1947); Russell, *Popular Music*, 211.

one of the best in Britain at the time, took positions at the Callender Works.[13] Throughout the next ten years, others followed from a variety of northern bands. The dramatic rise of the Kettering-based Munn and Felton Band, founded in December 1932, National champions by September 1935, owed much to imported soloists. Kettering undoubtedly had a deep-rooted band tradition, the band owing its foundation to the managing director's discovery that eighteen of his 400-strong workforce were bandsmen. However, despite this and the massive contribution made by the bandmaster, local cornet player and Munn and Felton employee, Stanley Boddington, it was the arrival of soloists from Yorkshire, Lancashire, Durham, and Scotland that raised the band to, and maintained it at, championship level.[14]

Finally, it is also significant that the success of individual bands, Luton and Callender's in the 1920s, City of Coventry in the 1940s, and Morris Motors in the 1950s, did not generally stimulate the movement in their localities in any dramatic way. Oxfordshire appears regularly in a tabulation of the counties of origin of prizewinners at the National in the 1950s, not because of an upsurge of high-quality bands in the county, but simply because of the continual success of Morris Motors. While more genuinely 'national' than many other forms of popular leisure—rugby league and crown-green bowling, for example—throughout the twentieth century the brass band has had its deepest roots in its earliest regional strongholds.

If geographical changes were less striking than has sometimes been suggested, there can be no doubt that, at least at élite level, the inter-war period heralded important changes with regard to the institutional nature of bands. In the nineteenth century, bands emerged from a variety of sources, but by 1914 they could broadly be placed into three categories: public subscription bands, which were probably in a majority; works bands supported by the workpeople, often involving deduction at source, perhaps coupled with an additional element of support from the employers; and works bands funded very largely by industrial concerns. Although little systematic information has been collected, it does seem that after 1914 very few new subscription bands were formed. The majority of new bands appear to have been works bands, or, from the 1950s, school and youth centre bands.

There is not space here to discuss works bands in the detail they deserve, although an extended study would make a useful contribution to the growing literature on industrial welfare policy.[15] It is worth noting, however, that, at

---

[13] Taylor, *Brass Bands*, 129; Taylor, *Labour*, 57.

[14] *Northampton Evening Telegraph* (2 Jan. 1933); *Brighouse Echo* (7 Sept. 1934); *British Bandsman* (12 Mar. 1938 and 9 Jan. 1954), for examples of northern soloists going to Kettering. This is, of course, not to ignore a flow in the opposite direction. Leading northern bands took young players from all over the country to help maintain their success.

[15] See especially Robert Fitzgerald, *British Labour Management and Industrial Welfare 1846–1939* (London: Croom Helm, 1988).

least in the private sector, a new element in the history of musical patronage by industrialists can be detected. Most of the works bands founded in the period up to about 1930 were either the products of individual paternalistic employers, such as John Foster of Black Dyke Mills, men with a particular love of music who wished to add the 'sacred art' to wider schemes of social welfare, or of limited liability companies with a pronounced interest in social welfare. Perhaps beginning as early as the late 1930s, but certainly marked from the early 1950s, a rather more obviously commercial spirit seemed to underpin the desire to support bands. The period was littered with bands which were born with, or quickly given, silver spoons, and went rapidly into the championship class, only to disappear as costs mounted and the return, both social and economic, diminished. Ferodo, Clayton Aniline, John White Footwear (although White himself was a great band enthusiast), and Crossley's Carpet Works, all top-flight bands for brief periods between 1954 and 1962, fall into this category to varying degrees.[16]

A brief survey of the Crossley Band from Halifax, West Yorkshire, demonstrates some of the shifting and sometimes uncertain thinking of the period. Originally comprising some fifteen Crossley workers and two 'borrowed' players, drawn together simply to accompany a single works carol service in December 1949 (perhaps revealingly, the management had first asked for an orchestra), the band quickly became a permanent and increasingly successful organization. The company's generous annual grants of between £200 and £1,000 played a key role here.[17] Gradually, the policy of recruiting players from outside the factory in order to raise the band's contesting profile led to a large reduction in the proportion of Crossley personnel; indeed, by the early 1960s, only about 20 per cent of the band were company employees. The publicity value of a successful contesting band was well known, with the band chairman seeing it as 'one of the best advertising mediums for the firm. We carry the prestige of the company with us.'[18] However, by June 1969, with Crossley Band inactive in the contest arena and burdened with an overdraft of almost £1,000 at a time when the parent-company was undergoing a critical merger with a leading rival, the directors used the argument that it was too expensive to maintain a band largely comprising 'outsiders' as the major reason for dissolving it.[19] Clearly, a policy acceptable in one economic climate had become less desirable in changing circumstances. Detailed case-histories are needed to clarify the processes at work in this period, but overall, the 1950s and 1960s do appear to form a bridge between the more deeply rooted support of the earlier period and the minimal-involvement sponsorship fashionable

---

[16] Taylor, *Labour*, 157–9.
[17] *Halifax Weekly Courier and Guardian* (1 Oct. 1965); Crossley's Carpet Works Band daybook, DC 1677, West Yorkshire Archives Department, Calderdale.
[18] *Halifax Weekly Courier and Guardian* (1 Oct. 1965).
[19] Balance sheets, DC 1681; *British Bandsman* (28 June 1969).

from the 1970s and 1980s. The history of the works band thus reflects a little of the wider passage of British capitalism from what might be termed a 'paternal' to a 'corporate' mode.

Works bands certainly came to dominate the contest field. For most of the period before 1914, despite the well-publicized success of bands like Black Dyke and Foden's, subscription bands dominated contesting. In the first four years of the newly constituted National (1900–4), for example, Black Dyke was the only works band to take a prize in the championship section. From about 1910 until 1923, a balance existed between the two types of works band on the one hand, and subscription bands on the other, with the prizes more or less equally shared. However, in 1923, works bands took four of the first six places and five in 1925. From this point, it was rare indeed for more than one subscription band to be among the National prizewinners. The pattern continued into the post-war period, and indeed reached its climax in the late 1950s and early 1960s. In 1955 and again in the years 1957–61, no subscription band finished in the final placings in the National championship class.

One further point in this context concerns the institutional origin of bandsmen (and, eventually, women) as well as of bands. Schools came to play a highly important role in the training of brass players, through both the establishment of bands and the work of peripatetic teachers with individual pupils. Although individuals had played brass instruments in the many school orchestras that grew up in the period after 1880, it was not until the 1920s that any serious consideration seems to have been given to the founding of school brass bands.[20] John Borland argued the case for small six- or eight-piece school bands in his *Musical Foundations*, published in 1927, and again in a series of articles in the *Musical Times* in 1935.[21] By the end of the 1930s a handful of bands had emerged, perhaps the first being the Marsden Senior School Band from the Colne Valley in the West Riding, founded in 1931. Another early band was that founded at Battersea Grammar School in 1938 by Harold Hind, who was later to play a major role in the movement in general, and among youth and school bands in particular. A National School Brass Band Association was founded in 1952, by which time the idea of the school band was becoming widely accepted.[22] The increasing popularity of the brass band among music educators owed much to the relatively rapid results which could be obtained by beginners, in comparison with novices in a traditional orchestra. There was, too, at least in areas with a band tradition, a keenness among some teachers to centre the children's musical experience in a culture that they understood, or at least had some awareness of. Although there remained a general feeling that the school music 'establishment' placed a

---

[20] For school orchestras, see Russell, *Popular Music*, 54–5.

[21] *Musical Times* (Sept., Oct., and Nov. 1935).

[22] Information from interview with Ron Massey, Honley, Huddersfield; V. Brand and G. Brand, *Brass Bands in the Twentieth Century* (Letchworth: Egon, 1979), 167.

higher emphasis on orchestras than on bands, there can be no doubt that increased intervention by the local state through the medium of the school did much to help supply a form of voluntary culture that was losing its own capacity to recruit.

This process was aided from the late 1940s by the establishment of local youth bands (some sponsored by education authorities, others by individuals), which recruited from school students in a particular area. The influential National Youth Brass Band was founded in 1952 by Denis Wright.[23] By the mid-1950s, many commentators believed that the band movement was increasingly becoming a youth movement, and not all were happy with the implications. Certainly, the rise of the youth at the expense of the subscription band does suggest that the brass band was becoming a specialist body, increasingly divorced from the broader popular social life that had once sustained it.

Nineteenth-century commentators had dubbed the brass band 'the working man's orchestra', and while the movement could not have prospered at any stage without some assistance from outside the working-class community, throughout the period to 1914, in terms of its players and to a very considerable degree its audience, the movement's social base was overwhelmingly working-class. Some commentators thought that they detected a significant change in this pattern in the 1930s. For example, in 1930, an article in the *British Bandsman* claimed that: 'The movement has so advanced in public opinion that we have now in our ranks a great percentage of artisans, clerks, shop assistants and the many others who years ago considered the brass band beneath their notice.'[24] Hard evidence is not plentiful for the period, but what there is does not suggest any great upward trend in the social base of the movement. It is surely significant that almost all of the considerable discussion in the band press of the disruption stemming from inter-war trade depression focused on the specific problems of manual workers. There are many passing references to the large role of miners in bands, and indeed, they probably represented the largest single occupational group among bandsmen.[25] Undoubtedly, given the changing demands of the economic system, there was a limited social mobility for working-class males in this period and some sons of working men would have obtained white-collar employment while still choosing their leisure from within the traditionally 'working-class' sphere.[26] However, comments like the *British Bandsman*'s almost certainly overestimated the extent of this change as it affected bands. The movement's public spokesmen were obsessed with presenting an upwardly mobile image,

---

[23] E. Howarth and P. Howarth, *What a Performance: The Brass Band Plays* (London: Robson, 1988), 203.
[24] *British Bandsman* (18 Jan. 1930).   [25] e.g. *Shields Daily News* (28 Sept. 1925).
[26] D. Glass, *Social Mobility in Britain* (London: Routledge & Kegan Paul, 1954), 98–159.

ORDER OF EVENTS

❖

Friday, October 19th, 1962

7.30 a.m.—Coaches leave "Eryl" for London.

12 noon—Lunch. The Fleece Hotel, Cheltenham Spa.

1.15 p.m.—Coaches leave parking enclosure behind the Fleece.

5 p.m.—Band Coach arrives at Cranstone's Ivanhoe Hotel, Bloomsbury Street, W.C.1.
(Telephone—Museum 5601)

6.30 p.m.—Dinner at the Hotel.

8 to 9.30 p.m.—Band Rehearsal
Hugh Myddleton Primary School, Bowling Green Lane, E.C.1.

10 p.m.— Return to Hotel by Coach.

NATIONAL
BRASS BAND CHAMPIONSHIP

THE ROYAL ALBERT HALL
Saturday, October 20th, 1962

Treorchy Secondary School Youth Band

Conductor—Ieuan Morgan, Esq.

aided by

THE PARENTS' ASSOCIATION
Chairman—Mr. Glyn Morgan.
Treasurer—Mr. D. Pugh.

for

THE FORCE OF DESTINY
(*Verdi*)

❖

Souvenir Programme

Saturday, October 20th.

7 a.m.—Rise and Shine.

7.30 a.m.—Breakfast at Hotel.

8 to 9 a.m.—Band Rehearsal at
Hugh Myddleton Primary School, Bowling Green Lane, E.C.1.

9 a.m.—Coach with Band leaves for the Royal Albert Hall.

9.30 a.m.—Arrival at Albert Hall but Band Members remain on Bus to know Order of Play.

N.B.—The Band may return to the School (above) for another Rehearsal, according to Order, as informed by Chairman and Treasurer.

Meals—Al Fresco—
10/- to each Bandsman

Sunday, October 21st.

7 a.m.—Rise and Shine.
Morning Free.

12.30 p.m.—Return to Hotel.

12.45 p.m.—Leave for
St. Sepulchre's Church, Holborn Viaduct, E.C.1.

1 p.m.—Lunch at
St. Sepulchre's Church.

1.45 p.m.—Rehearsal at the Church

2.30 - 3 p.m.—Break.

3 p.m.—The Bandsman's Annual Service.
Address—Eric Ball. Esq.
Organist—Francis Cameron, Esq.
Items—Treorchy S. S. Youth Band.
(Conductor—Ieuan Morgan, Esq.)

4 p.m.—Tea at St. Sepulchre's Church.

4.30—p.m.—En Route for Home.

7.30—p.m.—High Tea
Fleece Hotel, Cheltenham Spa

12 midnight—The return of ?

78

Figure 2.1*a, b, c.* The Treorchy Youth Brass Band. An alternative view of 1960s teenage culture. In 1962, the Treorchy Youth Brass Band, conducted by Ieuan Morgan, became the first youth band to qualify for the National Finals in the Championship Section. Its carefully planned visit to London was commemorated in a printed 'Souvenir Programme'. The editor of this volume bashfully occupies the position of second trombone.

and observations of this type were invariably made with an eye to enhancing status.

The period after 1945 undoubtedly did see a more significant widening of the social base. By the 1970s, Dobcross Band could include 'a director of a small winding mill, five schoolteachers, an executive engineer with the Post Office and one with the Water Board'.[27] It is not clear to what extent bands were actually attracting directly from the established middle class, or simply recruiting players from working-class families that had been educated 'out of their class' and into a range of white-collar professions, as a result of the expanded educational ladder of grammar school and technical college. The latter seems more likely, given the divorce of many middle-class musicians from the networks and organizations that would have led them into the band movement. Even in this period, however, the pace of change should not be exaggerated. There was probably considerable regional variation, but

[27] H. Livings, *That the Medals and Baton be Put on View* (Newton Abbot: David & Charles, 1975), 35.

certainly in the traditional band areas the overall 'flavour' of the movement was decidedly working-class. Brian Jackson and his co-fieldworker, Denis Marsden, certainly saw it as proletarian enough for inclusion in their classic study of working-class Huddersfield, *Working Class Community*. Marsden described the audience at the 1962 Open as 'almost entirely working class' and implied the same of players and committee-men.[28] The 'cloth-cap image' which so many writers in the 1970s claimed to be long outmoded, was undoubtedly still rooted in reality in the 1960s.[29]

The final 'structural' element demanding attention here concerns gender. 'Ladies' committees' had long been a crucial feature of the fund-raising mechanism, while women had, of course, also featured in the audience at concerts. One provincial paper even claimed that a number were present at the 1920 National contest, where the 'woman enthusiast . . . takes her knitting and makes a day of it'.[30] Whatever the validity of that comment, without any doubt the band itself was a rigidly masculine republic. It was not until the 1930s that any shift occurred. In 1930 at a concert in Batley, in the West Riding, Stanley Band featured cornet solos by two 9-year-olds, 'Master Willie' and (more importantly, in this context) 'Miss Mildred Holgate'.[31] They were almost certainly the children of local band trainer, Percy Holgate, and Mildred appears to have been part of a novelty act attached to the band, rather than a member of it. Two years later, the daughter of the Gainsborough Britannia bandmaster, Harvey Nuttall, was similarly featured as soloist, but then actually joined the band in 1933. In 1954, when the issue of female players was beginning to receive regular attention in the band press, Britannia happily claimed her as the first woman member of a brass band.[32] By 1938, a handful of other female players appeared. In March, a slow melody contest at Dinnington in south Yorkshire was won by 13-year-old cornet player, Grace Cole, of Firbeck Colliery Band, with 8-year-old Betty Anderson of Leicester Imperial in third place on tenor horn. In the same year, Patricia Parkinson, aged 15 and from Shipley in Yorkshire, became the first-ever girl to play in a National final when she appeared with Canal Ironworks.[33]

In a broadcast after the 1938 National, J. H. Elliot claimed that 'young women players in brass bands have recently become quite numerous', but there is little evidence to support his rather generous interpretation, and it was the outbreak of war that gave an important boost to the opportunities for women players.[34] As bands lost players to the forces, women players

[28] B. Jackson, *Working Class Community* (London: Routledge & Kegan Paul, 1972), 22–39, for a stimulating view of banding and its place in working-class culture.
[29] See e.g. *Sounding Brass*, editorial (Winter 1973–4).
[30] *Yorkshire Evening Post* (30 Oct. 1920).   [31] *British Bandsman* (23 Aug. 1930).
[32] *British Bandsman* (24 July 1954).
[33] *British Bandsman* (26 Mar. 1938); *The Times* (26 Sept. 1938).
[34] *British Bandsman* (8 Oct. 1938).

filled some of the vacancies, although, again, numbers do not seem to have been large. A further stimulus to this first generation of women players may have been the example of the all-female dance bands which emerged in the late 1930s, such as the Ina Ray Hutton Band and Teddy Joyce's Girl Friends.[35] After the war, the trickle of female players, nearly always school-girls or teenagers, increased again, although initially it may well be that they found more space and opportunity in either newly formed bands or school and youth bands than in the longer established ones. The Brecknock Estate Silver Band, founded in London just after the war, included seven girls, while as early as 1954, twenty-eight of the National Youth Brass Band (approxim-ately 15 per cent) were girls.[36] Most of the older established bands contained at the most only one or two women players. Nevertheless, a base had been laid for what was to become a considerable growth of women players from the 1960s and 1970s onwards.

The early women players were in no sense making a 'political' point—they were mostly too young to do so in any really coherent way—and nor were their families. Betty Anderson came from a banding family, and claimed that it 'did not occur to me at that time that girls did not play in brass bands. I thought everybody did.'[37] It was, though, an unorthodox and implicitly challenging action. It is a matter of interpretation as to whether their breaking into the band world represented the achievement of any significant level of social 'liberation' by women. At one level, of course, it did, in that a tightly male world had been breached. Nevertheless, it is equally the case that their place within the bands both reflected and was constrained by male values.

When discussing female players in the journals, writers often adopted a far more overtly 'human interest' approach than they did with males. Inevit-ably, this involved interrogation about their courting habits, a process which elicited such standard replies as: 'You have no time for marriage while you're playing the cornet.'[38] A similar mentality prevailed when, in 1964, the *British Bandsman* acknowledged the increasing size of the women's contingent by beginning a regular 'Bandswoman's Exchange' column.[39] The editor noted: 'The photographs will add some welcome glamour to our pages.' Women writers illustrated broadly similar attitudes towards sexual roles. Writing in the *British Bandsman* in 1954, Edith Alston argued that it was good for women to play, but stressed the need for them to maintain 'their poise and dignity',

[35] For an example of wartime opportunity as exemplified by Mrs Otter of Devon, see *British Bandsman* (3 Mar. 1945). On female dance bands, see *Melody Maker* (22 Jan. and 7 May 1938). Gracie Cole's move from brass to professional dance and show band work was partly facilitated by a spell with Rudy Starita's All Girl Band. See *British Bandsman* (7 July 1945).

[36] *British Bandsman* (25 Oct. and 10 July 1947).

[37] C. Bainbridge, *Brass Triumphant* (London: Muller, 1980), 92.

[38] *British Bandsman* (26 June 1954).

[39] This was written by Sheila Rushforth, a product of the pre-1939 recruitment phase who had later turned professional. *British Bandsman* (20 Feb. 1965).

and seemed to have trouble accepting the idea of women in uniform. Again, women players were seen by some writers to bring special 'feminine' sensibilities to banding, the long-established trainer and arranger James Brier seeing them as 'more refined in their tastes than men . . . more sensitive and emotional'.[40] Such sentiments, mild as they were by the standards of the period, and too 'soft' a target for detailed exposition, nevertheless serve to illustrate the atmosphere in which female players found themselves.[41]

Perhaps more significantly, there does seem to be a sense in which the movement's treatment of women mirrored their function in the wider society, as a reserve army of labour, to be used when the supply of males contracted.[42] It is no coincidence that the first trickle of women into bands around the period 1938 coincided with the recruitment problems at that time. In this way, too, any sense of women 'breaking through' is muted by the realization that they were gaining access to a male space at the very moment when it was losing status and standing within the general working-class culture. It should also be underlined that women's progress into the élite contesting bands was strongly resisted. In these bands, where male applicants were never in short supply, women made no headway. A woman's musical place was definitely not to be in a soloist's chair, or indeed in any chair, in a first-section brass band.

Writing in the 1960s, the sociologists Jackson and Marsden were struck, as had been many before them, by the sense of purpose and mission which surrounded much band work: 'The first thing they tell you is that this is the Brass Band Movement.'[43] Before moving on to explore the bands' musical life, it is important to consider the meaning and significance of this phrase in the post-1918 period, as it undoubtedly sheds much light on band culture and on the brass band's changing role in musical life.

Although the exact structure of the 'movement' in terms of personnel and organization was never actually delineated by contemporaries, its constituent parts are fairly obvious. At the core lay the contesting bands. Always a minority at any one time, they were nevertheless viewed as a musical vanguard, raising standards, showing banding's best possible public face. Non-contesting bands were wedded to the movement through a shared musical culture, by the constant supply of talent they provided to their competitive colleagues, and by the simple fact that many of them had contested in the past, and would do so again after passing through a process of rebuilding, financial retrenchment, or whatever.

By the 1890s, through the foundation of the first regional and local band associations to set rules for local contests and generally oversee the interests of bands, the movement had begun to generate a skeletal organizational infra-

[40] *British Bandsman* (24 May 1941).   [41] *British Bandsman* (25 Apr. 1964).
[42] P. Summerfield, *Women in the Second World War* (London: Croom Helm, 1984).
[43] Jackson, *Working Class Community*, 22.

structure, one that grew considerably from the 1920s. The increase in the number of band associations from the 1920s, the establishment of the Alexander Owen Memorial Scholarship (1922), the National Brass Band Club (1925), the National Brass Bands Federation (1931), and the Bandsmen's College of Music (1932) all illustrate an increased tendency toward cooperation and unity. However, no one central organizing body emerged. There was no compunction to join the local associations, and bands, especially the most successful ones, showed a cavalier attitude to them, joining and leaving as and when it suited their finances and their needs. The only really effective centralizing mechanism came with the establishment of the bandsmen's register immediately after the Second World War, set up by the organizers of the National Contest to settle the century-old problem of bands using borrowed players and professionals in contests. The establishment of a rigorous system of registration, at least for the most important event in the band programme, gave players the closest thing they ever had to a membership card for the brass band movement.[44]

Much of this organizational activity was generated at grassroots level. However, other key aspects—the establishment of the register, for example —were either instigated or encouraged by commercial interests. The large role played by such interests in the development of banding must be stressed, if only to illustrate the extent to which a supposedly independent, community-based form of leisure was to a degree structured by 'external' forces. The most important group was the band music publishers, and the most important of these was John Henry Iles. Almost all of the major specialist band publishers owned a newspaper or journal, advertising their products and generally reflecting their views. However, as owner of the music publishing house, Richard Smith and Company, and through that company the publisher of the *British Bandsman*, as well as being the controller of the two major contests, J. H. Iles exerted considerable influence on all aspects of banding. The *British Bandsman*, the only weekly publication and the one with the largest circulation, became almost the official organ of the movement. When discussing the views of the 'movement', we are often referring to Iles and his colleagues at 210 The Strand, his editors, and local correspondents.[45]

The involvement of national newspapers again illustrates the influence of commercial interests in shaping events. The *Daily Herald*'s decision, on taking over the National in 1945, to introduce a system of regional heats, was inevitably unpopular with many bandsmen in the 'traditional' areas, whose

[44] In recent years, the registration card has effectively become a membership card. Players retain their cards for three years after they end their registration with a band so that they 'still belong to the movement'. I am grateful to Ethel Beahan of the Registry for this information.

[45] For a brief biographical sketch, see P. Gammond and R. Horricks, *Music on Record*, i. *Brass Bands* (Cambridge: Stephens, 1980), 76–7. This useful book carries outline biographies of many of the key figures mentioned in this chapter.

chances of reaching the finals were limited by the regional structure. The subsequent complaints were overruled. The decision to proceed with a regional structure may have reflected the stated desire to widen the geographical base of competitive banding and increase opportunities for bands in previously marginal areas. However, it should also be viewed as an outcome of the *Herald*'s marketing strategy. Publicity director Jerome Chester was fully aware that if the National was to play a part in helping the paper recapture some of the market lost to the *Mirror* and *Express* since the early 1930s, it had to win publicity across the widest possible geographical area.[46]

In general, commercial and 'voluntary' groupings were able to agree on broad principles. The essential ideals underpinning the concept of a 'movement' appear to have been a belief in the bands' capacity to educate both their own members and a wider audience, great faith in the contest as the central agency of musical progress and loyalty to a clearly defined instrumentation, playing style and repertoire. There was, too, a profound, almost missionary zeal, as captured in an editorial in the *British Bandsman* in 1954:

The brass band is something of a social phenomenon, a brotherhood, part of the British way of life. Truly amateur bands are not merely haphazard groupings of players who happen to enjoy a 'blow'. They have a more serious purpose, part of which is to give opportunity for the unfolding of artistic skill and experience in those whose daily tasks are all too often monotonous and unsatisfying, although necessary.[47]

These almost Victorian ideas of rational recreation and self-improvement emerge again in this defence of the social value of youth bands by the secretary of the National Brass Band Club: 'Here may be the answer to the present increasing numbers of draped-coated, drainpipe-trousered gangs, who roam the streets of our cities. These youths are to be pitied rather than blamed . . . brass-banding is one excellent way in which to give the coming generation an interest in life. Anyway, it is worth thinking over.'[48]

There was, too, a remarkably strong emphasis on the outward respectability and discipline of those already in the movement. 'Remember, gentlemen,' warned the *British Bandsman*'s 'Downside' in 1930, 'that you are but part of a great movement, and your conduct in public may go a long way towards raising or lowering us in the eyes of the public. See to it that you do nothing that may let the brass band movement down.'[49] The adoption of uniforms at National Contests in the early 1930s, the result of a long campaign by *British Bandsman* editor Herbert Whiteley, and the determined efforts twenty years later by National Championship producer Edwin Vaughan Morris to make players put out cigarettes before they took the stage for the second half of

[46] For the *Herald*'s marketing problems, see H. Richards, '*The Daily Herald*, 1912–1964', *History Today* (Dec. 1981), 15.

[47] *British Bandsman* (20 Feb. 1954).   [48] *British Bandsman* (15 Feb. 1958).

[49] *British Bandsman* (9 Aug. 1930).

the massed band concert at the National, are just two of many attempts to improve public image. All this was partly to maintain the loyalty of moneyed supporters, but it was also hoped that the musical establishment might look a little more favourably on the movement if it was divested of its 'taproom feel'.[50]

Whether the led always took great notice of the leaders is doubtful. The interviews in Arthur Taylor's *Labour and Love* include many tales of high spirits (and sometimes just *spirits*), and of momentary clashes with the great men of the movement, who, if one believed the comments in the band press, supposedly had the permanent, unquestioned loyalty of their players.[51] Iles's annual attempts at conducting during the massed band concert at the National were a source of some ribaldry, while amiable but pointed calls of 'Hurry up, Henry' greeted his delay in announcing the winner at the end of the 1935 contest. At grassroots level, bandsmen could enjoy a genuine democracy. 'Joe, you're a nice fellow, but you're no bloody use as a conductor and you're sacked', are the words reputedly used by the Black Dyke cornet player, Willie Lang, when asked to express the band's views to their conductor, Joe Wood.[52]

The great significance of all this, however, lay not in these internal disagreements but in the overall sense of unity. Bandsmen had a strong sense of belonging. Initially fuelled by the location of bands in specific communities, and by the large role played by the family as an agent of recruitment, this feeling was made ever stronger by the rhetoric of the 'movement'. It gave bands strength and sustenance. The vitality of banding owed much (and still does) to the determined sense that something special and worthwhile was being done, something that must be continued whatever 'they' (the musical establishment, the public, the BBC, the Performing Right Society (PRS)—the Kluforming Klights Klan as they were referred to in the 1920s—or whatever enemy) might think. At the same time, of course, such inner strength might have been a source of weakness, cutting players off from some of the major social and artistic changes of the period. Traditional instrumentation, repertoire, and much else were clung to with a determination that annoyed many would-be reformers, unable to grasp the fact that hard-earned cultural capital was not easily given up. In this way, though, at least something of the bands' reduced position within popular musical life originated from within.

MAKING MUSIC

The brass band, although only one of many forms of popular musical society in existence before 1914, was a particularly privileged one. Especially in small industrial communities where the entertainment industry was less penetrative, it was central as an agent of both musical entertainment and education.

[50] Taylor, *Labour*, 67, 114.
[51] Taylor, *Labour*, 161–4, for one player's not exactly flattering view of Alex Mortimer.
[52] *Northamptonshire Evening Telegraph* (30 Sept. 1935); Taylor, *Labour*, 128.

This section investigates its changing place in local musical and social life from the 1920s.

The bands' varied musical life had fallen essentially into four activities: playing for dancing and public ceremonies, concert work, and contesting. The dance band function was the least important of the four, but it was more significant than has been realized. The history of popular urban dance in Britain has been seriously neglected but it is clear that for working-class youth in particular, dancing, in a variety of locales, was a major form of entertainment at least from the 1860s and probably earlier.[53] Some of the brass bands' contributions to this were unintentional: listeners simply took the chance to dance to whatever suitable music the bands had to offer. Such displays were sometimes discouraged, especially by Nonconformist recreational reformers, being viewed as unseemly, and opposed to the rational atmosphere deemed appropriate when music was being performed. In June 1871 at Bradford's first-ever corporation-sponsored park concert, the local paper noted that 'There was some dancing going on but of a furtive and disconnected kind, it being understood that the committee objected.'[54] By the 1890s, public dancing had lost some of its stigma and brass-as-dance-bands became common attractions at pleasure-gardens, fêtes, and a variety of other attractions, including public parks in some areas.

Engagement-work of this type seemed reasonably plentiful until about the mid-1920s, when brass bands were made effectively redundant by the emergence of specialist dance bands, performing American-style popular music. In 1926, when one Bradford Park Band Committee dispensed with brass bands and engaged dance bands 'proper', the first night of the new regime saw 1,500, a far larger crowd than had ever been attracted before, dancing to the Indiana Dance Band.[55] When Don Pedro's Mexicans were booked at the Rydings Park, Brighouse, in 1930, they drew 'one of the largest crowds ever seen in the Rydings'. The local paper expressed some disapproval that locals seemed to prefer 'jazz' bands, and foreign bands at that, to the 'excellent' local brass bands. ('Don Pedro' was in fact John Guy from Birmingham.[56]) Brass bands did continue as dance bands in certain settings, particularly at private, socially select gatherings. In 1930, for example, Brighouse and Rastrick in Yorkshire, Mere Band in Wiltshire, and Poole Town in Dorset, all found themselves playing for dancing at Conservative Party fêtes.[57] How long this kind of work continued is not clear, but it is apparent that by 1930, one of the links that held the brass band in the mainstream of popular youth culture had been broken.

[53] For a marvellous—albeit highly coloured—view of the Victorian dance hall, see J. Burnley, *Phases of Bradford Life* (Bradford, 1871), 157–68.

[54] *Bradford Observer* (5 June 1871).   [55] *British Bandsman* (10 July 1926).

[56] *Brighouse Echo* (20 June 1930); *British Bandsman* (5 June 1926).

[57] *Brighouse Echo* (1 Aug. 1930); *British Bandsman* (9 Aug. 1930).

Concert life was more central to banding, and initially more secure. In the course of the nineteenth century, bands had built up a flourishing concert circuit. Much of this was outdoor work, usually on summer evenings, and, dependent upon the strength of the local Sabbatarian lobby, Sunday after-noons. Even the smallest bands could usually be guaranteed work in their local parks, but an élite group undertook national tours of up to ten or twelve weeks' duration. In 1922, six such bands advertised themselves in the *Brass Band News* specifically as 'concert bands'.[58] From the late Victorian period, major concerts in parks and on seaside promenades could sometimes attract crowds of a size more normally associated with important sporting events. One of the largest of the inter-war period occurred at Oldham in August 1926, when an estimated 15,000 watched Durham-based Harton Colliery. The hard-ship of miners at this moment of industrial conflict, and a subsequent display of sympathy and practical financial assistance, may have swelled the audience here, but other attendances of several thousand were common.[59]

There was, however, a continuous rumble of concern in the band press from about 1930, suggesting that these concerts were losing their audiences, and that bands were losing some of their share of such engagements. Initially, there was little hard evidence, but by the late 1930s, the weight of argument had be-come convincing. The main concern centred on moves by concert organizers towards a much increased use of military bands and dance bands in public parks. Similarly, seaside resorts were clearly making less use of brass bands. In 1938, Southport Parks Committee cut the number of brass bands it hired from ten to five, while Eastbourne Council decided not to engage any at all. The *Eastbourne Gazette*, referring to the performances of what, perhaps significantly, they termed 'industrial bands', articulated an increasingly com-mon critique of their repertoire and approach:

It is true that these bands could well emulate their military brothers and introduce a little light variety into their programme. On the other hand, the correct presentation of brass band music hardly lends itself to modern tastes for variety and swing. It is quite a tribute to the catholicity of style in industrial bands that many dance band trumpeters were trained in the north.[60]

By the final months of 1938, the *British Bandsman* had become concerned enough to publish a detailed investigation of the policies of seaside entertain-ment promoters. The problem was clearly greatest in the south of England where bands were less centrally rooted in popular musical culture, but even entertainment managers in resorts like Scarborough and Yarmouth, with a large number of visitors from the bands' heartlands, and where the top bands were still popular attractions, admitted some evidence of changing taste. The

---

[58] *Wright and Rounds' Brass Band News* (5 May 1922). The bands were Foden's, Harton Colliery, Horwich RMI, Irwell Springs, St Hilda Colliery, and Wingates Temperance.
[59] *British Bandsman* (7 Aug. 1926).   [60] Quoted in *British Bandsman* (29 Jan. 1938).

consensus echoed the *Eastbourne Gazette*. 'Stage bands', as some dance bands were termed in this performing context, and, to a lesser extent, military bands, gave greater variety in the fullest sense, with their novelty acts, vocalists, and comedians. One manager claimed that a new generation was not content 'with sitting round a bandstand listening to 25 musicians, who are generally only on view from the chest upwards, putting over some rhapsody, which, the programme informs us, owes its birth to the Slavs'.[61]

It is significant that it was against this background that the St Hilda Band, professional since 1927, and probably the most commercially attuned concert band, folded in 1937. Its manager, Jimmy Southern, felt that worthwhile engagements were increasingly hard to find. That might be a comment on a particular band, but it reinforces the general pattern, and, highly significantly, coincides with the timing of the recruitment and disbanding problems noted above.[62]

Of course, the outdoor concert did not disappear in the 1930s. Élite bands did not abandon this work until the 1960s, and through the local park concert, it forms an important element in the activity of many bands to this day. It was, though, in long-term decline. The 1950s saw the real acceleration of the trend. Falling attendances and diminishing appeal were partly accompanied, partly caused, by a new rival, so-called 'canned music', the playing of current hit records over amplification systems. 'How ludicrous it is', commented Harold Hind in 1954, 'to see a crowd of people in deckchairs, sitting round an empty bandstand containing a loud speaker emitting the latest hits.'[63] It was, though, popular with audiences and cheap for local authorities, and virtually all forms of live bandstand entertainment suffered. By the early 1960s, many bandstands were rapidly becoming more monument to past taste than focus for live entertainment. The *Daily Herald* was referring to more than simply the outdoor concert when bemoaning the decline of banding in this lament from 1956, but it was undoubtedly one of the issues in mind: 'The public demand for brass bands has fallen lamentably since the war . . . one's fear is that brass bands may eventually have to play largely for their own enjoyment.'[64]

Inevitably, bands became despondent when playing to small and not always attentive audiences. One obvious response, gathering pace from the 1920s, was simply to move indoors, and thus attract only the serious and genuine followers. Indoor concerts have indeed become a central feature of band culture. For all their value, however, especially as a showcase for music which had previously been regarded as too specialist for park and pier audiences, such concerts were never to be as frequent as the outside engagements. Moreover, they lacked the direct link into popular social life that the older style engagements possessed. In the late 1930s, almost imperceptibly at first, but gathering pace from then on, audiences increasingly had to go looking for bands, rather

[61] *British Bandsman* (31 Dec. 1938).   [62] Taylor, *Brass Bands*, 132.
[63] *British Bandsman* (15 May 1954).   [64] Taylor, *Labour*, 109.

than simply meeting them during the course of evening, weekend or holiday social life. In this way, another link with the wider community withered.[65]

This process becomes clearer if the focus is shifted to the third category of musical function. The brass band movement's involvement in the ceremony and ritual of public communal life was established from the very earliest moments of its inception, and provided it with some of its strongest linkages with the wider popular culture, especially working-class culture. Sunday school walks and processions, trade-union galas, friendly society demonstrations, the opening of public buildings, and other civic high days and holidays were major events in the band calendar. This is underscored by the bands' emphasis on good appearance and deportment at these events, both to honour the community and to ensure a rebooking. Uniforms, not normal at the slightly more private world of the contest until the 1930s, were obligatory. Southowram Band, from a small village near Halifax, purchased a new uniform in 1920, at some inconvenience, specifically to do justice to the St Anne's Sunday School Whit Walk. In 1938, Batley Band launched a uniform fund after losing a ceremonial engagement they had held for twenty years because of their poor appearance.[66]

Quite simply, public displays of what might be termed 'civic culture' have declined significantly (or taken new forms) over the whole period, and especially since 1945. It is difficult to be precise about the patterns here; different forms almost certainly underwent changes at various stages, and regional variations will also have been significant. The decline of the Whit Walk might, however, prove indicative. As early as 1920, one West Riding local paper commented on the reduced presence of adults on the local walk, suggesting that the excursion was rapidly taking over as a focus of popular interest on the Whit holiday. By 1937, after almost two decades of falling church attendance and increased penetration of popular social life by the expanding leisure industry, the same paper could talk of a clear decline, not just in attendance, but in the actual number of walks. In the 1950s, the pace of decline seems to have quickened considerably. Obviously, there were still plenty of walking engagements. The trend, however, was clear. For brass bands, such changes were highly important; they had grown up within a pattern of local culture that was gradually being superseded, and could hardly avoid being hurt in the process.[67]

If the wider culture was increasingly hostile, then it was inevitable that bands took ever-prouder refuge in the central ritual of their own world, the

---

[65] We should not exaggerate the good behaviour of earlier generations of spectators. One reviewer commented in 1897: 'The selections abounded with hidden melodies – hidden by the noise of the children playing round the bandstand' (*Keighley Labour Journal*, 5 June 1897).

[66] *British Bandsman* (1 May 1920; 9 Apr. 1938).

[67] *Brighouse Echo* (28 May 1920, 14 and 21 May 1938). Whit Friday is, of course, still the scene of a number of quickstep contests in villages along the Lancashire and Yorkshire border, contests which in some areas can be traced back to late Victorian patterns of Whitsun celebration.

Figure 2.2. A brass band competing at the 1952 Belle Vue Contest. The band is unidentified, but the conductor is Harry Nuttall.

contest. The number of contests involving full bands undoubtedly fell after the First World War, as travel costs and trade dislocation took their toll, but even the most cursory glance at the band press illustrates how the great events of the contest season pervaded the whole mentality of banding. The importance of the contest lay in its capacity to satisfy the needs of so many groupings within the band community. For what one writer has termed the 'idealists', those who sought, as one bandsman expressed it to him, 'to make music better', the major contests provided the occasion for the release of the new repertoire that they believed would both raise standards and increase the respect in which the movement was held in the wider musical culture.[68] Both this repertoire and its impact will be discussed later.

For the commercial interest-groups, contests offered sizeable rewards. Certainly, only a very limited number were organized with major commercial intent. Some contests were organized by local band associations. Many others were promoted in order to raise funds for a particular institution—a band, a club, sometimes a charity. However, even the smaller events were an obvious

[68] Jackson, *Working Class Community*, 26.

The Great Championship Contest
for the
CRYSTAL PALACE ONE THOUSAND GUINEA TROPHY

LAST YEAR'S WINNER
FODEN'S MOTOR WORKS

11.45 a.m.—SECTION 1.—CHAMPIONSHIP. CONCERT ROOM.

Grand Championship Brass Band Contest for the Crystal Palace One Thousand Guinea Challenge Trophy, the "Daily Telegraph" Challenge Cup, and the W. W. Grant Memorial Cup and other Prizes.

*Adjudicators :—*H. BENNETT
F. WRIGHT
H. GEEHL (*Referee*)

PRIZES

FIRST PRIZE—FIFTY POUNDS, the THOUSAND GUINEA TROPHY for the Championship of Great Britain and the Colonies, and a Bronze Medal with bar and clasp for every Member of the Band. (Members of the Band winning the Trophy twice will be presented with Solid Silver Medals, and Members of the Band winning the Trophy three times will be presented with Solid Gold Medals) and Messrs. THE UNIFORM CLOTHING & EQUIPMENT Co., LTD., 10 & 11 Clerkenwell Green, London, E.C.1, will present one Bandmaster's Frockcoat Suit complete, design to be selected by the winner, to the value of TEN GUINEAS, and Messrs. WRIGHT & ROUND, 34 Erskine Street, Liverpool, will present to the Resident Bandmaster, one *Brass Band News* Gold Medal, valued at FOUR GUINEAS, and A GREAT LOVER OF THE

EUPHONIUM (lady) will present to the Euphonium Soloist of the winning band, a Special Box filled with Cigarettes.

SECOND PRIZE—FORTY POUNDS, and the *DAILY TELEGRAPH* CHALLENGE CUP, and Messrs. B. FELDMAN & Co., 125 Shaftesbury Avenue, London, W.C., will present to the Resident Bandmaster, one Conductor's Gold-mounted Baton.

THIRD PRIZE—THIRTY POUNDS, and the W. W. GRANT MEMORIAL TROPHY.

FOURTH PRIZE—TWENTY-FIVE POUNDS.

FIFTH PRIZE—TWENTY POUNDS.

1. CHAMPIONSHIP CONTEST

TEST PIECE: AN EPIC SYMPHONY ... ... Percy E. Fletcher

No.	Band	Conductor	Draw	Result
1.	Baxendale's (Manchester) Works	F. Mortimer		
2.	Besses o' th' Barn	W. Wood		
3.	Bickershaw Colliery	F. Mortimer		
4.	Black Dyke Mills	W. Halliwell		
5.	Blackhall Colliery	N. Thorpe		
6.	Brighouse and Rastrick	W. Halliwell		
7.	Carlisle St. Stephens	W. Lowes		
8.	Creswell Colliery	H. Moss		
9.	Crystal Palace	D. Wright		
10.	Enfield Central	E. S. Carter		
11.	Foden's Motor Works	F. Mortimer		
12.	Haswell	J. C. Dyson		
13.	Harton Colliery	W. Lowes		
14.	Jewell Springs	J. Jennings		
15.	Luton	F. Mortimer		
16.	Metropolitan-Works	H. Heyes		
17.	Morris Motors	S. V. Wood		
18.	Munn & Felton's Works	W. Halliwell		
19.	Rushden Temperance	T. Young		
20.	Scottish C.W.S.	J. A. Greenwood		
21.	Sheffield Transport Dept.	G. W. Heayo		
22.	Wingate's Temperance	W. Halliwell		

Admission to Concert Hall   TWO SHILLINGS

The Director's Office is in the Eastern Entrance Hall. At "The BRITISH BANDSMAN" Stand can be obtained "THE BOOK OF TEST PIECES"—Price 1/-.

FOR FULL REPORTS AND RESULTS OF THE CONTEST ORDER THROUGH ANY NEWSAGENT THE "BRITISH BANDSMAN" WEEKLY

The Head Quarters of the National Brass Band Club will be under the organ. Entrance at back of organ and Clubroom will be available for members and friends. Mr. J. H. Richenside, the Hon. Secretary, will be pleased to welcome them.

Visitors are strongly recommended to get their tickets for the Massed Bands Concert during the day to avoid the rush and frequent disappointment which is likely to arise through leaving it too late.

6

Figure 2.3. A page from the programme of the National Band Festival (Contest), held at the Alexandra Palace on 24 February 1938. The annotations are by a member of the audience.

and effective location for trade-stands advertising wares as diverse as musical instruments and gum for dentures. The two major national contests controlled by J. H. Iles, the National and the Open (under Iles's control from 1925) were the clearest examples of commercial motivation. Although it would be churlish to deny Iles's commitment to bands as forces of musical education and entertainment, it would also be foolish to overlook the extent to which the two big festivals were used as vehicles to publicize Richard Smith and Company, and the *British Bandsman*. Competitions also provided considerable sponsorship opportunities for organizations from outside the movement. The clearest example is afforded by the involvement of newspapers. By the mid-1920s, all of the classes at the National, with the exception of the One Thousand Guinea Trophy, were sponsored by a paper or magazine.[69] The most celebrated press involvement occurred in 1945 when the *Daily Herald* took over the running of

[69] The sponsors were the *Daily Telegraph*, *Daily Express*, *Daily Graphic*, *Daily Mirror*, *Pearson's Weekly*, the *People*, and *Cassell's Journal*.

Figure 2.4. The ostentatious 'One Thousand Guinea Challenge Trophy' was commissioned at vast expense for the Crystal Palace Choral Competition in 1872, when it was won by the Welsh Choral Union conducted by Griffith Rhys Jones (Caradog). It was first used for the brass band competition at the start of the 20th century. In deference to the Welsh Choral Union, the trophy is now kept at the Museum of Welsh Life, St Fagans, Cardiff.

the National from Iles, whose finances had never recovered following his bankruptcy after sustaining losses in the film industry in 1938.[70]

For the players, the rewards were enormous. Apart from the artistic pleasure and the sheer excitement of performing, contesting provided chances to travel, to renew old acquaintance, and in some cases to learn. Keen younger players and junior bands especially saw contests, again particularly the major ones, as a great stimulus, a chance to sample the best of their culture. At the National the main competitions were always followed by a concert, and the battle for seats was intense. Here the leading bands and soloists became heroes, as enthusiastically welcomed and studied in this fraternity as any jazz or dance band musician was in his.[71]

Finally, contests linked bands to their local community. Most bands took some supporters to contests, although the exact number varied according to location, importance and the state of trade. They gave proceedings something

[70] *British Bandsman* (27 Jan. 1945). For Iles's business problems, see obituary in *Isle of Thanet Gazette* (1 June 1951).
[71] Taylor, *Labour, passim.*

of a sporting flavour, many of them wearing band colours and favours. Press commentators could not avoid the Cup Final analogy. At least until the early 1950s, victorious bands could be assured of the type of civic welcome—crowds at the railway station, 'See the Conquering Hero Comes' played by another local band, speeches from the president, a procession across town for a celebration dinner—that had become almost a cliché of social behaviour by the 1870s.[72]

Even the contest, though, was not immune to changed circumstances. The gradual loss of interest in contest performance among the wider community from the 1950s is a further significant indicator of the bands' marginalization within popular musical culture. 'Thousands', for example, gathered to greet Brighouse and Rastrick after their National success in 1946, 'one thousand' after a similar achievement in 1968.[73] To an extent, this changed pattern of behaviour reflected new attitudes to community celebration, but also stemmed from a reduced level of media attention. In 1946, a Yorkshire journalist noted the enormous attention given to the National by the BBC: 'The first four placings were announced by Stuart Hibberd, Frank Phillips and others nearly a dozen times in the space of six hours.' The national press often gave quite substantial coverage to the major events. Almost forty years later, conductor Trevor Walmsley could argue that if 'Barnsley's left back breaks his bloody leg, it's more newsworthy than winning the National'.[74]

This emphasis on reduced status in popular musical life should not obscure the willingness of bands to make use of new opportunities to reach an audience that was proving increasingly fickle. In particular, they embraced wherever possible the growing technological mass media. Black Dyke had recorded as early as 1903, and the leading bands became regular recording artists. One band discographer has talked of a 'flood' of recordings from the 1920s, with St Hilda, Besses o' th' Barn, and Black Dyke especially prolific. St Hilda made some 160 '78s' up to 1937, while Black Dyke made twenty-six for HMV in 1938–42, and a further twenty-three for Regal-Zonophone from 1940 to 1943.[75] There were plentiful opportunities, too, for the leading cornet soloists such as Harry Mortimer, Jack Mackintosh, and Owen Bottomley. Bands were still to find a reasonable market for their LPs in the 1950s and 1960s. Obviously, these recordings made up only the smallest fraction of the total record market, but they did at least help bands counteract some of the antagonistic trends.

Bands were less happy about their relationship with the BBC, an issue which will be returned to later. For all the undoubted problems, however, from the

[72] See e.g. St Hilda's homecoming described in the *British Bandsman* (9 Oct. 1920).
[73] *Brighouse Echo* (25 Oct. 1946; 18 Oct. 1968).
[74] *Brighouse Echo* (25 Oct. 1946). Taylor, *Labour*, 262.
[75] See Frank Andrews, *Brass Band Cylinder and Non-microgroove Disc Recordings 1903–1960* (Winchester: Piccolo Press, 1997); Tim Munton, in Brand and Brand, *Brass Bands*, 175.

first band broadcast (almost certainly by Clydebank Burgh in April 1923) the BBC did provide another useful showcase.[76] The highest profile accorded to bands came during Harry Mortimer's period as the Corporation's brass and military band supervisor from 1942 to 1964.[77] His initial task was eased by the great demand for light music during the war. Broadcasts played a central role in keeping the band movement together at that time, providing a focus when normal activity was massively disrupted. The *British Bandsman* ran a weekly column on the performances, taking the medium more seriously in a critical sense than at any stage before. Mortimer was able to build on this: during one brief period in the later 1940s, he succeeded in transmitting between ten and fifteen half-hour programmes a week. There was a constant demand for more broadcasts, however, even during the best days. In 1945, for example, a petition of 10,000 names was handed to the BBC by the National Brass Band Club as part of a campaign for greater coverage. The issue has remained high on the agenda to this day.[78]

Before 1914, the brass band repertoire had served as a kind of repository of the main currents of popular musical taste (with the notable exception of music-hall song and drawing-room material). The need to fulfil a variety of musical functions had led to the development of an extraordinarily wide repertoire embracing, in almost equal proportions, elements of 'art', 'popular', or 'light' music, and specialist band music.[79] In essence, selections based on nineteenth-century opera had become the norm for contesting purposes, while a distinctive blend of operatic selections, musical comedy and operetta, marches, specialist solos, and hymn tunes formed the basis of the concert repertoire.

This mixed repertoire remained typical of band performance right through to the 1960s, and beyond in many cases. Concentrating momentarily on concert music, the continuity is quite striking. At least until the 1950s, the *structure* of the programme reflected very faithfully the shape and pattern that had been established by the Victorian bands. A typical programme invariably began with a march, which was followed by an overture and then a selection, usually operatic. From this point there was usually some scope for flexibility, but at least one more selection, a shorter piece such as one of the specialist tone poems, a solo usually for cornet, and finally an arrangement of a vocal item— a glee or, more commonly, a hymn—usually completed the performance. Such a relatively predictable structure clearly had advantages. Audiences knew what to expect, while the mixture gave variety to the programme, both in terms of length and mood of piece. This was a type of programme well suited to audiences with both mixed tastes and levels of interest. While most areas of

[76] Taylor, *Brass Bands*, 125.
[77] H. Mortimer with A. Lynton, *Harry Mortimer on Brass* (Sherborne: Alphabooks, 1981), 119.
[78] *British Bandsman* (3 Mar. 1945).   [79] Russell, *Popular Music*, 228–38.

musical performance have their own structures and patterns, the band concert does seem to have been slightly more standardized and ritualistic than most. The half-hour broadcast concerts generally followed this pattern, although the exact mixture might alter according to requirements. The 6.30 a.m. 'Bright and Early' slot that many bands filled in the 1950s was obviously likely to be much 'lighter' in tone than a Saturday afternoon concert.

There were obviously changes in the content of the repertoire. It is simply not possible to do justice to this topic here, but a few generalizations are useful.[80] There does appear to have been a diminution in the appetite for Italian opera over the period, with the classical and romantic symphonic repertoires increasingly favoured as sources for the 'serious' element of a performance. There was almost no use of the contemporary art-music repertoire, a clear example of the popular–serious divorce that so many commentators debated from the 1930s. The choice of musical comedy and show music simply reflected changing taste, new works moving in, and then almost as rapidly out, of the repertoire. Gilbert and Sullivan, of course, remained massively popular, and some musicals, such as Novello's *Dancing Years*, became brass band 'standards'.

Iles's use of Percy Fletcher's *Labour and Love* as the test piece for the 1913 National was undoubtedly a major turning-point in the contest repertoire.[81] It is sometimes argued that Fletcher was the first 'serious' composer to write for the medium, but Fletcher's standing was in fact a little lower in the contemporary hierarchy. His obituary in the *Musical Times* termed him 'a theatre conductor and composer of popular music'. Probably the first composer of any status to write for the brass band was Joseph Parry, who, in the late nineteenth century, produced the *Tydfil Overture*, while Granville Bantock composed both a brass *Festival March* and a setting for brass and voice of his wife's poem *Sons of Liberty*, as part of a work composed for the twenty-first anniversary of the Independent Labour Party in 1914.[82] However, as Paul Hindmarsh says elsewhere in this book, *Labour and Love* broke the hold of the selection-as-test-piece, and there was never any doubt that the event would from then on be dignified by an original commissioned piece. From the 1920s, a number of major British composers were persuaded to write works for the National, the best-known results being Holst's *A Moorside Suite* in 1928, Elgar's *Severn Suite* in 1930, Ireland's *Downland Suite* in 1932, and Bliss's *Kenilworth* in 1936.

[80] *British Bandsman* gave quite extensive coverage to individual band repertoires, especially after 1945, and provides, as in so many areas, a useful source. Obviously, the discussion here revolves mainly around bands of a fairly high standard.

[81] D. Bythell, 'Provinces versus Metropolis in the British Brass Band Movement in the Early Twentieth Century: The Case of William Rimmer and his Music', *Popular Music*, 16/2 (1997), 154, 157–62.

[82] *Musical Times* (Oct. 1932); T. Herbert, 'Repertory of a Victorian Brass Band', *Popular Music*, 9/1 (1990), 119; *British Bandsman* (11 Apr. 1914).

The Open continued with the operatic selection until 1924, but when Iles effectively took over the contest in 1925, he quickly adopted his National policy, commissioning a work from Thomas Keighley. Keighley's *Macbeth* was so successful that he came to dominate this contest for several years, with further pieces in 1926–8, 1932, and 1935. Apart from a period in the 1950s when the National organizers called upon Frank Wright to produce arrangements of a variety of nineteenth-century works, the major contest test pieces have been original works.[83]

Throughout the period, the brass band was undoubtedly developing its own 'canon', in the sense of a body of music specifically composed for bands, which had gained a favoured place in the taste of bandsmen and audiences alike. This included both shorter pieces such as the cornet solos *Carnival of Venice* and *Alpine Echoes* (1928), and test pieces like Fletcher's *Labour and Love* and *Epic Symphony* (1926), *Life Divine* (Jenkins, 1921), *Lorenzo* (Keighley, 1928), *Pageantry* (Howells, 1934), and *Resurgam* (Ball, 1950). While the best of these pieces undoubtedly stretched technique, placed heavier demands on the band as a whole rather than simply the soloists or 'cornermen', and explored the texture of band instrumentation far more inventively than before, it is also the case that the repertoire was becoming more highly specialized than had previously been the case. Much of this was music for an 'in-group'. One commentator's view that much of it was ' "non-music" . . . markable music', might be harsh, but it does point up the existence of a growing gap between the maturing band repertoire and wider popular taste.[84] To a degree, the development of the band as a musical medium took place at the expense of a more general popularity.

BRASS BANDS AND SOCIAL CHANGE

Both the band movement's decline in numbers and its loss of place in popular musical culture have already been touched on in a number of places. It is now time to consider possible explanations in real depth.

It must be stressed that the problems of the movement were not a specific creation of the years after 1918. Complaints about recruitment difficulties in particular had been prominent for several years before the war, with many a lament on the preference of young men for 'sport and the pictures' over banding. The First World War added further burdens. The band press featured many stories in 1914–15 of bands enlisting *en masse*, or losing large numbers to the forces in a very short time. Most survived by drawing on young players, and by Christmas 1919 were back to full strength.[85] Nevertheless, the count of Yorkshire and Durham bands noted above, although problematic, clearly

---

[83] Taylor, *Brass Bands*, 277–95.   [84] Jackson, *Working Class Community*, 39.
[85] *British Bandsman* (13 Nov. 1920) for the bandsmen's roll of honour.

suggests that some bands did not survive the war years. From this point, a movement already past its peak was threatened by the acceleration of the existing challenges and by the development of new ones.

Many factors have contributed to the changed status of the brass band. Rather than attempt to look at the issue chronologically, the ensuing discussion is grouped around economic, social (narrowly defined here as almost synonymous with 'recreational'), and musical changes. Economic processes at both macro and micro levels have undoubtedly played a highly significant role. The few writers who have considered the twentieth-century band movement have suggested that the economic depression and chronic unemployment of the inter-war period was a major reason for the fall in the number of bands at this time. The exact impact of the depression needs careful consideration. Economic historians now paint for us a complex view of the period 1920–39, those years during which the number of registered unemployed never fell below one million. Simplifying enormously, the period is now seen as one in which regional differentiation in unemployment levels was quite marked. Certain areas, especially those with an economic dependence on staples aimed at export markets, suffered appallingly. Unemployment in Jarrow reached 72 per cent in 1935, and 62 per cent in Merthyr Tydfil in 1934. In the new growth points of the economy, however, such as electronics and consumer durables, for example, outside of the worst crisis of 1929–33, unemployment was low, sometimes negligible: High Wycombe had a rate of only 4 per cent in the mid-1930s. This was not, however, simply a matter of divisions between north and south, between 'old' industrial and 'new' industrial regions, as the above examples might be taken to imply. Towns in the heart of the old industrial north, with a mixed economy or a specialism in a particular area such as engineering, often had unemployment rates close to those of the 'prosperous' south. These variables have to be taken into consideration and generalizations about the economy and the problems of bands made reasonably localized and subtle as a result.[86]

There can be no doubt that in areas of high continuous unemployment, the period from 1920 posed severe difficulties for the movement. Some bands did fold as a direct result of economic slump. At least five Durham colliery bands—Hebburn, Woodlands, Cornsay, Esh Winning and Kibblesworth—went out of existence for long periods between 1932 and 1938.[87] Economic depression does not, however, appear to have been a fundamental cause of the falling number of bands catalogued earlier. The timing of the acceleration of band closures seems crucial, occurring around 1938, after the worst impact of the depression had passed. Moreover, a town like Halifax, with a relatively low unemployment rate of around 6 per cent, lost four bands in 1938,

---

[86] The best brief introduction to this topic is S. Constantine, *Unemployment in Britain between the Wars* (London: Longman, 1980).

[87] *British Bandsman* (19 Mar. 1938).

suggesting that factors other than economic ones were in operation.[88] What depression did cause were the severe organizational and financial problems that so hampered and pressurized many bands in this period. Bands were often left, in movement parlance, 'short-handed', as players left to seek work in other areas. The regional reports in the band press recorded these problems with a level of exactness which gives events a certain poignancy, as when 'Downside', the Dorset and Wiltshire correspondent of the *British Bandsman*, noted the extreme difficulties of Bourton Band, caused by the closure of the local iron foundry and the subsequent migration of several players to new work in King's Lynn. By 1938, 'Red Rose' in the *British Bandsman* could talk of a 'little army' of bandsmen lost to Lancashire over the two decades. It is likely that the hardest-hit area of all was the Rhondda Urban District, which suffered the migration of 28 per cent of its population, some 47,000 people, between 1921 and 1935.[89]

Financial problems were legion, and it is not entirely surprising that a certain bitterness was directed by some bandsmen at some of the better funded works bands, especially in the south, which were generally little affected by such difficulties. New instruments, music, and uniforms were at a premium; travel became a luxury. Bands constantly found themselves appealing for funds, running raffles, collecting 'a mile of pennies', and going out playing with collecting boxes. There were impressive attempts at mutual aid when banding showed hints of moving from a purely musical to a social movement. In 1928, the North Wales correspondent of the *British Bandsman* encouraged his local bands to raise money for the 'bandsmen's kiddies' in the stricken South Wales coalfield. In December of the same year, the paper launched a 'Find A Miner A Job' campaign, encouraging bands away from the coalfields to fill their vacancies with unemployed miners, using government migration schemes to find them work. Whether this campaign achieved much is not known, but it illustrates the sense of fraternity that sometimes broke through the pettier elements of banding activity. There were, too, many modest acts of local assistance, as when, in 1938, Stourton Memorial Band near Leeds held a concert to boost the funds of struggling neighbours, Kippax Old.[90]

Successful bands were not exempt from these problems. In 1930, the wife of the Brighouse and Rastrick president raffled a gold watch to raise money for the band to travel to the Crystal Palace. Two years later, the band was again struggling to raise the £50 for travel, and only reached the target at the last moment. Wingates Temperance was less successful, failing to find the money for its London appearance in 1938.[91]

---

[88] The bands were Southowram, Norland, Rishworth, and Ryburn and Friendly (the latter soon recovered, in fact).

[89] *British Bandsman* (9 Aug. 1930; 31 Dec. 1938); Constantine, *Unemployment*, 22.

[90] *British Bandsman* (10 Nov. and 22 Dec. 1928; 5 Feb. 1938).

[91] *Brighouse Echo* (12 Sept. 1930; 16 Sept. 1932); *British Bandsman* (22 Oct. 1938).

Some of the smaller bands with no reserves to fall back on found themselves in disastrous situations. The records of the Idle and Thackley Band, a sixteen-strong band from a textile community on the northern edge of Bradford, make truly depressing reading, featuring as they do a number of small but decidedly unpaid bills. In 1933, the band managed to persuade Wright and Round to supply music on credit. The company acceded to this 'unusual request' (a form of words suggesting that the company neither liked nor greatly encouraged this form of transaction) as 'we remember you as very old subscribers and we want to help you as much as possible in these hard times'. The band's enthusiasm for Wright and Round's assistance is undoubtedly more than partly explained by Boosey and Hawkes's anxious enquiries in the same year about the whereabouts of 18s. 10d. owed on music purchased eighteen months earlier! The band seems to have struggled on, eventually dissolving during the war.[92] Public support, too, was affected by depression. A Welsh commentator noted a marked fall in attendance between two visits by St Hilda to Caernarfon Pavilion in May and August 1930, as 'industrial matters are bad at the quarries'.[93]

It has to be said, however, that the impression of a movement battling very hard and to a certain extent succeeding in living on reduced means and with reduced expectations—like so many sections of the working class in general in this period—is stronger than that of a movement dealt any kind of fatal blow. Alongside the various strategies for coping noted above, bands showed in general a determination to survive. A Durham newspaper was impressed that Brandon Silver Band could still win prizes three years after the local colliery where most of the players worked had closed down; the *British Bandsman* equally so by the efforts of some of the Rhondda bands.[94] Indeed, virtue was often made out of necessity, and periods of unemployment, and inactivity caused by strikes and lock-outs, were often used to the bands' advantage. Work was done on band rooms, extra time was spent on practice. The *British Bandsman* commented in 1920 that the coal strike was giving bands in areas where the shift system usually militated against midweek rehearsal, unexpected opportunity to practise. The Marsden Colliery bandmaster, Jack Boddice, claimed that the band had managed an unprecedented seventy-six full rehearsals during the 1925 coal dispute preceding its success at the National, while Harton Colliery undertook a twenty-six week tour in 1926, an opportunity that would not normally have presented itself.[95]

---

[92] Records of Idle and Thackley Brass Band, Bradford Archives, 54D 80/1/32. The band had gone bankrupt once before, in the first decade of the 20th cent.

[93] *British Bandsman* (23 Aug. 1930).

[94] *Durham County Advertiser* (26 Apr. 1928); *British Bandsman* (17 Nov. 1928).

[95] *British Bandsman* (30 Oct. 1920); *Shields Daily News* (30 Sept. 1925); *British Bandsman* (7 Aug. 1926).

Banding also provided a valuable source of income, both communal and individual. Some bands worked to raise money for local projects during periods of hardship. Welsh bands in particular were active during the miners' strike of 1926.[96] Probably, soloists and members of the élite bands benefited the most, as banding skills provided, in the words of one contemporary, 'the means of creating an opportunity for them to earn a livelihood, which would otherwise have been an impossibility'.[97] St Hilda Colliery's decision to become a professional band soon after the temporary closure of the pit is perhaps the most extreme response of this type to adversity.[98]

Many historians have been struck by the fact that 'Working people seem to have been extraordinarily resilient, or stubborn, in the face of the depression'.[99] That determination kept the bands and other elements of the rich (at least in traditional manufacturing areas) working-class associational culture alive. At the same time, through both the mechanisms noted above and a less quantifiable artistic contribution, bands undoubtedly played their part in softening the worst excesses of the period and in allowing people to sustain their dignity and resilience.

Mass unemployment on this scale was not to return again until the 1970s, and the 1950s and 1960s were periods of relative economic prosperity. Nevertheless, large changes were wrought by the decline in the numbers employed in certain traditional staple industries. The geography of banding as it stood in 1914 corresponded fairly faithfully to the geography of eighteenth- and nineteenth-century industrialization. As has already been shown, the 'classic' location of bands was the small industrial town or village. As that industrial pattern altered, the place of bands shifted with it. The most striking example is provided by the mining industry. In the early 1920s, 1,289,000 miners were employed in Great Britain. By 1974, that number had fallen to 246,000. The situation becomes even clearer if looked at in a local perspective. In 1923, 170,000 miners were employed in Durham. By 1939, the figure had fallen to 112,000, by 1960 to 87,000, by 1970 to 34,000. Seventy-five Durham pits closed in the 1960s.[100] Given the huge contribution made by miners to the band movement, it is hardly surprising that their falling numbers, and above all, the subsequent breaking up of pit communities and the distinctive social life that they spawned, have contributed much to both the decline in the number of bands and their diminished role in social life.

[96] *British Bandsman* (19 and 26 June, 24 July 1926).
[97] *British Bandsman* (31 Dec. 1938).   [98] Taylor, *Brass Bands*, 129.
[99] Constantine, *Unemployment*, 43. For a stimulating discussion of the relationship between associational culture and unemployment, see R. McKibbin, 'The "Social Psychology" of Unemployment in Inter-War Britain', in P. J. Waller (ed.), *Politics and Social Change in Modern Britain* (Brighton: Harvester, 1987), 161–91.
[100] M. Bulmer (ed.), *Mining and Social Change* (London: Croom Helm, 1978), 22; C. Jones, 'Coal, Gas and Electricity', in R. Pope (ed.), *Atlas of British Social and Economic History since 1700* (London: Routledge, 1989), 79.

Ultimately, however, relative affluence proved a greater threat than industrial depression and economic decline. There can be no doubt that, for those in regular employment, the period from 1924 to 1938 saw a significant and almost continuous rise in real wages.[101] Crucially, the period also saw a marked fall in basic working hours for many workers. Six and a half million workers enjoyed an average reduction of six and a half hours a week in 1919, and although this was the single largest such reduction, by the end of the 1930s, the forty-eight-hour week had replaced the pre-war norm of fifty-four hours for many workers.[102] The 1950s and 1960s were to see further extensions of these twin developments. Obviously, confident generalizations like these ride roughshod over the often massive hardships of some areas and some individuals. Nevertheless, it is clear that many people had both increasing amounts of disposable income and increasing amounts of spare time in which to spend it. The ensuing social changes undoubtedly touched the brass band world.

Bands themselves had benefited greatly from similar processes in the nineteenth century. Now they found that in an environment conducive to the expansion of leisure activities, rivals emerged. Concentrating for the moment on the inter-war period, challenges for popular commitment, loyalty and money came from a number of directions. Many of these challenges had first emerged in the years immediately before the war, but they undoubtedly gathered momentum. One such challenge was offered by sport, especially soccer, although rugby union in South Wales, and rugby league in its various enclaves in the north of England, could attract large support, as could league cricket, and the 'new' sports of the period, especially speedway and greyhound racing.

To a degree, bands coexisted with sport, providing half-time or pre-event entertainment at many venues. Again, it must be stressed that sport could suffer quite seriously from the same economic pressures that affected bands. First-division soccer attendances fell in the height of the depression in the early 1930s, while a number of sides in depressed areas, including Merthyr, Ashington, Thames, and Durham City lost Football League status as crowds fell and finances crumbled.[103] Gareth Williams has illustrated how Welsh rugby suffered from the loss of players in the 1930s, as top performers either turned professional with league sides or went to those West Country union clubs able to find them work.[104] Nevertheless, while such a broad view guards against simplistic analysis, there can be no denying the intensifying hold of sport in this period. Average attendance at football matches over the period

[101] S. G. Jones, *Workers at Play* (London: Routledge & Kegan Paul, 1986), 10–14, especially table 1.2, p. 13.

[102] Ibid. 15–20.

[103] D. Russell, *Football and the English* (Preston: Carnegie Publishing, 1997), 82–4.

[104] G. Williams, 'From Grand Slam to Grand Slump: Economy, Society and Rugby Football in Wales during the Depression', *Welsh History Review*, 11 (1983).

as a whole rose steadily, first-division averages rising from 25,300 in 1927–8 to 30,600 in 1938–9, and peaking at 40,700 in 1949–50. The sideshow nature of band performances at soccer matches seems suitably symbolic of wider shifts in popular loyalties.[105]

The cinema, too, was blamed by many commentators for the bands' difficulties. As with sport, there can be no doubt of its hold over popular audiences. Annual cinema attendances rose from 903 million in 1934 to 1,027 million by 1940.[106] Of some importance here was the high attendance of the boys and young men that bands were so keen to recruit. Clearly, spectator sport and the cinema were easy targets, especially in a period when many commentators made much of the division between 'active' (good) and 'passive' (bad) leisure pursuits. Less commonly selected for attack, because they were normally 'active', but actually representing serious competition, were the innumerable voluntary activities that absorbed the energies of so many. The number of junior football clubs grew from 12,000 in 1910 to 35,000 in 1937; the Scout movement grew from 108,000 to 420,000 over the same period.[107] One could play football (and be a Scout) and play in a band; many, including cornet virtuoso Jack Mackintosh, managed it. The point is simply that there were ever more choices—choices diminishing the bands' pool of recruits and supporters. After the war, although some of the leisure pursuits discussed here were now themselves suffering from declining patronage, a further set of social activities emerged to reshape leisure style. Television, DIY, and motoring were only three of the most talked about.[108]

Without any doubt, however, the most significant threat, and probably the single most important change of any type influencing the band movement, was the massive set of changes in popular musical tastes and habits which first became apparent in the period around the end of the First World War. At the very heart of this lay three interrelated developments: the growth of technological media; the so-called 'Americanization' of British popular music; and the accompanying rise of the dance band and a new style of dance music.[109] The term 'Americanization' is problematic, and is only used here as a working generalization, to refer to broad changes in British taste and repertoire that owed something to exposure to American influences. Similarly, 'dance band music' covers a range of evolving styles played by a variety of musical combinations, and again the phrase is loosely used here. The significance of these

[105] For attendances, see N. Fishwick, *English Football and Society, 1910–1950* (Manchester: Manchester University Press, 1989), 48–9.

[106] J. Richards, *The Age of the Dream Palace* (London: Routledge & Kegan Paul, 1984), 11.

[107] J. Springhall, *Youth, Empire and Society* (London: Croom Helm, 1977), 138–9.

[108] A. Marwick, *British Society since 1945* (London: Allen Lane, 1982), has useful material.

[109] For an invaluable introduction, see C. W. E. Bigsby, 'Europe, America and the Cultural Debate', in Bigsby, *Superculture* (London: Elek, 1975); S. Frith, 'Playing with Real Feeling: Jazz and Suburbia' and 'The Pleasures of the Hearth: The Making of BBC Light Entertainment', both in Frith, *Music for Pleasure* (Cambridge: Polity in association with Blackwell, 1988).

changes has to be traced over a long period, at least into the 1950s, in order to be fully appreciated, but the focus for the moment remains on the inter-war years.

This sea-change in taste has many strands, too complex to unravel in full detail here. Of major importance was the take-off of the dance hall. As already noted, dance halls were a feature of British popular musical culture from the mid-nineteenth century. However, they were generally deemed unacceptable by respectable middle- and working-class society, and it required the relative loosening of social constraints during the First World War (coupled with an increase in purchasing power) to generate a more tolerant attitude. From about 1919–20 there was, too, an important change in the marketing and structure of the dance-hall business, with the establishment of the highly respectable 'palais de danse'. The earliest halls to bear this name, at Hammersmith and Birmingham, were aimed at middle- and lower middle-class audiences (minimum admission at Birmingham in 1920 was 5s.), but over the course of the next decade this new style of hall became available to a far wider clientele. Together with the much larger number of venues that grew up in all manner of premises all over the country, they occupied an absolutely central place in popular social life from the early 1920s.[110]

With the new halls came new music. The older styles were not totally displaced. There was always a market for 'old-tyme' dancing among older age-groups, and indeed, in the late 1930s there was a considerable enthusiasm for 'Gay Nineties' nights in some northern halls among younger audiences. Bolton even witnessed a vogue for *ceilidhs* in 1938 which both worried local swing bands and raised listenership to Radio Telefis Eireann.[111] However, American styles predominated. After a brief flirtation with jazz music of the type associated with the American 'novelty' bands that visited Britain between 1916 and 1920, British bands rapidly adopted a much lusher, sweeter style, drawing in particular on the work of Paul Whiteman. Whiteman virtually set the agenda for British dance music in the 1920s. When he allowed Bix Beiderbecke to play 'hot' solos, British bands felt able to unleash their soloists in similar fashion. Similarly, in the later 1930s, American swing bands established the new canons of taste.[112]

The fact that the 'Americanization' of popular music in this period was often stimulated initially through *live* performance in dance halls, and indeed, in variety theatres, is a point sometimes overlooked. So, too, is the fact that throughout the rest of the period up to 1939, many first experienced new musical trends through the medium of live performance. Nevertheless, it would be hard to underestimate the key role played by the new technological media, partly the gramophone, but above all the wireless. The growth of these

---

[110] This paragraph draws extensively on M. Hustwitt, 'Caught in a Whirlpool of Aching Sound: The Production of Dance Music in Britain in the 1920s', *Popular Music* 3 (1983).
[111] *Melody Maker* (25 June and 30 Apr. 1938).   [112] Hustwitt, 'Caught', 16.

media in this period was striking. By 1928 there were an estimated 2.5 million gramophones in Britain, record sales having increased from 22 million to 50 million in the previous four years. The collapse of the record industry in 1929–30 slowed this growth dramatically, but a crucial base had been laid.[113] The growth of broadcasting was more significant still. In 1922, when the British Broadcasting Company (as the BBC was then known) was founded, only one household in every 100 had a licence. By 1930, the figure had become 30 in every 100, and by 1939 it had risen to 71.[114]

The spread of new technology fundamentally altered the context in which brass bands operated. First, it undermined the bands' function as a source of musical education and dissemination in the field of art music and even in some areas of light music. It was now so much easier for audiences to gain access to various types of music in the original form. J. H. Elliot's claim in 1936, that 'the old conception of the brass band as a mirror through which the classics could be displayed to thousands who could never see the actuality is no longer valid', may have underestimated levels of previous popular musical experience, as well as the continuing popularity of selections, but it underscores this fundamental change in the musical environment.[115]

Alongside this, wireless and gramophone gave massive exposure to the new, mainly American, styles of popular music. It is noteworthy that dance band record sales provided the biggest source of record company profit in the 1920s.[116] Dance band music formed a regular and popular broadcasting feature from the earliest days. The local stations that carried so many of the earliest transmissions before their absorption into the BBC regional networks from the late 1920s, regularly featured bands, and did much to stimulate local groups.[117] The BBC's first national dance band transmission went out in March 1923, and in the next month the Savoy Havana Band made the first of its many broadcasts. In 1928, the BBC formed its own dance band with Jack Payne as leader.[118] By the end of the decade, late evening dance band performances were an established feature of the schedule. From the early 1930s another source of dance music was supplied by the expanding network of continental commercial stations, which the BBC fought so persistently to destroy. Radio Luxembourg's powerful transmitter penetrated the whole country, although most of the other stations could only be clearly received in the South-East and Midlands.[119] For the few, there were also the American East Coast

[113] Hustwitt, 'Caught', 16–22.

[114] M. Pegg, *Broadcasting and Society, 1918–1939* (London: Croom Helm, 1983), 7.

[115] J. F. Russell and J. H. Elliot, *The Brass Band Movement* (London: J. M. Dent & Sons, 1936), 200.

[116] Hustwitt, 'Caught', 16.   [117] *Melody Maker* (29 Jan. 1938).

[118] A. McCarthy, *The Dance Band Era* (London: Studio Vista, 1971), 50.

[119] Pegg, *Broadcasting*, 116–26, 140–6; R. Nichols, *Radio Luxembourg: The Station of the Stars* (London: W. H. Allen, 1983), 12–47; R. Plomley, *Days Seemed Longer: Early Years of a Broadcaster* (London: Eyre Methuen, 1980).

shortwave stations, whose jazz programmes could be received quite clearly at certain times of the year, and to whose timetables the proselytizing *Melody Maker* gave considerable space.

The massively increased interest in American popular music, and in dance music in general, called into being a legion of dance bands. The existing literature on dance bands concentrates very largely on the top-flight professional bands, and pays little attention to the huge number of bands that grew up to service the needs of local halls. It is not possible yet to talk with confidence about numbers, growth rhythms, geography, or social class. First impressions suggest rapid growth, large numbers, a genuinely national coverage and a wide social mix, but still (at least at semi-professional level and below) a preponderance of working-class players. Gender issues are clear: almost all bands were male, although women players were not completely unknown.[120]

Bands playing some American-style music existed in London and the provinces by 1919–20. The involvement of the dance music publisher, Lawrence Wright, in the launch of *Melody Maker* in 1926 as largely a dance band musicians' paper, suggests a fairly advanced level of growth during the early 1920s.[121] By the 1930s, the dance band had become a major feature of musical life. In 1938, a local correspondent in *Melody Maker*, with an albeit ill-disguised enthusiasm for the musical prowess of his region, claimed that Bolton, Lancashire, had almost fifty 'gig' bands, with another twelve in the neighbouring district of Farnworth.[122] These would have ranged from scratch bands, probably surviving for very short periods in the 'lower' end of the market, hunting for work in the private-party, scout-hut dance market, to the élite semi-professional bands with residencies at local halls, recording engagements, and quite probably some success in the network of dance band competitions which *Melody Maker* established almost immediately after commencing publication. Most towns possessed a solid core of dance band players. Raymond Thomson's excellent study of dance in Greenock—albeit in the post-1945 period—suggests that in a town with a population of 70,000 about 100 musicians served the fifteen local venues.[123]

The significance of the dance band in this context lay not only in its new repertoire but in the challenge it posed to the hegemony of the brass band. Here was a rival instrumental organization of real strength growing up within the community at large. The spokesmen of the brass band movement were for the most part as hostile to 'jazz', as they (like so many other commentators) termed dance music of all types, as all other defenders of musical tradition

[120] *Melody Maker* provides a rich starting-point for primary research.

[121] C. Ehrlich, *The Music Profession in Britain since the Eighteenth Century: A Social History* (Oxford: Clarendon Press, 1985), 203.

[122] *Melody Maker* (19 Feb. 1938).

[123] R. Thomson, 'Dance Bands and Dance Halls in Greenock, 1945–55', *Popular Music*, 8 (1989).

based on formal notation, formal training, and a base in Western art music. They had not liked ragtime either, and they assumed that jazz would be a short-lived craze, as ragtime had been for many British audiences. Even many perceptive players made the same assumption; Harry Mortimer, as he wryly remembers in his autobiography, turned down the chance to play with Jack Hylton on these grounds.[124] It says little for the grasp of popular taste among many in the movement that, as late as 1938, contributors to the band press could still proclaim: 'it will be a glad time for brass bands when this craze dies out', 'let not the bands lose heart it is only a passing phase', and 'we believe and contend that "jazz" and "swing" music is a passing vogue'.[125] Their greatest worry was that dance bands would attract brass band players. Undoubtedly they did. Indeed, at least in the provinces, the brass band not surprisingly formed the major training ground for dance band brass players. They were greeted with some suspicion by some of their new colleagues, the brass band being seen by many as a profoundly unsuitable nursery. A writer, commenting on the quality of Billy Cotton's new trombonist in 1928, was paying a compliment when he said: 'Originally a brass band man, he has left all traces of that school behind.' Jock Bain, trombonist with Roy Fox, commented ten years later: 'some aver that the thorough brass band man never shakes himself free of staccato phrasing and thin tone—especially on the trombone'. Bain concluded that it depended 'on the man behind the gun'. By now, there were many gunslingers.[126]

In 1926, the *British Bandsman* presented the issue in simple terms of loyalty to a pure movement against short-lived financial gain: 'Is it worthwhile sacrificing all the comradeship, and maybe the healthy rivalry of brass banding, for a temporarily more lucrative spare-time occupation, which, in a year or two's time, the caprice of a fickle public may (as likely as not) have relegated to the limbo of forgotten things?'[127] Whatever the bandsman's musical taste or sense of loyalty, at that exact juncture the financial rewards were extremely high, as indicated by rumours that due to the huge demand for trumpet and trombone players for work of this type, theatre musicians were being paid ten times their normal fee to take dance engagements.[128] Throughout the 1930s, dance band work undoubtedly offered reasonable remuneration, probably higher than that available to most bandsmen.

Unquestionably, some players were lost to the movement in this way. These ranged from soloists such as George Swift, who went from St Hilda to Jack Hylton, to rank-and-file players.[129] However, bands had always suffered the

[124] Mortimer with Lynton, *Mortimer on Brass*, 106.
[125] *British Bandsman* (26 Feb. and 2 Apr. 1938).
[126] *Melody Maker* (Jan. 1928; 5 Mar. 1938).
[127] *British Bandsman* (31 July 1926).   [128] Ehrlich, *Music Profession*, 203.
[129] Admittedly, by the time of Swift's departure, St Hilda was a professional band anyway. *British Bandsman* (2 July 1938).

loss of personnel, whether to symphony orchestras or ice-rink bands, and it is probable that much of the contemporary complaint about heavy losses was exaggerated. Bandsmen had a long tradition of combining loyalty to their bands with semi-professional work, and this pattern probably continued over this period in the shape of men like Frank Wilby, cornet with Brighouse in the 1930s and trumpeter with the New Imperial Dance Orchestra in Huddersfield; Cliff Ward, conductor of Llanelly Silver and leader of Len Colvin and his Denza Players; and the cautious A. L. of South Shields, cornet player with a first-section band, who wrote to *Melody Maker* asking for advice about mouthpieces for dance band trumpeters who did not want to spoil their brass band work.[130]

This dangerously 'divided interest' worried band commentators almost as much as defections. They claimed, probably with some justification, that dance band engagements kept players away from rehearsals, and, less convincingly, that they developed in the dance hall 'a slipshod way of playing' that was undermining the movement's musical standards.[131] In the final analysis, however, probably more crucial to the long-term future of banding was the fact that dance bands recruited a new generation of musicians who might otherwise have gone into brass bands, and that this massive injection of new musical experience fundamentally shifted the taste of the younger generation.

The first point is difficult to substantiate, but there is no doubt that the 1930s in particular saw a rise in the sale of what had previously been relatively unorthodox instruments, most notably saxophones, but also accordions, guitars, mandolins, and many others. Musical instrument dealers were quick to respond to the new market opportunity, offering most of these instruments at weekly hire-purchase rates of between 2s. and 2s. 6d. per week.[132] On the second point, there can be no denying the massive appetite for American-influenced dance music in this period. Dance band programmes were consistently shown to be among the most popular form of radio entertainment, especially among younger audiences. In their 1939 study, *Broadcasting in Everyday Life*, Jennings and Gill noted that, when asked to name their favourite band conductor as a test of knowledge and discrimination, while 'the elder women showed complete indifference', 57 per cent of young women and 89 per cent of children put forward a name. The authors also noted the debate that took place within the community over interpretation of individual tunes by different bands, admitting with a little reluctance that 'even in homes where dance music flows on for hours at a time, a certain amount of discrimination is exercised'. They recorded, too, that national band leaders were

---

[130] *Brighouse Echo* (7 Sept. 1934); *Melody Maker* (16 July and 6 Aug. 1938).
[131] *British Bandsman* (31 Dec. 1938).
[132] *Melody Maker* advertisement columns provide an excellent source.

hero-worshipped, and that even local players gained enhanced status in their communities.[133]

This major set of changes in popular taste obviously accounts for some of the lost public engagements of the late 1930s and earlier. It must also have been central to the recruitment problems which were emerging just before the war. By the late 1930s, bands were having to draw from the first 'youth culture' that had been fully exposed to the new technological media. The changed taste of youngsters was a commonly cited reason for the bands' problems. When Southowram Band from just outside Halifax folded in February 1938, the decision hinged on the fact that it was hard 'to get youths to take up the instruments'. In the same month, Crookes Band in Sheffield, the third band to fold in the city in twelve months, claimed that 'they could not get youths to take up the instruments'. In the next month, when Barton's Band in Preston 'simply faded out', the *British Bandsman* claimed: 'The bands in the Preston district are getting concerned about the lack of interest which is beginning to show itself in the general public. They seem to be more interested in military bands and jazz combinations.'[134]

To an extent, some bands attempted to fight back with changes in repertoire and performance structure. Jazz pieces occasionally appeared in the publishers' journals, Munn and Felton making effective use of Feldman's brass band arrangement of the Original Dixieland Jazz Band classic, *Tiger Rag*, at the 1938 National concert. Played as an encore for *Labour and Love*, 'it caught the audience by surprise by its unexpectedness, but after the initial shock (as it were) everyone settled down to enjoy it, especially the drummer's effects'.[135] More common was the increased use of vocal or non-brass instrumental items, although such performers usually worked within the 'popular classic' rather than the 'popular' idiom. Probably the most successful of these acts was Roland Jones, euphonium soloist with Black Dyke and, from 1939, Bickershaw, who was regularly featured by his bands as an operatic tenor. Indeed, he went on to join Sadler's Wells as principal tenor in 1947. Ultimately, however, these tactics provided little defence. Although the *British Bandsman* writer who claimed in 1938 that brass bands 'couldn't swing' may have underestimated their potential for change, he nevertheless captured their limits in the new environment.[136] Under the impact of the 'Americanization' of popular music, the

---

[133] H. Jennings and W. Gill, *Broadcasting in Everyday Life* (London: BBC, 1939), 16, 18. Admittedly, most of their detailed research was based on a study of a working-class district of Bristol and some caution must be exercised when applying their findings to the national situation. Bristol did not, for example, have a strong brass band tradition.

[134] *British Bandsman* (5 and 26 Feb., 19 Mar. 1938).

[135] *British Bandsman* (1 Oct. 1938). *Tiger Rag*, of course, hardly represented the most modern element of popular music by 1938.

[136] Jones began his career with Gwauncaegurwen Band. On his vocal career, see *British Bandsman* (2 Apr. 1938; 7 Feb. 1964); *Leigh, Tyldesley and Atherton Journal* (14 Nov. 1947). *British Bandsman* (29 Jan. 1938). In some areas, another type of 'jazz band', the comic bands

brass band, that most British of musical institutions, had lost its privileged position in the popular musical culture of industrial Britain.

It may seem perverse to have spent so much time looking at the inter-war period, a time during which the bands' declining status in popular musical life was only just becoming apparent. However, it does seem that this period saw the establishment of new patterns of musical style and consumption that increasingly cut brass bands adrift from the wider community and, more particularly, the younger performers and consumers. To a large extent, the problems experienced in the 1950s and 1960s simply represented the working-through of the previous thirty years of social and cultural change.

The 1940s and 1950s certainly continued the process of change. The presence of American servicemen in Britain during the war further stimulated the popularity of swing. Revivalist jazz from about 1946, and the 'trad' jazz boom of the late 1950s and 1960s, may have represented a further challenge to the supply of brass players. Absolutely fundamental was the great change in the popular musical tastes of the young, beginning in earnest in 1956 and establishing a whole new pantheon of musical rivalries—rock 'n' roll, skiffle, and jive, words which, like jazz before them, many band writers could only bear to write down if sanitized by inverted commas. With jazz and dance music there could be coexistence, at least at the level of shared instrumentation and personnel. With the guitar-led 'pop' culture there was very little overlap. It can have been little consolation that the old rivals, the dance bands, were also damaged by the change.[137] Television theme-tunes and selections from shows like *South Pacific*, coupled with the not inconsiderable audience they retained for the standard band repertoire, still gave brass bands a footing in the wider popular musical culture. None the less, by the late 1950s they had become effectively divorced from the mainstream of popular youth culture. The passage from somewhere near the centre to the margin of popular culture had reached the point of no return.

A final consideration in this study of decline concerns the style of band culture. As early as the 1930s, but perhaps particularly from the 1950s, it may well have been the brass band's image and overall culture, as much as its music, that made it unattractive to new generations. Bands had always operated under a very tight discipline. Conductors or bandmasters who had won the respect of their players, usually through artistic achievements, could exert the authority of an officer over the ranks. Sometimes that discipline was natural, considerate, and unforced, at other times almost cruel. Tom Morgan,

armed with kazoos, watering cans, funnels, mouth organs, and all manner of instruments, might have also presented a challenge. They were certainly popular attractions at carnivals and processions. See E. Bird, 'Jazz Bands of North East England. The Evolution of a Working-Class Cultural Activity', *Oral History*, 4 (1976); R. Wharton and A. Clarke, *The Tommy Talker Bands of the West Riding* (Bradford: Ronnie Wharton & Arthur Clarke, 1979).

[137] Thomson, 'Dance Bands', 154.

conductor of Callender's, and indeed, an ex-military bandmaster, could generate an atmosphere in which 'sometimes you'd actually be sweating with fear'. J. A. Greenwood was another with a tendency to hardness.[138] All bandmasters placed high emphasis upon an almost military cleanliness, formality, and neatness. Black Dyke bandmaster, Arthur O. Pearce, stressed these elements very forcefully. In the late 1940s, solo cornet Willie Lang, forgetting his overcoat for a park engagement, was saturated in a subsequent downpour when Pearce refused to allow him to borrow a replacement. Afterwards, it was Lang who apologized for his improper dress.[139] At about the same period, at the beginning of a park concert on an exceptionally hot day, Pearce, tunic over arm, 'addressed the audience and asked them if the players could play with their tunics off. An immediate "yes" was voiced by the audience, so in coloured shirts and with caps on they played to a delighted crowd. This is a good exhibition of discipline and will be remembered for a long time.'[140]

Generally, those brought up in the movement seem to have accepted, and indeed been proud, of this discipline, but it must have appealed less to new recruits, especially as there were now attractive alternatives. Dance bands from the 1920s and pop groups from the 1950s, although in a sense adopting uniforms of their own, had an altogether more fashionable image. Interestingly, some of the uniform manufacturers who had serviced brass bands were quick to respond to the new opportunity, Beevers of Huddersfield, one of the oldest uniform firms, offering 'styles of the moment for dance bands'.[141] Again, although many were run in a fairly hard-headed way, there was a slightly more democratic feel about dance bands and groups. There was, too, an element of responsiveness, bands picking up rapidly on new styles and new repertoire. Brass bands were much more at the behest of publishers, contest organizers, conductors, and the sheer weight of tradition. Certainly by the 1950s, in an age when, for young men, uniform and discipline meant National Service, the essentially Victorian brass band subculture must have appeared somewhat anachronistic. It seems suitable that the brass band's major contest should have been sponsored by a daily paper, the *Daily Herald*, that was very much associated with the older generation of the 'traditional' working class.[142]

BRASS BANDS IN THE NATIONAL CULTURE

For most of the period up to about 1930, the band movement felt itself hugely neglected and underestimated by the musical and, indeed, the entire artistic 'establishment'. There were good grounds for this view. The 1927 edition of *Grove* almost ignored the movement altogether, and even the *Musical Times* failed to notice either Holst's or Elgar's test pieces in 1928 and 1930

---

[138] Taylor, *Labour*, 84, 49.   [139] Ibid. 126.   [140] *British Bandsman* (6 Sept. 1947).
[141] *Melody Maker* (1 Jan. 1938).   [142] Richards, *The Age*, 15–16.

respectively. When bands were mentioned, much of what was written was inaccurate and ill-informed. Probably the most infamous example of this is afforded by Beecham's speech to a luncheon club in Leeds in 1928 when he referred to the brass band as 'that superannuated, obsolete, beastly, disgusting, horrid method of making music'. This attack formed only part of a wild tirade against many aspects of British musical life, and some, like Iles, felt able to dismiss it as mere publicity-seeking or as simply another example of Beecham's idiosyncratic beliefs. 'I cannot take anything Sir Thomas Beecham says about music seriously', the editor of the *British Bandsman* told his readers. Others were furious and lengthy criticism of Beecham filled the band press for some weeks.[143]

As the twentieth century progressed, many leading figures within the brass band movement began to entertain great hopes that, through its alliance with 'serious' composers, the brass band would attain the kudos previously denied it, and take its rightful place in the mainstream of serious musical culture. Large claims followed each new test piece commissioned from 'outside'. Hubert Bath's 1922 test piece, *Freedom*, was deemed the first brass band symphony, the appearance of which 'marks an epoch in the history of the movement, and the year 1922 will become a date of outstanding importance in the world of music'. The 'capture' of Elgar in 1930 was greeted with particular rejoicing, well illustrated by Iles's strangled hyperbole as he made the announcement in the *British Bandsman*: 'The upward progress in our ambitions and aims for thirty years past is disclosed in the grandeur of our attainments today.'[144] By 1938, the *British Bandsman*'s editor, James Brier, could write: 'Bands have always been popular with the working-class people, but since our great composers began to realize the merit of our working-class brass bands they have risen to the dignity of professional orchestras in some cases.'[145]

Although these declamations—'movement' rhetoric at its most extreme—were hopelessly exaggerated, bands undoubtedly received greater attention from about the early 1930s. If the specialist music press failed to notice Elgar's *Severn Suite*, the national press certainly did not, and the ensuing publicity helped launch a modest 'discovery' of the movement. Two *Musical Times* articles by Denis Wright on 'Scoring for Brass Band' in 1932, later expanded into a book, continued the process. This was followed by Harold Hind's technical treatise *The Brass Band* (1934), Bliss's inclusion, albeit briefly, of a positive comment on bands in his 'A Musical Pilgrimage of Britain' for the *Listener* (1935), and J. F. Russell and J. H. Elliot's pioneering history, *The*

---

[143] *British Bandsman* (6 Oct. 1928), for the speech and Iles's and Whiteley's response. The 13 Oct. issue contained two pages of letters on the incident.
[144] *British Bandsman* (12 Aug. 1922; 16 Aug. 1930).
[145] *British Bandsman* (8 Jan. 1938).

Brass Band Movement (1936). Apart from the stimulus provided by Elgar, these publishing events also reflected a mild flurry of competition among music publishers for a potential new market, and, more importantly, a small part of the much wider 'discovery' of working-class culture that so marked the 1930s.

This flurry of anthropological endeavour encompasses the investigative journalism of Orwell, the documentary film movement, the establishment of mass observation, and much else. Some of the impetus for this investigation stemmed from sympathy with the plight of the unemployed, while much else reflected the contemporary debate over the 'Americanization' of British culture. Increasingly, especially among certain elements on the political left, the working class suddenly appeared a homely bulwark against the worst excesses of a shadowy and rarely well defined Americanism.[146] Some composers enthusiastically embraced the bands as a refuge against the American invasion. The clearest statement of this type came from Hubert Bath, writing about the 1930 National: 'It was a joy to me as a musician to know that the musical backbone of our country, north of Luton, is not and, it is hoped, never will be at the mercy of the American invasion. The breath of our good, honest, fresh brass air from the north was, and always will be, an invigorating tonic to the jaded, Americanised southerner.'[147]

After about 1940, composers and musical commentators could less often, and less glibly, admit their total ignorance of bands. An outburst like Beecham's of 1928 would have been inconceivable in 1948; indeed, in February 1947, he was engaged to conduct a mass band concert at Belle Vue, although fuel restrictions led to its eventual cancellation.[148] Certainly, between approximately 1930 and 1955, the national press gave the movement considerably more coverage than previously. Alexander Owen's death in 1920 received almost no mention, whereas Fred Mortimer's in 1953 even earned an obituary in some editions of *The Times*.[149]

The emergence of the brass band as a 'serious' artistic force was not, however, to become a reality. Very few composers ever produced more than one piece for bands and fewer still entered into anything resembling long-term relationships with them. To a degree this simply reflected the class base of the British musical élite. The band movement occupied a social position beyond the experience of most contemporary composers. Probably more influential, however, was the bands' rigid, almost ritualistic adherence to a specific instrumentation. As hinted at earlier, such an approach made perfect sense to members of a movement who drew much of their satisfaction and status from

---

[146] C. Waters, 'The Americanisation of the Masses: Cultural Criticism, the National Heritage and Working Class Culture in the 1930s', *Social History Curators Group Journal*, 17 (1989–90).

[147] *British Bandsman* (18 Oct. 1930).

[148] *British Bandsman* (16 Feb. 1947). I am grateful to Bram Gay for correcting my claim in *Bands* (Milton Keynes: Open University Press, 1991) that the concert had in fact gone ahead.

[149] *British Bandsman* (7 Aug. 1947).

mastering a particular medium that they exerted at least some control over. However, it was a form both alien to most formally trained musicians, and likely to appear restricted in scope to those who did discover it.

From about 1950, the movement thus passed from hopeful enthusiasm about its possible elevation in the artistic hierarchy to the ambivalent attitude it perhaps still shows. The musical and artistic 'establishment', especially the Arts Council, was increasingly viewed with suspicion and sometimes worse, and yet there was great pride in those bandsmen who graduated into symphony orchestras, and affection toward those composers and conductors who paid the movement some attention.[150] There was, too, an inferiority complex, reflected in a desire to flatter and be flattered by the élite musical community. Jack Howard's 'appreciation' at the beginning of Frank Wright's *Brass Today* (1957) illustrates this well. Howard, the managing director of Bessons, claimed that it would be 'invidious' to single out any of the many contributors for special mention, but then did exactly that, selecting first Sir Adrian Boult, and then Karl Rankl, former musical director of the Royal Opera House, Covent Garden. Both men had done much for bands, especially Boult, both as a guest conductor and through his work at the BBC, but it is highly significant that Howard felt obliged to emphasize *their* achievements, rather than those of some of the other contributors, many of whom had over thirty years' 'front-line' service.

Similarly, despite the heightened level of media coverage from the 1930s until approximately the mid-1960s, bands were never really able to maintain a strong position in the general popular culture. In their strongholds they were often respected and capable of generating quite considerable degrees of local and regional patriotism. The *Shields Daily Gazette* used St Hilda's National victory of 1920 for a strong defence of the cultural vitality of the north:

The southerner is apt to regard the northman—especially if the latter hails from an industrial or coal-mining area—as a somewhat grim and hard being, who has little use for the refining graces and arts of life. As a matter of fact, the North is, we believe, more musical than the South; that is, musical inclination and aptitude are commoner possessions of the people. The fame of its bandsmen, recruited almost entirely from the ranks of labour, affords one proof of that; its celebrated choirs and musical societies supply others.[151]

There was something of this almost missionary spirit behind the annual pilgrimage to London for the National, a northern cultural 'invasion' of the unenlightened south.

---

[150] It was proudly recorded in *British Bandsman* (9 Mar. 1957) that the trombone section of the Royal Opera House orchestra, Derek James, Harold Nash, and Haydn Trotman, all came from bands in South Wales.

[151] *British Bandsman* (23 Oct. 1920). See also *Shields Daily News* (29 Sept. 1925).

Figure 2.5a, b. Two images of the 1937 National contest, illustrating the essentially light-hearted treatment often accorded to bands by the media.

In general, however, in most parts of Britain outside of the band heartlands, and eventually even there to a degree, a strikingly different image of bands and industrial musical culture emerged. Ultimately, much of this stems from the representation of bands by a national press that often did not understand the culture it was portraying. Ignorant of the specialist nature of the music, reporters inevitably sought for 'human interest', given that this became the unifying element of so much journalism from the 1930s onwards. In general, treatment of bands was light-hearted. 'Characters' and atmosphere dominated. This was most noticeable in the use of photographic imagery. A set of clichés evolved, a favourite involving a very young player who was invariably featured either holding the largest instrument, or conducting the rest of the band (or, even better, older members of his own family) in some impromptu concert (see Fig. 2.5*a, b*[152]). The adjudicators' box was another object of interest and humour. Did they really stay in there that long, and what happened when they wanted to . . . ?

This generally humorous, light-weight treatment, which might usefully be termed the 'oompah-syndrome', was reinforced through a variety of other representations, such as the use of bands in advertisements for breweries. As a result of this, from at least as early as the 1930s, the brass band began to emerge as a convenient symbol for a rather comic-book northern-ness. Dennis Potter captured this in a *Daily Herald* review of *Man of Brass*, a 1963 BBC television play by Ron Watson, starring Jimmy Edwards as a double B♭ bass player named Ernie Briggs, who preferred his band to married life. This 'northern saga', commented Potter, 'grimly celebrating slate-grey rain and polished euphoniums, was firmly in the eeh-bah-goom heritage of lazy so-called North Country humour'.[153]

Much of this satire was understandable. In an ever more style-conscious age the bands' use of uniform and their maintenance of often clumsy Victorian names gave them a rather antiquated image in many eyes. There were also, of course, other more positive images, including the rather heroic 'dignity of labour through art' or 'sacrifice of labour for their art' depictions usually found in left-of-centre representations. The *Daily Herald* usually included one such item in its pre-National coverage, as in 1947, when the contest took place during a chronic fuel crisis. The paper noted: 'The musicians of the miners' bands had worked two shifts without rest last Thursday, to avoid a drop in production while away.'[154] (While this style of description tended to be overblown, it is hard not to be impressed by that particular act.) In general, though, comedy won out.

There was more to this than the simple use of bands as slight comic relief. It also represented the marginalization and even denigration of provincial

[152] I am extremely grateful to Angela Cartledge of Bradford Art Galleries and Museums for drawing my attention to these illustrations.

[153] *British Bandsman* (7 Dec. 1963).   [154] *Daily Herald* (3 Nov. 1947).

culture, and more especially northern working-class culture (the strong Celtic band tradition was little noted). In an age when, especially as a result of the BBC's centralizing tendencies, the metropolis was increasingly assumed to be the centre of British culture, and when an expanding media emphasized the international, the brass band (and by implication the 'north') appeared decidedly parochial.

The BBC's policy of 'cultural uplift'—its desire to raise standards of taste—added to the problem for the most part. The brass band was often treated as a rather deviant form, in need of being 'taken in hand', as the *Listener* once put it. The BBC did consider establishing its own band in the 1930s, but the idea did not come to fruition. In effect, Callender's served as the BBC house band, at least until Mortimer's arrival in 1942, making its 150th broadcast in January 1938.[155] The band was eminently suited to the role. Angry at missing out on the first prize at Belle Vue in 1928, it refused to compete there again, and threw away all its Smith and Company arrangements, subsequently proving highly sympathetic to the rather technical and specialist works that some BBC personnel felt bands should be playing. This combination of musical 'correctness' and hostility to the contesting world (combined with proximity to London) may have benefited Callender's, but other, more mainstream bands were regularly measured against the band in such places as the wireless notes of *Musical Times*, and found wanting. Conversely, when it suited programming needs, bands were made to look comical and unsophisticated, as when Lostwithiel Band was asked to play '*Flora* [sic] *Dance* at a much increased tempo so as to fit the time block [allocated to it on a particular programme]'.[156]

The ultimately rather cosy image of the working man at play that emerged from so many of these presentations allowed the brass band, rather in the way that George Formby and Gracie Fields operated in a much larger arena, to be appropriated by the media as a symbol of the working class in amiable, domesticated form.[157] In times of conflict, the bands were used to remind the middle classes of the essential 'decency' of the working class. In 1920, the *Croydon Advertiser* revealed much when informing readers: 'It was a delightful contrast to the dreadful strike of the miners that . . . many brass bands from colliery districts assembled at the Crystal Palace and joined in the competition.' The Victorian notion of music as the civilizing art clearly still had purchase; brass instruments made striking miners safe.[158]

The relationship between the band movement and popular political culture raised here is a key one. Before 1914, bands for the most part adopted a self-consciously non-political stance, seeking, for 'the good of the band', to appeal to and serve as wide a community as possible. This tendency remained equally

---

[155] Quoted in *Musical Times* (Jan. 1936); *British Bandsman* (29 Jan. 1938).

[156] Admittedly, this example does come from a later period when the bands were generally better treated by the BBC music department. *British Bandsman* (31 May 1958).

[157] Richards, *The Age*, 169–206.　　[158] *British Bandsman* (23 Oct. 1920).

marked in the period studied here. The movement's spokesmen continued to stress the need to avoid controversy and the band press remained generally mute on all major issues of domestic politics.[159]

Obviously, some chose a different path. In certain areas, especially in mining districts, relatively strong organizational and financial links were forged with trade unions. The Durham coalfield provides particularly strong evidence of this, with a number of lodges adopting and funding bands. The annual miners' gala in July became one of the great festivals in both the band and the union calendars. Some bands were prepared to display public loyalty to lodge politics. In 1922, St Hilda, Harton, and Marsden Colliery bands headed a procession for William Lawther, the Labour Party general election candidate for South Shields.[160]

In 1928, at a time of particular tension within the Durham miners' movement, two Durham colliery band conductors, W. R. Straughan, in charge of both Hetton and Houghton bands, and R. C. Lander of Lumley Band, claimed that they had been sacked by their bands because their political views were not acceptable to the Durham Miners' Association.[161] A letter from the Hetton secretary denied the charge, admitting to 'a little trouble between the union officials and Mr Straughan' but claiming that Straughan's sacking was the result of his being too busy with other bands.[162] Lumley's officials responded to the political charge by arguing that Lander was dismissed because of his 'reckless' use of money when engaging players and buying instruments. Lander and 'Mercato', the *British Bandsman*'s Durham correspondent, seem to have been one and the same person. In his last piece for the paper before he moved south after the collapse of his small business, 'Mercato' laid the accusation of corruption alongside that of socialism. 'So long as a conductor will sing the *Red Flag* and ask no questions as to what's happening with the £8 or £10 a month subscribed by the colliery workmen he is all right, but as soon as he wants a little information no time is lost in getting rid of him.'[163] While there is not really enough evidence to reach the essence of these disputes, it is obvious that some bands and their officials were anxious to defend the ideals of the labour movement within the wider mining culture.

In general, however, such events were the exception that proved the rule. It is significant that the bands which marched for Lawther in 1922 felt it necessary to defend themselves against a hostile letter in the local press, on the grounds that their action was simply an extension of their general community service

---

[159] Russell, *Popular Music*, 288–9.   [160] *British Bandsman* (2 Dec. 1922).

[161] The Durham coalfield witnessed some conflict between the Durham Miners' Association and the break-away Durham Miners' Non-Political Union between 1928 and 1930. See R. Waller, 'Sweethearts and Scabs: Irregular Trade Unions in Britain in the Twentieth Century', in P. J. Waller (ed.), *Politics and Social Change*, 213–28, for the wider context; and, more specifically, W. R. Garside, *The Durham Miners, 1919–1960* (London: Allen & Unwin, 1971), 232–4. On the sackings, see *British Bandsman* (28 Apr., 2 June, and 1 Dec. 1928).

[162] *British Bandsman* (12 May 1928).   [163] *British Bandsman* (15 Dec. 1928).

function. Harton's secretary argued, 'We did what we thought was our duty, the same as we did when we paraded the town for the Mayor's Carillon Fund, the Ingham Infirmary Fund, the Buffs' memorial day, and various other objects.' St Hilda's Jimmy Southern, while pointing out that 'St. Hilda's Lodge, through their generous weekly subscription rightly demands a claim on our services', offered his opinion that union parades did little to change people's minds and stressed that 'we rely upon the support of all sides and hope to meet a continuance of the same'.[164]

More important perhaps in this context were the links that were forged between bands and colliery management and owners. A number of bands, including some of the lodge bands, received important financial assistance from these sources. St Hilda Band was given £100 after winning the National in 1920, probably a fairly small cost for the publicity the company received.[165] Moreover, there must have been very close liaison between bands and managers in order to secure the often very substantial periods away from work required for contesting, and, above all, for concert tours of the type undertaken by St Hilda and Harton. Management could also exert a powerful hold over individuals; in the 1920s, Bill Blackett of Harton Colliery was threatened with dismissal if he played for another band. For an individual who stood to make £3 a week during band tours, as opposed to his normal rate of £1. 17s. 0d. as a platelayer, such threats had real force.[166]

Evidence of similar barriers preventing the bands from becoming a more central element of the labour movement can be found all over the country. There were, in fact, incidents that placed bands in confrontation with individual unions. The pre-war battle with the Musicians' Union over bands and bandsmen undercutting union rates persisted at least into the early 1920s. Some unions objected to bands' recruiting policies, several members of Horwich RMI Band losing their jobs in the early 1930s after railway unions complained that long-serving employees were being laid off at the expense of recently appointed bandsmen.[167] In general, the old-established 'business' mentality persisted, bands taking any engagement that would not alienate the local community, and taking necessary action where needed to distance themselves from controversy. St Hilda was reputed to have dropped 'colliery' from its title after the General Strike in order not to alienate potential customers. Gravesend Workers' Band changed its name in the same year, believing 'Workers' to be 'acting as a deterrent. Although, taken literally, this should not be the case, the existing prejudices of political opinion cannot be totally ignored.'[168] All these examples stem from the inter-war period, but there is little evidence of any great shift after 1945. Indeed, the incorporation of

---

[164] *British Bandsman* (2 Dec. 1922).   [165] *British Bandsman* (30 Oct. 1920).
[166] Taylor, *Labour*, 62.   [167] Taylor, *Brass Bands*, 123–4; Taylor, *Labour*, 46.
[168] Brand and Brand, *Brass Bands*, 101–2; *British Bandsman* (21 Aug. 1926).

colliery bands into welfare schemes after nationalization may have intensified this pattern.

It is instructive that neither the industrial nor the political wings of the labour movement ever really made serious efforts to encourage bands either politically or artistically. The *Miner*, the official paper (1926–30) of the Miners' Federation of Great Britain, for example, did much to encourage literary and artistic expression through 'Black Diamonds', its weekly page devoted to readers' contributions, yet barely mentioned bands, despite their centrality in the musical culture of many miners. In general, the labour movement's emphasis was much more on the creation of an oppositional popular culture, based on specifically created workers' sports clubs, theatre groups, cine clubs, choirs, and so forth, rather than on attempts to reshape or use existing configurations.[169] Such an attitude suggests many possibilities. Labour leaders may simply have been acknowledging the fact that they were dealing with a long-established associational culture with an essentially non-political approach that was not easily changed. It also suggests a lack of confidence in and perhaps, in the case of the intelligentsia on the political left, an ignorance of, the strength of the indigenous working-class culture. Whatever the reasons, an emphasis on 'politically correct' forms of high art generally formed the preferred vehicles for struggle through culture.

I have suggested elsewhere, with reference to the period before 1914, that banding helped reinforce some of the more conservative—perhaps consensual is a better term—forces within society.[170] A similar case could be made for this period. At the very least the tendencies of the less politically aware bandsmen were likely to have been reinforced by their absorption in this largely non-political culture. Moreover, musical activity directly rivalled politics for precious resources of time, money, and energy (although perhaps less precious than before 1914). Most importantly of all, banding offered considerable artistic, emotional, social, and, to a lesser extent, economic rewards. The sense of belonging to a movement, a sense quite possibly stronger after 1914 than before, had special importance here. It gave bandsmen a feeling of purpose, achievement, and collective identity, which otherwise might have found an outlet in the political sphere—particularly in the labour movement. To an extent, through their musical activity, band members found satisfactions denied them elsewhere, which limited their recourse to the political arena.

It is also worth considering whether the strict discipline, the respect for authority, and the great emphasis on hard work that bandsmen had imposed

[169] S. G. Jones, *The British Labour Movement and Film 1918–1939* (London: Routledge & Kegan Paul, 1987); S. G. Jones, *Sport, Politics and the Working Class: Organised Labour and Sport in Inter-War Britain* (Manchester: Manchester University Press, 1989); R. Samuel, E. MacColl and S. Cosgrove (eds.), *Theatres of the Left* (London: Routledge & Kegan Paul, 1985).
[170] Russell, *Popular Music*, 285–92.

upon and emphasized to them so often, shaped some individuals' world-view so as to prepare them better for service to the needs of the modern industrial state. Pushed to extremes, the belief that political consciousness can be defined by the structures and patterns of particular leisure pursuits tends not only towards mechanistic readings of social behaviour, but ignores the fact that the intellectual and attitudinal needs of capitalism are sometimes also those of political and industrial radicalism.[171] Socialists and trade unionists need discipline, an appetite for hard work, and so on. Nevertheless, it is hard to imagine either a works manager or a recruiting sergeant being unhappy with the precision of a band in full flight.

This chapter has dealt mainly with decidedly negative aspects of banding and it would be unfortunate if this emphasis masked completely the many achievements of bands over this period. The improvement in standard has been alluded to on a number of occasions; Brian Jackson's informant may not have been far wrong when claiming in the early 1960s: 'These big bands, it sounds funny to say it, like the Lindley Band that won the Belle Vue Championship in 1900—well they wouldn't have been able to *play* some of the stuff that our local band plays now.'[172]

Given the shrinking audience for band music, much of this endeavour was only appreciated by specialist audiences. However, a much wider public benefited, in the sense that, throughout the period, the brass band remained the single most important training ground for brass musicians of many different styles and persuasions. Maurice Murphy is perhaps the best known of those who maintained the long-established line of supply to the symphony orchestra; Eddie Calvert, Ted Heath, Kenny Baker, Joan Hinde, and Dawn Heywood are just a few of the many in the fields of jazz and light music who owed at least some of their training to brass bands.[173] There was also the great contribution that bands made to the *social* as well as the artistic life, particularly of their members, but also of the wider community. It must never be forgotten that a great deal of band work was a source of enormous fun and enjoyment.

Their decline in popularity is not, of course, peculiar to brass bands. It forms a small part of that massive process which we describe as 'the decline of "traditional" working-class culture'. It is dangerously misleading, in that it implies the existence of a static culture in the period from about 1880 onwards, when this traditional pattern began to emerge. But in the context of popular leisure, it does at least serve as a shorthand for the falling popularity of professional

---

[171] For an extreme view, which nevertheless raises interesting questions, see J. M. Brohm, *Sport: A Prison of Measured Time* (London: Pluto Press, 1978).

[172] Jackson, *Working Class Community*, 33.

[173] Frank Wright (ed.), *Brass Today* (London: Besson & Co., 1957), 116; *British Bandsman* (28 Mar., 25 Apr. and 27 June 1964).

soccer, the music hall, certain types of seaside holiday, and so on. The very specific problems of the band illustrate how careful we have to be with blanket phrases: the movement was clearly in some difficulty before 1939, although the 'decline' of working-class culture is normally regarded as having its roots in the 1950s. Brass bands were an early victim because they lacked the absolute centrality in the total working-class culture of some of the other institutions that experienced difficulties from the 1950s and because they were especially vulnerable to the changes in taste and attitude that were eventually to mark so much of British social life. The band movement showed early, and in revealing microcosm, the combined impact of an economic shift from a manufacturing toward a service-based economy, rising living standards and greater consumerism, and the nationalization and internationalization of popular taste made possible by a powerful, largely commercially controlled, technological media.

3

❦

The Musical Revolution of the Mid-Nineteenth Century: From 'Repeat and Twiddle' to 'Precision and Snap'

Vic and Sheila Gammon

Musical Worlds Apart

In 1928 Gustav Holst composed *A Moorside Suite* for brass band. This work was important as the first composition expressly written for brass band by a 'major' English composer, and it is significant that it was the test piece at the National Championship at Crystal Palace that year. Subsequently, the inter-war years saw brass band works by Elgar, Bantock, Howells, Bliss, and others. At last art-music composers were taking the brass band seriously.

Holst's suite was significant in that it drew, in idiom, on the work of recovery undertaken by folk music collectors and composers particularly in the

This essay is respectfully and affectionately dedicated to Reg Hall, musician, writer, enthusiast, and friend, whose ideas on traditional and popular music have been a constant source of stimulation and challenge. We have tried to make certain sections of the argument clearer and have introduced section headings, otherwise the structure and the argument of the essay remain substantially the same as the earlier version. Much of the empirical material on which the essay is based is reproduced and discussed more fully in Vic Gammon's other work referred to in the notes. We would gratefully like to acknowledge the help of Christopher Whittick of East Sussex Record Office and the Sussex Archaeological Society, Joyce Crow of the Sussex Archaeological Society, Chris Walsh of Lewes Town Council, and Richard Carter of Uckfield Community College. Trevor Herbert was an unfailing source of encouragement and advice.

years 1903–14. His daughter commented that the suite 'is a fitting acknow-ledgement of a twenty years' debt of gratitude for the solid and companionable help that folk song had brought him'.[1]

A Moorside Suite brought together the brass band—an institution Dave Russell has described as 'one of the most remarkable working class cultural achievements in European history'[2]—with an idiom which was thought by many to be the musical expression of the spirit of the English people. We might well ask why and how such an institution and an idiom ever lost contact; did they ever have any active relationship in the past?

Writers interested in the musical activities of English working people have something of a problem when such questions are raised.[3] Folk music collectors, who ranged areas of the country in the late nineteenth and early twentieth centuries, discovered a residual musical culture that, at least in some of its aspects, was unlike the mainstream of Western art music or the commercial popular musics of the nineteenth century. It was a stratum of music and musical activity that had a life and being of its own.

In recent years the work of these collectors has been subject to a strong and necessary re-examination.[4] Not surprisingly, the collectors have been found to be people of their own time, who articulated their own artistic and cultural concerns and prejudices through their work. The desire of some of the most significant collectors was to find a basis for popular musical and cultural regeneration, and a musical language suitable for the self-consciously English composer. This led them to emphasize in their selection and publication some of those elements in the music they discovered (for example, the use of 'church' modes) which they interpreted as archaic and deeply meaningful.

The folk music collectors undoubtedly rescued a great deal of music that would otherwise have perished. We value their work greatly. They also be-queathed succeeding generations a great many widely accepted yet ultimately very misleading ideas about folk music. Put briefly, the collectors (with the notable exception of Frank Kidson) tended to indulge in mythology rather than engage in historical enquiry. They erected a set of notions about music

---

[1] C. Bainbridge, *Brass Triumphant* (London: Muller, 1980), 69–70; I. Holst, *The Music of Gustav Holst*, 2nd edn. (London: Oxford University Press, 1968), 100.

[2] D. Russell, *Popular Music in England, 1840–1914*, 2nd edn. (Manchester: Manchester University Press, 1997), 205.

[3] We self-consciously write about England and English music in this essay, not through any narrow-minded nationalism, but because it is the country we have studied. Moreover, the social, historical, and musical processes which took place in Wales, Scotland, and Ireland were so entirely different from England that it is impossible to propose an account which fits them all.

[4] See particularly G. Boyes, *The Imagined Village: Culture, Ideology and the English Folk Revival* (Manchester: Manchester University Press, 1993); J. Francmanis, 'The Musical Sherlock Holmes: Frank Kidson and the English Folk Music Revival', Ph.D. thesis, Leeds Metropolitan University, 1997; V. Gammon, 'Folk Song Collecting in Sussex and Surrey 1843–1914', *History Workshop*, 10 (1980), 61–89; D. Harker, *Fakesong* (Milton Keynes: Open University Press, 1985); M. Pickering, *Village Song and Culture* (London: Croom Helm, 1982).

and music making among the lower orders of the eighteenth and nineteenth centuries which we feel have been very damaging, and remain so.

There is a great difficulty in trying to study popular music, mostly oral and aural music, from a period before sound recording.[5] It is very difficult to reconstruct or imagine what a town band or church band sounded like in 1830. We have to rely on scanty and indirect information, often from hostile witnesses, in an attempt to extend our understanding. Nevertheless, there is accumulating evidence which affirms that popular music making had a coherent style which differed markedly from the performance practices and conventions of Western art music. The institutions in which this older type of music making flourished included church bands, town, village and friendly-society bands, festivals such as friendly-society feast days and harvest homes, the home, the pub, and the street.

We now know something of the repertory and styles of performance of vernacular singers and instrumentalists in the century before 1850. Two striking features emerge from this work. First is the eclecticism of lower-class musical culture. This culture drew its repertory from a wide range of available sources, including oral tradition, ballad sheets, psalms, popular songs, popular church music, military music and popular dance tunes. It certainly included those items which late Victorian and Edwardian collectors were to describe as 'folk song' and 'folk music', but these by no means constituted the whole repertory.[6]

Secondly, the musical performances of vernacular singers and instrumentalists articulated a pervasive musical style, which, although at times it might have been influenced by aspects of art music, was in essence its own thing, following its own conventions and idioms. For economy and ease of reference we have described this formation of institutions, repertories, and performance style as the 'plebeian musical tradition'.[7]

PROBLEMS OF INTERPRETATION AND UNDERSTANDING

Some writers have obviously found it difficult to understand such ideas. It is worth pausing for a moment to explore why this is so. The point is best illustrated by examples. Golby and Purdue, in their 'populist' reading of cultural

[5] V. Gammon, 'Problems of Method in the Historical Study of Popular Music', in D. Horn and P. Tagg (eds.), *Popular Music Perspectives* (Exeter: International Association for the Study of Popular Music, 1982), 16–31.

[6] V. Gammon, 'The Performance Style of West Gallery Music', in C. Turner (ed.), *The Gallery Tradition* (Ketton: S. G. Publishing in association with Anglia Polytechnic University, 1997), 43–51, and V. Gammon, 'Popular Music in Rural Society: Sussex 1815–1914', D. Phil. thesis, University of Sussex, 1985, generally.

[7] Following E. P. Thompson in 'Patrician Society: Plebeian Culture', *Journal of Social History*, 7 (1974), and in *Customs in Common* (London: Merlin Press, 1991), esp. pp. 16–96. For recorded examples of traditional performance the 20-CD set, *The Voice of the People*, an anthology edited by Reg Hall (Topic Records TSCD 651–670, 1998), is indispensable listening.

history, choose Mr Punch as 'the indomitable spirit of English popular culture'. They see a double theme in this history. One aspect is the domestication and taming of popular culture, the other is the continuity of its almost anarchic dimension, including its refusal to be serious or rational.[8]

There certainly are aspects of the old popular culture that could be described as anarchic, that refused to be serious, but it was not all like that. To imply that it was is a gross caricature. One process clearly evident in the work of these writers is homogenization: popular culture is perceived as a unity, and not seen as constituted by different and often conflicting elements. If Mr Punch is a figure of English popular culture, so are Bunyan's pilgrim, Robin Hood, and the heroic men and women who inhabit popular ballads.[9] Many of the songs widely current in the eighteenth and nineteenth centuries attest to a level of seriousness rarely attained by modern popular songs, and many vernacular instrumentalists showed enormous devotion to their music.[10] According to Golby and Purdue, the popular culture of 'the day' broadly expresses 'the aspirations and desires of most men as most men are'.[11] Many feminists would probably agree, but what our authors are expressing is a naïve belief in an inherent and eternal human nature transcending history and culture.

Given this unpromising start, it is hardly surprising that, citing Vic Gammon's work on the expulsion of the old church bands and the suppression of the old-style popular church music,[12] the authors can conclude that by the late 1850s, 'No doubt the quality of music was improved, but to the impoverishment of the labouring classes whose active participation in church services was greatly reduced.'[13]

If we ignore the fact that great pains were taken in Gammon's work to show that the main performers in church bands were village artisans, not labourers, we must ask why there is 'no doubt the quality of music was improved'? On whose terms can such a statement be made? Whose music, whose quality? Thus we find the opinions of middle-class reformers transmuted into a statement of historical fact. Many of the old church musicians did not think the changes an improvement and articulated their opinions. We find here a

---

[8] J. M. Golby and A. W. Purdue, *The Civilisation of the Crowd* (London: Batsford, 1984), 14–15.

[9] A. L. Morton, '*Pilgrim's Progress*, A Commemoration', *History Workshop*, 5 (1978), 3–8; R. B. Dobson and J. Taylor, *Rymes of Robyn Hood* (London: Heinemann, 1976); J. C. Holt, *Robin Hood* (London: Thames & Hudson, 1982); S. Knight, *Robin Hood: A Complete Study of the English Outlaw* (Oxford: Blackwell, 1994). D. Dugaw, *Warrior Women and Popular Balladry, 1650–1850* (Cambridge: Cambridge University Press, 1989).

[10] V. Gammon, ' "Not Appreciated in Worthing?" Class Expression and Popular Song Texts in Mid-Nineteenth Century Britain', *Popular Music*, 4 (1984), 5–24.

[11] Golby and Purdue, *Civilisation*, 13.

[12] V. Gammon, ' "Babylonian Performances": The Rise and Suppression of Popular Church Music, 1660–1870', in E. Yeo and S. Yeo (eds.), *Popular Culture and Class Conflict 1590–1914* (Brighton: Harvester, 1981), 62–88.

[13] Golby and Purdue, *Civilisation*, 106.

transcendent and universal notion of what constitutes music, the perfect complement to the ahistorical and acultural notion of 'men as most men are' that informs the work of these two writers. Populism deserves better!

Dave Russell has produced a second edition of his excellent, interesting, and rewarding book, *Popular Music in England, 1840–1914.* He has some positive things to say about the earlier version of this essay.[14] He has conceded a great deal of ground to us: 'it is hard to disagree with some of their points. There clearly were ways in which the process of formalisation and restructuring that took place in the early and mid-nineteenth century dispossessed, almost "deskilled", some musicians'.[15] We are, however, criticized for making 'bold claims', and for overstating our case about what happened to popular music making in the mid-nineteenth century.

We still feel that there are significant points of difference between us, or perhaps (to put it in more postmodern terms) his background, approach, and the materials upon which he has drawn, do not allow him to see things as we do. The focus of his work tends to be towards the public, the organized, the institutional, and historically visible aspects of music making. We would want to add to these vital areas more emphasis than he gives to insights into the domestic, the *ad hoc*, the informal, and generally 'hidden' aspects of music making.[16]

Russell admits that industrialization brought fundamental changes to the structure of popular musical life:

To see that life survive and perhaps even progress during the early industrial phase is at first sight somewhat surprising to the historian of popular recreation, so used to viewing the period *c.*1780–1850 as one of disaster for so many popular pastimes. While numerous areas of traditional recreation, such as 'folk' football or blood sports, came under attack from the forces of evangelicalism and utilitarianism, the pattern of popular music-making was left altered, but substantially unscathed. Often firmly rooted in evangelical culture and carrying strong overtones of moral health, it was allowed to continue and indeed actually encouraged. While upper- and middle-class acceptance was essential to survival, however, the resilience of the working population was arguably the most crucial factor.[17]

Whereas Russell sees music as different from other areas of traditional recreation that were attacked between 1780 and 1850, we see a consonance between old street-football and the plebeian musical tradition, just as we see a consonance between strictly regulated eleven-a-side association-football matches and strictly regulated twenty-four-a-side brass band contests.

[14] V. and S. Gammon, 'From "Repeat and Twiddle" to "Precision and Snap": The Musical Revolution of the Mid-Nineteenth Century', in T. Herbert (ed.), *Bands: The Brass Band Movement in the Nineteenth and Twentieth Centuries* (Milton Keynes: Open University Press, 1991), 120–44.
[15] Russell, *Popular Music*, 199.
[16] Gammon, 'Popular Music in Rural Society', generally.
[17] Russell, *Popular Music*, 198.

We would not wish to take issue with a notion of resilience ('the act of rebounding or springing back' or 'the power of resuming the original shape or position after compression, bending etc.'[18]) but we think Russell's account greatly underestimates the alteration that took place in popular music making in the mid-nineteenth century. The phrase 'altered, but substantially unscathed' is unclear to us: we would argue that popular music making was substantially altered and qualitatively changed in the period. Russell is right in seeing upper- and middle-class acceptance as a significant part of the process, and there are some elements of continuity. Nevertheless, we hope to show that he underrates, or because of the nature of his sources is unable to see, the significance of the change that took place within lower-class music making in the period.

We are well aware that the notion of 'revolution' is overworked in historical writing, but we could not come up with a better term to describe what we see as a complete change in a relatively short period of time. We are accused of suggesting a notion of 'musical revolution' that implies a 'forcing of plebeian musicians into unwanted directions', whereas 'Northern musicians, at least, appear to have swum with the tide, rather than against it'.[19] In many circumstances it is very wise to swim with the tide, particularly if the likely alternative is drowning.

A central theme of our work is that change, in this case musical change, entails losses as well as gains, no matter how enthusiastically that change is endorsed. We would not want to deny that the brass band movement created musical opportunities and that bandsmen were enthusiastic about their bands and music. But the opening of one set of musical and social possibilities usually involves the closing off of others. At bottom, we feel that Russell does not fully appreciate the richness of the vernacular musical tradition before what he has unhelpfully termed 'the emergence of a popular tradition' in the nineteenth century. The fundamental prerequisites of this popular tradition, he thinks, were 'printed music, instruments and tuition'.[20] Though all of these can be helpful, supportive aspects of a popular musical tradition, we see none of them as essential. In a dominantly oral/aural musical culture, the key prerequisites are ears, mouths, and situated learning through immersion in the musical experience.

There are significant gaps in Russell's work and these tend to cluster in the area of informal music making. Nowhere is there a discussion of the printed ballad trade, probably the most significant medium by which songs were circulated in the nineteenth century. This trade was in decline by 1840, but still a potent force. Traditional dance and its accompanying music, be it social dances, 'Cotswold' morris, or the processional clog dances of Lancashire, get

---

[18] *The Shorter Oxford English Dictionary*, 1807.
[19] Russell, *Popular Music*, 200.   [20] Ibid. 171 ff.

short shrift. There is a growing body of scholarly work on these areas.[21] It is notable that Dave Russell nowhere cites the work of Ian Russell, who has done so much to document the pub carol-singing tradition of South and West Yorkshire. This is an autonomous, century-and-a-half-old tradition, a remnant of a musical practice that refused to die when the old style of church music and its practitioners with their customary observances were forced from the church. This vibrant tradition suggests that there is some compelling evidence of 'stresses and tensions' in the transition from one type of musical practice to another, even in the industrial north.[22]

History is largely written by the victors, or, at least, the survivors, but that does not mean that we should unquestioningly accept their accounts. Our wish to rescue the poor ballad singer, the old-style church musician, and the traditional dance player from the enormous condescension of musical posterity, seems to be in the best tradition of social history writing that we know.

MANY MUSICS, NOT ONE MUSIC

If confusion and misunderstanding are to be avoided, there is a need to explore further a point about musical perception. There exist what we would term one-dimensional and multi-dimensional views of music. A one-dimensional view of music sees it as a unitary phenomenon. In such a view, an assessment of a performance (or a piece, or a style of music, or often all three at once) takes place on what we can visualize as a straight line stretching from bad to good.

If, however, we take a multi-dimensional view of music—a view that acknowledges that the world contains a multiplicity of musics—then we have to disentangle judgements of quality from an understanding of musical stylistic difference. Let us take the examples of jazz and symphonic music. Both can be performed excellently or poorly, but an excellent performance of a Beethoven symphony can never aspire to be a piece of jazz and a wonderful jazz performance cannot adequately be judged by criteria customarily applied to a symphony.

A unitary or one-dimensional view of music confuses questions of quality and style. Judging all music by one set of criteria, derived from one type of music, means that any music that does not meet those criteria is categorized as inferior or bad. All musical styles have practitioners of more and less ability,

[21] See e.g. K. Chandler, *Ribbons, Bells and Squeaking Fiddles: The Social History of Morris Dancing in the English South Midlands, 1660–1900* (Enfield Lock: Hisarlik Press, 1993).

[22] A. Gatty, *A Life at One Living* (London and Worksop, 1884), 34–8 (I owe this reference to the kindness of Ian Russell). I. Russell, *A Song for the Time* (Unstone, 1987), 32–4, a booklet that accompanies a cassette recording of the same name. I. Russell, 'Traditional Singing in West Sheffield 1970–2', 3 vols., Ph.D. thesis (University of Leeds, 1977). There are ten recordings in the *Village Carols* series produced by Ian Russell.

more and less competence or mastery of the idiom. Judgements about the competence of performers can only be made within the established boundaries of a musical style. A crucial misunderstanding takes place when a competent performance in a particular musical style is judged as incompetent because of the application of criteria from a different musical style.

It is not simply a matter of liking one type of music and not liking another. Judged by the standards of bebop, the *Eroica Symphony* is a dismal failure. As a piece of sustained improvisation *The Rite of Spring* is a non-starter. These examples verge on the ridiculous, but we think they illustrate our point. For convenience (borrowing a concept from Bourdieu) we will term this judging of one musical style by the criteria of another musical *misrecognition*. Linked to social power, musical misrecognition is historically significant; it can have very material outcomes in shaping musical activity.

In an artistically liberal and avowedly multicultural society, when 'serious' composers are experimenting with new sounds and forms of music, and when jazz gets state sponsorship and can be studied at the Royal College of Music, it is easy to discount the historical importance of one-dimensional views of music and musical misrecognition. We would venture to say that a non-pluralist view of music has been dominant for most of human history. Many people still see Western art music as the summit of a musical pinnacle and the yardstick by which all else is to be judged.

The thesis we propose is that the plebeian musical tradition, and what became established as the tradition of brass banding, operated from quite different stylistic bases; different in terms of their conventions and criteria, their musical procedures, and their notions as to what constituted excellence.

We know that in the terms of the critical standards prevailing in brass banding there were (and are) 'crack' championship-winning bands and poor bands, the butt of adverse comment in the brass band (and other) press. Some ensembles played superbly within the conventions of the plebeian musical tradition, but some instrumentalists playing within the plebeian tradition did so incompetently. Excellence and virtuosity exist in both aural-based and notation-based musics throughout the world, but so do aspirations which outstrip competence.

The crucial point is this: we must not mistake quality for style; we must not judge one musical style by the standards of another. To do so will inevitably result in the judged style being found deficient, wanting, inadequate. It is worth noting that competence is always situated, always applied, always competence in doing something specific.

QUESTIONS OF EVIDENCE

In the study of popular musics of the past, different sorts of evidence can be brought into play.

- The historian wishing to enquire into the history of types of music that predate sound recording is often forced to make use of evidence from the pens of hostile witnesses, witnesses who judge a type of music by alien criteria, be it Indian music, Arabic music, black American music, the music of Gaelic Scotland, or the plebeian musical tradition of eighteenth- and nineteenth-century England. By looking for consistencies within hostile accounts, one can distil both elements of outlook common to the observers and consistent elements of style in the music being observed.
- Comparative evidence from societies with dominantly aural musical traditions can provide insights into changes in nineteenth-century music making.
- Used regressively, information and material recorded from traditional musicians in England over the past ninety years can provide us with vital understanding of the older tradition.

This range of evidence provides comparisons, generates questions, and assists in the formation of interpretations.[23] It is surprising that some historians seem willing to take on trust the testimony of hostile observers, without subjecting it to the full rigour of historical criticism.

The Musical Revolution—The Uses of Musical Literacy

No piece of music is good or bad until specific and often unconscious criteria are applied to it. In this sense, beauty is in the ear, or rather the brain, of the listener. The brain is no naïve organ. Musical perception is the result of a complex process of musical enculturation: the assimilation of the norms and conventions of a particular style or styles. The degree to which we respond to and are able to understand differences *within* a particular musical style is conditioned by the degree to which individuals 'master' the stylistic norms and conventions.

Having mastered one set of musical norms and conventions, one style, individuals have historically tended to judge all other types of music by the internalized criteria of the assimilated style. The fact that this is an intellectually invalid procedure has not stopped it being a potent historical force; nor do we feel society is free of this force today, even though there is more real 'polymusicality', more real response to and valuing of different musical styles, and more ability to play in different musical styles than probably at any time in the past.

Between about 1830 and 1860, a great deal of what was distinctive about the music making of artisans and the labouring poor was destroyed or went underground. A different and in many ways (at least initially) alien set of

---

[23] See n. 5. On general questions of evidence in relation to the history of popular culture see P. Burke, *Popular Culture in Early Modern Europe* (London: Temple Smith, 1978).

musical values, élite and middle-class in origin, was promulgated and gained ascendancy. That vernacular music making flourished under the new conditions is testimony to a sort of resilience, but this should not lead us to think that lower-class music making resumed its original shape or position. The most public aspects of vernacular music making were metamorphosed in the period; the less public aspects retained something of the old musical culture, but were increasingly marginalized. The most important agent in this profound change, although it was not the only one, was the brass band.

Not to see the enormity of this change is a failure of both assessment and imagination. Given the degree of misunderstanding and misinterpretation of these issues, there is obviously a need to spell out in detail the nature of this musical revolution. We will try to do this by a series of comparisons of before and after, briefly illustrating the points we make.

Musical literacy was known within the plebeian musical tradition. Manuscript music books for church band and country dance musicians survive in considerable quantities, and we have good evidence that town and village bands made use of lovingly copied manuscripts. Sheet music was very expensive in the eighteenth and early nineteenth centuries, and hand-copying provided one of the only practical ways of getting hold of unknown music.

The use of musical notation is significant, and provides evidence against the damaging notion of a purely oral/aural folk tradition. Yet we should not protest too much. It seems certain, from the evidence we have considered, that the majority of instrumentalists active in the first third of the nineteenth century were ear-players, who learnt their playing without reading the notes. No doubt within bands there was quite a lot of direct teaching of melodies and parts. The importance of memory, and, in many cases, the ability to recreate melody parts, is crucial within dominantly aural musical traditions. It is precisely that sort of tradition which encourages such abilities.

Brass bands used copied-out manuscripts, but with the development of cheaper printed music produced specially to supply the need, print took over from manuscript. Performance increasingly became print-based. No doubt there were (and still are) good ear-players whose grasp of musical notation was not well developed but who, if performing with good readers, would grasp their parts well enough. Yet as the pressure for excellence grew, the pressure to read well must also have grown.

The great advantage of the existence of a score and of parts is that the coordination of large groups of musicians playing prearranged music becomes a practical possibility. The benefits and potentialities of this are still being explored. Ethnomusicologists have noticed that the introduction of notation has often accompanied and been causal in fundamentally changing musical practice.[24] Musical notation gives a system of classification which has the

---

[24] B. Nettl, *The Study of Ethnomusicology* (Urbana: University of Illinois Press, 1983), 329.

potential for structuring the way we think about and conceive musical sound. Once we have acquired it, we tend to try to fit all musical experience into its framework; it becomes incorporated into our sense of reality. (In Bourdieu's terms it becomes *doxic*, a self-evident part of the mental equipment with which we interpret and cope with the world.) 'Every established order tends to produce (to very different degrees and with very different means) the naturalization of its own arbitrariness.'[25]

Anyone who has tried to transcribe traditional music into Western musical notation knows how hard it is to get timings and pitch variations down accurately. Bartók's system for doing this produces a score which is monstrously complicated. Such music is not made for Western notation, and Western notation is not made for it. Yet once the mental habit of perceiving music through Western notation is acquired, that which will not fit within the regularities of the notational system (for example, crotchet beats, exact subdivisions, and semitone pitch divisions) is considered anomalous, offensive, dangerous, incompetent, or wrong.[26] Alternatively, the exotic element is not perceived at all—because no mental structure exists for its perception, that aspect of performance is simply not noticed. Most usually, it is interpreted (misrecognized) as a failure within a system of which it is not even a part. In his support, Bartók realized that he was dealing with a coherent musical system, and struggled to understand and appreciate it. Brass band teachers of the nineteenth century simply wrote off expressions of the older popular style as ignorance and incompetence.

We are not suggesting that an aural musical culture is somehow more tolerant than a literate one. Both operate from a system of classification, and both tend to intolerance. But we think the mechanism of response and the reasons for that intolerance are very different. The former is deeply traditional, absorbing acceptable change often without noticing it, but rejecting that which is too alien to be absorbed; the latter, in operating from a notational base, projects that which is learnt from notation (in origin a descriptive system) onto all musical experience (thus making it prescriptive).

Nor are we arguing that an aural musical culture is inherently superior to a literate one. We can see positive aspects to both. What we would want to oppose is a notion that an aural musical culture is necessarily or inherently inferior to a literate one. What we are trying to understand in this essay is something of the nature of the change from the one to the other. Given the profound significance of this change, it is worth taking some space to explore

---

[25] P. Bourdieu, *Outline of a Theory of Practice* (Cambridge: Cambridge University Press, 1977), 164.

[26] M. Douglas, *Purity and Danger* (Harmondsworth: Penguin, 1970); P. Stallybrass and A. White, *The Politics and Poetics of Transgression* (London: Methuen, 1986), 19–20, 72–3, and generally.

the implications of a shift from a dominantly aural to a dominantly literate musical tradition.

Written down, the musical piece gains a permanence it never had in a world dominated by memory and re-creation. The existence of a score encourages people to treat that score as a source of authority, a final arbiter in case of dispute. Notation is not music, but, in a dispute, the appeal is not to what sounds best to the performers, but to a notion of authorial correctness. 'Permanently available and amenable to rationalistic verbal explication, the score rapidly usurps the sound experience of music as the focus of verbal attention and becomes the key stone of an eminently verbalizable conception of what "music is".'[27]

In a dominantly aural but partly literate musical culture, written music can have the effect of stabilizing a repertory, of transmitting music from past to present *without* stopping processes of elaboration, decoration, and variation which are usual features of aural tradition. It has been argued that oral/aural cultures live in a world of the permanent present where, even if innovation takes place, it is absorbed without fuss and often without recognition. The past is often adjusted to suit the present.[28]

Musical notation probably originated as a mnemonic device. Within a dominantly aural culture, such as early nineteenth-century England, it probably retained much of that function, but it has the potential to grow to dominate musical practice. It is difficult for us to grasp the profound changes in the conceptualization of music that the coming of musical literacy implies. In the main, this is due to our ignorance of, and our lack of empathy for, the aural/oral mind within a dominantly aural/oral culture.[29] To a band instructor of the 1880s (and to many of his contemporaries and successors), knowledge of music was equated with knowledge of musical notation: 'Supposing, now, the case of a band is taken which starts without any knowledge of music. The first thing necessary is to get the rudimental part well into the minds of the pupils.' His method was to drill his students 'after the manner of an ordinary school-lesson'. 'By the end of that time most of the members could read the notes, and also count the time tolerably well. One of the best results of this method was it got rid of those who were not in earnest about the thing —in a word the drones.'[30]

It is a commonplace of the study of oral poetry that literacy disables the oral poet. He or she is no longer able to combine motifs, to improvise, to

[27] T. Wishart, 'Musical Writing, Musical Speaking', in J. Shepherd, P. Virden, G. Vulliamy, and T. Wishart (eds.), *Whose Music?* (London: Latimer, 1977), 136. For a recent discussion see P. Théberge, *Any Sound You Can Imagine* (Hanover, NH, and London: Wesleyan University Press, University Press of New England, 1997), 178–84.

[28] J. Goody (ed.), *Literacy in Traditional Societies* (Cambridge: Cambridge University Press, 1968), 30–4.

[29] W. J. Ong, *Orality and Literacy* (London: Methuen, 1982), generally.

[30] *British Bandsman* (Mar. 1888), 106.

rhapsodize, once written language has entered his or her consciousness.[31] Although there is a great deal of evidence of musical literacy and oral tradition coexisting and interacting in nineteenth-century England (and many other periods and places), it is equally clear that expanding musical literacy is destructive to aural methods of musical creation and re-creation.

In aural musical cultures it is often the case that the mental skills of memorization and re-creation using formulas are often highly developed; in literate musical cultures these mental skills tend not to be developed, and are in a sense replaced by sight-reading and musical reproduction. If musical notation is combined with an outlook on the world that posits, within strict limits, correct and incorrect ways of doing things, the result, given the possibility of an appeal to authorial correctness, is to change the musician from a musical speaker to a musical reproducer.[32] As Nettl puts it, 'a Western concert is to a large extent an exercise in mental and dexterous ability'.[33] George J. Bowles, advising aspiring band contestants in 1888, wrote:

The special points to work for are: accurate rendering in a mechanical sense, that is, as to notes and time; expression of light and shade, correct phrasing, etc., playing in time and quality of intonation. The extra and unusual efforts put forth by the individual members of a band to gain the above points in preparing for a contest must necessarily raise the status of that band, for these are the essential points which go to make up the best quality of performance.[34]

The musical score reduces sound to graphic representation, the aural to the visual. Its material form presents us with a reification of music. It promotes an elision of thought which transforms lived aural experience existing in time into lines and dots existing on a flat page. The process is complete when we describe such a representation as music. (A fascinating contrast to this is offered by the fact that country musicians in southern England used the noun *music* to mean a musical instrument.) Print suggests to us that what is represented has a reality apart from musical performance. As Wishart argues, the permanence and scrutability of the text fundamentally challenged 'the immediate dialectic of musical action and musical experience'.[35]

No notational system can prescribe exactly what a piece should sound like. Western notation is moderately good at prescribing pitch and timing, less good at prescribing dynamics, hopeless at prescribing timbre. At any time, within a defined context, there exist practical conventions which regulate how a score is to be interpreted. These change over time, and the musicians may be largely unaware of their existence. Thus even within a musical system strongly

---

[31] A. B. Lord, *The Singer of Tales* (Cambridge, Mass.: Harvard University Press, 1960); Ong, *Orality.*

[32] Wishart, 'Musical Writing', generally.   [33] Nettl, *Ethnomusicology*, 328.

[34] *British Bandsman* (Apr. 1888), 131.   [35] Wishart, 'Musical Writing', 136.

reliant on notation, there exists a residual aural tradition in which conductors, musical directors, adjudicators, and music teachers play a central role.

All performance is re-creation, but a performance from the exact memorization of a part is profoundly different from a performance in which an aural musician reassembles and remakes a piece he or she has played, perhaps hundreds of times, before. We are therefore making a conceptual distinction between playing from memory ('aural') and memorization ('literate'). In a predominantly aural musical culture, the instrumentalist absorbs the music he or she knows, and makes it part of his or her being. This assimilation operates in a way that makes possible the re-creation of a piece from schemata and fragments stored in memory, in a literal sense a combination of recollection (re-collection) and improvisation within known conventions. In a dominantly literate musical culture, memorization, where it occurs, tends to be by rote. It is interesting that, in 1887, a contributor to the *British Bandsman* stressed the importance of memorization of all aspects of a part—'all marks, rallentandos, pauses, etc.'—to a soloist.[36] This suggests (as does a great deal of other evidence) that musical literacy induces notation dependence and diminishes the ability to play from memory.

This tendency to make the musically literate notation-dependent has been widely observed. Although there are exceptions, few musicians with a high degree of musical training ever really seem to break this dependency. Those who do, often those who reach a high state of proficiency, break the dependency through memorization, not through the aural processes of recollection and re-creation.

In some circumstances literate musicians with less training do seem to be able to break away from notation dependency. There are many examples of types of music that have a notational base but which loosen their ties and their dependence. Examples would be New Orleans street music and jazz, Bohemian polka music as performed in Texas, and Jewish *klezma* music.

Music reading did not simply take over from aural transmission as the dominant form of access to a musical repertory; taking the society as a whole, it is probable that aural forms of musical communication remained numerically greater in nineteenth-century England. The significance of the brass band movement is that musical literacy gained the prestige associated with what we might call the leading sector of popular music making. Henceforth 'real' musicians were perceived as literate musicians and aural musicians relegated to a secondary status.[37]

Specialist musicians appear in many different societies. A purely aural musical culture will produce differing musical competences, but a society in which literate and aural modes of transmission are current inevitably produces a greater degree of musical, social, and cultural fragmentation. In nineteenth-

---

[36] *British Bandsman* (Oct. 1887), 22.   [37] Goody, *Literacy*, 68.

century England, the huge culture shock and social revolution of industrialization and urbanization increased these tendencies.

Music literacy can be a 'mystery', a means of integrating initiates into a craft and excluding others. For complex reasons, one of which was the middle-class belief in the social utility of music for the working class, the mystery of music literacy was extended in nineteenth-century England as thousands learnt to read staff and sol-fa notation. Nevertheless, the increase in musical literacy had the effect of increasing the significance of the division between musical literates and illiterates.

The role of Western musical notation might usefully be compared in some ways to that of Latin within medieval society—a *lingua franca* which cut across linguistic barriers allowing the communication of ideas and material among those initiated into its use. The effect of musical literacy on significant sections of the nineteenth-century working class was to make them feel a connection with the prestigious art music of Europe, however modified and adapted were the forms in which they encountered it (for example, selections of themes from 'great' composers).

It is possible to view an aural musical culture as a kind of 'restricted code', performances being limited by a traditional repertory, traditional conventions, known ways of performing, and a limited vocabulary of musical reference. It is reasonable to argue that musical literacy extends the range of music that can be performed. Both systems of musical production, aural and literate, are, however, limiting in their different ways. Both systems leave the musician without the ability to grasp music radically different from that with which he or she is familiar.

Freed from dependence on memory and encounter, literacy means that written-down music from the past becomes available, and composed and notated music becomes communicable over great distances. Musical notation liberates music from the tyranny of the present, but it does not open up all musics from the past—just that tiny fraction which has been developed through the use of musical notation.[38] Only sound recording can make all musics available for scrutiny.

It might be thought that musical literacy would encourage critical attitudes and a relativist approach to the subject, by showing the music of the past to be different from that of the present. Instead, musical writers of the nineteenth-century proposed a developmental, and later an evolutionary, model of musical progress, in order to justify the present in relation to the past. In this way they dealt with this potentially unsettling knowledge about musical difference. They also developed the 'great man' or 'genius' theory of musical creation, a concept in tune with nineteenth-century individualism.[39]

---

[38] Goody, *Literacy*, 53.
[39] e.g. H. Parry, *The Art of Music* (London: Kegan Paul, Trench, Trubner, 1893), generally.

CHANGE IN STYLE AND REPERTORY

The change from a dominantly aural to a dominantly literate musical practice underlay significant change in performance style. Our understanding of the older plebeian musical style is derived from both a reading of contemporary source material and close listening to English performers of vernacular music who have been recorded over the last ninety years. These players, whose dominantly aural music making forms a direct continuity with their nineteenth-century predecessors, are the inheritors of the plebeian musical tradition.

The church choir-bands, village and town bands and musicians performed their music in a style which drew its conventions from traditional practice. There is good evidence for believing that the major elements of their way of playing included an emphasis on volume, with relatively little use of dynamics (although these are sometimes indicated in manuscript books). When, in 1859, a band was employed to play for a celebration of the Mid-Sussex and Southwater Benefit Association, an observer noted, 'the band of music engaged was certainly very superior to the noisy apology for music which is generally heard at annual festivals of this kind'.[40] A use of embellishment, decoration, and elaboration in the different lines played seems to have been common. In 1831, J. A. La Trobe accused the country church musicians of 'throwing in, according to their notions of beauty, shakes, turns, cadences, and other frivolous ornaments'.[41] Sometimes the music would make use of a controlled flexibility of tempo, playing slightly before or behind the beat, emphasizing the off-beat in dance music. The musical conventions of these early bands were known and used by the musicians themselves in their playing, and although we have no doubt that elements of élite musical practice were sometimes imitated and absorbed, the configuration of elements that made up the plebeian musical style was in many ways quite different from professional and élite amateur musical practice.[42]

Sometimes we catch a critical echo of the older plebeian style of playing in the brass band literature. In 1861, in an appreciation of Richard Smith, the *Illustrated News of the World* compared him to other performers:

As a cornet player he is one of the best in the kingdom, both as to tone and true musicianlike feeling. Not like some quack performers we could point out, who get themselves paroted [*sic*] in some spluttering cornet solo, in the shape of a polka, with stupid variations, and who could not read correctly, under any circumstances, a simple melody, as far as regards time or phrasing.[43]

[40] *Sussex Agricultural Express* (16 July 1859), 2.
[41] J. A. La Trobe, *The Music of the Church Considered in its Various Branches, Congregational and Choral* (Thames Ditton, 1831), 138.
[42] Gammon, 'Popular Music in Rural Society', generally; Gammon 'Performance Style'.
[43] Quoted in *British Bandsman* (June 1888), 166.

The consonance between La Trobe's 'frivolous ornaments' of 1831 and this writer's 'stupid variations' thirty years later is notable. Other writers report in a critical vein on what may reasonably be interpreted as examples of a popular semi-improvisational style of playing. George Bernard Shaw noticed musicians 'busking' (improvising inner parts—Shaw called it 'vamping') on more than one occasion.[44]

By the last third of the century, the dominance of the score coupled with professional interest and direction, contesting and adjudication, led to an emphasis on playing the music exactly as written, on precise timekeeping, on the 'correct' interpretation of dynamics, and on the production of a good and even tone. A writer of 1887 informs us that a good player:

must know how to express and how to shape tune particles by the process called phrasing. Again, he must learn to recognize the composer's purpose and mode of thought, as revealed in the various forms of musical design. Then he must have a trained perception of proportion in combining sounds, and in the exact adjustment of time measurements and rhythmical formations.[45]

George Bernard Shaw, writing appreciatively on the Salvation Army in 1906, articulated a favourite theme which was strikingly in tune with his political views—the need for strong direction from the musically able before much could be achieved: 'But mere enthusiasm could not have produced the remarkable precision and snap in their execution. They must have worked hard and been well-coached by their conductors.'[46]

Because the brass band movement performed the works of famous composers, thereby linking with the great tradition of European art music, the musical theory underlying the practice was established, elaborated, and widely published. It is notable that an important conductor like Edwin Swift was able to teach himself transposition, harmony, and arranging from published works.[47]

No doubt there were differences in performance style within the plebeian musical tradition. Even within living memory and the age of sound recording, traditional instrumentalists from Sussex, East Anglia, and Northumberland demonstrate marked regional variations, musical accents if you like, in the way they play, although they work within the broad outlines of the plebeian musical tradition. The significant point is that, whereas the musical standards of the plebeian musical tradition were generated within that tradition, the musical standards of the brass band movement were absorbed from music professionals and members of the middle class. The most important agency

[44] G. B. Shaw, *London Music in 1888–89 as Heard by Corno Di Bassetto* (London: Constable & Co., 1937), 203.
[45] E. H. Turpin, 'A Preamble', *British Bandsman* (Sept. 1887).
[46] G. B. Shaw, *Shaw's Music*, iii (London: Max Reinhardt, The Bodley Head, 1981), 589.
[47] A. Taylor, *Brass Bands* (St Albans and London: Granada Publishing, 1979), 74.

Figure 3.1. A group of unnamed brass players photographed in the Lewes area of East Sussex, *c.*1860s or 1870s.

for cultural standardization and the setting of musical models was the brass band contest.

Repertory changed along with style. Early nineteenth-century bands played a repertory which consisted of what we would call traditional dance tunes, marches (often these two were interchangeable), some popular song airs (such as 'Rule Britannia' and 'God Save the King'), and, if they were church musicians, they played the old-style church music which included the so-called fuguing tunes. Interestingly, a considerable proportion of this repertory got onto contemporary barrel organs and part of it survives as regimental marches. Having listened to early recordings of military bands playing such pieces, it is clear that their style of performance had little in common with the way traditional dance musicians play the same pieces. The brass bands in the second half of the century played a very different repertory. In some ways it was very modern, and included recently composed quadrille sets and other dance music such as polkas, together with popular-song and hymn arrangements, but most noticeably selections from operas and strung-together themes from 'great' composers, with titles like 'The Works of Beethoven'. In 1869 the *Sussex Agricultural Express* reported a harvest home celebrated in West Hoathly:

The proceedings were enlivened during the afternoon by the excellent performance of the Ockenden Band, which attended by permission of W. W. Burrell, Esq. The following programme was gone through in masterly style:

Pas Redouble—'Kadour'	Gurtner.
Selection—'Faust'	Gounod.
Valse—'Corn Flower'	Coote.
Galop—'Belgravia'	C. R. Bloe.
Glee—'Chough and Crow'	Bishop.
Quadrille—'Winters night'	Marriott.
Polka—'Levy-A'-than'	J. Levy.
Valse—'Blanche'	H. Farmer.
Quadrille—'Sicily'	D'Albert.
March—'Come where my love lies dreaming'	Christy's Minstrels.
Pas Redouble—'Monte Christo'	J. Rivère.
Selection—'Orphée Aux Enfers'	Offenbach.
Galop—'Impetuous'	Pironelle.
March—'Lucia di Lammermoor'	Donizetti.
Valse—'Juliet'	C. Coote jun.
Glee—'Red Cross Knight'	Callcott.
Quadrille—'Donnybrook'	R. Smith.
Galop—'Cupid's Arrows'	C. Barthman.
Polka—'Rataplan'	H. Koenig.
March—'Toll the Bell'	Christy's Minstrels.

God Save the Queen.[48]

Sir Walter W. Burrell, Bart, MP, local landowner of Cuckfield and West Grinstead Park in Sussex, was patron and financier of the Ockenden Band, which was named after his house in Cuckfield. The *Sussex Agricultural Express* of 7 January 1879 has the description 'Sir W. W. Burrell's own private Band'.

DEVELOPING STANDARDIZATION

In the older bands, as in the military band tradition, the emphasis was on ensemble work. The adoption of operatic selections, including arias, created the conditions for the emergence of the star soloist. The instrumentation of

---

[48] *Sussex Agricultural Express* (11 Sept. 1869), 2.

Figure 3.2. One of the many popular reproductions of Thomas Webster's *The Village Choir* (1847). Engraved by H. Bourne, this version lacks some of the figures and the background shown in other versions. In spite of its jokey 'genre' quality, it is the best and most celebrated picture of a West Gallery band that is known. The original painting is owned by the Victoria & Albert Museum.

the early bands was highly variable. In churches there might be almost any combination of fiddles, cellos, flutes, clarinets, bassoons, and/or other instruments, numbering from two or three to a dozen or more. Occasionally brass instruments crept into church bands, and there are cases of double basses and serpents being used. Town bands had combinations of wind and generally rather primitive brass instruments. In Lewes Town Hall there is a painting dating from 1830 by A. Archer entitled, *Arrival of William IV and Queen Adelaide at 'The Friars', Lewes* (Fig. 3.3). The Lewes Town Band is shown in one corner, and there is a list of the band members attached to the picture. The instrumentation of the band seems to have been:

3 clarinets
2 clarinets or oboes
2 french horns
2 bugles
1 flute
2 bassoons
1 trombone
1 bass drum

Henry Burstow listed the Horsham Town Band of around 1835 or 1840 as:

Figure 3.3. Detail from a painting dating from the 1830s by A. Archer, entitled *Arrival of William IV and Queen Adelaide at 'The Friars', Lewes*. The Lewes Town Band is shown in one corner, and there is a list of the band members attached to the picture. The painting hangs in Lewes Town Hall.

> 1 flute/fife
> 3 clarinets
> 2 keyed bugles
> 1 trumpet
> 2 trombones
> 1 french horn
> 1 serpent
> 1 drum[49]

Source material provides many variations on these types of combinations.

It must be said that, whilst some of the instruments that have come down to us from the period are obviously well made, the quality of others must have been variable. Some church band musicians made their own instruments, as did James Nye who lived near Lewes in Sussex.[50] Metal fiddles and cellos have

[49] H. Burstow, *Reminiscences of Horsham* (Norwood, Pa.: Norwood Editions, 1975), 50.

[50] J. Nye (ed. V. Gammon), *A Small Account of my Travels Through the Wilderness* (Brighton: Queen Spark Books, 1982), 45.

been reported from different parts of the country, one assumes mostly the work of local smiths.

It would be good to think that industrial progress in the second half of the century brought with it a reduction in the price of instruments and a general improvement in quality. The standardization of instruments certainly helped bands perform together without the difficulty of ill-matched instruments, although many non-standard combinations, making use of old instruments and playing skills, existed throughout the century. Also many instrument makers in the nineteenth century produced cheap and shoddy goods. No doubt those manufacturers who struck up good working relationships with bands, and attended contests in order to do business, were reputable and made instruments of reasonable quality. Nevertheless, if the positive aspects of Victorian musical instrument making were craftsmanship combined with industrial production, the negative aspect was the widespread distribution of poor-quality goods.

Interestingly, the production of relatively cheap instruments also influenced the remnant of the ear-playing musicians: cheap concertinas, melodeons, mouth organs, penny whistles, and banjos—all in their way nineteenth-century inventions or adaptations—provided the characteristic instruments for traditional pub music in the later nineteenth and early twentieth century.

The earlier bands tended to be smaller than the later brass bands. Church bands had anything from two or three to a dozen players—occasionally, as in the case of West Tarring, Sussex, as many as fourteen. (In contemporary records, in the context of the church bands, the terms 'band' and 'choir' are used fairly interchangeably; both could refer to a group consisting of instrumentalists, singers, or most usually both.) Town bands usually counted their members in double figures, but rarely more than twenty. Not that all brass bands achieved the approved numbers and balance of instruments of the 'classic contesting bands',[51] as many old photographs show. The development of what has been termed a music service industry in the second half of the nineteenth century no doubt improved retail services for musicians. The increasing availability of cheap printed music was a luxury undreamt of by instrumentalists earlier in the century. The development of hire purchase no doubt facilitated instrument buying.

Yet we think there is a significant difference between early and later bands in terms of control and ownership of instruments. Although there are examples in churchwardens' accounts of parish funds being used for the purchase of strings, reeds, and particularly the more expensive lower pitched instruments, cellos, and bassoons, the general impression is of individual ownership of instruments. Different patterns existed later in the century, but corporate ownership and control of instruments was by no means uncommon. Collectively and

---

[51] Taylor, *Brass Bands*, 72–3.

institutionally owned sets of instruments can be found in a number of museums, or mouldering away in cupboards and under stages of village halls.

If we consider the events at which bands played we find some continuity and, significantly, some radical change. The early bands tended to play for social events in which the music was simply an adjunct to the event, be it a church service, a parade, a celebration such as a benefit-club feast day, or a dance. Even the *ad hoc* ensembles that played in pubs did so as an accompaniment to drinking and socializing. Clearly much of this pattern continued into the era of the brass bands, although the 1840s and 1850s saw the wholesale expulsion of the church bands from religious services. As well as undertaking many of these older customary functions, brass bands increasingly played in contests and concerts, events at which the music was the central, if not the only, reason for the performance. This change of emphasis was highly significant in popular perceptions of music—for the first time, the music itself became a central focus of attention, not just a necessary component of an event, the main function of which was non-musical.

LEARNING STYLES: CONTINUITY AND CHANGE

We have no doubt that the enthusiasm of particular individuals was vital in inspiring and holding together a band in the early nineteenth century.[52] The family tradition was also very important. The Horsham town band, observed for posterity by the young Henry Burstow, had no less than seven Potters in a band of twelve players.[53] There is some evidence of itinerant teachers of music training choirs for a short period and then moving on, but we do not believe these shadowy people had a very great influence in sustaining church bands. In the main, amateur enthusiasm kept the church bands going.

Enthusiastic individuals were obviously of vital importance in the success of brass bands, and the significance of particular families remains to the present day. Many bands selected their own trainer from among their ranks, but increasingly there was a trend towards the use of professional and semi-professional trainers and conductors. The influence on the movement of such legendary figures as John Gladney, Edwin Swift, and Alexander Owen is well documented. The movement also provided professional or semi-professional work for a large number of other people.[54]

Consideration of the role of trainers and conductors leads on to a consideration of educational styles within bands. In the earlier tradition there seemed to exist a great deal of autonomy in learning style, a great deal of the sort of 'learning by doing' which has been widely observed by ethnomusicologists.

---

[52] Gammon, 'Popular Music in Rural Society', 34.   [53] Burstow, *Reminiscences*, 50.
[54] Gammon, 'Popular Music in Rural Society', 127 and 289–90.

Keith Swanwick makes the following observations and reflections on John Blacking's work on the Venda people of South Africa:

Reading Blacking's description of the way in which the Venda learn music, I am reminded of my own experience as a boy in a Midlands village brass band. Music was to some extent learned in the context of other social activities; we knew that we would be playing at Remembrance Day services or garden parties or on parade at other village events. I mastered the technique of the E flat tenor horn informally, without instruction—the band master never quite got round to *instruction*. Most of the playing was of whole pieces or long sections with very little fragmentation into part-learning or analysis of particular difficulties. In fact, Blacking's description of the Venda fits perfectly: 'The main technique of learning was by observation and listening, trial and error, and then frequent rehearsal'. It was also considered vital to be playing with others. Few members of the band seemed to practise at home very often or for long and most technical progress seemed to be achieved when playing together. I suspect that this pattern of learning is still prevalent today in church choirs, amateur orchestras, rock bands, folk groups, the Salvation Army, steel bands and many other variations of our rich musical culture.[55]

It would seem reasonable, therefore, to assume that such a learning process was common in brass bands as it had been in earlier ensembles. We should, however, notice a growing emphasis on training, instruction, and discipline, and some of the sources suggest that fragmentation into sectional part-learning and the analysis of particular difficulties was a favoured nineteenth-century practice within the brass band movement. The method of the brass band teacher previously quoted was 'to devote one night in each week, for a period of two months, to exercises written upon a blackboard to be learnt and repeated by the pupils, sometimes singly, and sometimes together'. He practised fragmentation into parts, and made a great use of scales and exercises. He emphasized the need for home practice and stressed that teaching should be 'systematic, progressive and persevering'. One senses little feeling of joy in this approach.[56] Sets of rules are not unknown for early bands, but the most common ethos one encounters is that of a voluntary association. Early bands were renowned for an independence of attitude, pride, and confidence in what they did, and what we would describe as an exuberant hedonism, which was often expressed in quite extravagant actions.[57]

RATIONAL RECREATION AND QUESTIONS OF CONTROL

Acts of 'masculine gaiety', the expression of disgust at contest decisions, and unruliness were features of the brass band movement, yet such actions are

---

[55] K. Swanwick, *Music, Mind and Education* (London: Routledge, 1988), 128.

[56] *British Bandsman* (Mar. 1888), 106. For an interesting comparison see B. Jackson, *Working Class Community* (London: Routledge & Kegan Paul, 1968), 21–2.

[57] Gammon, 'Popular Music in Rural Society', 31.

always contrasted with a normative idea of what behaviour should be. In some respects, the 'sporting' ethos of the brass band movement is inherited directly from an aspect of the old popular culture of the eighteenth and nineteenth centuries. The interplay of the ethos of rational recreation, aggressive competitiveness, and what Golby and Purdue describe as an 'appetite for beer and sensation',[58] forms one of the most fascinating dynamics within the brass band movement. Temperance sponsorship of bands, with subsequent lapsing or defection of members, is a recurring motif, but amusing anecdotes of this type should not lead us to think that temperance did not have a solid base in the working class and among many bandsmen. The use of uniforms is significant in this context. A uniform implies subservience of the individual will to disciplined behaviour—uniforms were rare among early bands outside the military.

Discussion of behaviour leads us on to a discussion of patronage and questions of control. The church bands flourished in a particular set of ecclesiastical conditions where clerical authority was weak and musicians exercised considerable autonomy and gained a significant control over the music of the parish church. Certainly church and chapel provided a basis for musical activity, but it is misleading to describe what the church generally did for the church bands as patronage. It was the reimposition of clerical authority which led to the expulsion and suppression of church bands. Both church and early town bands drew most of their membership from artisans, a traditionally independent group who had sufficient income to finance an interest in music, as well as flexible 'pre-industrial' work patterns which ensured blocks of time in which to practise.[59] The 'classic' brass band is very different. In the case of subscription bands, something of the old independence could be retained, but even here support from wealthy members of the community could be of crucial importance and could exercise a decisive influence. An account of the formation of a town band at Ashford in Kent in 1859 gives a fascinating insight into the attitudes and values in play:

Ashford Town Band—A meeting was held on Monday evening in the lower Public Room, for the purpose of taking steps to establish a town band. Mr. Wills was chairman. Mr. Farley said he had sketched a few resolutions, which he would read seriatim:—1st,—That a good band is required in this town, to contribute to the recreation and amusement of the inhabitants more especially of those engaged in daily toil, and also to assist in cultivating a musical taste.

2nd,—That a committee be appointed, and requested to solicit donations, and make necessary arrangements with a proper band master and band.

3rd,—That two evenings in every week be set apart for the band to play in public.

---

[58] Golby and Purdue, *Civilisation*, 14.

[59] Gammon, 'Popular Music in Rural Society', 32 and 121; E. Hobsbawm and G. Rude, *Captain Swing* (Harmondsworth: Penguin, 1983), p. xxiv; Thompson, *Customs in Common*, 352–403, particularly 373; K. Thomas, 'Work and Leisure in Pre-Industrial Societies', *Past and Present*, 29 (1964), 50–62.

4th,—That by the kind permission of Mr. J. Lewis, the band play in the field adjoining Mr. Epps' garden once each week: and, in case the S. E. R. Company with their officers and servants approve and support the project it shall play in the triangle of the New Town the other evening in each week; otherwise it shall play both evenings in Mr. Lewis's field.

These resolutions were put by the chairman and unanimously adopted. The Rev. J. P. Alcock then proposed an additional resolution, to the effect,—that as the object of this meeting is to promote innocent recreation, and to cultivate a taste for music, the band shall not meet for practice at any inn or public house. This met with some opposition, but was eventually carried.[60]

In the case of works' bands, the situation is sometimes clearer. Owners who put in significant support could exercise a control and direction over band policy unknown to earlier bands. They often provided a band room, and could also finance professional instruction if they felt inclined, as was the case with the previously cited Ockenden Band of Cuckfield financed by Sir W. W. Burrell, and many industrial examples. In the case of Volunteer bands a layer of military-style discipline could be added.

In all cases, enhanced status within a community and the resultant self-esteem were important motivations for participation in music making. In the case of competing brass bands, the additional confirmation of competition success was a possibility. A significant number of bands incorporated references to their contest-winning prowess in their titles.

In the case of both earlier and later bands, taking part could lead to supplementary income for the bandsmen. This could be in money or in kind, often in the form of beer and food. This aspect of banding forms a continuity, although when brass band competitions started the additional possibility of prize money existed.[61]

The image of the brass band as a product of the industrial regions, a land of mills and pit villages, is an overdrawn stereotype. Certainly the industrial heartland of Yorkshire and Lancashire was the cradle of the movement, and produced most of the champion 'crack' bands. Nevertheless, the movement was much more widespread, and its influence went far beyond the northern manufacturing counties. Bands from the south of England existed in their hundreds and probably thousands, although they seldom achieved much at the national contests.

MUSIC IN SOCIAL AND GEOGRAPHICAL SPACE

In social terms, the brass band movement was essentially working-class. In the south as well as the rest of the country, significant industrial and social changes

[60] *Sussex Agricultural Express* (21 June 1859), 2.
[61] Burstow, *Reminiscences*, 50; Shaw, *Shaw's Music*, ii. 122.

worked against the continuation of the leisure patterns of the past. Small workshops and independent artisans with their task-oriented notions of time declined, as methods of hand production were co-opted into industrial processes. Sometimes hand production was stimulated by the factory system, but even here, intensified demand led to a breakdown of 'pre-industrial' work patterns and the development of 'sweated' labour. Mobility and enforced migration also had a negative influence on old ways.

Russell has noticed that the strength of the band movement was in the relatively small industrial villages of Yorkshire and Lancashire.[62] This is a very important point. The industrial revolution transformed old villages and created new industrial ones, which provided new and different social conditions. Initial dislocation was followed by relatively stable settlement in a close environment, and this sort of pattern seems to have been a very suitable seedbed for band development, but it was not the only one. The 'forest' communities of north Sussex, Horsham, Crawley, Horsted Keynes, Nutley, Fairwarp, Turners Hill, West Hoathly, and East Grinstead were veritable hothouses of band activity in the later nineteenth century.[63] These were market towns and villages partially enmeshed in what some observers have seen as an archaic type of economy.[64] Brass bands seem to have flourished in small-scale communities, but with the present state of our knowledge, it does not seem possible to generalize beyond this observation.

We have tried to show that, while there were some continuities in the activities of the amateur bands that performed in the nineteenth century, the major discontinuities were far more significant. The middle decades of the nineteenth century witnessed a remaking of the musical activities of many working people. A new style of music emerged, new instrumentations, new forms of organization and institution—most significantly the brass band contest. This amounts to significantly more than a pattern of popular music making 'left altered, but unscathed'.[65]

On the negative side, the middle decades of the nineteenth century witnessed the destruction of church bands, a purposeful and deliberate act. The 1850s also witnessed the reform of military music—one wonders how much because of its neglected state, and how much because the style of playing of military musicians was out of step with élite musical tastes. On the positive side, we believe that the nineteenth century increased opportunities for participation in active music making. It would be quite wrong to see the changes

---

[62] Russell, *Popular Music*, 206–9.

[63] Gammon, 'Popular Music in Rural Society', 129; R. Hall, *I Never Played to Many Posh Dances . . . Scan Tester, Sussex Musician, 1887–1972* (Rochford: Musical Traditions, 1990), 102–8, 110.

[64] M. Reed, 'The Peasantry of Nineteenth-Century England: A Neglected Class?', *History Workshop*, 18 (1984), 53–76, generally.

[65] Russell, *Popular Music*, 198.

of the mid-nineteenth century as simply a defeat for indigenous vernacular musical culture—as wrong as to see the changes as the manifestation of the ever-forward march of progress. In trying to sort out the gains and losses, the result would probably depend as much on each individual's approach and attitude to music as on the evidence produced.

It was not that the plebeian musical tradition was destroyed by the advent of the brass band and the related changes of the mid-nineteenth century; rather, it lost its place as the basis of much vernacular music making, and went underground. Its dynamic force was present in the activities of numerous urban and rural amateur musicians, and was still audible in some aspects of the music hall. Significantly, the fast developing musical instrument industry found there were profits to be made in catering for the needs of vernacular musicians whose way of doing things harked back to older musical practices.

The example of the concertina neatly illustrates the point. To most people, a concertina is a concertina, but actually there are three distinct types, really three distinct instruments, all developed in the nineteenth century and each of them serving different needs.

The English concertina is a fully chromatic instrument, and has the same bottom note and roughly the same range as the violin, for which it was often substituted. The notes of the scale of C are placed on alternate sides of the instrument with accidentals placed adjacently. The English concertina lends itself to solo line playing, and although it is possible to play in thirds and to play chords, it is not easy to provide melody *and* substantial accompaniment on the instrument. It was marketed as a drawing-room instrument and came in various sizes from treble to bass, to be played in ensembles and concertina bands. These concertina bands modelled themselves on brass bands, dressed in uniforms, played a standard brass band repertory from brass band scores, and had contests organized at Belle Vue and Crystal Palace. A number of concertina bands were active until the inter-war period.

The duet concertina is also fully chromatic, but has a wider range than the English concertina, larger models covering most of the notes on a piano keyboard. The left hand plays the lower notes, the right hand the higher; on larger models there is a substantial overlap of notes on the two sides, allowing considerable flexibility. There are different systems of note layout, ergonomically designed, apparently quite illogical on the surface, but all allowing the playing of complex music with full self-accompaniment. The duet concertina was the instrument of the musically ambitious player, and was much used by professionals as well as by aspiring amateurs.

The anglo (or more properly Anglo-German) concertina offers a very different note arrangement from the other two. The duet and English both play the same note on the push as on the pull; this is not so on the anglo. Its notes are arranged in rows so that if one pushes on, say, a C row, one gets the notes of the tonic chord CEGC′, and if one pulls, one gets the other diatonic notes DFAB. Usually there are two diatonic rows, most often in G and C. Better instruments have a third row containing chromatic notes not available on the two diatonic rows. Its note arrangement makes it very similar to those other highly popular instruments, the melodeon and the mouth organ. The push/pull arrangement of the notes makes it hard to play in a legato style, but when playing diatonic dance music, the instrument itself fairly dances, producing a lively, forceful, and jumpy sound.

Needless to say, the anglo was the instrument most favoured by ear-players in the nineteenth century. The three types of concertina neatly demonstrate the differentiation of the nineteenth-century instrument-buying public. In a sense, they also graphically illustrate the fragmentation of working-class musical culture in the nineteenth century. Professionals and high-flyers played the duet; middle-class people and musically literate, respectable working-class members of concertina bands played the English; ear-players and the musically disrespectable played the cheaper anglo. The prices were stratified according to the complexity of the instrument and the nature of the market.

CROSSING MUSICAL BOUNDARIES

In a wider perspective, we have seen how two musical value systems could operate within popular music making. This raises the question of how people experienced and coped with this clash of values. Could people move between different types of music making?

The evidence is contradictory but interesting. On the one hand, the adoption by significant portions of the working class of a value system derived from Western art music, which categorized music as good and bad according to particular criteria, must have had the effect of devaluing much self-made, vernacular music. On the other hand, there is significant evidence of many musicians being able to play different types of music, able to move between sight-reading in a band and playing by ear and from memory. 'Trombone Billy', a friend and musical associate of Scan Tester, the Sussex anglo concertina player, was both a trained bandsman and an able pub musician, who could play hornpipes for stepdancing on his trombone.[66] This ability to move easily between different musical styles, which we might term 'polymusicality', has been raised into an educational goal by recent writers.[67] There is evidence, however, that ear-playing musicians, able musicians who greatly enjoyed their music, must often have been rejected from ensembles where reading musical notation was seen as an absolute necessity. This happened to Scan Tester himself—one of the few English traditional musicians to have been extensively recorded. In the 1960s, he told Reg Hall:

[66] Hall, *Posh Dances*, 31–2.   [67] Swanwick, *Music, Mind*, 115–17 and generally.

the bandmaster wanted me to join the band. Well, he wanted me to join like the others to learn music. . . . Well, the man what was the bandmaster of the band, he used to be a shoemaker and used to go down there, and he used to be pointing this music out to me trying to learn me. He was a cornet player and, 'course, I couldn't learn that music, you know. I wasn't no good. I tried! I tried hard enough to learn it, but I couldn't, and they all thought I was going to learn music, because I was good on any music [musical instrument]. I was playing a music, but as for to learn the music to read it off, I couldn't, and I never did, and that was the reason why that I come out of the band . . .[68]

Yet even when instrumentalists were able to move between contrasting styles of playing, the effect of the existence of different musical value systems operating within lower-class culture must have been to devalue the older and now less esteemed ways of playing. The fragmentation of working-class culture must have led to a great loss of cultural class-cohesion. One significant impetus within the culture was for people to become upwardly aspirant, willing to accept and absorb middle-class values, but disowning that which they had owned in the process. Another response was for people to cling, at times defensively, to what they had known and valued.

THE WIDER CULTURAL CONTEXT

It is worth considering the wider implications of this analysis in terms of debates about popular culture and class relations in nineteenth-century England. Historians have rightly become sceptical about the efforts and achievements of middle-class reformers, rational recreationists, and moral crusaders. Whatever feelings of self-satisfaction reformers' efforts brought them, they often did not bring the results desired. No doubt some rational recreationists deluded themselves about the success of their efforts. It would be totally naïve of us to think that any attempt at reformation would be successful in a simple or linear way. In a dynamic and contested social field, the end result of such efforts would inevitably be different from the aims and aspirations of the reformers. Yet it would be equally naïve to believe that such efforts were without effect in changing and modifying lower-class culture in profound and significant ways.

The mid-nineteenth-century encounter between autonomous lower-class culture and middle-class taste and reforming zeal led to the marginalization and devaluing of many positive elements of the old plebeian musical tradition. This encounter created the conditions for the incorporated, patronized, and denigrated culture of the brass band, albeit a culture in which a new, and in many ways positive, identity could be forged. Ironically, considering the aspirations of middle-class rational recreationists, the changes created the conditions for the success of commercial provision of popular music, which filled the cultural partial vacuum created by the decline of the older tradition.

[68] Hall, *Posh Dances*, 103.

CHANGING TRADITIONS

The older musical culture did not die, although a fairly systematic attempt was made to destroy it. Nor did it simply fade away. What survived of it tended to go underground, to become part of the defensive and insular culture that characterized the later nineteenth-century working class. In part the old tradition was replaced by music and musical activities approved by the middle class, although, as in the case of the brass band, these were sometimes transformed in non-approved ways by working-class practitioners, a process Russell has described as the 'working class capacity to extract the maximum benefit from rational recreation while ignoring or deflecting its ideology'.[69] In part, something of the idiom and style of the old tradition found its way into music hall, and thence into popular music generally, perhaps to be 'reabsorbed' by the public-house singing tradition. Something of the old spirit was retained in the populist evangelical music of the Salvation Army—brass instruments, anglo concertinas, and all. Aspects of the old tradition survived to be picked up in selected places by Edwardian folk music collectors and later enthusiasts.

There is even some evidence that after training and drilling in the rigours of music literacy, some ensembles seemed to revert to something like older aural styles of playing. Mention has been made above of bands of literate musicians who have taken their ensemble playing away from strict reproduction of exact pitches and time values. Playing for dancing seems to promote among brass musicians that specific quality that jazz musicians call 'swing'. Recordings of brass players playing for the Britannia Coconut Dancers from Bacup and the Helston Furry Dance testify to this. Adapting Ong's phrase, we must consider this phenomenon 'secondary aurality', a state where musical literacy has had and retains a marked influence.[70]

When all this is considered, the marginalization and residualization of the old, dominantly aural, plebeian musical culture is an inescapable fact, as is the dominance of a musical ideal derived, if somewhat adapted, from Western art music. We think this can justifiably be described as the incorporation of lower-class music making into the musical-aesthetic world of élite and bourgeois taste. This was achieved, though never totally, and never in an uncontested way, centrally through the brass band.

This acceptance by a significant portion of the working class of what were initially alien musical conventions meant a rejection of the plebeian musical tradition as a basis for musical development. This represented a denial of self-worth and contributed to a further fragmentation of working-class culture. Simultaneously and crucially, it ensured a subordinate, sneered-at but safe place for working-class music making within bourgeois culture. 'Our aims', stated the *British Bandsman* in its prospectus of 1887, 'are to stimulate, and,

---

[69] Russell, *Popular Music*, 213.   [70] Ong, *Orality*, 137.

where it is non-existent, to create and foster in bandsmen a desire for, and a love of good and high-class music . . . and lastly to urge a claim for a higher status in the musical world for band professors'.[71]

The low esteem of band professors is but one aspect of the low status of brass bands in the musical world. The acceptance of some central and vital aspects of middle-class musical taste meant that the working-class musical culture could easily be judged by prevailing musical standards, and by those standards be judged wanting:

Plenty of instances could be found in which wealthy amateurs, often large employers of labour, have promoted the establishment of brass or reed bands, by aiding in the purchase of instruments, and the engagement of teachers. It is, of course, a matter of opinion whether a brass-band is very much of a musical blessing, but that does not interfere with the motive of the person who aids it with his money.[72]

When considering musicians to accompany a choral society, Fisher felt that a local teacher might be thankful to get mediocre woodwind players, but 'might consider himself fortunate if no member of the local brass band offered his services on the trombone'.[73] H. E. Adkins, writing in the 1920s, commented: 'The Military Bands of our towns and villages were nondescript organizations, being, more often than not, the manifestation of goodwill towards music on the part of certain members of the community, but just as frequently they were exhibitions of the inefficacy of goodwill without proper direction.'[74] Such disparaging remarks about amateur bands are common.

One way to deal with such judgements was to assail the heights of excellence as a contest-winning 'crack' band. Yet even this did not ensure respect and value from social and musical 'superiors'. No doubt many working men derived enormous pleasure and satisfaction from playing in a brass band, but perhaps we should seriously question whether the loss of a socially independent stylistic basis for the development of working-class music making was worth what was gained. What happened is what happened. In the plebeian musical tradition there was the basis for a very different musical and social development. From our position in the late twentieth century this is hard to see, but that does not mean we should not make the effort.

Our aim in this essay has *not* been to say that the brass band movement was a bad thing—clearly tens of thousands of people obtained enormous pleasure and satisfaction from playing in brass bands. Rather, our desire has been to approach positively the aural musical world of the early nineteenth century and before;[75] to challenge Whiggish interpretations of musical history which

---

[71] *British Bandsman* (Sept. 1887), 1.

[72] H. Fisher, *The Musical Profession* (London: J. Curwen & Sons, n.d. (1888)), 113.

[73] Ibid. 101.

[74] H. E. Adkins, *Treatise on the Military Band*, revised edn. (London: Boosey, 1958), 8.

[75] Ong, *Orality*, 175.

base themselves on an uncritical notion of progress; to point out that all changes in musical practice are the product of contestation within cultural fields and inevitably involve losses as well as gains.[76]

Frederick Jones, veteran of the Falmer and Stanmer Church Bands, lived through the changes in musical style and regretted the loss of the older music: 'Alas they were indeed happy meetings, notwithstanding the disdain, shall I say contempt with which a more educated public regarded our old compositions with their repeat and twiddle.'[77]

Ultimately we favour aesthetic tolerance, or at least a form of musical relativism which accepts and does not deny real (objective) and experienced (lived and felt) differences in styles and in responses. Intolerance which does not recognize itself as such (a common fault of much liberalism) is still intolerance. Musical taste as a social and cultural marker has for centuries been, and will continue to be, used in social and cultural conflict, whether we favour tolerance or not.

The routes that led to our starting point, Holst's 1928 *A Moorside Suite*, are complex. In the mid-nineteenth century, working-class music making took a great step towards embracing European art music. In the early twentieth century, some English art-music composers found a new basis for their work in 'folk song', an aspect of the previously despised and rejected music of the English lower classes. *A Moorside Suite*, the work of a socialist composer who had played the trombone in a theatre band, represents the coming together of these two highly significant musical impulses.[78] We find the irony compelling.

---

[76] P. Bourdieu, *Distinction* (London: Routledge & Kegan Paul, 1984), generally; P. Bourdieu, 'Intellectual Field and Creative Project', in M. F. D. Young (ed.), *Knowledge and Control* (London: Collier Macmillan, 1971), 161 ff.

[77] K. H. MacDermott's MS, i. 54 (letter of 25 May 1917), in the library of the Sussex Archaeological Society, Lewes.

[78] Holst, *Music of Gustav Holst*, 100 and 140; I. Holst, *Gustav Holst*, 2nd edn. (London: Oxford University Press, 1969), generally.

4

⨯

Instruments and Instrumentation of British Brass Bands

ARNOLD MYERS

INSTRUMENTS OF THE EARLIEST BRASS BANDS

The first all-brass bands of the 1830s departed from the centuries-old band tradition of accompanying melody played on woodwind with harmony played on brass. The common wind band instrumentation of clarinets with horns and other brass instruments was varied to produce the brass band: cornets as principal melody instruments, accompanied by a variety of brass instruments of middle and low tessituras. The widespread adoption of the new instrumentation would seem to have been a matter of taste: a preference for the sound of concerted brass instruments made possible by the inventions of the early years of the nineteenth century. The price lists of D'Almaine and Jordan (Appendix 1) show that the expense of equipping a band with cornets would have been slightly more than for providing the same number of clarinets.

The rise of the all-brass band seems to follow hard on the heels of the invention of the cornet in the late 1820s and its introduction to Britain shortly after. All-brass groups would have been possible earlier: the keyed bugle was a popular melody instrument, and horns, trombones, and ophicleides were already used in military and civilian wind bands. There is no evidence that any brass bands were formed in Britain with all the upper parts played by keyed bugles.

Surviving descriptions of the make-up of bands are not plentiful. Listings of the instrumentation of early brass bands, usefully assembled by J. L. Scott,[1] show a wide variety of groupings used in the period up to 1845. Cornets and

---

[1] Jack L. Scott, 'The Evolution of the Brass Band and its Repertoire in Northern England' (Ph.D., University of Sheffield, 1970).

keyed bugles were variously accompanied by french horns and trumpets (probably mostly valved horns and trumpets), trombones, ophicleides, bass horns, and serpents. The bass drum and side drum did not differ from those used in other bands which performed outdoors and on the march.

Often clarinets were used in what were otherwise all-brass groups, a usage which continued throughout the nineteenth century and into the twentieth, though not in major contests from the 1870s. The presence of clarinets did not alter the essential nature of the brass band: they replaced one or more Bb cornets, or were used to provide brightness in the upper register in the role usually played by the soprano cornet. Later, in the 1890s, and again in the 1970s, some bands sought to improve the effect of this topmost voice by using high Eb trumpets in place of the difficult Eb soprano cornet. The principal melodic line was always taken by the Bb cornet (often crooked into Ab in the 1840s, 1850s, and 1860s).

The early nineteenth century was a particularly fruitful time for the development of new instruments. The second decade saw the invention of successful keyed brass instruments (keyed bugle and ophicleide) and of the valved brass. Although the valve was at first envisaged as a means of effecting a rapid change of crook on the trumpet and the horn, the possibility of new families of chromatic brass instruments was quickly conceived and explored. The full range of valved instruments used in the brass band was produced as early as the 1820s, at least in embryonic form.

The Trombones

Of the instruments used by brass bands in the 1830s, the trombone (invented by the fifteenth or early sixteenth century) was the oldest.[2] Its concept was so simple, and its early form so satisfactory, that its development has been in matters of detail such as bore size and the interior profile of the mouthpiece. The tuning slide was added in the middle of the nineteenth century: even as late at 1889, Higham's cheaper models lacked this useful feature. Although the tenor size (mostly pitched in 8-foot C or 9-foot Bb) has been the most widely used, the standard complement was a set of alto, tenor, and bass. These might ideally have been disposed either in F, C, and G, or in Eb, Bb, and F; in practice, the make-up of trombone sections varied widely, and rarely conformed to one of these 'ideals'. The trombone had virtually disappeared in Britain for most of the eighteenth century,[3] but in the first quarter of the nineteenth century it returned to fashion, frequently with a forceful style of playing which gave it associations only now being thrown off, but no doubt appealing to many bandsmen and bandmasters. The alto, capable of less volume than the tenor and bass, and not as full in tone as valved horns, was less popular in the early

[2] Anthony C. Baines, *Brass Instruments* (London: Faber, 1976).
[3] Trevor Herbert, 'The Trombone in Britain before 1800' (Ph.D., The Open University, 1984).

bass bands, and does not appear to have been much used at all after the 1860s. The bass in G, more manageable than the F bass (with both, the outer slide was controlled by a handle), had a particular appeal to players in Britain; they were as numerous in early bands as tenor trombones and also became the standard bass trombone in the orchestra.

Some trombones were made with valves (usually three) instead of a slide. Valve trombones are arguably easier to learn to play, especially for those who already play a valved instrument, and are more robust, but they have never equalled the slide trombone in quality of tone. They were used by some brass bands, but became less common towards the end of the nineteenth century.

The French Horn and the Trumpet

These instruments were used by military and other wind bands at the time of the formation of the first all-brass bands, and naturally, early brass bands used them. At that time, valved and natural horns[4] and trumpets[5] were in use, but it appears that the valved instruments were preferred for bands. Both were used more to fill out the harmony and add their different voices to the tone-colour of the band rather than as leading melodic instruments. Both were pitched most commonly in F (the horn with a 12-foot tube length, the trumpet 6-foot) and provided with crooks for Eb, D, C, etc. It was not until later that orchestral players ceased to use crooks and played music in all keys entirely with the valves, so it would be reasonable to assume that horn and trumpet players in brass bands made some use of crooks, even though in any one band the music was probably arranged using a relatively small range of key signatures. As clavicors and saxhorns were adopted in bands in the 1840s and the 1850s, the use of french horns and trumpets fell away.

The Serpent and Bass Horn

The serpent,[6] being a popular bass instrument, was adopted by some of the earliest brass bands. It was nearly always made of wood (often walnut) with leather binding; the crook and sometimes the mouthpiece were of brass. It is usual to class it as a 'brass' instrument on account of its being played with a mouthpiece, which is comparable in size to that of a euphonium, but with a cup-shape approximating to a hemisphere. The inventor is invariably cited as Edmé Guillaume, a canon of Auxerre, and the date of invention as 1590; research has not produced other contenders to take the credit. Its role as a support for vocal music in churches continued through to the nineteenth century.

The serpent was most commonly built in C, with an eight-foot tube length. The compass extends down to C_2, not very low, but the serpent in a group of

[4] Reginald Morley-Pegge, *The French Horn*, 2nd edn. (London: Benn, 1971).

[5] Philip Bate, *The Trumpet and the Trombone*, 2nd edn. (London: Benn, 1978).

[6] Reginald Morley-Pegge and Philip Bate, 'Serpent', in S. Sadie (ed.), *The New Grove Dictionary of Musical Instruments*, iii (London: Macmillan, 1984), 347–52.

instruments can give the impression of an instrument an octave lower. It is not a loud instrument, but can add a telling effect of depth. As with other brass instruments, there is no upper limit to its range, but above G_4 the tone loses character. The fact that the finger-holes are grouped in two sets of three to suit the human hand rather than spaced out along the tube (as on a recorder, for instance) means that the fingering cannot define the pitch of the tone that is being played very precisely—the player has to pitch the notes by fine control of lip tension. Often, two notes a semitone apart have identical fingering, and most notes can be 'bent' up or down by the player to a greater extent than on any other brass instrument. Towards the end of the eighteenth century, three or four keys were sometimes used. It was probably most frequently a three-keyed serpent that was used in the early brass bands. In its most developed form, it had fourteen keys with all the holes covered and placed to best effect. This was not necessarily a better instrument for either player or listener, and the serpent finally yielded as a popular instrument to the ophicleide and the valved brass basses. With its adoption as a band instrument, the serpent became more widely played in its old age than in its youth. It was used considerably in France, Britain, Germany, and Italy. Several modified versions were made and favoured in different countries, generally easier to carry around and of a narrower bore than the serpent. The 'bass horn' enjoyed a certain popularity in Britain alongside the serpent. It was invented in the 1790s by a Frenchman exiled in London, Louis Alexandre Frichot, and is of brass or copper in the form of a V with a large curving crook.[7] It had three or four keys, retaining the serpent's six finger-holes in widely spaced groups of three and its rather unfocused tone-colour. Bass horns were usually pitched in C. Few were made after 1835.

The Keyed Bugle

The keyed bugle was invented and patented in 1810 by a militia bandmaster living in Ireland, Joseph Haliday (born in Baildon, Yorkshire in 1774),[8] and gained immediate acceptance. It was a flexible and versatile instrument, the only soprano brass instrument of agility that was fully chromatic. Although the keyed trumpet was already in use in continental Europe, the keyed bugle appears to have been an independent invention. The conical bore and the large, well-spaced tone-holes (see Fig. 4.1) proved satisfactory acoustically: the disparity in tone-quality between notes with the keys closed and those with the keys open can be reduced with practice to be as negligible as on woodwind instruments. The most widely used size was the 4-foot C or 4½-foot B♭—in Britain, bugles were generally built in C, but more frequently played with a short, looped crook to give a B♭ instrument. The smaller E♭ bugle (similarly

[7] Reginald Morley-Pegge and Anthony C. Baines, 'Bass-Horn', in *New Grove Dictionary of Musical Instruments*, i. 175.

[8] Ralph T. Dudgeon, *The Keyed Bugle* (Metuchen, NJ, and London: Scarecrow Press, 1993).

Figure 4.1. Keyed bugles in E♭ (Pace) and C with B♭ crook (Greenhill), both *c*.1840.

playable in D♭) seems to have been used less frequently in the early brass bands. The original maker of the keyed bugle was probably Matthew Pace. His move to London from Dublin in 1816 no doubt furthered the popularity of the bugle in England. Although used alongside cornets, its popularity waned after 1840, and bugle tone-colour was later supplied in bands by the flugel horn.

The Ophicleide

The keyed bugle's popularity was matched—and outlived—by that of the ophicleide, invented by 1817 in Paris by the maker J. H. A. Halary, and patented by him in 1821.[9] The ophicleide was conceived as the bass member of a family of three sizes. The alto ophicleide, falling between the bass and the keyed bugle, had less success, and is not known to have been used in Britain.

[9] French Patent No. 1849, Mar. 1821, cited in Clifford Bevan, *The Tuba Family* (London: Faber, 1978), 59.

Figure 4.2. Contrabass saxhorn in E♭ (Courtois, *c.*1865), and ophicleide (Smith, *c.*1840).

Halary deserves credit not only for developing the ophicleide (*ophis* = serpent, *kleis* = cover or stopper), but also for producing it in a form which required little modification in its fifty or more years of popularity.

The distinguishing features of the ophicleide (Fig. 4.2) are its almost perfectly conical bore and its relatively large tone-holes, all of which are covered by keys. Most ophicleides have either nine or eleven keys. With the latter, each semitone in the lowest octave has its own key, but two fingers of the right hand have each to operate two keys; with the nine-key instrument, each finger (except the left-hand little finger) has only one key to operate, but two notes in the lowest octave require accurate control of lip tension as the forked fingerings give little help to the player. The accusation that the ophicleide was cumbersome with rattling keys is wrong: the surviving repertoire shows how agile it could be. The keywork was mechanically similar to that of the saxophone (which was, in fact, developed from the ophicleide), and needed to be no more noisy than that of the saxophone when well regulated.

Ophicleides are pitched in 8-foot C or 9-foot B♭; Halary's original idea was to use different crooks on one instrument in the manner of the B♭ crook for the

C keyed bugle, but separate instruments were soon found to be preferable. Unlike later valved basses, they make regular use of all the fundamentals: their compass is three octaves and more from B_1 and A_1 respectively. The sound is firm and clear—not with the full mellowness of the euphonium or the reediness of the saxophone, but somewhere between the two.

The Cornet

The valve, invented no later than 1814 by Heinrich Stölzel and Friedrich Blühmel in Prussia, was first applied to the horn and the trumpet.[10] Within a few years, however, Stölzel and others were making valved brass instruments in a variety of sizes and shapes—in essence the present kinds of brass band instrument. The names given to them (*Bass-Trompete*, *Chromatisches Basshorn*) we would now find misleading. Although the initial development of these instruments was in Germany and Austria, it was largely the French remodelling of these instruments which was imported and copied in Britain.

The cornet, a valved version of the then-popular post-horn, was invented *c*.1828. It is not known who made the first cornet (it may well have been Halary in Paris) but its popularity was immediate, especially in France and Britain. In Britain, it was made by Pace and others. In addition, large numbers were imported from France and Germany by the end of the 1830s. It was first known as the cornet-à-pistons in France and the cornopean in Britain, though this latter term is now reserved for the early form with Stölzel valves and a single 'clapper' key for trills (see Fig. 4.3) that was a feature of instruments made for the British market. This model had a wide mouthpiece receiver, and used a mouthpiece indistinguishable from that of a keyed bugle; alternatively, a trumpet mouthpiece could be used.

Like the keyed bugle, the two principal sizes were the $3\frac{1}{4}$-foot E♭ and the 4-foot B♭, the latter being far more numerous and providing the leading voice of the band. Like french horns of the time, cornets were supplied with crooks. The E♭ soprano cornet was frequently played crooked into D♭ in the 1850s and 1860s. The B♭ (more rarely C) contralto was usually supplied with shanks for B♭ and A, and crooks for A♭ and G, and sometimes for F and low E♭ also. Shanks (straight lengths of tubing up to 8 inches long) and crooks (longer lengths with one or more loops) are inserted between the mouthpiece and the body of the instrument to lower the entire pitch range. Shanks and crooks were generally used to put the instrument in a different key to facilitate reading music parts; other advantages were a more mellow sound and a downwards extension of the compass. The mouthpiece for the early cornet was deeper and more funnel-shaped than that used towards the end of the nineteenth century.

---

[10] Herbert Heyde, *Das Ventilblasinstrument, seine Entwicklung im deutschsprächigen Raum von den Anfangen bis zur Gegenwart* (Leipzig: VEB Deutscher Verlag für Musik, 1987).

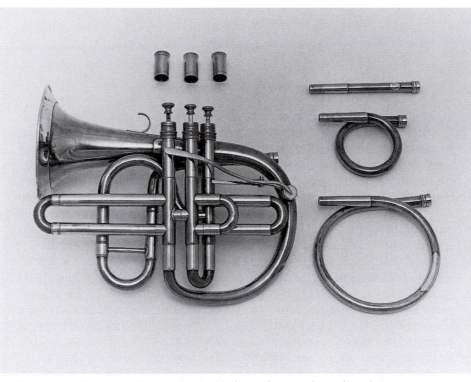

Figure 4.3. Cornopean (Pace, *c.*1845) with clapper key, crooks, and touchpiece protectors.

The Clavicor

Among the derivatives of the early German experimental valved brass instruments of the 1820s developed in France were Guichard's valved ophicleide (1832) and 'Clavicor' (1838).[11] The latter could fill the middle of the harmony of the band, offering a horn-like instrument of alto or tenor tessitura more suited to marching bands than valved french horns. The clavicor (or 'alt horn') was latterly made in Britain also (see Fig. 4.4) and was used by a significant number of brass bands in the 1840s and 1850s.

Instrumentation

These, then, were the brass instruments available in the movement's first decade. Some of the earliest surviving published music for brass band consists of parts of *Wessel & Co.'s Journal for Brass Band*, the arrangements being by William Childe, dating from the early 1840s.[12] We must presume that the

---

[11] Anthony C. Baines, 'Clavicor', in *New Grove Dictionary of Musical Instruments*, i. 426–7.
[12] *Wessel & Co.'s Journal for Brass Band* [*c.*1840–5], British Library.

Figure 4.4.
Clavicor in D♭
(Pace, *c.*1840).

instrumentation is fairly typical of the better bands of the time, although the bandmaster of a band buying the publication would have been expected to make adaptations for the forces at his disposal. Showing how far brass bands had developed by the time Sax's instruments were introduced, in No. 15, *Fantasia on Scotch Airs*, the instrumentation is:

1 cornet-à-pistons in E♭ and D♭
2 cornets in A♭
1 cornet in A♭ and B♭
2 french horns in E♭
1 valve trumpet in E♭
1 alto trombone
1 tenor trombone
1 bass trombone
1 ophicleide
tympani

Other music in the same series calls for similar instruments, but standing in different keys: in No. 12 (*Gems from the Opera*) the soprano cornet (in D) is optional; the solo cornet is in A; the other two cornets are in G; the horns are in E♭/D and C/E; two trumpets (in C and D) are called for; and there are optional parts for two more horns in G.

The instrumentation of the successful and well-equipped Cyfarthfa Band has been described elsewhere.[13] In both the Childe arrangements and the Cyfarthfa part-books, the ophicleide part is far from being a simple bass line: it is wide-ranging and often rapidly moving, similar to the solo euphonium part in later brass band music.

INVENTIONS, HOPEFUL AND FRUITFUL

The valve, as we have seen, was invented by 1814, and within a few years not only were familiar instruments like the horn, trumpet, and trombone equipped with valves, but new instruments, such as the clavicor, were developed.[14] The importance of the invention was that it gave freedom to construct instruments with any desired bore profile, and consequently a variety of tone-qualities. Previous chromatic brass instruments had been limited to those of largely cylindrical bore with slides (trombone and slide trumpet), those of conical bore with tone holes (serpent and keyed bugle families), and the french horn when played in the upper part of its compass with the difficult technique of hand-stopping. With valves, medium- and wide-bore instruments could be built with intermediate profiles, partly cylindrical and partly 'conical'. The cornets, horns, euphoniums, and basses of the modern brass band are just such intermediate bore-profile instruments.

The original form of valve, the Stölzel valve, was a piston valve in which the piston casing itself was continued into the main tubing of the instrument at the lower end, the windway following right-angled bends inside the pistons.

---

[13] Trevor Herbert and Arnold Myers, 'Instruments of the Cyfarthfa Band', *Galpin Society Journal*, 41 (1988), 2–10.

[14] Arnold Myers, 'Technology since 1800', in T. Herbert and J. Wallace (eds.), *The Cambridge Companion to Brass Instruments* (Cambridge: Cambridge University Press, 1997), 115–30.

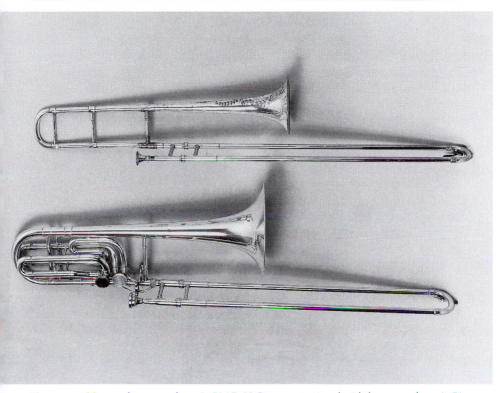

Figure 4.5. Narrow bore trombone in B♭ (G. H. Pace, *c*.1895) and wide bore trombone in B♭ with valves for F and G (Boosey & Hawkes, *c*.1980) as currently used for bass trombone parts.

Since the piston diameter was that of the bore of the instruments, the bends inside the pistons were necessarily abrupt. This form of valve was used on the early cornets (cornopeans) and clavicors in British brass bands until the late 1840s and early 1850s (see Figs. 4.3 and 4.4). It continued to be used in some cheaper imported cornets for a further thirty or forty years.

The rotary valve also seems to have been conceived by Stölzel and Blühmel in 1814, but was not developed until 1828 (when Blühmel patented a form with three windways in the rotor), and 1835, when Joseph Riedl in Vienna patented the form which has continued to the present day with two windways in the rotor. The bends inside the rotor are also right-angled, but less abrupt than in the Stölzel valve. Although widely used in Germany, Austria, and Italy, the rotary valve has been less popular in Britain. A small number of brass bands have used instruments imported from Germany and Austria; Joseph Higham in Manchester made some rather elegant rotary valve instruments. With the recent adoption of the B♭ + F trombone, however, most brass bands now boast one or two instruments with one rotary valve, or occasionally two: (see Fig. 4.5).

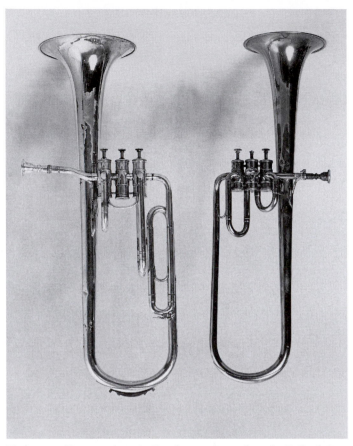

Figure 4.6. Tenor saxhorn in F and contralto saxhorn in B♭ (both Sax, imported by Distin, *c.*1845).

The Berlin valve was also a piston valve, conceived by Stölzel in 1827 and modified in 1835 by Wilhelm Wieprecht and Carl Wilhelm Moritz, with a wide-diameter piston. The windway goes straight through the piston when the piston is not depressed, but takes two right-angled turns when the valve is operated. The use of this valve in Britain only extended to some early instruments by Adolphe Sax in the late 1840s (see Fig. 4.6), and to some cornets by the maker Köhler of London.

The design of piston valve now used universally is that of the Parisian maker Étienne François Périnet (1839). The piston diameter is wider than that of the Stölzel valve, but narrower than that of the Berlin; the windways are compactly arranged with gentle curves in three dimensions, minimizing the disparity in resistance between natural and valved notes. The fine cornets by Courtois and Besson imported from Paris in the mid-1850s which established

Figure 4.7. Cornet in B♭ (Besson) presented to Alexander Owen as a prize at the 'First Sight' contest at Mossley in 1874. A typical cornet of the British brass band.

the model for the standard brass band cornet (Fig. 4.7) had Périnet valves. Since then, the vast majority of valved brass band instruments made at home or imported from abroad have used them (see Fig. 4.2).

The other continental valve designs, such as the Vienna valve, saw little service in Britain; the ingenious valves being developed in America at the same time were unknown. There were, however, some native inventions. In England, John Shaw patented 'swivel valves' in 1838.[15] In these, a rotating disk abutted a fixed disk. The main tubing of the instrument led to and from the fixed disk, and the rotating disk carried two loops of tubing, long and short. If the touchpiece of the valve was not depressed, the shorter loop of tubing connected the two parts of the main tubing; if the valve was operated the disk rotated so that the longer loop made the connection. The difference in the lengths of tubing in the loops was calculated to give the desired difference

[15] John Shaw's first patent for a valve design was No. 5013 of 7 Oct. 1824 for 'Transverse Spring Slides for Trumpets, Trombones, French Horns, Bugles . . .'. His disk valve patent was No. 7892 of 1 Dec. 1838 for 'Swivel or Pivot Plate' valves.

in total tube length, and hence the desired difference in pitch. Few Shaw valve instruments have survived. The idea was modified and marketed by Köhler in his 'Patent Lever' instruments, which were shown at the 1851 Great Exhibition.[16] In the Köhler adaptation, the rotating disk carried only two small knuckles of tubing which were much lighter and easier to rotate. These connected the two parts of the main tubing, either directly or via a fixed loop. Difficulty in maintaining airtightness is usually given as the reason for the discontinuation of these valves.

In 1862, George Samson patented his 'Finger-Slide' valves,[17] which showed some similarity to the earliest British trumpet valves of Pace, in that the casing in which the piston moved was extended into a windway at both ends, the touchpiece connecting with the piston through a slot in the side of the casing. Instruments with Samson valves, which were made by Rudall, Rose, Carte & Co., show a very high standard of workmanship, but the complexity must have led to both high initial expense and difficulty of maintenance. These must be regarded as the only commercially successful valve designs to have originated in Britain, and even this success was short-lived. Several 'Patent Lever' instruments, mostly cornets, and a handful of 'Finger-Slide' instruments survive.

Basses

Stölzel, extending the application of the valve from existing to completely new instruments, developed 12-foot F bass valve instruments in the 1820s.[18] Parallel developments took place elsewhere. In Paris, for example, the maker Guichard patented a valved ophicleide in 1832. The name *Bombardon* was given in Austria to relatively wide-bore valved basses from 1829. In Berlin, the enterprising bandmaster Wilhelm Wieprecht had already introduced valved instruments into Prussian military bands when, in 1835, he developed a wide-bore bass with Berlin valves in conjunction with the maker Carl Wilhelm Moritz, with the name *Bass-Tuba*.[19] Although some Austrian and German instruments were imported into Britain, it was not until the tuba was remodelled by Adolphe Sax as a member of his family of saxhorns in 1843, and subsequently promoted by Britain by the Distin family, that it was widely adopted by brass bands.

The basses are easier to carry on the march when wrapped round the player, the weight resting on the shoulder rather than held or strapped in front. These

---

[16] Köhler's 'Patent Lever' instruments are described in *The Crystal Palace and its Contents: An Illustrated Cyclopaedia of the Great Exhibition of 1851*, 285–6.

[17] George Robert Samson, 'Improvements in Valves or Cylinders for Wind Instruments', Patent No. 1245 of 29 Apr. 1862.

[18] Clifford Bevan, 'Tuba (i)', in *New Grove Dictionary of Musical Instruments*, iii. 664–8.

[19] Wilhelm Wieprecht, 'Die Chromatische Bass-Tuba', Prussian Patent No. 9121 of 12 Sept. 1835. Translated into English in Bevan, *Tuba Family*, 201–11.

'circular basses' were used by many brass bands in the latter half of the nineteenth century. (The term 'helicon' was not widely used in Britain at the time.) The American derivative of the circular bass, the sousaphone, has seen very little use in British brass bands.

Saxhorns

Adolphe Sax, the Belgian-born inventor and maker of wind instruments who worked in Paris from 1842, met with considerable opposition from rival makers when he took out a patent in 1843 covering the instruments which came to be known as saxhorns,[20] and became ruinously embroiled in litigation in defending the patent. He can, of course, be given credit for producing well-made instruments in a family of consistent design and graded sizes, but the members of the family were not new in themselves: comparable instruments had been in use in Germany and elsewhere for some years. He initially used the Berlin valves (see Fig. 4.6). Ignoring the extreme sizes, which were rarely used, the family consisted of: a soprano in 3-foot F or 3¼-foot E♭; a contralto in 4-foot C or 4½-foot B♭; a tenor in 6-foot F or 6½-foot E♭; a baritone in 8-foot C or 9-foot B♭; a bass in 8-foot C or 9-foot B♭; and contrabasses in 12-foot F or 13-foot E♭ (later also in 18-foot B♭). The bass was distinguished from the baritone by its larger bore. The tenor and baritone saxhorns differed little from the instruments already known variously as clavicors or althorns, a source of confusion in nomenclature that has persisted to this day. The contralto was somewhere between the relatively narrow-bore cornet and the wider-bore valved bugle (flugel horn).

The fact that British brass bands adopted the saxhorns so readily is largely due to Sax's association with the Distin family, stemming from their meeting in Paris in 1844,[21] and the promotion of Sax's instruments by the Distins in Britain. The Distin family enjoyed a popularity and esteem in Britain in the mid-nineteenth century with which only that of the Mortimer family in the twentieth century can be compared, and their agency in London for Sax instruments was highly influential. Saxhorns were marketed by Henry Distin from 1845. When, five years later, he started making similar instruments, Sax appointed Jullien as his London agent. The adoption of saxhorns by the brass bands of Britain was remarkable in its rapidity: the prize-winning band at the well-documented Burton Constable contest of 1845[22] was already using several. The Mossley Temperance Band purchased a full set of saxhorns in 1853, and won the first prize at the Belle Vue contest that year. Many bands

---

[20] French Patents cited in Malou Haine, *Adolphe Sax (1814–1894): Sa vie, son œuvre et ses instruments de musique* (Brussels: Éditions de l'Université de Bruxelles, 1980), 196–7.

[21] Adam Carse, 'Adolphe Sax and the Distin Family', *Music Review*, 6 (1945), 194–201.

[22] Enderby Jackson, 'Origin and Promotion of Brass Band Contests', *Musical Opinion and Music Trade Review* (1 Nov. 1896), 101–2.

took names such as 'Hawick Saxhorn Band', even if they retained trombones and ophicleides in addition to the Sax model instruments.

After a time, similar instruments by other makers were frequently called 'saxhorns'. The tenor horns (or simply 'horns') and baritones of the present-day brass band are tenor and baritone saxhorns. The bass saxhorn was replaced by the very similar euphonium, and the contrabasses, alternatively known as bombardons in bands (and tubas in orchestras) are now, in brass band parlance, merely 'basses', E♭ or BB♭ ('double Bs').

The Euphonium

The fact that the term 'bass saxhorn' or 'B♭ bass' gave way to the Austrian name, *Euphonium* or *Euphonion*, for virtually the same instrument as that developed by F. Sommer in 1843[23] is probably due partly to the attractiveness of the word, and partly to the role played by the instrument, which, like that of the ophicleide latterly, was not to play the bass of the harmony, but to provide an independent melodic line at tenor pitch. Like the ophicleide, the euphonium has a wide compass and is capable of virtuoso performance. It contributes much to the characteristic rich sound of the full brass band.

The Flugel Horn

The keyed bugle was more rapidly replaced by valved bugles in German-speaking countries than in Britain. Even when the keyed bugle was no longer used, it was not always replaced in brass bands except by cornets. The desire for an alternative tone-colour at the pitch of the principal melody line led to the adoption of the *Flügelhorn*, the name for the valved bugle prevalent in Austria, rather than the contralto saxhorn. Although the Distin family quintet appeared to have been using a flugel horn in 1845, it was only widely taken up by bands in the 1860s. In the 1870s, some bands appear to have used two or three flugel horns, but the present-day complement of one soon prevailed. It has never had the importance in Britain that it has in Austrian bands, and even if there were two or three in a brass band in the 1870s, they mostly doubled two or three of the cornet parts. The single 'flugel' in a brass band has usually doubled the principal or 'repiano' cornet line in the tuttis and contributes its own occasional solo, though in modern scoring it can equally be grouped with the horns or be given an independent part.

THE PATTERN OF MANUFACTURE AND IMPORT 1845–1873

When all-brass bands arrived, there were a number of British makers who were capable of producing the instruments required. The firms of Pace, Percival,

---

[23] Bevan, *Tuba Family*, 90–100.

Key, Greenhill, Roe, Smith, Wigglesworth, Metzler, and Sandbach produced high-quality instruments from their workshops. Some of their work has survived in museum collections. The expanding market also absorbed a flood of imported instruments (especially the cornopeans which were needed in large numbers) mostly from France and Germany. Often British dealers would stamp their own name on these imported instruments.[24] Many of these imports were very cheap compared with the hand-crafted British models, though some high-quality instruments from firms such as Halary and Sax were sold in Britain.

After acting as agent for Sax for five years, Henry Distin decided that he could more profitably make instruments, and set up his own workshop in 1850. In 1868 he sold his thriving business to Boosey & Co. for £9,700, though the name Distin was retained for trading purposes for several years. Other makers[25] who commenced manufacture of brass band instruments in mid-century were Köhler & Son (active throughout); William Brown (from 1851); Rudall, Rose, Carte & Co. (already making woodwind, they added brass on joining with Key & Co. *c.*1857); F. Besson (from 1857, though a related firm was making from 1837 in Paris); George Butler (from 1858 as a branch of a Dublin firm); and Rivière & Hawkes, later Hawkes & Son (already repairing, they added manufacture in 1875). All these were in London; the principal provincial makers of brass band instruments were Joseph Higham (from 1842) in Manchester, and James Gisborne (from *c.*1839) in Birmingham.

Supply and Use of Instruments 1845–1873

Very useful evidence of the kinds and numbers of instruments being used by the leading brass bands in the early 1860s has survived. Over eighty forms used by bands entering contests are preserved in the archive of Enderby Jackson papers formerly in the care of Raymond Ainscoe.[26] Since only bands reasonably certain of their balance of instruments would enter a contest at the national level, we can assume that the instrumentation of these bands represents the 'state of the art' at that time.

The thirty-four surviving forms from the 1860 Crystal Palace contest show that the average band (eighteen players) consisted of:

[24] An example is a german silver cornopean in the Edinburgh University Collection of Historic Musical Instruments, which is inscribed 'Sold by M. Corcoran, Dublin' and also bears the mark of Metzler (London). The design and material of construction, together with the inscriptions on the tuning-slide, shank, and crooks (B for B♭, Es for E♭) indicate that the instrument was imported from Germany by Metzler.

[25] William Waterhouse, *The New Langwill Index: A Dictionary of Musical Wind-Instrument Makers and Inventors* (London: Tony Bingham, 1993).

[26] The Enderby Jackson papers, formerly in the collection of Raymond Ainscoe of Kirkby Lonsdale, are at present in the care of the author. A partial list is given in Roy Newsome, *Brass Roots: A Hundred Years of Brass Bands and Their Music (1836–1936)* (Aldershot: Ashgate, 1998), 223–4.

1–2 sopranos, mostly in D♭, but some in E♭
5 cornets, mostly in A♭, but some in B♭
0–1 alto saxhorns in A♭
2–3 tenor saxhorns or alt horns, mostly in D♭, but some in E♭
1–2 baritones, mostly in A♭, but some in B♭
1 tenor trombone, mostly in C, but some in B♭
1 bass trombone, mostly in G
1–2 ophicleides, mostly in C, but some in B♭
1 Sax bass or euphonium, mostly in B♭ or A♭, some in C
2 contrabass saxhorns or bombardons, mostly in E♭, but some in D♭

There was a scattering of soprano saxhorns, alto trombones, flugel horns, clarinets, trumpets, french horns, and BB♭ contrabasses. In each band there was usually a mixture of instruments from the E♭/B♭ and the D♭/A♭ dispositions of valved instruments, and the F/C/G and E♭/B♭/F dispositions of trombones, though some maintained a 'purer' instrumentation. One band, the Darlington Temperance Brass Band, consisted entirely of instruments standing in natural keys: soprano in D; six cornets in A; alt horn in E; two alt horns in D; valve tenor trombone in C; baritone in B♮; euphonium in A; two ophicleides in C; and two bombardons in D.

We cannot be certain to what extent the valved instruments were built in keys such as D♭ and A♭. Most of the surviving instruments are in F, E♭, C, or B♭, and we can surmise that these instruments were commonly used with crooks, alternative tuning-slides or tuning-slide extensions. The fact that it is mostly the smaller instruments which are in the D♭/A♭ disposition would support this: it could only be a nuisance to deal with a crook or an extended tuning-slide for a euphonium or a bombardon. Where crooks or tuning-slide extensions were used, we would expect it to be for reasons of tone-colour preference in the case of cornets (cornopeans), and in order to extend the range downwards in the case of bass instruments.

Several bands gave the names of side drummer, bass drummer, or both, and sometimes a cymbal player: the form of the Darwen Temperance Band, Lancashire, listed 'Drummer, but will not bring his drum of course'. As was to be the case for over a hundred years, percussion instruments were not allowed in contest playing. However, the 1862 entry form for the South Yorkshire Railway Company's Brass Band included 'Bass drum, of course will be required for street playing', perhaps indicating that the band would march from the railway station to the Crystal Palace.

There are twenty-three surviving entry forms for the 1861 Crystal Palace contest. The average size of the bands was slightly smaller (seventeen players). There were relatively fewer ophicleides. One band, however, still sported a keyed bugle: the Wakefield Foresters commenced their form with 'Bugle in D♭', and went on to include three ophicleides in C. The bombardon player of the

Mossley Amateur Brass Band near Stalybridge is cited on the form as being the 'first public player on a four-keyed bombardon'. If this was in fact the case, he was the forerunner of many future E♭ bass players in bands where either one or both E♭ basses were equipped with a fourth valve. The entry form of W. L. Marriner's Band (also the Band of the 35th York Rifle Volunteer Corps), Keighley, listed a unique instrument, the double-slide contrabass trombone in B♭ which has been described by this author elsewhere.[27] One would dismiss this invention as an aberration were it not for the fact that its player actually won the prize for the best bass player in this contest.

The thirteen surviving forms from the 1862 Crystal Palace contest show still fewer ophicleides, but half the bands now use flugel horns. W. L. Marriner's Private Brass Band listed two flugel horns (they entered none in 1861), and the E♭ bass sonorophone which was their prize for the best bass player the previous year. The sonorophones were a family of bell-forward rotary-valve instruments patented in 1856 by James Waddell, and marketed by Metzler & Co.[28] The circular coils of the main tubing are held in front of the player like a steering-wheel. They can occasionally be seen in photographs of bands in the late nineteenth century. In terms of sound-quality and response to the player, they did not differ markedly from the other valved instruments used in brass bands. The Allendale Saxhorn Band boasted valved trombones in E♭, B♭, and F. Overall, about one in ten trombones were listed in these forms as valve trombones: the actual proportion may have been a little higher, since none is listed specifically as a slide trombone.

The five forms surviving from the 1863 Crystal Palace contest, and the seven surviving from the Order of Druids' Brass Band Contest at the Royal Park Garden, Leeds, in the same year, show the same trends continuing. Only one ophicleide is mentioned, and trumpets have disappeared altogether.

THE BUSINESS OF INSTRUMENT MAKING

Improvements in the design of valves, and refinement of the design of instruments, led to the models which have continued to this day: the cornet, the flugel, saxhorns, euphonium, and the basses. After the last of Enderby Jackson's Grand National Crystal Palace Contests in 1863, the annual contest at Belle Vue, Manchester, was the most prestigious and influential. Following the incident at the 1873 contest in which a Black Dyke euphonium player played trombone solos on a valve trombone, the rules were tightened. Valve trombones were excluded, and our present-day band instrumentation can be said to have crystallized from this date. Of course, it took some time for the rules of other contests to follow, and the instrumentation of non-contesting bands

[27] Arnold Myers, 'A Slide Tuba?', *Galpin Society Journal*, 42 (1989), 127–8.
[28] George Metzler and James Waddell, 'Improvements in the Construction and Formation of Valve Musical Instruments', Patent No. 1836 of 12 Aug. 1858.

has never been standardized. We can safely assume that some small village bands carried on using valve trombones, clarinets, and, no doubt, ophicleides, throughout the century.

The brass instruments specified by the major contests have been as follows.[29]

1 soprano cornet in E♭
8 cornets in B♭
1 flugel horn in B♭
3 tenor saxhorns ('tenor horns') in E♭
2 baritones in B♭
2 tenor trombones in B♭
1 bass trombone
2 euphoniums in B♭
2 basses in E♭
2 basses in B♭

This gives a total of twenty-four players; sometimes one extra player has been allowed who would double one of the parts: a fourth trombone or, more usually, a further cornet. The numbers of each kind of instrument have been determined by the repertoire of test pieces rather than the contest rules. The body of published compositions and arrangements for brass band has both grown more rapidly and been musically more satisfactory as a result of being written for a standard combination. The conventional instrumentation has four parts for the B♭ cornets: solo, second, third, and repiano. The 'solo' part is played by four cornets (usually), unless a single player is specified. The 'repiano' part, often shared with the flugel horn, has an independent line on occasion, but frequently doubles the solo cornet line. (There is no repiano part in Salvation Army scoring.) The tenor horns and baritones have separate parts for each player. The euphoniums and basses have only one part each, occasionally marked 'divisi'.

Although the kinds and numbers of brass instruments in the full contesting band have not changed since the mid-1870s, the instruments themselves have evolved, and the sound of a full brass band today is noticeably different from the sound of bands to be heard in early recordings. In general, the modern band is louder and thicker, the late Victorian band brighter, lighter, and crisper.[30] The evolution of the instruments of the brass band has followed

---

[29] 'National Brass Band Championships of Great Britain, Rules', in Allan Littlemore (ed.), *The Rakeway Brass Band Yearbook 1987* (Hollington: Rakeway Music, 1987), 419–22.

[30] Some early recordings of brass bands are preserved in the EMI Music Archives, such as Gramophone 018 238c, Black Dike Mills Band, *Gems from Sullivan's Operas* No. 3 of July 1903, and Gramophone GC-2-28, Besses o' th' Barn Band, *Henry VIII Morris Dance* (Edward German) of May 1904. The recording methods, however, do not allow a fair assessment of the sound quality of these bands. Clearer impressions of the sound of the brass band playing at high pitch on narrow-bore instruments are given by recordings of the 1930s, such as Regal Zonophone MR 2244, Foden's Motor Works Band, *Kenilworth Suite* (Arthur Bliss) of Dec. 1936.

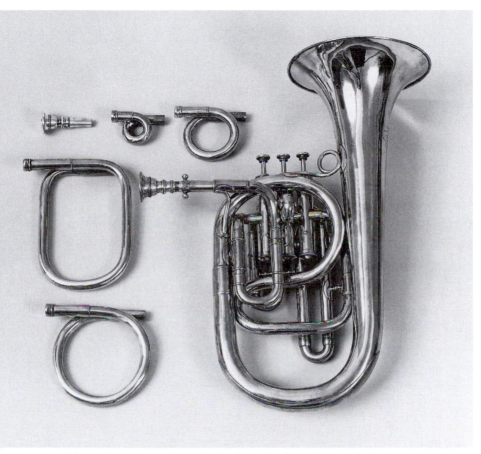

Figure 4.8. Tenor tuba (tenor saxhorn) in F with crooks for E, E♭, D, and D♭ (Henry Distin, *c.*1855).

the evolution of the instruments of the British orchestra, and the overall sound quality has changed similarly.

Mass Production

In general in the history of musical instruments, the invention of successful new instruments leads to experimentation with ensemble and the formation of new musical groupings. If these in turn are successful, a repertoire is established, and makers find that there is no demand for new kinds of instruments, only for improvements in the existing ones. Although instruments basically similar in bore profile to saxhorns (such as Distin's 'Tubas' (Fig. 4.8), 'Ventil Horns', and 'Tenor Cor', Metzler's 'Sonorophones', and Courtois's 'Koenig

Horns') were introduced, none gained wide acceptance in brass bands, though individual bands certainly used them here and there to play tenor horn parts. Besson's 'Cornophones' (a family of instruments similar to Wagner tubas) might have made a useful contribution to the instrumentation of the brass band, but their launch in the 1890s was fifty years too late for this.

In the 1870s and 1880s, the number of brass bands was increasing dramatically, and the market for sales was better than at any time before or since. Nearly every community seemed to support a band, not necessarily of a particularly high standard, so there was a demand for inexpensive instruments. Also, the proliferation of contests fostered an increase in the number of more competent bands which could and did afford instruments of better tone-quality, dynamic range, compass, intonation, and response to the player.

In the second half of the nineteenth century, most of the instruments for brass bands were made by the larger firms—those capable of mass production such as Boosey, Hawkes, Besson, and Higham. Imports continued, still mostly of cheap models, but including some fine instruments such as the Viennese instruments used by the Cyfarthfa Band, and the Courtois instruments imported from Paris by S. A. Chappell. Makers had a vested interest in the brass band movement, and regularly gave presentation instruments to prizewinners in contests.

The advertisements of the leading makers were quick to enumerate the prize-winning bands using their instruments after each major contest. Gisborne & Co. of Birmingham claimed in 1905[31] that its instruments were used by Besses o' th' Barn, Black Dyke, Kingston Mills, Irwell Springs, and Wingates, among others. Besson & Co. claimed in 1907[32] that bands playing its instruments had won three of the last four Belle Vue contests (also citing Wingates).

The number of makers of instruments was also at its highest at the end of the nineteenth century. The largest firms employed considerable workforces.[33] In 1890, Besson & Co. employed 131 hands at its Euston Road workshops, turning out 100 brass instruments per week, and had the addresses of over 10,000 British brass bands on its books. In 1895, Hawkes & Son moved its workshops from Leicester Square to 3,500 square feet of new premises in Denman Street, Piccadilly Circus; the company was then employing nearly a hundred men. In 1924 it established the factory at Edgware now operated by Boosey & Hawkes. In 1875, Boosey & Co. appears to have set a limit of 100 hours for a

[31] Gisborne & Co. Ltd., advertisement, *British Bandsman* (22 July 1905), 338–9.
[32] *Besson's Brass Band Budget* (1907), 8.
[33] Algernon Rose, *Talks with Bandsmen, a Popular Handbook for Brass Instrumentalists* (London: William Rider, [1895]; facsimile edn. London: Bingham, 1995). This book gives fascinating, if somewhat anecdotal, accounts of the leading makers of brass band instruments and their specialities: Gautrot, Silvani & Smith, George Potter & Co., Rudall Carte & Co., George Butler, Besson & Co., Courtois & Mille, Brown of Kennington, J. Higham, W. D. Cubitt, Boosey & Co., William Hillyard, Charles Mahillon & Co., and Hawkes & Son.

workman to make an instrument.[34] Peter Robinson, the son-in-law of Joseph Higham and a proprietor of the firm of J. Higham, was, according to different accounts, employing either seventy or over ninety men in 1892. The Salvation Army made instruments (for its own use) from 1889 to 1972. It established a factory in St Albans in 1901, and turned out sixteen instruments a week.[35] However, no British firm was as large as that of Gautrot in France, which employed 560 in the 1880s.

These larger firms produced all the brass band instruments in a range of qualities, typically 'Class A', 'Class B', and 'Class C', the cheapest being half the price of the top models. Silver-plating was an optional extra, generally available from the 1870s, and elaborate engraving of the bell (occasionally the whole instrument) was yet another extra. Not surprisingly, most of the instruments surviving from this period are silver-plated, Class A instruments of quality: we can safely surmise that the large numbers of cheaper and unplated instruments that were sold have long since deteriorated beyond worthwhile repair—today, cheap, 'educational' instruments hardly last five years. The widespread use of silver-plated instruments gave rise to some brass bands taking the name 'Silver Band'. This little ostentation did not signify any difference at all in instrumentation.

Improvements

The improvements in the instruments themselves were real, if not quite as important as the makers claimed. A clear passage of the windway through the valves was the aim of numerous designs.[36] Distin's 'Equisonant Pistons' and Higham's 'Clear Bore' pistons were typical of the valve designs of the more expensive models.

Lightness of valve-action and minimized length of travel were also design objectives. In 1907, Boosey & Co. introduced 'Solbron', and later 'Silbron', valve pistons with special bronze which (very effectively) reduced friction. From 1922 the same firm produced 'N. V. A.' (New Valve Action) valves for cornets, in which depressing the piston extends a spring. Most cornets have top-sprung valves in which the spring is compressed when the valve is operated; most larger instruments are bottom-sprung, also with compression springs. These minor modifications were typical of many with which manufacturers hoped to increase their market share.

---

[34] The Archives of Messrs Boosey & Hawkes, London, contain records of instruments made by Distin & Co. and Boosey & Co. at the end of the 19th cent., giving workmen's names and the hours spent on each instrument. (Per Lloyd P. Farrar.)

[35] Brindley Boon, *Play the Music, Play! the Story of Salvation Army Bands*, 2nd edn. (London: Salvationist Publishing and Supplies, 1978), 172–5.

[36] John Webb, 'Designs for Brass in the Public Record Office', *Galpin Society Journal*, 38 (1985), 48–54.

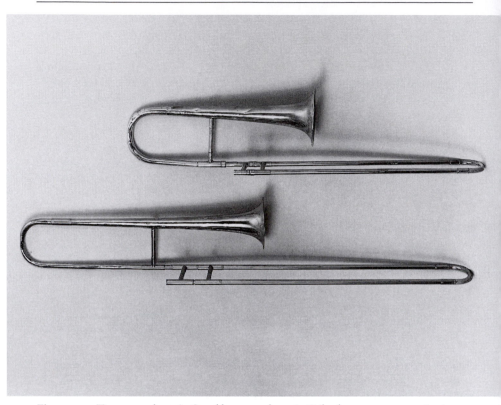

Figure 4.9. Tenor trombone in C and bass trombone in G (both anonymous, *c.*1845).

At the end of the century, cornets were still supplied with shanks for playing in B♭ and A (sometimes also with a crook for A♭). Though most bands were using cornets in B♭, the cornet was widely used orchestrally, with the parts frequently written for cornet in A. 'Bayley's Acoustic Cornet' of 1862 (made by Kohler) was one of the first to incorporate a fixed mouthpipe—it was supplied with tuning-slides of different lengths instead of terminal crooks. Rudall Carte's 1903 patent instrument[37] had a fixed mouthpipe, and a change to A was effected by pulling out an auxiliary tuning-slide. Other makers, such as Besson, provided a 'quick-change' rotary valve. The fixed mouthpipe for brass band cornets surprisingly only became standard after the Second World War.

The first brass bands appear to have used trombones based on German, medium-bore models. The tenor in C at Cyfarthfa Castle Museum, Merthyr Tydfil (Fig. 4.9) has a bore of 11.7 mm descending, and 11.9 mm ascending; the tenor in C by Wigglesworth at Cliffe Castle Museum, Keighley (probably

[37] Arnold Myers and Frank Tomes, 'PCB Cornets and Webster Trumpets: Rudall Carte's Patent Conical Bore Brasswind', *Historic Brass Society Journal*, 7 (1995), 107–22.

imported from Germany) has a bore of 10.9 mm descending and 12.6 mm ascending. The G bass in Fig. 4.9 has a bore of 12.5 mm in both inner slide-legs, and a G bass by John Green of London (*c*.1835) in the Edinburgh University Collection of Historic Musical Instruments has a bore of 12.9 mm. By the 1870s, the narrow-bore French model had become as universally used in brass bands as it had in orchestras. These trombones were often played with a deep funnel-shaped mouthpiece rather than the wide-cupped profile now used.

The B♭ tenor in Fig. 4.5 by G. H. Pace and the standard instruments of Hawkes and Besson have a bore of 11.4 mm. The tenor trombones made by the Salvation Army were slightly narrower at 10.8 mm descending, 11.0 mm ascending. The highly popular Besson Class A bass trombone in G of the 1890s has a descending bore 12.0 mm, 12.4 mm ascending. These figures can be compared with the 13.9 mm bore of the Conn 8H B♭ tenor model as a present-day point of reference. The effect of this use of narrow-bore trombones, which continued until the 1950s, was to emphasize the contrast between trombones on one hand, and baritones and euphoniums on the other, and to exploit the vocal qualities of the instrument in quiet passages, and the crispness of attack of narrow-bore trombones in loud passages. The forceful attack possible on a trombone with half the cross-sectional area of the modern instrument made a valued contribution to the sound of a band, particularly in contest playing where percussion was not used.

The most interesting developments in instrument design concerned the euphonium and basses. These developments were the forms of compensation applied to valved instruments by Boosey & Co. and Besson & Co. The need for these compensating systems arises from the fact that a valve adds a fixed length of tubing to the instrument. Two valves which separately add the correct lengths of tubing will, when operated simultaneously, add a length which falls short of that required to sound in tune. With a large instrument such as an E♭ bass, if the first valve allows a D♭ to be played in tune, and the third valve allows a C to be played in tune, the first and third valves together will cause a B♭ that is noticeably sharp, and actually needs a further 10 cm or so of tubing to be added to bring it into tune. On instruments with a fourth valve, the fourth valve will give a B♭ in tune, but there are further intonation problems if the fourth valve is used in combination with any of the basic three. The problem is most acute with the euphoniums and the basses, since these instruments are frequently used in the lowest parts of their compass which require the valves to be used in combination, and the moving in and out of tuning-slides by the player in the course of performance is not practical.

One solution, offered by Higham and Besson, was to make instruments with five valves, offering the player a choice of fingering for many notes and allowing a reasonable in-tune option for any given note. Although economical, five-valve instruments were not widely used in bands, though a number of professional tuba players did use them. The compensating system, however, gives improved intonation without the player having to learn new fingerings. In a three-valve compensating instrument, the tubing brought into play by the third valve is actually led back through the first and second valves; if the first and third valves, say, are operated together, an additional loop of tubing attached to the first valve is brought into play. In the case of the Eʙ bass, this will give the required 10 cm. Brass band valved instruments with this system of 'Compensating Pistons' have been made by Boosey & Co. (and, latterly, Boosey & Hawkes) since 1874. Boosey's works manager, David James Blaikley, has been given credit for inventing the system.[38] It was not, however, a new invention, though this was the first commercially successful application. Hawkes & Son and Besson & Co. also made a number of instruments with compensating valves, presumably under licence, before merging with Boosey & Co.

Besson & Co. made numerous brass band instruments with 'Enharmonic Valves', a system which it patented in 1903[39] (see Fig. 4.10), but which, again, was not actually new. It is superior to compensating valves in that the windway is not required to pass through each valve more than once. In a three-valve 'enharmonic' instrument, the mouthpipe leads into the third valve. If the third valve is not operated, the windway leads through the first and second valves, which act in the usual way, back through the third valve to the bell. If the third valve is operated, the windway is led through the first and second valves by a different route including a third valve tuning-slide, and in going through different passages in the first and second valves, will be directed through separate, longer, loops of tubing if either the first or the second valve is operated simultaneously with the third. (This is the principle of the 'full double' french horn.) The fact that a three-valve instrument with 'enharmonic' valves has two completely different valve-loops, each with its own tuning-slide, makes for a rather heavy instrument. A four-valve 'enharmonic' instrument is heavier again than a four-valve compensating instrument—this is the only reason that can be put forward to explain why Boosey's compensating valves have continued to be made and Besson's 'enharmonic' valves have not.

Hawkes & Son, their sales of euphoniums probably suffering from the competition, brought out four-valve instruments under the appellation 'The Dictor'. These instruments employ a simplified form of compensation, in which the tubing brought into play by the third valve passes through the fourth valve; if the fourth and third valves are operated together, an additional loop of tubing attached to the fourth valve is brought into play.

Boosey's 'Compensating Pistons' and Besson's 'Enharmonic Valves' were applied to all valved instruments except the Eʙ soprano cornet. With the cornet and the flugel horn, the extra cost and the added weight led to a limited uptake by bands; with the tenor horn and baritone, the relative importance

---

[38] D. J. Blaikley, Patent No. 4618 of 14 Nov. 1878.
[39] Besson & Co., Patent No. 12,849 of 12 May 1904.

Figure 4.10. Euphonium with four valves, 'Enharmonic Patent' (Besson & Co., 1911).

of the lower tessitura similarly limited adoption. Virtually all the best bands, however, adopted compensating euphoniums and basses. It is probably a tribute to the higher musical standards being attained by British brass bands in the 1870s and later that the subtle refinement in intonation was thought to justify the considerably greater expense of these complicated instruments.

In recent years, cornets and flugels have been equipped with 'triggers' which extend the first and third tuning-slides manually. These permit a player to correct the intonation of notes which require the valves to be used in combination, without adding significantly to the weight of the instrument.

Mergers

After the First World War, the depression hit the instrument trade, and the smaller makers only survived on repair work. Boosey & Co. and Hawkes & Son merged in 1930, and were joined in 1948 by Besson & Co., and later by Rudall Carte & Co., which, however, had ceased making brass instruments in the 1930s. J. Higham was taken over by Messrs Mayers and Harrison in 1930, and ceased manufacturing soon after.

In the inter-war period, which saw the most important additions to the brass band repertoire, there were no significant developments in instrument design. Mutes, however, were increasingly used. In the *Severn Suite*, Elgar wrote for muted euphoniums—a request not complied with at the time. Straight or pear-shaped cornet and trombone mutes of fibre or metal were the most commonly used. The modern repertoire requires mutes for all the brass instruments in the band, and often several different kinds (such as cup and harmon), as well as straight for the cornets and trombones.

MORE RECENT CHANGES

The instrumentation of British brass bands has remained remarkably consistent since it crystallized in the late nineteenth century. There was a practice in the 1870s of using up to three flugel horns, so that the second and third cornet parts were doubled by flugels as well as the ripieno (repiano in brass band parlance) cornet part. At the same time there were often four tenor horns.

The Salvation Army bands have never been restricted by contest regulations, though the music published for full band by the Salvation Army (and, as is pointed out in Chapter 5, until very recently not available for use outside the Army) has closely followed the instrumentation of 'outside' bands. Many of the larger Salvation Army bands, however, have been considerably larger than the contesting bands, with much doubling of parts. In these circumstances, the use of more than one flugel horn has been common, and there is often a specially written part for a fourth trombone.[40] The Salvation Army has also regularly published music for a smaller band. The 'Triumph' series is arranged for a reduced instrumentation, flugel doubling second cornet, and omitting third tenor horn. The 'Unity' series was arranged in four parts, with a choice of instrument for each part, and percussion; in recent years, arrangements have been published with an independent fifth part for euphonium. These arrangements can also be played by full bands.

There have been frequent suggestions that brass bands should incorporate saxophones, french horns, and trumpets, etc. In the early years of the twentieth

---

[40] Many passages in brass band compositions published by the Salvation Army in their 'Festival' and 'General' series are scored for a quartet of trombones. There is not a separate printed part for fourth trombone—the first part is divided and requires two players.

century, a number of bands (especially in the Salvation Army) did actually use up to four saxophones.[41] A change of instrumentation today would involve rearrangement (or abandonment) of the very substantial repertoire on which bands draw. Brass bands, like military bands, have made use of echo cornets, post horns, xylophones, and other instruments, in a solo capacity.

Low Pitch

In the 1960s, brass bands were persuaded to make a change which, in retrospect, could have been made forty years earlier, but even so was accepted reluctantly by many bands. It was announced in April 1964[42] that the instrument makers (that is, Boosey & Hawkes and the Salvation Army) were to cease making high-pitch instruments, and that, as a consequence, in course of time, all British brass bands would have to change to low pitch.

As far as we can tell from surviving instruments, the earliest brass bands probably played at a pitch not far from the modern international standard, A_4 = 440 Hz. As pitch-levels rose in the middle of the nineteenth century, the brass bands apparently kept in line with orchestral and other instrumental practice, which settled at 'Old Philharmonic' pitch, A_4 = 452.5 Hz. To reduce strain on operatic and oratorio singers, lower pitch standards were adopted by professional orchestras towards the end of the century, quickly followed by amateur orchestras. British Services military bands changed to low pitch, A_4 = 439 Hz, in 1929, leaving British and Commonwealth brass bands as the only sizeable area of musical activity at high pitch. Many bands did not participate in performances alongside orchestras or organs. Some that did used alternative tuning-slides to bring their instruments down to low pitch. The present standard was agreed internationally in 1939.

By the 1960s, band instrument makers were producing more instruments at international pitch for export than at high pitch for the home market, and put forward reasons of economy to justify their decision to cease making high-pitch instruments. Once it was clear that the change was inevitable, some bands had all their instruments converted by fixed extensions to the tuning-slides (damaging both appearance and intonation), and some bought new sets of instruments, while others used both means in part. One of the first bands to change was York Citadel Salvation Army, who were playing at low pitch by July 1964. The International Staff Band of the Salvation Army was in low pitch by the autumn of that year. There were complaints from traditionalists that the sound of the brass band would lose brilliance in lowering the pitch.

---

[41] Alf Hailstone, *The* British Bandsman *Centenary Book: A Social History of Brass Bands* (Baldock: Egon, 1987), cites contemporary reports of short-lived attempts to introduce saxophones into brass bands.

[42] Eric Ball, ' "Low" Pitch for Brass Bands: Definite Plans at Last', *British Bandsman* (4 Apr. 1964), 1, and Dean Goffin, 'Advantages are Incalculable', *British Bandsman* (4 Apr. 1964), 2.

They may have been right—it was the orchestral string players, seeking brilliance, who had raised the pitch a century previously—but the difference in tone-quality due to the change in pitch has been less marked than that due to the adoption of wide-bore instruments. By the end of the 1960s, most of the best contesting bands had changed to low pitch, and those bands remaining at high pitch did so out of inertia rather than conviction.

Although the decision of the manufacturers in 1964 to cease production of high-pitch instruments must have resulted in economies in production costs, it made brass bands a marketing target for American and Japanese makers, who were not slow in seizing the opportunity. In November 1964, Barratts of Manchester Ltd. ran an advertisement which read: 'Have you realised that the most exciting advantage of the change to low pitch is that you and your band can now, for the first time, experience the joys of playing a famous Conn instrument?'[43] Before long, medium-wide and wide-bore American trombones were being used by leading bands. Cheap instruments have been imported from Eastern Europe and China ever since. Makers such as Yamaha (Japan) and Courtois (France) now offer the whole range of brass band instruments. In England, Brass Band Instruments Ltd. (subsequently Sterling Musical Instruments Ltd.) started making band instruments, adding to the keen competition which prevails now, as it did a century ago.

Percussion

Bass drum and side drum have always been used by brass bands on the march, and often cymbals also. The change from rope-tension bass drums as deep as they were wide, to shallow drums with rod tension, has been very gradual, starting in the middle of the nineteenth century, and only completed in the middle of the twentieth. Bands needed to buy a new bass drum only if the old one was badly damaged, not to help win a contest. Similarly, deep rope-tension 'Guards pattern' side drums and shallow rod-tension drums were both in use over the same period. For concert work, the band's drummer could until recently make do with little more—or could use a small kit including timpani, tambourines, castanets, triangle, and others, especially if the band indulged in 'novelty' numbers. There have been no percussion instruments peculiar to brass bands.

For years, composers had written parts for percussion instruments in contest test pieces as well as in 'entertainment' music. *Journey into Freedom* (Eric Ball, 1967) is typical in calling for side drum, bass drum, cymbal, triangle, and tambourine, with optional timpani; but these parts were only played in concert performance, and the music makes sense without them. Similarly,

[43] Barratts of Manchester Ltd., 'Low-down on Low Pitch' (advertisement), *British Bandsman* (14 Nov. 1964), 5.

Vaughan Williams included a celeste in *Variations for Brass Band* (1957), knowing that the part would not be heard at all at the National Championships for which the work was commissioned. The first major contest to allow percussion was at Belle Vue in 1969. The test piece for this event, Gilbert Vinter's *Spectrum*, is scored for the usual brass instruments plus bongos, claves, wood block, tambourine, triangle, cymbal, side drum, and bass drum. Like most subsequent test pieces, it is less than satisfactory if the percussion parts are omitted. The percussion instruments now called for in test pieces for top-section bands include virtually the full complement normally carried by the orchestral percussion section, and occasional imports from dance band drum kits and the Latin American tradition.

Wide-Bore Instruments

Having followed orchestras down in pitch, bands followed in the adoption of wider bore instruments in the 1970s. The difference in sound and response to the player is most striking in the case of the trombone, but noticeable from E♭ soprano to BB♭ bass. During the Second World War, production of instruments ceased as the factories were required for war work. When production of instruments resumed, the export market was given priority, and instruments were only available on the home market from May 1946.[44] From this time, medium-bore trombones were offered (before the war, their main use in Britain was in dance bands). The Besson 'Academy' model and the medium-bore Boosey & Hawkes 'Imperial' model were widely adopted by brass bands. Apart from student models, all the instruments now made for brass bands are wide-bore versions of traditional designs, capable of great power but requiring to be 'well-filled' by the players to achieve the richness of sound characteristic of a good brass band.

For a short period in the 1970s, some bands adopted the bass trombone in G with a valve lowering the pitch to D (comparable with the F valve on a B♭ trombone) that had been the British orchestral bass trombone of the 1930s and 1940s. By the end of the 1970s, the wide-bore B♭ + F trombone (sometimes with a second valve giving G, E, or D—see Fig. 4.5) had replaced the traditional G bass trombone, which has never evolved into a wide-bore version. Medium-wide and wide-bore B♭ + F trombones have also been used for tenor trombone parts in many bands.

It is ironic that brass bands should have adopted the instruments originally designed to allow symphony orchestras to fill concert halls seating thousands, some fifty to sixty years after the time when the bands could themselves attract audiences of thousands to their concerts.

[44] Boosey & Hawkes Ltd. advertisement, *British Bandsman* (4 May 1946), 3; Besson advertisement, *British Bandsman* (25 May 1946), 5.

Figure 4.11. BB♭ bass (Besson & Co., 1900), formerly used in Wombwell Town Band. This model of BB♭ bass was very widely used in brass bands from *c*.1880; some were still in use *c*.1990.

5

God's Perfect Minstrels:
The Bands of the Salvation Army

Trevor Herbert

Your temptation will be to play what is pleasing, what will bring out the music, what will impress the people with its charm—and with the ability of those who produce it. But beware! Let us have good music, but music which has a message in it. Tunes that whenever and wherever they are sung will bring God, and Calvary, and Eternity nearer.[1]

In January 1992, a press release was issued from the International Head-quarters of the Salvation Army in London: 'The Salvation Army, after more than a hundred years, is scrapping the regulation, which has prevented its instrumental music from being sold to, or performed by, non-Salvation Army musicians. For too long The Salvation Army has had a ghetto mentality when it comes to music.'[2] It went on to announce the abolition of all restrictions on the sale and consumption of Salvation Army music. This meant that, for the first time since the opening decade of the Army's existence, anyone was free to buy and perform music which the Salvation Army published, or for which it

Much of the research for this chapter was conducted at the International Heritage Centre of the Salvation Army in London (IHC), and at the American Heritage Centre (AHC) at the USA Headquarters in Alexandria, Va. I am especially grateful to the curators of these archives, Gordon Taylor and Susan Mitchem respectively, and to their colleagues, for the generous assistance which I received. I am particularly grateful to Gordon Taylor, who brought to my attention inaccuracies which would otherwise have gone unnoticed. Documents and data relevant to this chapter are given in Appendix 2.

[1] General William Booth in the *Local Officer* (Oct. 1897), 65–6.
[2] IHC Music Publishing/Publications Music Dept., file 5. Press release dated 22 Jan. 1992. The order was made effective from 1 Mar. 1992.

held the copyright. Previously, the Army had sold music only to its own members, who were themselves bound to play only Salvation Army music and use (where possible) other Salvation Army products. Such restrictions had prevailed since 1885, when a directive was issued from the Chief of Staff which instructed bands that 'henceforth Army bands must use only music published by the Salvation Army'.[3] The historic change of policy was, according to the *Salvationist* of January 1992, 'by inspiration of the Holy Spirit'.[4] In fact, more temporal considerations were also at the root of the change: copyright protection on some of the Army's most popular composers was due to expire within a couple of decades anyway, and the controllers of the Army's finances realized that it was in its interests to reap the benefits of an open market.

By 1992, the restriction may not have been as strictly observed as it had been a couple of decades earlier, but it was in place, and was intended to be kept. Salvationist Publishing and Supplies Ltd. (originally called the Trade Department; the S.P.&S. Ltd. name started being used in 1916/17) had been set up to serve Salvationists, and to ensure that they were protected in both practical and spiritual terms from the fickle whims of open capitalism. The Music Department was established in October 1883 to oversee all matters concerning the publishing of music. Its task was partly pragmatic, and partly doctrinal and censorial.[5] The Salvation Army movement needed a ready supply of music which was affordable and of high quality. Also, as the repertoire of music expanded, there were concerns that its development should, by its nature and tone, sustain the doctrinal principles upon which the Salvation Army was based. The notion that the character and practices of music could be prescribed by regulation came directly from the Army's founder. On the face of it, it is remarkable that the Salvation Army, one of the most practical and socially proactive religious denominations to have existed, should ever have ordained such a restricting and dogmatic maxim—let alone applied it for so long. This is a religious movement which swept aside every vestment and almost every morsel of traditional church ritual, in favour of direct evangelicalism and practical, expedient, social reform, and which pragmatically borrowed its tunes from sources as disparate as American gospel music, Romantic *Lieder*, vernacular folk song, and music hall. And yet, until the closing decade of the twentieth century, it sustained a rule which sought to prevent a note of Salvation Army music being blown by men or women who did not hold within

---

[3] General Order published in the *War Cry* (May 1885).

[4] *Salvationist* (25 Jan. 1992), 2.

[5] An Outfit Department was established at Headquarters for the supply of uniforms in 1881. There was already by this time a Book Department which supplied books and periodicals. These different operations eventually came under the remit of a more general Trade Department. The 1917 Yearbook was the first to be published under the imprimatur of the Salvationist Publishing and Supplies Ltd. The Music Department was established in 1883 under the supervision of Herbert Booth.

them the absolute conviction of Salvationism, and had not signed a pledge to promise such conviction. It is within this context that Salvation Army brass bands must be seen.

In order to understand the story of Salvation Army bands, one has to understand the origins and nature of Salvationism, and the scale of the influence of William Booth, the Army's charismatic founder, and his equally impressive wife, Catherine Booth, who, as well sharing her husband's unremitting faith, was a woman of superlative eloquence and intellect. William Booth had been a Methodist preacher. He turned to a more evangelical ministry, founded on a strong belief in the need for people to receive spiritual salvation through the enactment of the message of Christ's gospel. He further believed that this vision could be realized through a religious agency which sought to combat vice and promote social reform. The urgent need for his mission was, to him, abundantly and starkly evidenced by the condition of the urban poor.

The Salvation Army was originally founded as the East London Christian Mission in 1865. Within ten years, it had expanded beyond London and had thirty-two Mission stations. The Mission took on a quasi-military organization in 1878, and adopted the 'Salvation Army' name. The name was formally adopted by deed poll two years later, by which time Parliament had confirmed it to be a properly constituted religious body.[6] The speed at which the Army grew at the end of the nineteenth century was impressive. Indeed, many of its regulations, which were always authoritarian rather than democratic, came about because the recruitment of soldiers was so stunningly successful that orders had to flow thick and fast to control them.

The brass bands of the Salvation Army have always been formally separate from the brass band movement as a whole, and secular bands are often referred to in Salvation Army writings as 'outside' bands. But despite this separation, there is an obvious symbiotic influence between the two sectors, and it is especially intriguing and complex because the Salvation Army's founder was careful to avoid such influences. The cross-fertilization between the two sectors cannot be attributed to any formal links between secular and Salvation Army bands, for there have never been such links, but rather to the common ground which both types of bandsmen, as individuals, have occupied. They have observed and experienced each other's practices, and there has been a level of migration between the two sectors. Latterly the process has been made more obvious through the common consumption of each other's performances in a range of mass media.

---

[6] The standard Salvation Army history is the 7-vol. *The History of the Salvation Army.* Vols. i–iii were written by Robert Sandall (London: Nelson, 1947, 1950, 1955). Vols. iv and v were by Arch R. Wiggins, (London: 1964, 1966). Vols. vi and vii are by Frederick Coutts (London: Hodder & Stoughton, 1973, 1986). A more recent work on the early history of the Army is Glenn K. Horridge, *The Salvation Army, Origins and Early Days: 1865–1900* (Godalming: Ammonite Books, 1993).

Brass bands were famously 'introduced' into the Army by Charles Fry, a builder from Salisbury. Fry was born in 1837. He led the local Wesleyan Methodist choir, and had been a cornet player with the 1st Wiltshire Rifle Volunteer Band. The source details concerning the alleged first use of a brass band in a Salvation Army campaign are sometimes contradictory, but it seems that Fry and his three teenage sons, Fred, Ernest, and Bert, played at an open-air meeting in Salisbury in March 1878.[7] They performed, so it seems, primarily to deflect the attention of hooligans from other Salvationists, rather than for any musical reasons. Their action was successful, and Booth got to hear of it. His attention had already been drawn to the value and practical utility of using brass instruments a year earlier while on a tour of the north-east. He noted in his diary:

The last Sabbath we had a little novelty, which apparently worked well. Among the converts are two members of a brass band—one plays a cornet, and to utilise him at once Brother Russell put him with his cornet in the front rank of the procession from South Stockton. He certainly improved the singing and brought crowds all along the line of march, wondering curiously what we should do next.[8]

In 1880, Booth issued his first 'Orders for Bands' in the *War Cry*, which drew attention to the 'the great utility of musical instruments in attracting crowds to our open air meetings and indoor meetings' and entreated 'the formation of bands throughout the country'.[9] The Fry family subsequently accompanied the Founder on some of his most challenging and important early campaigns. Though Charles Fry, who died near Edinburgh, four years after the Salisbury event, at the age of 44, has always been credited with being the first Salvation Army bandmaster, the Fry band is not regarded as the first Salvation Army corps band. Indeed the preoccupation of determining which was the first brass band is one of the many features that Salvationists share with their secular counterparts.

In April 1906, the *War Cry* ran a light-hearted article under the heading, 'The First Band: Interesting Question to be Settled'.[10] Bandsmen and soldiers whose recollections reached back as far as the founding days of the Army were invited to submit information which would resolve the vexed question. A

---

[7] A family portrait photograph of the Fry family shows the father with a cornet, and the sons with a cornet, an euphonium, and a valve trombone. The photograph shows them in Salvation Army uniform, so it must have been taken between 1878 and 1882, when Charles Fry died.

[8] William Booth's journal, *Christian Mission Magazine* (Oct. 1877), 264–5; quoted in Ian Bradley, 'Blowing for the Lord', *History Today* 27/3 (1977), 190–5. There are many reported instances of instruments being played in the early days of the Army which predate the Salisbury event. Music figured prominently in the work of the Christian Mission, and the Mission brought out two publications of hymns, *Revival Music* (1876) and *The Christian Mission Hymn Book* (1870).

[9] *War Cry* (27 Mar. 1880).   [10] *War Cry* (14 Apr. 1906).

committee of inquiry took stock of the available evidence under the supervision of the Chief of Staff, who was able to announce:

. . . a small band had been got started and was in active operation with the Consett Corps during the latter part of 1879.

With the complete evidence before it, therefore, the Board of Inquiry has no hesitation in awarding the palm to Consett—to which corps we extend our sincere congratulations.[11]

The Consett corps did indeed have a band at an early date but, despite this apparently definitive utterance, one commentator has suggested that another contender might have been overlooked. It appears that a band was formed in Manchester in 1879. It was not cited in the correspondence in the *War Cry*, perhaps for diplomatic reasons, since it was formed by the General's second son, Ballington Booth.[12]

The importance of such detail pales into insignificance compared to the speed at which banding grew in the Salvation Army in those early days. Bands were quickly incorporated into Booth's campaigns as a routine feature, and the 'War Congress' held on Monday 5 August 1878 (based upon Methodist-style 'Conferences') included 'Processions led by a band of musical instruments . . . [which marched] to and from Fieldgate after the morning and afternoon meetings and before the evening meeting'.[13] By 1883 the *Salvation War* was claiming that:

. . . the formation of hundreds of brass or other bands with over 5,000 instruments during this year is an event which must needs leave its influence on the future musical history of the country. . . . The playing of these bands has been made a great ground of complaint against us everywhere but so far from there being any sign of them being objectionable, this is one of the surest evidences for their virtues.[14]

The author added optimistically, 'the simple truth is that the band empties the public houses far and near'.[15] As more corps and citadels were founded, so the number of bands and players grew. An audit conducted in 1916 showed there to be 24,477 senior bandsmen and 4,270 junior bandsmen.[16]

Bands were incorporated into the Salvation Army for a number of complementary reasons. Brass instruments are robust, durable, and easy to play, and are suited for indoor or outdoor use. By the late 1870s, they were cheap, and a large stock of them was on the second-hand market. Though the Army was claiming in 1900 that the vast majority of bandsmen had acquired their

[11] *War Cry* (21 July 1906).   [12] Horridge, *Salvation Army*, 46–8.
[13] *Christian Mission Magazine* (Aug. 1878), 224.
[14] IHC, *The Salvation War* (London: Salavation Army Book Depot, 1883), 60–1.
[15] Ibid. 61.
[16] *Salvation Army Year Book* (1918), 26. The report referred to an audit conducted two years previously.

knowledge of music since their conversion,[17] many early Salvationists had probably been members of brass or volunteer bands, so there is likely to have been a core of efficient, musically literate players. Such practicalities explain why brass instruments rather than violins, concertinas, or any other group-ings, gained the ascendancy in the Army,[18] but there were other factors at work too. Brass bands complemented Booth's particular brand of charismatic evangelicalism and the metaphor which permeated every aspect of it. From the time that the East London Christian Mission became the Salvation Army, the military allegory was all-pervading.

The renaming of the Mission had almost literally been instigated with a stroke of a pen, when Booth, reading a draft of his annual report, changed a casual description of the Mission's workers from 'volunteer army' to 'salva-tion army'.[19] The 'army' epithet originated from his vision of Salvationism as a 'fighting religion' in a war against the devil and his works; but the use of this imagery had important practical ramifications. The adoption of the name was catalytic and led to the entire organization operating according to a strict military structure, and it was this which made it possible for such diverse, widely distributed groupings of individuals to carry the same message with a single meaning and tone. The military infrastructure was crucial; it flowed from the urgent necessity to form a fighting force which was absolutely cohesive, and uncluttered by dissent, controversy, or indiscipline. It was imperative that the chain of command was clear and the message unambiguous, and that it should be understood and obeyed in the smallest units as well as in the move-ment as a whole. The reason that this ambitious and complex objective was so successfully achieved is that, to Booth and his fellow leaders, this was no mere metaphor; it was literally an army, and the enemy was real and apparent before their eyes. Salvation Army soldiers throughout the land acquiesced readily in militaristic discipline and authority, because they too shared the literal interpretation of this message and were willing to apply it unproblem-atically to their endeavours.

Brass instruments have associations with militarism in many cultures, and such associations were especially resonant in the late Victorian period, because of the ever-present image of military imperialism and the common sight of brass bands in volunteer exercises and ceremonies. Such well-established symbolisms, and the shimmering clarity of the sound of brass combined with

[17] Supplement to the *Field Officer* (Dec. 1900), 1–2.
[18] The Salvation Army found brass bands to be especially popular and practical, and this for-mation became the main focus for its instrumental music. But it never discouraged any other instrumental combinations, and also published music for such groups. Indeed Booth's 1880 order urged corps to form bands from any instruments: 'This includes violins, bass viols, concertinas, cornets or any other brass instruments . . . or anything else that will make a pleasant sound for the Lord.' See also Brindley Boon, *Play the Music, Play!*, 2nd edn. (London: Salvationist Publishing and Supplies Ltd, 1978), ch. 19.
[19] *Encyclopaedia of Religion* (London: Macmillan, 1982), s.v. 'Salvation Army'.

drums, gave added substance to the metaphor. Brass bands also had other advantages: they were loud and vibrant, and contributed to a spectacle which must have been truly eye-catching. Amid the throng, the uniforms, the swirling flags, the happy, optimistic, self-confident exhortations of hope, the singing, and the beating of tambourines and drums, the stirring sound of brass band music added a significant dimension to the vivid image of Salvationism. Performance and display was one of the crucial ritual instruments of the Army's campaigns.[20] Booth had stated that the 'first necessity of the movement' was 'TO ATTRACT ATTENTION. If the people are in the danger of the damnation of Hell, and asleep in the danger, awaken them—"to open their eyes". These and other methods attract their attention, secure a hearing for the gospel, and thousands repent, flee to Christ from the wrath to come, and are saved.'[21]

Booth also favoured the brass band because of its potency as a current popular music form. It was one of the ways in which he harnessed aspects of popular culture to his cause. Such devices met his need to reach a popular mass congregation, a class of people whom he saw as being forgotten by society as a whole, and who found the message of traditional, organized religion not just unapproachable but largely incomprehensible; referring to his experiences as a Methodist, Booth observed that: 'I found that ordinary working men in their corduroys and bowler hats could command attention from their own class which was refused point-blank to me with my theological terms and superior knowledge.'[22] The establishment of what was, in effect, a large, widely dispersed, vernacular clergy, turned out to be the most powerful weapon of the Salvationists.

Brass bands were a part of the strategy, and were as subject to discipline as any other part of the Army. They were a powerful weapon in an aggressive attack against the greatest adversary. But to Booth, bands provided a challenge to his image of total cohesion. On the one hand, he recognized their essentially utilitarian merits, but on the other, he also saw them as a danger. For the whole of his life, Booth was alert to what he perceived to be the seductive qualities of music, its power to evoke irrepressible passion, the temptation for its practitioners to indulge in barren virtuosity, and the omnipresent threat that Salvation Army bands would assume an independent identity within the Army. It seems likely that Booth had observed the development of the brass band movement,[23] and he must also have been acutely aware of the much-publicized problems which the volunteer force was having with its brass

[20] See Diane H. Winston, 'Boozers, Brass Bands, and Hallelujah Lassies: The Salvation Army and American Commercial Culture 1880–1914' (Ph.D. thesis, Princeton University, 1996).

[21] William Booth, *All About the Salvation Army* (London, 1882), 9. Quoted in Horridge, *Salvation Army*, 48–9.

[22] Hulda Friederichs, *The Romance of the Salvation Army* (London: Cassell & Co., 1907), 2 ff.

[23] As a Methodist minister, Booth had worked in Brighouse in the West Riding of Yorkshire, one of the great centres of the brass band movement.

bands. (See Chapter 1 for a discussion of the volunteer bands.) Many of the 1859 Volunteer Corps had been reduced to a nonsense because their bands had used the movement as a pragmatic and convenient framework for their music making, and disregarded, mocked, and even usurped authority through self-interest. Booth had successfully instigated a radical strategy which relied on a complex interplay of popular culture and religion, but this strategy contained within it the danger that the Army would become absorbed into and corrupted by the very culture which it sought to subvert. He saw brass bands as the most visible manifestation of this threat.

Regulations for the Army were enshrined in *Orders and Regulations for Field Officers*, which, from its earliest editions, contained an annex of 'Orders and Regulations for Bands'. Booth's concerns are both explicit and emphatic. The Field Officer should:

... acquaint himself with the advantages and dangers of Bands ... and avoid the dangers attending their use ... each bandsman should feel he is using his instrument for the saving of souls ... The F.O. must be ready to check the first beginning of anything like a separate feeling betwixt the Band and the Soldiers ... The F.O. must watch against professionalism.[24]

These sentiments were consistent with an announcement made in the *War Cry* early in 1881, which had the status of a General Order and was signed by Booth's son, Bramwell, who by that time was Chief of Staff:

In order to prevent misunderstanding, and to secure the harmonious working of the Brass Bands with the various Corps to which they are attached, the following regulations are to be strictly observed:—

1. No one will be admitted or retained a Member of any Band who is not a Member of The Army.

2. All the Instruments in every Band are to be the property of The Salvation Army, no matter by whom they may be purchased, or through whom they may be presented.

The words 'Salvation Army Brass Band,' followed by the number of the Corps, must be marked on every Instrument.

In no case are Instruments to be used to play anything but Salvation Music, or on any but Salvation Army service.

3. In the event of any Member of the Band resigning his position as such, he will leave his instrument behind him.

4. In no case will any Committee be allowed in connection with any Band.

5. In every case the Captain of the Corps to which the Band is attached shall direct the movements of the Band, and shall appoint the Bandmaster.

6. In no case will any Band, or Member of any Band, be allowed to go into debt, either for Instruments, or for anything else connected with the Band.

---

[24] *Orders and Regulations for Field Officers* (1907), 'Orders and Regulations for Bands'. The *Orders* are revised as necessary. They usually carry minor revisions; less frequently there are major revisions. The current *Orders* contain vestiges of the original texts.

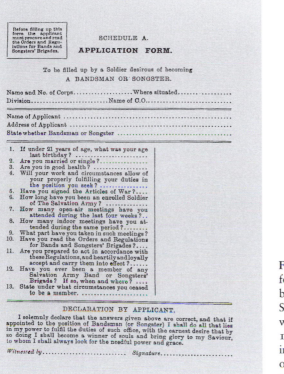

SCHEDULE A.

APPLICATION FORM.

To be filled up by a Soldier desirous of becoming

A BANDSMAN OR SONGSTER.

Name and No. of Corps...................Where situated........ ....
Division.......................Name of C.O...........................

Name of Applicant ....
Address of Applicant ....
State whether Bandsman or Songster ....

1. If under 21 years of age, what was your age last birthday ? ....
2. Are you married or single ?.................
3. Are you in good health ? ....
4. Will your work and circumstances allow of your properly fulfilling your duties in the position you seek ? ....
5. Have you signed the Articles of War ?....
6. How long have you been an enrolled Soldier of The Salvation Army ? ....
7. How many open-air meetings have you attended during the last four weeks ?..
8. How many indoor meetings have you attended during the same period ?........
9. What part have you taken in such meetings ?
10. Have you read the Orders and Regulations for Bands and Songsters' Brigades ?....
11. Are you prepared to act in accordance with these Regulations, and heartily and loyally accept and carry them into effect ?......
12. Have you ever been a member of any Salvation Army Band or Songsters' Brigade ? If so, when and where ? ....
13. State under what circumstances you ceased to be a member. ....

DECLARATION BY APPLICANT,

I solemnly declare that the answers given above are correct, and that if appointed to the position of Bandsman (or Songster) I shall do all that lies in my power to fulfil the duties of such office, with the earnest desire that by so doing I shall become a winner of souls and bring glory to my Saviour, to whom I shall always look for the needful power and grace.

Witnessed by.......................... *Signature*.........................

Figure 5.1. An application form for prospective bandsmen or songsters in the Salvation Army. Such forms were introduced late in the 19th century, and were printed in the *Orders and Regulations* of the Army. This example was published in 1902.

7. In no case is the practising of the Band, or any Members of it, to interfere with the meetings of the Corps.

8. It is strongly recommended that in cases where a Treasurer or Secretary is required by a Band, the Treasurer or Secretary of the Corps to which it is attached shall act in that capacity.

9. Any Band that may have been, or may be formed, which does not carry out this Order will not be recognised as a Salvation Army Band, and must not in future be allowed to take any part in the operations of The Army.

10. Any Band failing to carry out this Order will be at once disbanded.[25]

William Booth's first General Order of March 1880 (the full text of which is given in Appendix 2) had appealed merely for instrumentalists. This, the first substantial set of regulations for musicians, refers to 'brass bands'. It is difficult to believe that its authorship was not stimulated by some practical necessity, and these orders signal a concern of Booth's which persisted to the

[25] *War Cry* (24 Feb. 1881).

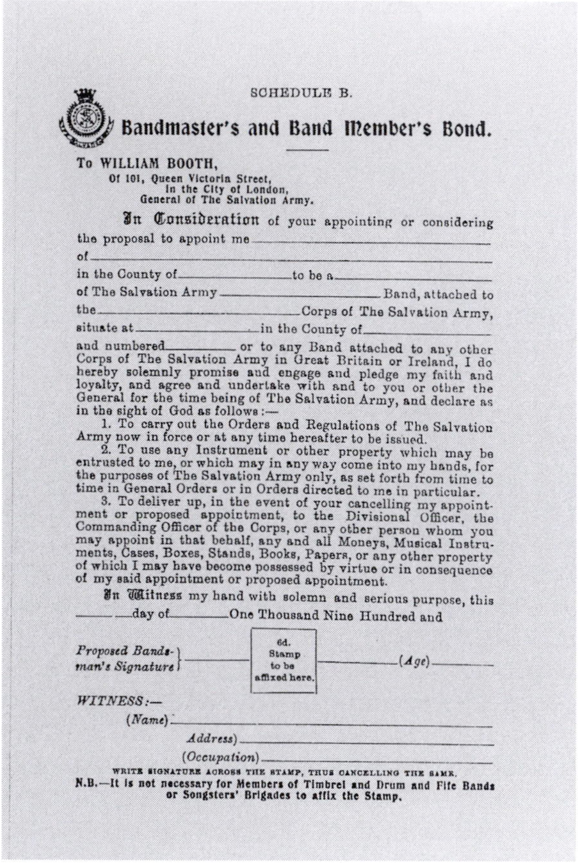

SCHEDULE B.

Bandmaster's and Band Member's Bond.

To WILLIAM BOOTH,
Of 101, Queen Victoria Street,
In the City of London,
General of The Salvation Army.

In Consideration of your appointing or considering the proposal to appoint me ______ of ______ in the County of ______ to be a ______ of The Salvation Army ______ Band, attached to the ______ Corps of The Salvation Army, situate at ______ in the County of ______ and numbered ______ or to any Band attached to any other Corps of The Salvation Army in Great Britain or Ireland, I do hereby solemnly promise and engage and pledge my faith and loyalty, and agree and undertake with and to you or other the General for the time being of The Salvation Army, and declare as in the sight of God as follows:—

1. To carry out the Orders and Regulations of The Salvation Army now in force or at any time hereafter to be issued.
2. To use any Instrument or other property which may be entrusted to me, or which may in any way come into my hands, for the purposes of The Salvation Army only, as set forth from time to time in General Orders or in Orders directed to me in particular.
3. To deliver up, in the event of your cancelling my appointment or proposed appointment, to the Divisional Officer, the Commanding Officer of the Corps, or any other person whom you may appoint in that behalf, any and all Moneys, Musical Instruments, Cases, Boxes, Stands, Books, Papers, or any other property of which I may have become possessed by virtue or in consequence of my said appointment or proposed appointment.

In Witness my hand with solemn and serious purpose, this ______ day of ______ One Thousand Nine Hundred and

Proposed Bandsman's Signature ______ 6d. Stamp to be affixed here. ______ (*Age*) ______

WITNESS:—
(*Name*) ______
Address) ______
(*Occupation*) ______

WRITE SIGNATURE ACROSS THE STAMP, THUS CANCELLING THE SAME.

N.B.—It is not necessary for Members of Timbrel and Drum and Fife Bands or Songsters' Brigades to affix the Stamp.

Figure 5.2. The Bandmaster's and Band Member's Bond from the *Orders and Regulations for Bandsmen*, 1902.

point of obsession. He even appealed to the wives of bandsmen. In an article entitled 'Self-denial of bandsmen's wives', he specified 'important work' for them, explaining that: 'A bandsman has special temptations that do not cross the path of an ordinary soldier . . . they are often in spiritual danger . . . There is likewise a possibility of musical interests and activity usurping the Salvationist ideal . . . What a chance a wife has of watching the rise of these various kinds of danger.'[26]

In fact, Booth was especially keen that brass bands should contain women as well as men. One of the founding principles of the Army was that every office should be equally available to women as to men—at the time of Catherine Booth's death in 1890, there were reckoned to be 5,000 female officers in the Army—and while the male gender is usually used in Army writ-

[26] *Musical Salvationist* (May 1897), 68–9.

ings when referring to 'bandsmen', it was not unknown for women to play in bands (though the majority of the early bands were all-male). In 1880, Booth had issued an order on the subject: 'we do here express our desire that as many of our officers and soldiers generally, *male and female*, who have the ability for so doing shall learn to play on some suitable instrument'.[27] The first woman band player is reported to have been Mrs Captain Abram Davey,[28] and many Salvation Army bands went on to recruit women players, a practice which was not entered into by secular bands. But by the end of the century it was necessary to provide more encouragement. The *Officer* noted:

Cannot some of our enterprising D. O.s and F. O.s introduce the innovation of our Swedish comrades? A D. O. of that country assures us that there is not half the trouble in managing such mixed bands as with those where the men have everything their own way. For one thing, it is almost impossible for seceders to carry off the whole band in case of trouble. The women can usually be reckoned on to stick to their guns, even if the men quit their post. Knowing this, the men seldom desert, in fact they are ashamed to show the white feather.[29]

William and Catherine Booth's talent for administrative and organizational detail found particularly strong expression through the Army's quasi-military structure. It possessed lucidly defined spheres of authority through chains of command and regulations, and vested supreme authority on earth in a single supreme commanding officer: the General. The transparency of Booth's personal conviction, together with his personal charisma, his unashamed autocracy, and above all, the consistency and clarity of his utterances, ensured that his legacy lasted. He was always an autocrat, and seldom relaxed his zealous control of bands, though towards the turn of the century one senses, perhaps because of his awareness of the self-evident success of bands in the Army, the signs of a less ardent need to restrict their musical endeavours. This might have been because the Music Department was operating effectively. Indeed in 1900, he seems to have felt the need to take (perhaps was encouraged to take) a conciliatory tone towards bands, though this fell very short of an apology: 'perhaps I have not said and done for you all that I might have done', he admitted, but his actions sprang from his concern that 'every band in the Salvation Army [should be] soul searchers'.[30]

Because early Salvation Army bands were founded on the basis of expediency rather than design, they had no formal instrumental line-up. By the

[27] *War Cry* (27 Mar. 1880). Quoted in Boon, *Play the Music*, 14.
[28] *War Cry* (31 July 1880). Quoted in Boon, *Play the Music*, 15.
[29] *Officer* (Jan. 1895), 27.
[30] Supplement to the *Field Officer* (Dec. 1900), 1–2. One senses a change in Booth's attitude to band music at about this time. The Music Board had a powerful grip on the progress of band music, and he was surrounded by people whom he trusted and who shared his ideology. Within a few months of this statement, Booth relaxed regulations concerning the relationship of instrumental music to sung texts.

TABLE 1. *The Instrumentation of 22 Salvation Army Brass Bands, Musical Salvationist, 10 (1896), 47*

	1	2	3	4	5	6	7	8	9	10	11	12	13	14	15	16	17	18	19	20	21	22
Soprano	–	–	–	–	–	–	–	–	–	–	–	2	–	–	–	1	1	–	–	–	–	–
1st Cornet	7	4	6	6	6	6	5	5	6	7	6	5	7	5	5	5	6	5	5	5	4	5
2nd Cornet	4	4	4	4	2	2	4	4	2	2	3	3	2	4	2	4	4	3	3	2	2	2
1st Tenor Horn	3	3	2	3	2	2	3	2	2	2	2	2	2	2	2	2	1	2	2	1	1	2
2nd Tenor Horn	3	2	3	1	2	2	–	3	2	2	2	1	2	2	2	1	1	2	1	2	2	2
1st Baritone	3	3	1	2	1	1	2	1	2	2	1	2	–	1	2	1	–	1	1	2	1	1
2nd Baritone	2	2	1	1	2	1	1	1	2	1	1	1	1	2	1	2	2	1	2	1	1	1
1st Trombone	2	1	1	2	1	1	3	1	2	1	2	1	1	2	1	1	2	1	2	–	1	1
2nd Trombone	2	1	2	1	1	1	1	1	1	1	1	2	1	1	2	1	–	2	1	1	1	1
Bass Trombone	1	–	1	1	1	–	1	–	1	1	1	1	1	1	1	1	–	–	–	–	1	–
Solo Euphonium	3	4	2	3	4	3	3	2	2	4	2	2	1	2	2	2	2	3	2	–	2	–
B♭ Bass	2	4	1	4	1	4	4	4	2	3	4	2	3	2	2	3	3	2	4	4	1	2
E♭ Bombardon	3	3	3	3	3	2	2	3	1	2	3	2	3	3	3	2	2	2	2	2	2	1
B♭ Clarionet	–	5	5	1	2	4	–	1	3	–	–	1	–	–	–	–	–	–	–	–	1	–
E♭ Clarionet	–	–	2	1	2	–	–	1	–	–	–	–	1	–	–	–	–	–	–	–	1	–
Cymbals	1	–	–	–	1	–	1	–	1	–	–	1	1	–	–	–	–	1	1	–	–	–
Side Drum	1	1	1	–	1	1	1	1	1	1	1	1	2	1	2	–	2	1	–	1	1	1
Bass Drum	1	1	1	1	1	1	1	1	1	1	1	1	1	1	1	1	1	1	1	1	1	1
TOTAL	38	38	36	31	34	33	32	31	31	30	30	29	28	28	27	27	27	26	24	23	23	20

1 Clapton, Congress Hall 2 Nunhead 3 Bristol I 4 Barrow I 5 Portsmouth I 6 I HQ 7 Penge 8 Northwich 9 Boscombe 10 ITHQ
11 Oldham I 12 Exeter 13 Regent Hall 14 Hull II 15 S. Shields 16 Luton II 17 New Brompton 18 Ramsgate 19 Worthing 20 Luton I
21 Northampton 22 Doncaster

late 1870s, secular bands were moving closer to a standard instrumentation because of the influence of contesting. Salvation Army bands did not enter contests, so there was no need for a standard instrumentation (see Table 1), and early publications reflected this. The musical manifestation of Salvationism —at least as far as bands were concerned—was therefore not especially idiomatic until the twentieth century, when specific genres developed and more sophisticated and idiomatic publications emerged. In the later nineteenth century, virtuosity and the type of homogeneity which preoccupied non-Salvation Army brass bands were of little concern to their Salvation Army counterparts.

The major concerns of a Salvation Army brass player would have been twofold: serving explicitly functional purposes in Salvation Army events, and protecting oneself and one's instrument from the injury which could arise from the gratuitous violence to which virtually all Salvationists were at times subjected. Violence against the Salvation Army was strongest when a corps was making its first 'attack'—expanding into a new area. Some writers have pointed out that violence against the Salvation Army was little more than a manifestation of the traditional mob reaction against anything which deviates from the norm.[31] The wilful conspicuousness of the Army inflamed would-be adversaries into 'rough musicing' it—the phrase widely used for such hooliganism.[32] Some such opposition was premeditated. For instance, the 'Skeleton Army' consisted of groups of urban youths—mainly from the better-off working class—who taunted the Salvationists. It was a loose formation (the term is more a generic description than a signifier of a movement), but they were well organized, and in Honiton in 1882, a one-penny paper with the title the *Skeleton* was circulated, declaring its intention to 'stamp out the fanaticism and blasphemy of the Salvation Army, which is doing so much to bring Christian religion into ridicule'.[33]

Victor Bailey has pointed out that such behaviour was exclusively confined to the southern part of the country and may well have reflected a rejection of the radicalism of Salvationism by a more affluent sector of the working class.[34] It is also worth remarking that attacks on Salvation Army bands were most prominent in areas of the country where the secular brass band movement was weakest. It is, of course, impossible to prove a causal relationship between such mob violence and geographical patterns of brass banding. But the worst violence occurred in places such as south-coast seaside resorts, where the

---

[31] See Horridge, *Salvation Army*, ch. 4.

[32] Ibid., and Victor Bailey, 'Salvation Army Riots, the "Skeleton Army" and Legal Authority in the Provincial Towns', in A. P. Donajgrodzki (ed.), *Social Control in Nineteenth Century Britain* (London: Croom Helm, 1977), 231–45. The term 'rough musicing' became well known; it was one of a number of terms used generically to describe a type of hooliganism involving taunting and physical violence.

[33] Horridge, *Salvation Army*, 123.   [34] Bailey, 'Salvation Army Riots', 233–5.

secular brass band tradition was not strong. What is certain is that being a Salvationist called for a very special kind of self-sacrifice. Official figures released by the Army in 1882 quoted 669 soldiers being brutally assaulted, 251 of them being women, and 23 being children.[35]

Salvationists had reason to protect themselves not just from physical attacks, but also from flagrant abuse in the press, and frequently from litigation. Salvationists were by nature outgoing—their evangelism called for constant outreach—but their persecution also drew them together; they sought nourishment and support from a shared sense of community and purpose. One senses that, from the earliest days, there was a need for Salvationists to look after themselves, to enshrine their spiritual and material values in an enterprise which was, in the best sense, self-serving. One of the immediate needs was uniforms. Early bands wore ex-army stock which was often blood-stained. The establishment of a uniform-manufacturing operation may well have provided the prototype for the beginning of its instrument and expanded sheet music operation.

The first musical instrument 'factory' began in east London in 1889, and was staffed by two men and a boy. Among the first orders was one for the repair of instruments smashed by the Skeleton Army at the Eastbourne riots of that year. By 1893, the factory was manufacturing valves and was able to manufacture every brass band instrument. The first complete set made entirely by the Salvation Army was supplied to a corps in Luton in 1894. In May of that year, a Captain Woodward claimed in the *War Cry* that, since the factory's foundation, it had made 'over 1,500' instruments. By 1904, the same paper claimed that the annual production was 1,000 instruments.[36] In 1901, it was decided to expand the works, in order that it could do its own plating. A suitable site was found in St Albans in Hertfordshire, where it stayed for the rest of its existence. Captain Woodward's article had pointed out that every instrument was individually tuned by Brigadier Fred Hawkes and Brigadier Arthur Goldsmith, both members of the Music Department. It was also claimed that the slide-maker there had previously worked for Distin's, Higham's, and Boosey's, three of the most important brass instrument manufacturers of the nineteenth century.

Despite Booth's concerns that bands should not become too sophisticated, there is evidence even before his death of a more imaginative interpretation of his doctrine, and a greater creative freedom of approach to musical matters. The three most influential figures in the development of musical life in the early days of the Army were Fred Fry, who, as a teenager in 1878, had stood beside his father in the Salisbury campaign; Henry Hill, a former police man from Hull; and Richard Slater, whom most Salvation Army historians regard as

[35] Horridge, *Salvation Army*, 97.
[36] IHC, musical instrument factory file—loose cuttings.

Figure 5.3. The instrument factory of the Salvation Army, 1930s.

the seminal force in Salvation Army music. The three worked in London, and shared Booth's confidence and respect. They appear to have been first-rate musicians. Slater was not a brass player but a violinist, and had an especially sophisticated knowledge of the art-music canon. He was a prolific composer of Salvation Army music, and because of the highly centralized authority structure, he exerted an important influence on Salvation Army music throughout the country and beyond. The three also seem to have been responsible for stimulating the expansion of the repertoire, the development of the manufacturing and publishing wings of the Army, and the fostering—in fits and starts—of more élite groups of Salvation Army musicians.

The first such group had been formed in 1887 as the 'Household Troops' (see Fig. 5.4). It appears to have been modelled on an earlier band known as the 'Lifeguards'. Each member was taught how to play a brass instrument, and playing in the band was part of their duties. They wore a distinctive uniform based around a Norfolk jacket trimmed with red braid, with the words 'Salvation Army' embroidered on it. The holistic training they received included scriptural study as well as physical exercise. Because the band rehearsed every day,

Figure 5.4. A late 19th century photograph of the Household Troops Band.

it soon became not just efficient but impressive. It was a big band, and the sight of it marching in its eye-catching uniforms was striking. It was the first Salvation Army band to tour abroad when it visited Canada and the USA in 1888–9.[37]

It was wound up within six years of being founded, almost certainly because it was perceived by Booth as acquiring those features of vanity and virtuosity against which he was so anxious to guard. During its existence, it had nurtured a number of the Army's senior musicians of the future. It had been the first showpiece Salvation Army band, but it was not the last. Within a couple of years, a band was started at the International Headquarters. It was not especially proficient in the early days, but its proximity to the main influential figures of the Army gave it a special advantage in its musical development. Initially, it was called the 'Salvation Army Staff Band', because it was no more than that: a band made up of the members of staff of the Salvation Army HQ.[38] It was to become the 'International Staff Band of the Salvation Army' (see Fig. 5.5). Though some corps brass bands—Chalk Farm, Hendon, Croydon, Clapton, Cardiff Canton, Tottenham (later Enfield), and many others—were

[37] Boon, *Play the Music*, 21–6. See also *War Cry* (2 Mar. 1887).

[38] Bands were formed in several of the Army's staff establishments: e.g. a Trade Headquarters Band was formed in 1885, a Salvation Army Assurance Society Band in 1924, and a Salvationist Publishing and Supplies Band in 1928.

Figure 5.5. Undated photograph of the International Staff Band in the posture of an American big band.

to acquire reputations for excellence, it was this central band which was to be the showpiece of Salvation Army banding in the UK.[39]

Booth died on 20 August 1912, but his influence was to be pervasive for most of the century. He was succeeded by his son, William Bramwell Booth, and the fact that his wife, sons, and daughters—and their offspring—were equally dedicated Salvationists ensured the continuity of the Boothian ideal and the practices which underpinned it. It is hard to exaggerate the extent of the Founder's personal influence and the primary paradigms which he ordained concerning the place of music in Salvation Army ritual, but this influence has combined with other potent forces to shape Salvation Army banding during the twentieth century.

From the closing years of the nineteenth century, two forces coexisted which were to determine these developments, and the repertoire and practices of Salvation Army bands in particular. The first was the institutionalization of the musical activities of the Army, a process which was most potently manifest in the establishment in 1896 of the International Headquarters Music Board. Band music was performed for the review of the Board by the International

[39] See B. Boon, *ISB: The Story of the International Staff Band* (London: Record Greetings Ltd., 1985).

Staff Band. The Board was to be the focus of musical power and influence. The publications which it approved, and the other organizational structures which it spawned, derived directly from the Army leaders' sustained ambition to rationalize and standardize Army music, and to ensure that the place of music in worship and evangelicalism should develop according to a centrally determined design. The policies of the Department were intended to be consistent with relevant sections of the *Orders and Regulations for Officers*. Though there was much talk of the Department existing to ensure a high standard for the Army's music, it is hard to avoid the impression that control and censorship were also in the foreground, stemming from a fear of the potential for brass bands to stray from the doctrinal principles upon which all Salvationist endeavours were supposed to be based. The process of institutionalization and standardization succeeded, *almost* completely, in controlling the production and consumption of Army music. This sphere of control also ensured fairly consistent parameters of style and performance practices.

The second force might seem to be in complete contradiction to the first, but it was not. It came from Salvation Army musicians who sought to interpret Army regulations about music, and their aesthetic implications, in a way which give more or less free rein to the creative spirit. Predictably, these two forces gave rise to occasional tensions, but the Salvationists who emerged as the best band composers appear to have had few problems in reconciling the dual criteria of doctrinal orthodoxy on the one hand and instinctive creativity on the other. But while there is only a little evidence of composers or performers deliberately circumventing Salvationist strictures in order to further their musical ambitions, many seemed to have used intellectual acrobatics to rationalize their music making as being in line with Boothian orthodoxy. The catch-all rationale that eventually emerged was that creative endeavour originating in and dedicated to a spirit of holiness was legitimate. Thus, any creative process or genre was legitimized by the sincerity of its offering in the spirit of worship. This rationale accounts for the fact that, when doctrinal tensions appeared, they seem to have been low-key, because for most of the twentieth century, the Music Department and the Music Board of the Army was staffed by a succession of officers who were not just fine musicians, but also entirely convinced and dedicated Salvationists. It was these officers who were among the main composers. There were splits and controversies, but these seem to have been caused more by individual circumstances than by a simmering feud between the Army's leaders and its musicians. The utterances of the most influential musicians in the Army's history are as replete with statements about evangelical ideals and Salvationism as they are with talk of playing techniques and styles, and unfailingly they have the ring of sincerity about them.

There are striking comparisons to be drawn here between what emerged as the musical practices of brass bands in the Salvation Army and wider debates about music which have prevailed from time to time in the Protestant church.

At the heart of such debates, one always finds a tension between aesthetic and doctrinal principles, a merging of artistic and scriptural dictates, and—eventually—a solution which is more a consensual resolution than a compromise. Such was the case with the Salvationists in the twentieth century as they engaged on a process of continuous reconciliation between the spiritual and the aesthetic ideals.

In September 1901, following a review of a memorandum from the Music Board, William Booth decided to relax some of the rules which controlled the development of Salvation Army music. Latitude was given to the Music Board to determine appropriate instrumentations, styles, and genres. More significantly he decided to allow the composers to write music which did not derive directly from other works—mainly hymns—which carried religious texts. Thus for the first time there was the prospect of the development of instrumental music as an independent genre. It was never intended that religious references should be withdrawn from Salvation Army compositions, but it did mean that Salvation Army composers were free to be entirely original in their thematic material. This was not an especially risky strategy, because the members of the Music Board were, in fact, the Army's main composers, and they had Booth's trust. But within three years of his death, his son, General Bramwell Booth, set up an inquiry into all matters relating to Salvation Army music. It was the first and most important such commission. The Council of Inquiry, which was chaired by Commissioner John Carleton, was made up of senior Army officers. Evidence was taken from twenty-three witnesses, including seven corps bandmasters. The Inquiry, which reported its findings in 1916, concluded that bands had three broad functions in the Army: to attract the attention of people to Salvation Army events; to accompany singing at services and other religious rituals; and to convey spiritual messages through the performance of suitable music: 'to speak directly to the hearts of the people'.[40] These three broad parameters embraced all of the Army's musical endeavours. The first and second of them were straightforward; after all, it was precisely these qualities that had led Booth to replicate the Fry family's example in 1878. But the third provided the opportunity for increasingly creative expression on the part of composers, and a freer rein for lyricism and virtuosity on the part of performers. There was also a concern that the musical content of Salvation Army works would start to be characterized by complexity and inventive cleverness at the expense of clarity and comprehensibility. William Booth's famous maxim that people needed 'a real tune, that is a melody with some distinct air in it, which takes hold of them and goes on humming in the mind' was widely shared.[41] Indeed Richard Slater had re-emphasised

[40] See Boon, *Play the Music*, 152.
[41] Quoted in Boon, *Sing the Happy Song: A History of Salvation Army Vocal Music* (London: Salvationist Publishing and Supplies Ltd., 1978), 5.

this to Salvation Army musicians at the close of the century: 'To reach the masses the music called for is that which goes direct to the souls of men, not such as demands a measure of culture and an intellectual process for its comprehension.'[42]

In order to understand how Salvation Army brass band repertoire developed in the twentieth century, it is necessary to understand the place of music in Salvation Army practices and rituals. Predictably, the procedures for such events are enshrined in a set of regulations.[43] Salvationists prescribe the use of bands in four main settings. They are used in open-air or indoor Salvation Army meetings intended to attract unbelievers and turn them to salvation, and here they might play a march to attract attention, and accompany hymns. They are also used in a number of routine services for those who are already converted. Such events include 'Holiness Meetings', in which the emphasis is on prayer and spirituality, and 'Praise Meetings' which, while also concerned with prayer and spirituality, are more celebratory of the gift of salvation. 'Gospel Meetings', intended for the unconverted, are generally called 'Salvation Meetings', and are typically held on Sunday evenings. Bands are used in this context to accompany singing. In 'Praise Meetings', which are often held on Sunday afternoons, in addition to accompanying hymns, the band may perform a march, a more substantial work, or even an *air varié* solo which features one of the band players. There are also special events in which bands are used, the most common of which is the 'Festival'. Festivals are the Salvation Army equivalent of concerts, and may bring together Salvationists from a number of corps, and here, a freer, larger scale celebration is in order. Because Festivals are, by their nature, special, large-scale, and celebratory, they have been the forums in which more ambitious works have had most conspicuous exposure.

A distinct Salvation Army repertoire developed primarily, but not exclusively, within those services which were intended for practising Salvationists rather than the army's outreach activity, especially Praise Meetings and Festivals (though many Salvationists would recognize Festivals as having an important outreach function). More opportunities to develop idiomatic repertoire came with the rise of élite bands such as the International Staff Band and some of its foreign equivalents which toured abroad and in their home countries. It is hard to see the performances given on such tours as more than a form of concert dedicated to the praise of God, even though they included prayers and some hymns. Many Salvationist soloists became as virtuoso as any found in the secular band movement.

---

[42] Richard Slater, 'The Music of the Salvation Army', *Musical Salvationist*, 13 (1898–9), 131.
[43] *Orders and Regulations for Field Officers* contain sections on the practices to be observed at meetings.

Throughout the period when this repertoire was developing, there was a constant concern that Salvation Army instrumental music could be a mere vehicle for artistic expression, and thus have no qualities which distinguished it from secular music. If the music was indistinguishable from the secular, its performers and listeners had no special incentive to behave differently from secular musicians and audiences. Consequently, all Salvation Army music had to be referentialist, and the reference had to be to a tune or text which evoked the spirit of salvation. There were also sustained concerns that Salvation Army meetings were becoming no more than an excuse for music making. In 1929, Fred Hawkes, who did as much as anyone to develop band music, lamented, 'In many places undue importance is attached to instrumental music . . . the original intention was merely to assist in leading singing';[44] and two years later, in an article which further articulated the view that bands were ignoring their spiritual function and flouting discipline, James Hay reflected on the fact that 'Only recently, twenty-five out of thirty-two Bandsmen said that they had not so much as read the "Orders and Regulations for Bands"'.[45]

By this time, the genres which were to be most popular with Salvationists were already being used. Marches and even *airs variés* were written on hymn motifs, or at least carried a title redolent of a spiritual message which its hearers would recognize. The relaxation in 1901 of the rules which required instrumental music to include a direct thematic reference to a hymn tune did not sweep away the practice of basing compositions on such material, and it never entirely died out. The first marches were hymns in duple time to which bands and other soldiers marched. The prototypes for two other main forms used by Salvationists which were not for singing or marching appear to have been introduced by Richard Slater.[46] The first of these is the *air varié*, which, in type, is more or less indistinguishable from the solos played by secular bandsmen, apart from the fact that hymn tunes are used as themes. The first Salvation Army *air varié* to be thus called is taken to be 'While the days are going by', by Frederick Hawkes, written in 1926. Another purely instrumental form utilized by Salvationists is the 'selection'. This was originally a medley of appropriate tunes; indeed, the first, written by Slater, carried the title 'Old Song Memories', and was distributed free to bands as a novelty in January 1902. The selection was widely used, and the fact that Slater had a good knowledge and love of art music laid the seeds for others to follow his example in arranging art-music works. But the need for a genre which could provide some aesthetic satisfaction for Salvationist composers and band

---

[44] F. G. Hawkes, 'Instrumental Music versus Vocal Music: Is the Former Progressing to the Detriment of the Latter?', *Staff Review* (1929), 102.

[45] James Hay, 'Regulations: Why Permit Them to be Neglected?', *Staff Review* (1931), 253.

[46] For a biography of Slater, see Arch R. Wiggins, *Richard Slater: The Father of Salvation Army Music* (London: International Headquarters, 1945).

players, without contradicting the doctrinal principles of Salvationism, gave rise to the only musical form which is unique to the Salvation Army: the 'meditation'.

The meditation also originates in the work of Slater, and was taken further by two other members of the Music Department in the first part of the century, Frederick Hawkes and Arthur Goldsmith. Hawkes had been a member of the celebrated Household Troops Band. Goldsmith was a cornet player in a military band, and became corps bandmaster at Poplar at the age of 15. The meditation derives from the practice of performing hymn tunes as a purely instrumental form and treating each verse differently in both harmonic and textural terms. Because meditations were based on well-known hymn tunes, they, and the religious messages which they conveyed, were easily recognizable to listeners. Brief, freely composed episodes between the hymn verses provided an additional opportunity for the composer to express himself. Similarities between the meditation and existing art-music forms, especially the choral prelude, are obvious, but claims that it really is unique to Salvationism are well founded, because of the particular evangelical context in which it has evolved, and also because it has always been directed to a brass idiom.[47]

The first prototype of the meditation was written by Slater in 1902, and was a setting of his own chorale, *Jesus, Hope of Souls Repentant*. It was described by him as a 'fourfold arrangement . . . so that the whole gives, as it were, a different setting of the four verses of a song, the aim being to bring out the different aspects and moods of the same piece'.[48] Other important early uses of the form were by Hawkes in his *Rousseau* (1913), and Arthur Goldsmith in *Rockingham* (1920). The latter work was the first to be actually described as a meditation.

Ronald Holz has identified different stages in the development of the meditation,[49] but in 1965, Ray Steadman-Allen, one of the best latter-day Salvationist composers, provided a 'recipe' for a typical meditation which serves as a good general summary of the genre:

A Introduction: original or tune-derived, perhaps a 'motto'
B First verse: simple, mellow, restrained
C Episode 1: lyrical; a melody (perhaps in 'duet') or melodic sequences—perhaps going on to a touch of 'dramatic action' and a modulation to the minor

[47] Any serious study of purely instrumental music in the Army should take account of the evolution of its hymn repertoire. The best work on this topic is Gordon Taylor, *Companion to the Song Book of the Salvation Army* (London: Salvationist Publishing and Supplies Ltd., 1989).

[48] Ray Steadman-Allen, 'Army's Instrumental Meditation has No Parallel Elsewhere', *Musician* (23 Oct. 1965), 695.

[49] Ronald Walker Holz, 'A History of the Hymn Tune Meditation and Related Forms in Salvation Army Instrumental Music in Great Britain and North America 1880–1980' (Ph.D. thesis, University of Connecticut, 1981).

D Second verse: scheme (*a*) euphonium or horn solo with a cornet *obbligato* scheme (*b*) a quartet of some kind (whatever is decided on, it will be contrasted with the first verse)

E Episode 2: (*a*) agitated figuration or (*b*) *fugato* entries on a subject derived from the tune

F Third verse: tonic major; florid bass or polyphonic writing

G Conclusion: grandiose, jubilant or fading as appropriate[50]

The function of the Music Board has been quite unique in British musical life. No other agency, from the Church of England to the British military establishment, has sought to centralize the control of its musical repertoire by vesting authority in a single office, and imposing a total restriction on any repertoire which does not pass through it. Such a singular sphere of authority has had consequences for the evolution of musical style and taste. Bandsmen's Councils have been held since 1899. Councils too are a unique feature of Salvation Army work; they are meetings for spiritual teaching and encouragement, and sometimes include technical instruction for musicians and musical leaders. Composition competitions have been held periodically since 1905, and there have been several initiatives to provide band players with a musical education. Such educative ventures have included training events, but the emphasis has been on the production of didactic literature. Perhaps the most ambitious publication of this type was produced between 1940 and 1947: a full-scale, systematic correspondence course for band conductors, which covered a wide range of skills and was complete with self-assessment tests.[51] The writing is both authoritative and authoritarian, and guides students through three channels of development: Rudiments of Music, Practical Music, and Salvationist Doctrine. Thus the self-assessment tests produce challenging juxtapositions such as 'What is the meaning of Da Capo . . . ?', 'Indicate the movement of the baton in four four time . . .', and 'Name two attributes of God'.[52]

The authors of the *Bandmaster's Correspondence Course* included Frederick Hawkes, who described a variety of instrumental line-ups for Salvation Army bands of different sizes. Standard instrumentations for band publications were introduced early in the Army's history, but there was never an assumption that all bands should have the standard instrumentation, or that they would be able to raise a band with the line-up of the International Staff Band,

---

[50] Steadman-Allen, 'Army's Instrumental Meditation', 695.

[51] AHC Ref. *The Salvation Army National Headquarters/The Bandmaster's Correspondence Course* (later known as the *Band Training Course*). Many authors contributed to the course and the material is arranged as a series of 'parts', 'sets', and 'sheets', rather than following conventional pagination. It is impossible to tell the exact date of publication from the material, but the project was begun in 1940, and the material was still being distributed up to the 1970s or even later.

[52] Ibid., part I, set II, sheet 2.

which played most publications before they were released. Many bands, including the Staff Band, also doubled parts. Hawkes's line-up for bands of different sizes takes into account the instrumentations for which the Army's publications were produced, and the variety of circumstances which confronted corps bandmasters throughout the country. (See Tables 2 and 3.)

The Salvation Army has produced several different series of publications to serve the needs of bands. In 1884, the first *Band Journal* was produced, cloning aspects of the format of secular brass band journals. It became known as the 'Ordinary Series', and later the 'General Series', and was the most widely used publication. In 1921, a 'Second Series', later known as the 'Triumph Series', was published for smaller, less proficient bands. To this was added in 1923 the 'Festival Series', which carried more idiomatic compositions for brass band; and in 1957, a further series, the 'Unity Series', was published for very small bands, containing selections, hymn tunes, and marches. Though there have been occasional publications which do not figure in these series, between them they embrace most publications for Salvation Army brass bands. In some countries outside the UK the Salvation Army has other publications along similar lines.

From the 1930s, Salvationist composers have expanded the range of types of composition used by brass bands. Eric Ball introduced the suite in *Songs in the Morning* (1936), and the tone poem in *Exodus* (1937). Philip Catelinet produced the 'Festival arrangement' *A Glorious Hope* (1937), and the hymn-tune arrangement *Weber* (1944). Other leading Salvationist composers have included Bramwell Coles, George Marshall, Dean Goffin, Ray Steadman-Allen, and Edward Gregson. The two latter composers have also written for secular bands. The works of foreign Salvationists have also been used in the UK, especially those of Emil Söderström and Erik Leidzén. Perhaps the two most major international figures to have written for the Army are John Philip Sousa, whose march *The Salvation Army* (1930) was composed at the request of Evangeline Booth, and Vaughan Williams, who wrote *Prelude on Three Welsh Hymn Tunes* for the International Staff Band in 1953. Eric Ball may have been the most talented and prolific composer of Salvation Army music. He is certainly the one who has written most for both Salvation Army and secular brass bands. He possessed a distinctive musical voice, and a total mastery of the brass band idiom, and evocations of religious, spiritual, and moral themes are frequently present in his works. It is difficult to identify another composer whose work juxtaposes doctrinal and aesthetic elements more successfully and consistently.

Ball held the rank of major when appointed Conductor of the International Staff Band in July 1942, succeeding George Fuller; but two years later, amidst shock and controversy, he resigned from the Salvation Army. The direct cause of his resignation was his interest in and practice of spiritualism and extra-sensory perception. He had written to General George Carpenter late in the

TABLE 2. *Composition of Brass Band from 10 to 20 Instruments, Minus Drums, 1940s*

	10	11	12	13	14	15	16	17	18	19	20
Soprano E♭	–	–	–	–	–	–	–	–	–	1	1
1st cornet B♭	3	3	3	3	3	3	3	4	4	4	4
2nd cornet B♭	1	1	2	2	2	2	2	2	2	2	2
1st horn E♭	1	1	1	1	1	1	1	1	2	2	2
2nd horn E♭	1	1	1	1	1	1	1	1	1	1	2
1st baritone B♭	1	1	1	1	1	1	1	1	1	1	1
2nd baritone B♭	1	1	1	1	1	1	1	1	1	1	1
1st trombone B♭	–	–	–	1	1	1	1	1	1	1	1
2nd trombone B♭	–	–	–	–	1	1	1	1	1	1	1
Bass trombone G	–	–	–	–	–	1	1	1	1	1	1
Solo euphonium B♭	1	1	1	1	1	1	1	1	1	1	1
Bombardon E♭	1	2	2	2	2	2	2	2	2	2	2
Medium bass B♭	–	–	–	–	–	–	1	1	1	1	1
TOTAL NUMBER	10	11	12	13	14	15	16	17	18	19	20

TABLE 3. *Composition of Brass Bands from 21 to 36 Instruments, Minus Drums, 1940s*

	21	22	23	24	25	26	27	28	29	30	31	32	33	34	35	36
Soprano E♭	1	1	1	1	1	1	1	1	1	1	1	1	1	1	1	1
Solo cornet B♭	3	3	3	3	3	3	3	4	4	4	4	4	4	4	4	4
1st cornet B♭	2	2	2	3	3	3	3	3	3	3	3	3	3	3	3	4
2nd cornet B♭	2	2	2	2	2	2	2	2	2	2	2	3	3	3	3	3
Flugel horn B♭	1	1	1	1	1	1	1	1	1	1	1	1	1	1	1	2
Solo horn E♭	1	1	1	1	2	2	2	2	2	2	2	2	2	2	2	2
1st horn E♭	1	1	1	1	1	1	1	1	2	2	2	2	2	2	2	2
2nd horn E♭	1	1	1	1	1	1	2	2	2	2	2	2	2	2	2	2
1st baritone B♭	1	1	1	1	1	2	2	2	2	2	2	2	2	2	2	2
2nd baritone B♭	1	1	1	1	1	1	1	1	1	1	1	1	1	1	1	1
1st trombone B♭	1	1	1	1	1	1	1	1	1	1	1	1	1	2	2	2
2nd trombone B♭	1	1	1	1	1	1	1	1	1	1	1	1	2	2	2	2
Bass trombone G	1	1	1	1	1	1	1	1	1	1	1	1	1	1	1	1
Solo euphonium B♭	1	2	2	2	2	2	2	2	2	2	2	2	2	2	2	2
Bombardon E♭	2	2	2	2	2	2	2	2	2	3	3	3	3	3	3	4
Monstre bass B♭	1	1	2	2	2	2	2	2	2	2	2	2	2	2	2	2
TOTAL NUMBER	21	22	23	24	25	26	27	28	29	30	31	32	33	34	35	36

previous year 'that the path of psychic-spiritual unfoldment . . . is one which I have been definitely led to tread'.[53] His interest in these practices came not from a mere curiosity, but from an idiosyncratic interpretation of angelicism. He had, apparently, been impressed and moved by Evangeline Booth's image of her father gazing at her from the battlements of heaven, and sought to extend his own religious experience through spiritualism. The work which is arguably Ball's best—certainly his best known—*Resurgam* (I shall rise again), has often been taken to be his most mystical.

Ball was not the only Salvationist musician to cross from the Salvation Army to the world of secular brass bands. The division between the two sectors has not been entirely watertight. It could be argued that Salvation Army and secular bands have lived under the restraining influence of two different but equally prescriptive orthodoxies: the contest ethos on the one hand, and the musical controls which have emanated from doctrinal and organizational imperatives on the other. These forces have caused the growth of the two sectors to be independent, discretely standardized, and stylistically stilted. But all brass players and composers have been subjected to a number of core cultural influences, and these have had an effect on the way that music is written and played. Both sectors have contributed significantly to the musical profession, in that citadels as much as band rooms have been the breeding grounds for many of the best professional players. The proximity of the two sectors was underlined when Robert Redhead became the first serving Salvation Army officer to be asked to write the test piece for the National Brass Band Championships. The work which he composed, *Isaiah 40*, was the test piece for the 1996 National.

In the 1960s, brass bands in the Salvation Army seem to have been susceptible to the same trends which affected the secular band movement. This was almost certainly due to a wider cultural phenomenon which saw traditions and innovations collide, and which left many traditional practices as casualties. The widespread interest in rock and pop groups had its manifestations in Army music as it did elsewhere. For a time Salvation Army 'pop' groups such as The Joy Strings provided a popular alternative focus to bands. There were also important changes to the infrastructures which supported brass banding within the Army. In February 1964, a meeting was held in which the instrument manufacturer Boosey & Hawkes informed the Army's British Commissioner of its intention to stop production of high-pitch instruments. Boosey & Hawkes and the Salvation Army were, by then, the only producers of high-pitch instruments.

In March 1964, it was announced that the Music Board had taken an unanimous decision for Salvation Army bands to change from high to low pitch.[54]

---

[53] Peter M. Cooke, *Eric Ball: The Man and his Music* (Baldock: Egon, 1991), 80–1.
[54] *Musician* (21 Mar. 1964), 1.

The decision was inevitable, because a change to a lower pitch by Boosey & Hawkes would have left the Army's instrument factory as the only place where high-pitch instruments were produced, and British Salvation Army bands as the sole users of high-pitch instruments. These instruments could not even be used to play solos with piano accompaniment without adjustment. The fact that Boosey & Hawkes were in consultation with the Army at all perhaps suggests a tacit acknowledgement that not all Salvation Army band players were playing Salvation Army instruments. Memoranda were circulated to Salvation Army corps, informing them that sets of tuning slides to lower the pitch could be purchased for between £100 and £180. The ensuing economic ramifications may have affected corps bands as they had civilian bands. But the Army was anxious to emphasize that the change would be gradual. The *Musician* carried a carefully worded announcement under the subheading 'Gradual Change from High Pitch Advised', which stressed that, 'Inevitably such a transition would take a considerable time to accomplish fully; there is no suggestion at all of any need for haste. What is accepted is that this move is desirable and to be recommended.'[55]

The ramifications of this change for the Army's instrument factory may well have been considerable—especially in terms of the implied need for new investment in manufacturing processes. In any case, general trading conditions had been slack, and questions hung over its viability. Though the production of tuning slides and the prospect of work in adjusting instruments from high to low pitch provided important short-term extra income, there were new competitors for the attention of Salvation Army band players. As was the case with secular bands (see Chapter 4), the change to the commonly used international pitch standard meant that players could choose a new instrument from virtually any manufacturer who sold instruments in the British market. Analyses within the Army showed that the factory had registered losses every year since 1957 and, with the exception of 1964 (presumably because of the sale of low-pitch slides), the loss was greater each year than in the year before.[56]

The St Albans workers were given notice that their employment with the Army would end on 24 February 1972. An amicable agreement was struck with Boosey & Hawkes which made for a smooth transition and ensured the immediate futures of the staff at St Albans. These events were described to Salvation Army band players in a short announcement under the heading 'Instrument Factory Changes' in the *Musician*:

In order to meet, adequately and economically, the growing demand for instruments for our bands throughout the world, it has been agreed for Messrs. Boosey & Hawkes

[55] *Musician* (21 Mar. 1964), 1.
[56] Salvation Army regulations forbid the direct quotation of documents at the IHC concerning the change to low pitch and the closure of the musical instrument factory.

Ltd., to rent our Musical Instrument Factory at St. Albans. Our craftsmen there, in conjunction with that firm, will continue to make the popular current models of the 'Bandmaster' cornet and the 'Triumphonic' tenor horn. The other 'Triumphonic' instruments will be discontinued.

Orders for all instruments should be sent, as before, to S. P. & S., Ltd., and we will be able to give competitive terms for those instruments bearing our own insignia, and those from Boosey & Hawkes and other makers. Repairs and reconditioning will also be undertaken, and used instruments will be traded-in and sold as previously.[57]

The withdrawal of the independent instrument manufacturing facility was symbolically important for the Army, even though it did not especially damage it in the longer term; indeed, the inevitable mainstreaming may well have benefited aspects of it. One source claimed that in 1980 there were 40,000 bandsmen worldwide, and that 'In England and Wales alone, the majority of the 800 local corps units can muster a band of some sort . . .'.[58] By 1997 the number had dropped to 25,183.[59]

Perhaps the most lasting and compelling influence of the Salvation Army on the world of music can be found not in Britain, but beyond. Booth's vision was of an international army which would challenge the devil throughout the world, and turn the multitudes towards salvation. The speed at which this diaspora occurred is striking. It had spread to the USA and Australia in 1880; France in 1881; Canada, Sweden, India, and Switzerland in 1882; South Africa, New Zealand, and Ceylon in 1883; throughout Europe and South America four years later; and then to the Far East and Russia. Without much design, but rather by the precipitous enthusiasm of its soldiers, the Salvation Army spread to sixty-three countries by 1916.[60] By 1941 it was in 97 countries and 103 by 1997.[61] As it went, it acquiesced to the tones and textures of local cultures—the popular cultures—in order to reach the masses and to be comprehended by them. With its message it took its repertoire, and for the same practical and utilitarian reasons that brass instruments proved so successful in a field in Salisbury in 1878, they were used in the streets of Bombay, Tokyo, Auckland, and Johannesburg, on the American prairies, and anywhere else where Booth's message was being articulated. It is in the nature of Salvation Army campaigns that converts become soldiers. Thus, brass instruments fell into the hands of indigenous populations. Throughout the world, Western brass instruments have become a part of popular music culture; some estimate that

---

[57] *Musician* (19 Feb. 1972), 115.

[58] *Sounding Brass* (Summer 1980), 21. *Salvation Army Year Book* (1981), 50, gives 41,481 senior bandsmen.

[59] *Salvation Army Year Book* (1998), 38. Statistics given as at 1 Jan. 1997.

[60] *Salvation Army Year Book* (1917).

[61] *Salvation Army Year Books* (1942) and (1998) respectively. One has to take into account that some of these statistics reflect changes in federations, colonies, and dependencies.

Figure 5.6. The Salvation Army was active in the USA from the 1880s. In California, the Salvation Army War Chariot was a familiar sight. This 1893 photograph shows the Charioteers on their way to a mining camp meeting.

there are 800,000 brass bands in India alone.[62] The music they play and the techniques they use owe little to Western influences, because the process of cultural assimilation has been so thorough, but irrespective of how such assimilations have been manifested, one need look no further than colonizing and missionary influences to see how they originated. Booth's disciples carried the message throughout the world at the turn of the century, in a manner which reflected those images which had been common in the British experience. Indeed, it is hard to see any single religious denomination—excepting perhaps the Roman Catholic Church—as a more powerful agency in terms of spreading a particular type of music culture worldwide than the Salvation Army.[63]

---

[62] Rob Boonzajer Flaes, liner notes to *Frozen Brass Anthology of Brass Band Music*, i, *Asia*, Pan, 2020CD. The *Frozen Brass* series is an aural record of an extensive research project into brass bands in non-Western cultures conducted by the Dept. of Visual Anthropology at the University of Amsterdam.

[63] See Trevor Herbert and Margaret Sarkissian, 'Victorian Bands and their Dissemination in the Colonies', *Popular Music*, 16/2 (1997), 165–79.

6

The Brass Band in the Antipodes: The Transplantation of British Popular Culture

DUNCAN BYTHELL

INTRODUCTION

When we speak of an international popular culture today, especially in music, we are likely to think of an American-dominated world whose origins lie in the gramophone record and whose current symbols are the transistor and the personal stereo. But at the beginning of the twentieth century, there was a rather different European-derived musical popular culture, whose essence lay in making music rather than merely listening to it. Amateur bands playing popular works by contemporary European composers, on various combinations of cheap, mass-produced wind instruments, were a major element in this culture, which was carried round the world not by the airwaves or in electronic devices, but in the heads, hearts, and hands of tens of thousands of ordinary European emigrants who took their home-grown customs, institutions, and pastimes with them when they put down new roots in strange places. The *British* strand within this transplanted popular culture was particularly important, and it was best able to thrive unchecked and little-changed in those small and distant communities where immigration from places other than the United Kingdom was negligible, and where cultural links with the 'Old Country' were kept strong by being continuously renewed. Not surprisingly, Australia, New Zealand, and Canada met these conditions perfectly in the late nineteenth and early twentieth centuries.

The diffusion throughout the Empire (and especially the White Dominions) of the British brass band in this period is a prime example of this process at work; in the musical world, other examples could be found in the proliferation of choral societies and competitive music festivals, while in the wider sphere, the process is evident in the games people played and the literature they read. Whether any other European society exported so much of its popular culture undiluted in the late nineteenth century is doubtful, although one is reminded, for example, of the way in which Italian immigrants to South America carried their love of opera with them to São Paulo and Buenos Aires. Still, we must never forget that there were probably no other societies in the world so obviously 'colonial' as Britain's antipodean outposts in 1900.

In its modern form, the British brass band began to take shape around the middle of the nineteenth century, and reached its zenith at the beginning of the twentieth. This period coincided exactly with the spectacular development of Britain's 'settlement' colonies in the south Pacific. Australia, whose white population numbered less than half a million in 1850, was approaching the five-million mark by the outbreak of the First World War; whilst the rate of population-increase in New Zealand, where colonization had barely begun in 1850, was even more rapid. In both cases, the arrival of successive waves of immigrants from the United Kingdom meant the creation of new communities on the coasts and in the interior, as the frontier of settlement advanced and natural resources were explored and exploited. The development process also involved the elevation of a handful of these communities—in the case of Australia, the state capitals of the six separate colonies which united to form a Commonwealth in 1901—into major cities, whose residents provided the houses, the everyday goods, and the vast range of services which an affluent and rapidly growing local population required. Whether large or small, these new urban communities in the antipodes quickly replicated both the physical forms and the social institutions familiar in Victorian and Edwardian Britain. It is not surprising that so quintessentially Victorian an institution as the brass band should have been prominent among them.

In broad outline, the social, economic, and political development of Australia and New Zealand followed similar lines during this period; and it is tempting, especially from a British perspective, to lump them together under the convenient epithets 'antipodean' and 'Australasian'. Up to a point, this practice can be justified—not least because, in both economic and cultural terms, there were many close links between the colonies on both sides of the Tasman Sea. In the great age of the passenger steamer around 1900 it was easier to travel from Sydney or Melbourne to Auckland and Dunedin than to Perth in distant Western Australia. Consequently, as the brass band movement gathered momentum in both countries, it was possible for leading New Zealand bands to enter major Australian contests, and vice versa. Invercargill Garrison Band led the way by contesting at Melbourne in 1897; and, in 1910, Wanganui Garrison became the first New Zealand band to win Grade A at Ballarat's prestigious South Street competition. Likewise, individual bandsmen

migrated readily in both directions across the Tasman in search of new opportunities to work and to play; and from the earliest days the organizers of
contests in New Zealand looked to their larger neighbour for adjudicators of
appropriate experience and impartiality.

Yet despite the links and the similarities, key differences between Australia
and New Zealand must not be forgotten. Apart from the very different circumstances under which colonization began, and the fact that New Zealand
remained outside the Commonwealth of Australia in 1901, there were dis-
similarities in the timing and the character of economic development which
had implications for the brass band movement. The fact that New Zealand (and
especially the north island) was booming in the 1890s, when much of eastern
Australia was in serious economic recession, must help to explain why its brass
band movement appeared to forge ahead during that decade after a late start.
Nevertheless, Australians still outnumbered New Zealanders by nearly five to
one at the outbreak of the First World War. Despite the pride of their city fathers
and the splendour of their public buildings, Auckland, Wellington, Christchurch, and Dunedin remained small provincial towns in comparison with
Australia's two great metropolises, Sydney and Melbourne, whose combined
populations equalled that of the whole of New Zealand at the beginning of the
twentieth century. This disproportion between the two countries which make
up Britain's 'antipodes' is reflected in the following pages, where Australia
receives considerably greater coverage than New Zealand. Selectivity has, of
course, been necessary at every level in an introductory sketch of this kind; but
this particular disparity also results from the fact that, whereas the author has
worked at first hand on some of the relevant Australian sources, he has depended
largely on the published works of others for information about New Zealand.

This chapter has three main aims: first, to consider why the history of the
brass band in the antipodes has been largely neglected; secondly, to provide an
outline of the growth of the brass band movement between the 1850s and the
1930s; and thirdly, to suggest some of the ways in which developments in
Australia and New Zealand diverged from the British model. A fourth theme
—a comparison between developments in Australia and in New Zealand—
will occasionally be touched upon; but more work, by other hands, will be
needed before this subject can be satisfactorily explored. Other topics meriting
further research will be indicated in the chapter's concluding section.

CONSPICUOUS, BUT NEGLECTED: THE BRASS BAND IN ANTIPODEAN HISTORY

That brass bands were a prominent and ubiquitous feature of the musical and
social life of Australia and New Zealand in the late nineteenth and early twentieth centuries is evident from the magnificent rotundas which still adorn

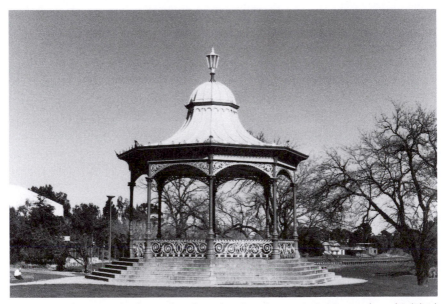

Figure 6.1*a*, *b*. Rotundas for outdoor brass band performances in Newcastle and Adelaide, Australia.

public parks and gardens, from the major cities down to the smallest country towns. That such bands, although by no means defunct, no longer play so important a part is suggested by the fact that, in parts of Australia, these fine structures—whether elegant, ponderous, or merely bizarre—are nowadays more commonly used as picturesque and convenient settings for wedding ceremonies than for musical performances. However, to capture a real sense of the brass band's place in antipodean history, we need to go beyond these evocative, if decaying, artefacts to the close-printed pages of local newspapers of eighty to a hundred years ago. Even a cursory glance will show that few occasions in public life—whether one-off events like laying a foundation stone, or annual rituals such as the Australian trade unions' celebrations of Eight Hours Day—were complete without at least one band in attendance to add solemnity, dignity, or a festive air to the proceedings, as appropriate.[1] Nor were brass bands on hand simply when pomp and circumstance were the order of the day. They entertained the crowds at sporting fixtures; gave their services free for worthy causes—fifty-two bands were said to have played at various Melbourne venues for 'hospital Sunday' in 1929;[2] added to the jollity of trade-union picnics and Sunday School outings; and provided a relaxing background to such outdoor routines as late-night shopping on a Friday, and post-prandial perambulation on a Sunday afternoon. And whilst secular bands—with municipal permission, of course—might make their distinctive contribution to sabbath ritual, their religious counterparts in the Salvation Army were also active in harnessing this popular form of music making to the stern task of accomplishing the Lord's work in new places.

A few moments' reflection will make it clear that, in an age when gramophone, radio, and other electronic means of storing and reproducing music were lacking, and when all music was necessarily 'live', the brass band must have played a major part in the musical education of both performers and audiences in Australasia, as elsewhere in the Western world. Until the advent of radio in the 1920s, bands provided most of them with their only real opportunity to hear concerted instrumental music, and with their first (and often their only) acquaintance with the popular classics. Similarly, it was only by learning a brass instrument that many young men could have been introduced to the pleasures of developing their own musicianship. In fact, an interesting list could be compiled of Australians, later prominent in many walks of life, who were bandsmen in their youth: it would include John Brownlee, the opera singer (1900–69); Frederick Curwen, sportsman, lawyer, and president of the Young Australia League (1894–1964); and Gordon Chalk, the Queensland

---

[1] A standard eight-hour working day was one of the proudest achievements of the Australian trade unions in the late 19th cent. It was celebrated annually in each of the major cities by a public holiday, which involved a procession of trade unionists with banners and bands, followed by a gala and sports day. A brass band contest was sometimes incorporated into the programme.

[2] *Australasian Band and Orchestra News* (Melbourne), 25 (Oct. 1929), 5.

politician.[3] In addition, it should be noted that a handful of men who began their musical careers in brass bands moved successfully into the 'serious' profession as orchestral players: the Partington family from Tasmania provided brass players for several Australian symphony orchestras for a considerable part of the twentieth century.[4] Most impressive of all, the cornet player, Percy Code (1888–1953)—whose bandmaster father had groomed him to be the Alexander Owen of the antipodes—ended his life rather as the Adrian Boult, being chief conductor of the Australian Broadcasting Commission's orchestras in the 1930s and 1940s.[5]

Finally, in recalling the former role of brass bands in colonial life, it must be remembered that they also offered a new type of team game and spectator sport to societies which took such things seriously. Brass band contests—at local, state, and even national level—were frequent and widespread from the 1890s to the 1930s; and the band associations which grew up to regulate contesting in both Australia and New Zealand served to create the sense that there was indeed a brass band *movement* there. From 1900 until it went into abeyance in 1924, the annual South Street contest at Ballarat was regarded as 'the Mecca of Australasian bandsmen', and crowds of 20,000 and more would gather to watch the marching, listen respectfully to the playing, and cheer on their favourites.[6] Sometimes, partisan spirits boiled over on the contest field with unseemly consequences. There were notoriously ugly scenes at the final of the New South Wales contest in Sydney in 1931, when a large part of the crowd disputed the verdict of the distinguished British adjudicator and composer, Cyril Jenkins. The judge's tent was besieged, and instruments were 'played in a derisory fashion'. Order was only restored when the police had been called and the conductor of the losing band had personally escorted Jenkins to the safety of a waiting motor car.[7]

Yet despite their contribution to so many different aspects of life, brass bands have so far largely escaped the attention of historians both of Australian music and of Australian leisure and popular culture. Not that band histories are completely non-existent: the brass band press everywhere has always been fond of filling odd corners with potted histories and old photographs of individual bands; and if Australian bands have been neglected, those of New

[3] On J. Brownlee, see *Australian Dictionary of Biography (ADB)*, vii (Melbourne: Melbourne University Press, 1966–), 450–1. On F. Curwen, see *A Biographical Register: Notes from the Name-Index of the ADB* (Canberra: Australian Dictionary of Biography, 1987), i. 154. On G. Chalk, I am indebted to Prof. Cameron Hazlehurst for private information.

[4] On the Partington family, see D. Madden, *A History of Hobart's Brass Bands* (Davenport, Tas., n.d., unpaginated).

[5] *ADB* viii. 48.

[6] On the early history of the South Street contest, see *Australian Musical News*, 1/1 (1911), 10; 3/12 (1914), 357; *Australian Band Leader* (Ballarat), 1/1 (1971), 13.

[7] *Sydney Morning Herald* (27 Jan. 1931). See also D. Bythell, 'Class, Community, and Culture: The Case of the Brass Band in Newcastle', *Labour History* (Australia), 67 (1994), 149–50.

Zealand have found a champion in Stanley Newcomb.[8] For the most part, however, band histories have been written by band enthusiasts rather than by professional historians. Their style tends to be narrative and anecdotal, their chronology vague, and their content dominated by tales of heroic individuals and their achievements on the contest field. Why, then, have scholars overlooked them?

It is easy to demonstrate the extent of their neglect in the standard histories of Australian music. For example, W. A. Orchard's classic account, published in the early 1950s, while devoting some space to amateur choral societies, contains a bare handful of brief and scattered references which testify merely to the existence of brass bands. Only in an appendix, entitled 'New South Wales Provincial Towns', and written not by Orchard but by a series of local correspondents, is the place of brass bands in Australia's musical history taken seriously; and not until literally the last page of the book, in a brief section on Bathurst, is a brass band actually described as 'the City's greatest and most honoured musical institution'.[9] This refusal to admit the brass band to a place in orthodox musical history is, of course, nothing new. It parallels British experience, and can presumably be explained in the same way. To those brought up in the bourgeois tradition of European classical music, brass bands were amateur bodies, and amateurism could easily be equated with low standards of technique and musicianship; at best, they played only inauthentic arrangements of 'great' music, while at worst they played trash; and finally, to the serious musician, the vulgarity and the false motives associated with band contests must have been more reminiscent of the football stadium than of the concert hall. When Henri Verbruggen, director of the New South Wales Conservatorium of Music, invited Melbourne's Malvern Tramways Band to share a platform with his symphony orchestra in 1921 after he had heard them play at Ballarat, it was hailed as 'the highest compliment yet paid to an Australian brass band'; but there is little to suggest that this was anything more than a token gesture.[10]

But if musical—and social—snobbery, together with that deference to all things British which some have called 'cultural cringe', easily explain why brass bands have been written out of Australia's musical history, it is less easy to understand why the new generation of social historians have generally overlooked them, given their strong interest in the history of other leisure pursuits.[11] Bands go unmentioned, for example, in Spearritt and Walker's

[8] S. P. Newcomb, *The Music of the People: The Story of the Band Movement in New Zealand 1845–1963* (Christchurch: G. R. Mowat, 1963).

[9] W. A. Orchard, *Music in Australia* (Melbourne: Georgian House, 1952). The references to Bathurst are on pp. 221–2.

[10] A. E. Zealley and J. Ord Hume, *Famous Bands of the British Empire* (London: J. P. Hull, 1926), 60.

[11] For 'cultural cringe', see J. Rickard, *Australia: A Cultural History* (London: Longman, 1988), 138–9, 222, 264–5.

collection of essays on *Australian Popular Culture* (1979), and are commemorated pictorially in that splendid bicentennial extravaganza, the ten-volume *Australians: A Historical Library,* by only one photograph of a Salvation Army band and one of the rotunda at Stawell, Victoria.[12] The only extended treatment of their place in community life by an academic social historian known to me is J. McEwen's doctoral thesis, 'The Newcastle Coalmining District of New South Wales, 1860–1900'. It may be, of course, that this neglect is unconscious: even so, one cannot avoid the suspicion that the brass band has been ignored because it does not fit easily into any of the currently fashionable approaches which characterize much recent work by Australian social historians. For instance, historians interested in the distinctively 'Australian' aspects of their society would, understandably, have had little time for an institution which was self-evidently an import from Britain and a prime example of the derivative and colonial character of Australian culture at the time. Nor is it surprising that the brass band has failed to excite the enthusiasm of left-inclined historians, who might easily have interpreted its development as an obvious example of bourgeois cultural hegemony and a sinister form of 'social control', designed to take the workers' minds off more serious matters. Finally, since the brass band was, until recently, an exclusively male preserve, one cannot blame Australia's feminist historians for failing to see anything interesting in it.

If these are indeed the reasons for the neglect, it must be admitted that they have some validity. Nevertheless, it would be unwise to put too much emphasis on arguments about 'social control' until we know more about how, when, and where bands were set up, who joined them, how they operated, and how they related to their local communities. It would be even less sensible to dismiss the brass band as merely a British cultural export until we have examined the ways in which it was subtly modified over the years, as it took root and developed in its new environment. A proper understanding of the history of colonial society and culture depends on striking the right balance between the similarities and differences which came to exist between the colonies and the 'Old Country', especially in the period of recurrent mass migration from the gold rushes of the 1850s to the depression of the 1930s.

It must be stressed that this chapter is introductory, and its conclusions are often speculative and tentative. If it can stake a modest claim to being one of the first words on the subject, it cannot pretend to be the last. Indeed, there are many issues, particularly with regard to quantification, which it cannot consider at all. How many Australians and New Zealanders actually played in brass bands? Were antipodean bandsmen more numerous than British

[12] P. Spearritt and D. Walker (eds.), *Australian Popular Culture* (Sydney: G. Allen & Unwin, 1979). F. Crowley, A. D. Gilbert, K. S. Inglis, and P. Spearritt (eds.), *Australians: A Historical Library* (Broadway, NSW: Fairfax, Syme & Weldon, 1987), iii. 444, and viii. 386.

bandsmen in proportion to population? How did the number who joined bands compare with, say, the number who regularly played cricket on an organized (but amateur) basis? Knowing how many bands existed at a given time would not, of course, solve the central problem, which is how many men played in a band *at some time in their lives*? Life-long bandsmen, who gravitated gracefully down the ranks from solo cornet to E♭ bass as lips got slack and breath got short, were, almost certainly, greatly outnumbered by young men whose band careers took up a mere part of that brief interlude between leaving school and getting married. Unanswered questions such as these will require detailed work on local sources which only a historian based permanently in the antipodes could hope to undertake. It is important, therefore, to give a clear indication of the materials which have gone into the production of this preliminary sketch.

Being small, informal, and voluntary organizations, individual brass bands tended to generate relatively little paper in their ordinary course of business, although they often left behind plenty of photographs. Given that they were often also ephemeral bodies, little of even this meagre documentation was likely to survive a band's demise. Certainly, very few band archives have yet found their way into academic libraries and record offices, though some material must surely still remain locally and in private hands. One particularly well-documented band is that which existed at Tooth's Brewery, Sydney, between 1927 and 1932, since its records are preserved with the firm's archives at the Australian National University (ANU); but, for reasons which will become apparent, Tooth's band was hardly a typical outfit.[13] In the absence of this basic material, what follows has been built up from fragments collected from a wide range of sources, many of which are only indirectly concerned with brass bands and their activities.

Among printed materials, undoubtedly the most important for tracing the activities of individual bands and assessing their role in community life are the local newspapers, which proliferated throughout Australia and New Zealand at precisely the same time as the bands themselves; and it is certain that historians wishing to examine the rise and decline of brass bands in detail in particular localities will find these, overall, the most valuable source of information. In addition, as bands became more common, a specialist brass band press developed to cater for enthusiasts and provide a mouthpiece for 'the movement'. Like its British counterpart, its editors relied heavily on local correspondents and band secretaries for information about the activities and achievements of individual bands. The New South Wales-based *Australasian Bandsman* and the Victoria-based *Australian Band News* both seem to have

---

[13] The records of Tooth's Brewery are deposited at the Australian National University, Canberra, in the Noel Butlin Archives of Business and Labour (hereafter ANU/ABL). The papers relating to the Brewery band are classified at N 20/4016–4038.

started life around 1900, but the earliest file of these publications that I have been able to locate, in Sydney's Mitchell Library, dates from 1926, just before they merged to form the monthly *Australian Band and Orchestra News*. Among other specialist publications, it should be noted that the Salvation Army in Australia ran a monthly paper for its own bandsmen and songsters entitled *The Musician,* but unfortunately this only began publication in 1947. Other ephemeral periodicals may have existed locally, but, like the Ballarat-based *Australian Band Leader* (1971–2), probably lasted only a short time before expiring for lack of readers and advertisers.

Apart from the specialist and general newspaper press, the activities of brass bands can also be studied intermittently, but sometimes in revealing detail, in the surviving records of the labour movement, with which they had many links. They can also be followed in the archives of local municipal bodies, with which they were often associated on civic occasions, and to which they generally looked for funding. A partial survey of trade-union, Trades-Hall, and Eight Hours committee records in the ANU's Archives of Business and Labour, and the Melbourne University Archives, together with a somewhat cursory sampling of the wide variety of local material available in the Newcastle (New South Wales) City Library, proved particularly fruitful in illuminating the ways in which records of this kind can cast light on Australasia's neglected brass band history.

THE GROWTH AND DECLINE OF THE BRASS BAND MOVEMENT

By the end of the 1890s, the British brass band—that is, the specific combination of cornets, saxhorns, and trombones which had become standardized in Britain, thanks to the growth of contesting and the activities of the music publishers and instrument makers—had also become established as the normal type of wind band operating in Australia and New Zealand. As in Britain, there had, of course, been earlier groupings of brass and woodwind instruments which served as forerunners of the 'movement'. Military bands accompanied the troops sent to police the Australian penal colonies from the very beginning, and they were present in New Zealand until British regiments were withdrawn in 1870 following the end of the Maori wars. More significantly, informal civilian bands obviously established themselves in many of the small new communities which sprang up in the pioneering days of the 1860s and 1870s, and were no doubt happy to use whatever instrumental talent was available: the first 'brass' band at Westport, in New Zealand's south island, boasted only nine players—four of them percussionists—at its formation in 1869.[14] Only as towns and villages became bigger, more settled, and more affluent, and as band contests grew in popularity, did bigger bands, of standard

---

[14] Newcomb, *Music of the People,* 21, 33.

Figure 6.2. The Christchurch Bicycle Band at the turn of the century. Bicycle bands were not uncommon; there are several examples of them in Italy and the USA. There are instances of mounted bands taking up bicycles as an alternative to horses.

instrumentation, become more common. Photographic evidence suggests that the classic British brass band formation had displaced older, informal combinations by the early 1900s—although a full complement of players may still have been an aspiration rather than a reality in many cases. There is, however, no known British prototype for the remarkable bicycle band which existed briefly in Christchurch in the 1890s (see Fig. 6.2).

The successful transplantation of the brass band to the colonies in the late nineteenth century should not surprise us, given the importance of ordinary, wage-earning immigrants from Britain in building-up Australasia's population and developing its communities and institutions. The contribution of British-born bandsmen to Australian banding is particularly noticeable in mining areas whose counterparts in 'the Old Country' were major centres of the movement. Thus McEwen has attributed the popularity of bands in the Newcastle coalfield district of New South Wales to the concentration there of migrants from the colliery villages of north-east England; while Philip Payton has drawn attention to the vigorous band tradition which Cornish miners created in South Australia's 'Little Cornwall'.[15] In terms of named individuals, approximately one-third of the thirty or so men noticed in *The Biographical*

[15] J. McEwen, 'The Newcastle Coalmining District of New South Wales, 1860–1900' (Ph.D. thesis, University of Sydney, 1979), esp. ch. 6; P. Payton, *The Cornish Miner in Australia* (Trewolsta, Cornwall: Dyllansow Truran, 1984).

Register of the Australian Dictionary of Biography as having brass band connections were British born;[16] while in New Zealand it has been observed that the first known trio of slide trombones in a brass band (1885) included Messrs Hepplestone and Charlesworth, respectively from Batley and Linthwaite, in Yorkshire. However, probably the dominant figure in the movement's early days in New Zealand was Thomas Herd. Born in Yorkshire, and gaining his early experience with bands in west Cumbria and County Durham, he emigrated in 1885, and soon began a long and fruitful association with Wellington Garrison Band which, under his leadership, had become the country's most successful contesting band by 1900.[17] Finally, Australasian banding received a further boost from Britain when the Salvation Army began its operations. The establishment of the first Salvationist band followed the arrival in Adelaide in 1881 of Captain Thomas Sutherland, who, we are told, led his musical forces through the streets playing his pocket-cornet, and 'marching backwards in the approved Christian Mission style'.[18]

Not only was the link between British and colonial bands established and sustained by the continued flow of migrant bandsmen. In the early twentieth century, colonial standards were maintained, and the purity of the transplanted traditions preserved, by the frequent appearance of adjudicators from Britain at major band contests, such as South Street, Ballarat. James Ord Hume—a prolific composer and arranger of band music—visited Australia and New Zealand in 1903 and again in 1924, and is credited with having persuaded New Zealand bands to give up the valve trombone in favour of the authentic slide version preferred in Britain.[19] More important still, colonial bands relied heavily on importing both their instruments and their sheet music from Britain via such establishments as Palings in Sydney. Virtually all advertisements for brass instruments in the Australian specialist press in the 1920s were for the popular Besson and Boosey models made in England; and, although the major instrument suppliers in the cities undertook repairs, I have found no significant evidence of the actual manufacture of brass instruments in Australia or New Zealand. Likewise with music: when Sydney's Professional Musicians Band wished to add the overture 'Morning, Noon, and Night' to its repertoire in 1931, it was unable to do so, because Palings did not have the parts in stock, and it would have taken too long, and cost too much, to import them from Britain.[20] Not surprisingly, Australasian banding

---

[16] I am grateful to Ann Smith, of the staff of the *Australian Dictionary of Biography*, ANU, for her assistance in analysing the name-index prior to the publication of the *Biographical Register*.

[17] Newcomb, *Music of the People*, 36. There is a profile of T. Herd in *New Zealand Mail* (Wellington, 7 Jan. 1897), 21.

[18] *The Musician* (Melbourne), 1/7 (Mar. 1948), 111.

[19] Newcomb, *Music of the People*, 65–6.

[20] ANU/ABL Records of the Musicians Union of Australia. T7/6/1 Minutes of the Professional Musicians Band, 3 Mar. 1931.

produced its own composers. Outstanding among them was Alexander Lithgow (1870–1929)—the 'Sousa of the Antipodes'. Glaswegian by birth, but emigrating with his parents at the age of 6 to Invercargill, he ultimately dominated Tasmanian banding, and enjoys the rare distinction of a full-scale entry in the *Australian Dictionary of Biography*.[21]

The traffic between 'home' and 'colonies' was, in fact, two-way. In one of his less happy entrepreneurial ventures into the brass band world, John Henry Iles, proprietor of the *British Bandsman* and initiator of the National championship at the Crystal Palace from 1900, organized a tour of the United Kingdom by an antipodean band as early as 1903: the 'Hinemoa' Band, handpicked from New Zealand's leading players and led by Thomas Herd, played in 'a hundred British towns' before their trip was aborted amid recriminations about bad organization.[22] Four years later, Iles masterminded the memorable and successful world tour by Britain's Besses o' th' Barn Band under Alexander Owen, which took in both Australia and New Zealand; and 'Besses' paid a second visit to Australasia at their own initiative in 1910. Equally memorable in the opposite direction was the 1924 visit to Britain of the Newcastle Steelworks Band, from New South Wales: intending primarily to play at the British Empire Exhibition at Wembley, the visitors confounded the British brass band fraternity by carrying off the first prize at Belle Vue. But the logistics and high costs of international tours and exchanges made them exceptional until after the Second World War. Malvern Tramways Band—generally regarded as Australia's best in the 1920s—would have liked to follow Newcastle Steelworks and tour Britain; but their bandmaster Harry Shugg (1891–1968) had to be content with organizing a private conducting and adjudicating trip for himself.[23] Other prominent Australian bandsmen also visited Britain on an individual basis: Percy Code and Percy Jones (1885–1948) both completed their musical training in the United Kingdom; while Frank Wright (1901–71), Australia's leading cornet player in the generation after Code, emigrated permanently to Britain in the 1930s, was quickly appointed organizer of concerts in London's parks for the London County Council, and established himself as a leading figure in the British brass band world.[24]

---

[21] *ADB* x. 119–20.

[22] For the 'Hinemoa' band, see Newcomb, *Music of the People*, 56; for J. H. Iles, see D. Bythell, 'Provinces versus Metropolis in the British Brass Band Movement', *Popular Music*, 16/2 (1997), 144–55.

[23] *Australian Band News* (Avoca, Vic.), 20 (May 1925), 12; 25 (July 1929), 6; *Australian Band and Orchestra News*, 21 (Apr. 1926), 15. For Newcastle Steelworks, see Bythell, 'Class, Community, and Culture', 148–9.

[24] On P. Code, see *ADB* viii. 48. On P. Jones and H. Shugg, see *Biographical Register*, i. 378; ii. 257. There is an obituary of Frank Wright, discussing his early career in Australia, in *Australian Band Leader*, 1/1 (Oct. 1971), 10.

Given the original links and continuing connections between British and colonial bands, it is not surprising that their role in both the musical and the social life of their respective countries showed many essential and enduring similarities. As our discussion of Orchard's history has indicated, Australian bands, like their British counterparts, were a distinct and largely separate stratum of the musical world, ignored and despised by an establishment which saw opera, chamber recitals, choral festivals, and symphony concerts as the only legitimate forms of serious music. Their detachment from the educational system seems equally complete. School bands were not unknown in Australia —indeed the St Vincent Boys' Band (Melbourne) and the St Augustine's Band (Geelong) achieved very high standards, and a number of other residential educational establishments seem to have maintained bands at various times both for their current pupils and their alumni.[25] But in a scathing editorial in 1929, the *Australasian Band and Orchestra News* lamented the apparent lack of interest in fostering bands in state day schools, despite the beneficial effects which an early introduction to banding was alleged to have in promoting the physical and moral health of young men.[26] The result was that, as in Britain, youngsters usually had to learn brass instruments outside the context of formal schooling, and thus one possible channel for maintaining a steady flow of recruits into 'the movement' was blocked, at least until recent years.

Socially, it is clear that Australian bands fulfilled the same functions for bandsmen and their families as they did in Britain. Men joined and stayed with their bands because of the mixtures of conviviality and cameraderie, of music making and money making, which membership brought. In lean times, the band could provide a network of emotional and material assistance, and there are several examples in the 1930s of bands using the proceeds of the collecting tin specifically to support their unemployed members.[27] Similarly, although women players seem not to have been accepted in brass bands until after the Second World War, there were various opportunities for wives and girlfriends to support their menfolk. Few bands appear to have been without a ladies' committee which would run dances, euchre parties (the Australian equivalent of whist drives), and other social events to help raise funds. Organizationally, too, brass bands in the antipodes closely resembled their British equivalents. Although it is proper to talk of a brass band *movement*, the fact

---

[25] The Newcastle district may have been exceptional in fostering school bands: there were said to be six in existence in 1902 (*Newcastle Morning Herald*, 7 July 1962). See also Bythell, 'Class, Community and Culture', 150.

[26] *Australasian Band and Orchestra News*, 25 (Oct. 1929), 1.

[27] e.g. in the winter of 1931, Hamilton Citizens Band gave the major part of the profits derived from concerts and engagements to twelve of its players who were out of work (Newcastle Public Library, Local Collection, A 2519, Hamilton Municipal Council, Correspondence, Box 2, File 6/170; Letter from Band Secretary to Town Clerk, 30 June 1931). South Melbourne Band used the proceeds of collections in a similar way (*Australasian Band and Orchestra News*, 25 (Sept. 1929), 16; and 25 (Dec. 1929), 14).

remains that each band was an independent, voluntary, and self-governing organization, owning its own property, determining its own business, and disciplining its own members. Each band came into being through some exercise of local initiative, and survival depended on its current membership having both the will and the means—in terms of both human and material resources—to carry on.

Because of the essential independence of each individual band, it is difficult to generalize with any precision about the rise and decline of the movement in Australia and New Zealand, or to make exact comparisons with Britain as regards chronology. However, it seems likely that, as in many other areas, there was something of a time-lag between British and colonial experience. Dave Russell's work on brass bands in Yorkshire suggests that, numerically speaking, they reached their peak in the first decade of the twentieth century, and found it increasingly difficult to keep up their appeal, both to players and to audiences, in the face of an ever-growing range of alternative attractions thereafter.[28] In the long run, of course, the same cultural and social processes which slowly made brass bands unpopular and unfashionable in Britain also operated in Australia and New Zealand. My general impression is that contesting only really caught on there in the 1890s and early 1900s, and that the heyday of the movement lasted into the 1920s in Australia, and the 1930s in New Zealand. Certainly, contesting seems to have remained popular in Australia, despite the unhappy suspension of the Ballarat competition in 1924, and there is evidence of new bands being formed (although there are also signs of defunct bands in some smaller county towns) down to the end of the 1920s.[29] What seems quite clear, on the other hand, is that the depression of the early 1930s had a sudden, severe and lasting effect on Australian bands in particular, and greatly accelerated the decline of the movement in many parts of the country. Tooth's Brewery Band folded in 1932 as a result of a loss of members through unemployment, a decline in financial support from the brewery, and a lack of paid engagements.[30] Palings stopped importing musical instruments from Britain between 1930 and 1933 in the face of declining demand.[31] Most revealing of all, the *Australian Band and Orchestra News*

[28] D. Russell, 'The Popular Musical Societies of the Yorkshire Textile District, 1850–1914' (D.Phil. thesis, University of York, 1979), 104–6.

[29] e.g. during the course of 1925, the *Australian Band News* reported the establishment of new bands at Tongala (near Echuca), Red Cliffs (near Mildura), the Glen Iris brickworks, St Mark's Church Fitzroy, and among Melbourne's Seventh Day Adventists. On the other hand, the *Australasian Band and Orchestra News*, 25 (Dec. 1929), 17–21, in a lengthy survey of the country bands of New South Wales, reported that the bands at Gundagai, Braidwood, and Nowra were defunct.

[30] For a fuller account of Tooth's Brewery band, see D. Bythell, 'Brewers and Bandsmen', *ABLative* (the Newsletter of the ANU Archives of Business and Labour), 8 (1988), 3–5.

[31] E. Keane, *Music for a Hundred Years: The Story of the House of Paling* (Sydney: O. Ziegler, 1954), 64.

changed its name in 1937 to the *Australian Dance and Brass Band News*—
an obvious sign that it was seeking to appeal to a new market of amateur
musicians. Even in Newcastle—which generally disputed Ballarat's claim to be
the centre of Australia banding—there is the very strong sense of a movement
in decay in the late 1930s. Despite a successful contesting record, Hamilton
Citizens Band, in a desperate plea for help to the local municipal council,
claimed in 1937 that it had 'nowhere to practice, nowhere to meet, and no
money to pay for a meeting place. Their debts amounted to over £100, principally due to the bandmaster.'[32]

Some Characteristics of Australasian Brass Bands

Different chronologies of expansion and contraction are only one of the ways
in which the brass band movement in the antipodes diverged from the British
model. Another contrast can be found in the geographical distribution of
bands. As in Britain, there were clearly areas which, in proportion to their
populations, were 'over-banded', and others which were correspondingly
'under-banded'. It is impossible at present to express these differences in a
quantitative fashion, but my general impression is that banding was particularly strong during the early twentieth century in the Newcastle coalfield, in
the Victorian and Western Australian goldfields, in the copper-mining district
of South Australia, and in remote Broken Hill—which suggests that the traditional British association between brass bands and mining communities also
applied in Australia. Similarly, it is likely that the importance of the band
in community life was even greater in small, up-country towns than in the
major cities: the towns of northern Tasmania, for example, seem to have been
enthusiastic centres. Nevertheless, there seems to be a striking difference in
the active and central role of the Australian state capitals in the movement,
as compared with London's distinctly modest place back home. According to
its headed notepaper, of the New South Wales Band Association's fifty
affiliated bands in 1930, twenty-six were 'metropolitan' and twenty-four
'country'; while a graded listing of the sixty competing bands registered with
the Victorian Band Association in 1925 indicates that about half of those
in the top three grades—and a majority of those in Grades A and B—were
Melbourne-based.[33] These figures refer, of course, only to affiliated bands
which were likely to be interested in contesting, and it is probable that many

---

[32] Minutes of a joint meeting of band committee and council subcommittee 1937 (Newcastle
Public Library, Local Collection, A 2519, Hamilton Municipal Council, Correspondence, Box 2,
File 6/170). For further details on Hamilton Citizens, see Bythell, 'Class, Community, and
Culture', 149.

[33] Various letterheads of the Band Association of New South Wales for the late 1920s were
found in the correspondence files of Tooth's Brewery Band (ANU/ABL N 20/4021). A graded list
of Victorian bands appeared in *Australian Band News*, 20 (Aug. 1925), 11.

country bands, with little prospect of taking part in state contests, were unregistered. Nevertheless, the apparent strength of the movement's metropolitan bases, compared with Britain, is remarkable.

Also noticeable are several differences in the types of brass bands. Again, current knowledge permits only an impressionistic picture to be painted: but the relative insignificance of workplace-based (and company-subsidized) bands is striking, and was the subject of a lengthy editorial in the *Australasian Band and Orchestra News* in December 1929, which reckoned that there were 'not more than ten in the whole of Australia'.[34] Even some of the so-called works bands received only minimal support from the company with which they were associated. The Newcastle Steelworks Band of the mid-1920s went to some pains to stress its financial independence of the Broken Hill Proprietary Company;[35] while the Queenstown (Tasmania) Band, on appealing to the local Mount Lyell Mining Company for a grant in 1905, was brusquely informed by the company secretary that 'music does not come within the scope of the company's operations'.[36] The position of Malvern Tramways Band in the 1920s is revealing: although it proudly boasted that it was 'a purely private organisation' and 'a tramway band in name only', the Tramway Trust none the less provided it with a band room, and 'offered employment to players worthy of the band', with the result that three-fifths of the members were tramway workers.[37] It looks as if the short-lived Tooth's Brewery Band was exceptional in having its instruments and uniforms entirely paid for by the company—at a cost of £1,000—when it started up in 1927.[38]

If corporate sponsorship was uncommon, public funding was often helpful. A marked peculiarity of the movement in New Zealand in its early days was the leading role played by garrison bands. It seems to have arisen because, until the introduction of compulsory military service in 1911, the bands associated with the old volunteer regiments enjoyed a degree of government funding which must have given them significant advantages over civilian bands when it came to acquiring instruments and uniforms. Not surprisingly, the earliest 'national' contests revolved around the friendly rivalry of these bands:

[34] *Australasian Band and Orchestra News*, 25 (Dec. 1929), 1.

[35] The Steelworks band received a grant of £50 from the Broken Hill Proprietary Company in its foundation year, 1916 (*Newcastle Morning Herald*, 2 Feb. 1917). However, in 1924 the band's secretary maintained that the Band 'does not receive any subsidy from the B. H. P. Co. or any other source whatever' (V. Beacroft to Town Clerk of Hamilton, 8 February 1924, Newcastle Public Library, Local Collection, A 2519, Hamilton Municipal Council, Correspondence, Box 2, File 2/15).

[36] G. Blainey, *The Peaks of Lyell*, 4th edn. (Melbourne: Carlton South, Vic.: Melbourne University Press, 1978), 234. The Company became more generous in its support of local bands in the 1920s.

[37] Zealley and Ord Hume, *Famous Bands of the British Empire*, 59.

[38] By the end of 1927, Tooth's Brewery had spent £796 on instruments and stands, and £225 on uniforms and medallions (ANU/ABL N 20/4016, memo from R. C. Middleton to General Manager, 22 Dec. 1927).

between 1895 and 1912, the winner, almost invariably, was either Wellington Garrison Band under Thomas Herd, or Wanganui Garrison Band under James Crichton.[39] A number of Australian bands, too, enjoyed links with local volunteer regiments around the turn of the century, but they never dominated contesting to the same extent. Increasingly, individual bands seem in many cases to have become identified with particular localities and municipalities, and their names suggest that they were seen, at least in part, as essentially civic organizations enjoying a special association with the public and community life of their own town or city. However some of the leading bands in the movement's early days, in the 1890s and early 1900s, carried the name not of their town but of their leader and founder. Thus Melbourne had Code's and Riley's bands, Ballarat had Prout's and Bulch's, and Newcastle had Barkel's. Some of these bands were subsequently adopted by a local municipality, and acquired official town-band status.[40] The origins of most antipodean bands will remain obscure until more local research has been done, but the implication is that, although reliance on municipal patronage came to be a feature of banding in the colonies, it was not necessarily the case that municipal initiative had established bands in the first instance—although some may have been originally set up as 'subscription' bands with the patronage of an *ad hoc* committee of leading citizens.[41] The relationship between brass bands and other voluntary organizations—such as churches or social clubs—also calls for further investigation before any definitive statements can be made. Is it, for example, of any significance that 'temperance' bands appear to have been almost non-existent? Perhaps not, in view of the fact that the word 'temperance' ought not to be taken literally when used in the titles of British bands. Again, how important was the Salvation Army's input into the development of Australasian banding? The impression is that the Army's bands were less isolated from, and better integrated with, the ordinary 'civilian' bands than was the case in Britain, but detailed local testing is needed before we can be certain.[42]

---

[39] Newcomb, *Music of the People*, chs. 3–7.

[40] e.g. Turner's Brunswick Band (Melbourne) was officially adopted as the Fitzroy Municipal Band in 1925, although only after some acrimonious debate in the Council Chamber (*Australian Band News*, 20 (July 1925), 15). Similarly, in 1918, Merewether Council recognized and subsidized the Band of Park Street Methodist Church Young Men's Club, which had been founded two years earlier, as its municipal band (*The History of Merewether* (Newcastle, 1935), 63–4, an anonymous official history, commemorating the fiftieth anniversary of the Municipality, copy in Newcastle Local Collection).

[41] Interestingly—in the light of its later importance as a centre of Australian banding—Newcastle was only 'relieved from the odium of being the only city in the Southern Hemisphere without a town band' in 1879 by a zealous citizens' committee, which set about raising a public subscription in order to transform the existing Volunteer Artillery Band into the City Band (*Newcastle Morning Herald*, 14 Oct. 1879).

[42] e.g. some Salvation Army bands seem to have enjoyed municipal subsidies (*The Musician*, 1/6 (Feb. 1948), 1).

In giving momentum to the movement as a whole, it is probable that contesting was of even greater importance than it was in Britain. This is partly because the commercial interests—the music publishers, instrument makers, and so on—who stood to gain financially by actively promoting the expansion of the movement on the 'supply' side in Britain, did not exist in Australia and New Zealand. Establishing governing bodies to regulate contesting did not prove easy, however. In the case of New Zealand, the first 'national' contests were run either by the military authorities for the garrison bands as part of annual manœuvres, or by the management committees which decided to include a 'one-off' contest as part of one of many international exhibitions which took place in the colony's leading cities at this period. The 1891 Dunedin contest was said to have been the first to be organized by the bands themselves, under the auspices of a United Brass Band Association. Unfortunately, local jealousies caused this body to split into separate north-island and south-island associations in the early twentieth century; and until they came together again in 1931, each organized its own annual contest, sometimes on the same dates.[43] As regards Australia, some of the individual state band associations seem to have been in existence by the early 1900s. Eventually, these bodies were responsible for laying down contest rules, grading affiliated bands, and registering their players: nevertheless, it seems likely that local contests in more remote communities remained informal and relatively unpoliced for many years.

If contesting was vital in creating and sustaining the sense of a movement, it would appear that contesting practice came to diverge from the British pattern at several points. For obvious reasons of time, cost, and distance, nation-wide contests were particularly difficult to organize in Australia, as few bands could afford to travel far outside their own localities. It cost Hamilton Citizens Band (from Newcastle) £200 to take part in the 1925 Brisbane contest;[44] and only a handful of eastern bands were able to make it to the 1929 West Australian contest held to celebrate that colony's centenary, despite the organizers' offer of £150 'appearance money' to each band.[45] The prospect of useful inter-state advertising was not enough to persuade Sydney's Tooth's Brewery to fund visits by its band to Perth, Maryborough (Queensland), or even Ballarat.[46] In order to encourage 'outside' bands to attend the 1938 New South Wales state contest at Newcastle, the organizers had to make elaborate provision for meals and accommodation for visiting bandsmen, and set up a special

[43] Newcomb, *Music of the People*, 46–8, 62.

[44] Balance sheets of the Hamilton Citizens' Band, Newcastle Public Library, Local Collection, A 2519, Hamilton Municipal Council, Correspondence, Box 2, File 6/170.

[45] *Australasian Band and Orchestra News*, 25 (Sept. 1929).

[46] ANU/ABL. The estimated cost of sending Tooth's Band to Perth was £1,200 (N 20/4018, memo from R. C. Middleton, 8 Mar. 1929). More modestly, an appearance at Ballarat was estimated to cost £275 (N 20/4019, letter from Band Secretary to Managing Director, 16 May 1932).

camp-site for them.[47] The difficulty of organizing an effective national structure for contesting may be one reason why the brass band movement in Australia failed to throw up an entrepreneurial figure like John Henry Iles, who dominated the British contest scene for most of the first half of the twentieth century.

But if the scope of Australasian contesting remained essentially regional down to the 1930s, there can be no doubt that contests had an enormous appeal, both to bandsmen and to audiences. In its heyday, the New Zealand national contest lasted for a whole week, and was described as 'an event of importance in the life of the dominion'. It included solo classes for all instruments, as well as a range of competitions—own choice, test piece, march, hymn tune, and even sight-reading—for full bands grouped into three different grades; about 150 different bands were said to have been involved in the 1933 contest at Dunedin.[48] By contrast with Britain, the emphasis in both Australia and New Zealand was on visual spectacle as well as on efficient playing, and quick-step march competitions, with the bands executing elaborate manœuvres while playing on the march, became a major feature of most contests. The rules for marching contests eventually achieved a terrifying complexity, with the marks being awarded more for smart appearance and successful drilling than for musicianship. In New Zealand, according to Stanley Newcomb, 'the most exacting requirement . . . is to march the measured distance of 100 yards taking exactly 120 paces in precisely 60 seconds. Inaccuracy is penalized at the rate of one point for every one fifth second or each pace out.' It is small wonder that Harry Mortimer, who adjudicated at the New Zealand national contest in 1953, was led to remark: 'I hate to think what some of my best bands would sound like if they had to play on the march as your men have done. I've never seen anything like it.'[49]

The first quick-step march contest ever staged in Auckland, in 1905, drew a crowd of 20,000; and similar contests continued to attract huge audiences until the 1950s. But the impact of a small local contest on a quiet country town must have been even more spectacular in terms of entertainment value. The two-day programme for a contest at Cessnock (near Newcastle) in 1935, involving just five Grade B bands, gives something of the flavour. It began with the bands marching from the railway station to the sports ground on Saturday afternoon, and ended with the adjudication and presentation of prizes at 10.30 p.m. on Sunday evening. In between times, the audience were treated to two demonstrations of massed band marching and two of massed band playing, together with four rounds of competition: quick-step march, waltz,

---

[47] See the introductory *Brochure* for the 1938 New South Wales Championship at Newcastle. (Copy in Newcastle Public Library, Local Collection, Cuttings File, 'Bands'.)

[48] J. F. Russell and J. H. Elliot, *The Brass Band Movement* (London: J. M. Dent & Sons, 1936), 202.

[49] Newcomb, *Music of the People*, 92–4.

own-choice light opera selection, and test piece.[50] It is not surprising that keen Victorian bandsmen in the late 1920s lamented the temporary collapse of the South Street contest, and blamed the alleged backwardness of the movement in their own state on this untimely (and perhaps unseemly) event.[51]

Among the other differences which emerged, it is also possible that, for a variety of reasons, Australian brass bands were more fragile and ephemeral than their British counterparts. The frequent and bewildering changes of name among Hobart bands, for example, suggest that they were constantly forming, becoming defunct, and reforming. Likewise, the historian of Dunedin's musical life, writing at the end of the Second World War about a city whose population peaked at 100,000, was forced to conclude that it had had 'so many bands that it is well-nigh impossible to give a complete account of them. Some have been of short duration, names and conductors have changed with bewildering speed, and scant material in the form of authentic records is available.'[52] The relative lack of a sense of community identity and loyalty, the migratory tendencies of Australian workers compared with their stay-at-home cousins in Britain, together with the vagaries of unemployment and the lack of public welfare provision, may all have contributed something to instability and a rapid turnover in band membership. Once again, detailed local research will be needed to verify this hypothesis, but the problems which particularly affected bands in small country towns are well indicated in the following account from the secretary of the Ararat Citizens' Band (Victoria) in 1925:

We are experiencing the usual luck of country bands, good players leaving: cannot be helped, as players must seek employment where it is to be found. We were fortunate in obtaining work for a good cornettist . . . but we will soon lose a good boy cornettist whose family are removing to the city. We have only one eupho [*sic*] player, and badly require another, and have no baritones. Want of balance in band, but we cannot help it at present.[53]

These sentiments were echoed five years later in the comment of the bandmaster of Hughenden Town Band (north-west Queensland) that 'it is a very

[50] A copy of the 'Souvenir Programme' is in the pamphlet collection, Newcastle Public Library, Local Collection.

[51] The Ballarat contest went into abeyance after 1924 because of disputes between the management of the South Street Society (which organized the whole *eisteddfod*) and the Victorian Bands Association (under whose rules the all-important competition for bands was conducted). See *Australian Band News*, 20 (Jan.–Feb. 1925). Attempts by the Ballarat-based Victorian Bands Association to establish a contest independent of South Street in the later 1920s proved unsuccessful, and in the following decade the Association was replaced as the governing body of Victorian banding by the Melbourne-based Victorian Band League. See *Australian Band Leader*, 1/3 (1971), 10. The Ballarat contest was successfully revived after the Second World War.

[52] See Madden, *Hobart's Brass Bands*, *passim*. M. Campbell, *Music in Dunedin* (Dunedin: Charles Begg, 1945), 61.

[53] *Australian Band News*, 20 (June 1925), 3.

hard uphill fight to keep the band going in a town like Hughenden'. Part of the trouble was the low motivation of some of the players, who 'played only when there was free admittance to a show or races', but the real difficulty was that Hughenden 'having no industry in the town, it is very hard to secure jobs for bandsmen, so there is nothing left but to teach the boys'.[54] Nor was this problem necessarily peculiar to country bands. One of the major reasons why Tooth's Brewery Band established itself so quickly and successfully in the late 1920s was that the company was initially persuaded to give priority in employment to experienced players from outside who would strengthen the band; but, for understandable reasons, this policy could not be continued once depression struck hard in 1930, and by February 1931 the band's secretary was lamenting the loss of key players as a result of the brewery's retrenchment of its workforce: 'our bass section is practically wiped out, our fine euphonium player lost to us, and our trombone trio split'.[55] However, it was not only hard times which could rob a leading band of several key players at a stroke. When Harry Shugg was persuaded to leave Geelong Harbour Band for Malvern Tramways in 1914, he took with him 'eight or nine' of its leading instrumentalists, who were found jobs by the Tramway Trust. As a result, the Geelong Band, which had enjoyed considerable contesting success during four years under Shugg's leadership, had to disband.[56]

If local and cyclical unemployment among other things made it difficult for bands to hold on to their players, it is also possible that they could not offer some of the other financial inducements which made long-term loyalty attractive in Britain. We have already noted that bands could try to help their members in material ways in hard times; but what happened in good times? Published and unpublished band accounts suggest that it was common practice in Australia to pay the bandmaster an annual retainer, and to cover players' travelling expenses; but how widespread was the British custom of an annual 'dividend', whereby the year's operating profit, often derived from Christmas playing, was shared out among the players? The elaborate rules of Tooth's Brewery Band provided for such a share-out, but band finances only permitted one dividend during its five-year existence: the sum involved (£5 a head) was roughly equivalent to a week's wages.[57]

In raising this issue, we are forced to explore the entire financial basis on which Australasian bands operated; and it is here that some of the biggest contrasts with Britain seem to emerge. In general, of course, brass bands tend to live from hand to mouth and from year to year, and when extraordinary expenditure is called for—on instruments, uniforms, or contest expenses—extra

[54] *Australasian Band and Orchestra News*, 25 (Jan. 1930), 17.
[55] ANU/ABL, N 20/4023, letter from Band Secretary to Managing Director, 10 Feb. 1931.
[56] Zealley and Ord Hume, *Famous Bands of the British Empire*, 60.
[57] ANU/ABL, N 20/4019, band accounts for the year ending 15 May 1930.

efforts will be made to raise extra income. It is also true that the published balance sheets of many brass bands do not necessarily reflect the real extent of their annual turnover, since, with so many small cash transactions, it is easy to dip into the collecting tin at the end of a day's playing in order to defray some immediate expense. Apart from occasional windfalls—and few bands can have been so fortunate as Singleton Town Band (New South Wales), which won a major prize in the State Lottery in 1935[58]—most band income was derived either from the fees charged when the band was hired for an engagement, or from collections and admission charges when the band sponsored its own public appearances. Unfortunately, paid engagements, though greatly prized, were often only obtained by competitive tendering, while the proceeds of public collections were entirely unpredictable. At the same time, it must be remembered that bands were often expected to give their services gratis on public occasions and for charitable causes. What all this could mean over a year's activities is indicated by the following account of the Bendigo (Victoria) Municipal Band in 1929: 'During the year, the band has assembled together on 124 occasions, as follows: 88 rehearsals, 7 paid engagements, 21 free concerts (for charity and other public functions), 8 recitals for band funds'.[59]

Given that many band activities would not generate income, and that many others yielded variable and unpredictable amounts, it was obviously desirable to have other more reliable sources of revenue. Although, as we have seen, genuine works bands were uncommon in Australia, individual bands may well have benefited from the private benevolence of local worthies: for example, it can surely have been of no disadvantage to the Collingwood Citizens Band that its president for many years was that enigmatic entrepreneur and *éminence grise* of the Labour Party, John Wren! Similarly, the Wallsend Band was probably not unique in the Newcastle coalfield in being supported by a monthly levy of 3d. per member raised by the local Miners' Lodge.[60] But for the most part—and in recognition of their public and civic role—many Australian bands came to rely on a regular annual grant from their local municipal council.

Quite why, or when, this began is difficult to say: and the generosity of city fathers was, in any case, very variable. During the 1920s, Brunswick Council (Melbourne) gave its band £200 a year, Kogorah (Sydney) and Hobart £150, but Brisbane only £39.[61] In small country towns, the grant could be no more than a token gesture: Forbes Town Band had to be content with £15, and the

---

[58] *Australian Band Leader*, 1/4 (1972), 6 and 8.

[59] *Australasian Band and Orchestra News*, 25 (Nov. 1929), 11.

[60] *Official Souvenir* of the 'Back to Wallsend Week' (Wallsend, 1935). Copy in Newcastle, Local Collection, Cuttings File 'Wallsend'.

[61] *Australian Band News*, 20 (Jan. 1925); *Australasian Band and Orchestra News*, 25 (Sept. 1929), 24; 25 (Oct. 1929), 10; and 26 (Feb. 1930), 23.

Leeton District Band received only £5.[62] Direct cash grants were not the only form of municipal support, however. Sometimes, the local band would be given shared use of a council-owned building as a rent-free band room: on occasions, this might be the sports pavilion on the town playing fields, although in Coburg (Melbourne) the band was given the use of the local maternity clinic in the evenings![63] The provision of a rotunda (or bandstand) in the local park or on the beach was also a civic responsibility, and the weekly roster of bands engaged to play there could, in Sydney or Newcastle, give councils another form of patronage to be shared around the local bands. Nevertheless, municipal funding was often criticized by bandsmen for being unreliable and parsimonious. 'Band subsidy', which seems often to have been earmarked for paying the bandmaster's stipend, was an obvious target for economy when public finances were under strain, as in Newcastle during the 1930s depression; while the reorganization of local government in the same area in 1938 served only to eliminate some of the smaller councils which had formerly supported 'their' band.

More seriously, it seems that relying on local authority grants could even be counterproductive: in the first place, it carried with it the obligation to turn out gratis for civic events and charitable causes; and second, it may have discouraged private donations, even on those occasions when the collecting box could be passed round, on the grounds that the band didn't 'need' more money, because it already enjoyed a council subsidy. The experience of Forbes Municipal Band, from rural New South Wales, is illuminating: on one occasion in 1930 they collected the grand total of 48s. from an audience estimated at more than 3,000 people. According to the *Sydney Morning Herald*, 'the sum was made up of 220 pennies and £1 in three penny pieces. There was a sprinkling of nails and buttons.'[64]

BRASS BANDS AND THE LABOUR MOVEMENT

Finally, it is worth examining the links between brass bands and the local labour movement in order to suggest some further divergences from the British pattern. To deal with this question adequately, it would, of course, be necessary to know more about the social composition of Australian and New Zealand bands. This would raise the further problem of whether the class structures of Britain and the colonies were indeed identical in the late nineteenth and early twentieth centuries. Neither of these important issues can be pursued in a preliminary sketch of this kind, and we must be content to

---

[62] *Australasian Band and Orchestra News*, 25 (Oct. 1929), 9; 25 (Dec. 1929), 15.

[63] Report to the Minister of Public Health on the Welfare of Women and Children (*Parliamentary Papers of Victoria*, 2/9 (1926), 550). I am grateful to Phillippa Mein Smith for this reference.

[64] *Sydney Morning Herald* (16 Jan. 1930), 12.

note that the links between brass bands and organized labour were many and complex. We have already commented on the popularity of brass bands in mining districts, and it is easy to demonstrate, from both local newspapers and union archives, how extensively trade unions used bands for processions, demonstrations, and social occasions. Indeed, some specifically trade-union bands existed. The Victorian Boot Trade Band, established literally to drum up support when the union was at a low ebb in the depression of 1896, is a notable example: subsidized by the union to the extent of £26 a year (which paid the bandmaster's salary), the band was much in evidence at labour functions in Melbourne until 1905, when it was formally taken over by the Trades Hall Council and renamed the Trades Hall Band.[65] Although the Sydney Boot Trade Unions failed in their attempts to set up a similar band in 1905, there were 'Labour' and trade-union bands in—among other places—Adelaide, Fremantle, and Broken Hill. Tom Mann, the British socialist and trade unionist, who spent most of the first decade of the twentieth century in Australia, started a boys' band in connection with his Victorian Socialist League, and on occasion played the big drum himself![66]

Even where 'labour' bands did not exist, there was certainly an assumption among union officials that local bands would and should lend their support—preferably gratis—at labour rituals. Yet such assumptions were not entirely justified, as the experience of the Ballarat Eight Hours committee suggests. In the late 1880s, the organizers of the annual commemoration regularly hired up to eight local bands for the procession, for a donation of two guineas each. But in the early years of the twentieth century, the minute books suggest a growing reluctance on the part of the bands to appear for this nominal payment, especially if it meant loss of wages to their members. Matters came to a head in 1911, when the City Band put in a tender of ten guineas, and Prout's Band one of five guineas: the committee felt obliged to appoint a deputation 'to wait upon the bands urging upon each the claims of the 8 Hours Day Movement to sympathetic consideration from a working-class standpoint with respect to the attitude of the bands'.[67]

In fact, trade-union and Trades Hall records in Sydney and Melbourne indicate that, regardless of whether bandsmen were workers or trade unionists, it was normally assumed that those who wanted the services of a band must expect to hire it at the going rate: and the consideration of tenders from rival bands was normally an agenda item when a metropolitan union was planning

[65] The history of the Victorian Bootmakers' Band can be traced in the minute books of the union's general and committee meetings between 1896 and 1908 (ANU/ABL T5/1 and T4/1/2).

[66] Attempts to establish a Bootmakers' Band in Sydney are referred to in the Boot Trade Council Minutes of 18 Oct. 1905 and 14 Aug. 1906 (ANU/ABL T4/9 and T4/1/2). For other 'labour' bands, see Bythell, 'Class, Community and Culture', 153.

[67] The Minutes of the Ballarat Eight Hours Anniversary Committee are in ANU/ABL. For 1911, see the meeting of 23 Mar. in E97/4/2.

its annual picnic or its contribution to Eight Hours Day. However, a different link between bandsmen and unionists was highlighted in the early twentieth century in both of Australia's leading cities by the unseemly disputes which broke out when the Professional Musicians Union sought a monopoly of trade-union playing for its members, and protested at the unfraternal behaviour of 'amateur' bands who took jobs at less than the union rate.

In Sydney, the problem surfaced soon after the Professional Musicians Union affiliated to the Trades and Labour Council in 1900. The union— whose membership, mainly employed in the orchestra pits of theatres and cinemas, included a particularly large number of cornet players—tried from time to time to organize a wind band from its own ranks. From an early date, it sought to impress upon the Trades and Labour Council and its constituent members that, on good union principles, it had 'a right to supply all musical wants to all the trade unions'.[68] In practice, the union could not raise enough professional wind players to meet all the requirements of a major event such as Eight Hours Day; and it had to be content with securing priority of employment, at official union rates, rather than a monopoly. For its part, the Trades and Labour Council tried at least to ensure that the amateur bands engaged privately by individual unions included only men who were members of their own appropriate union, and it was regarded as improper that notorious anti-unionists should be employed on trade-union occasions. As a result of this compromise, the 1904 Eight Hours procession was headed by a sixty-strong band of professional musicians, while fifteen other 'first class bands' also took part.[69] The union's secretary believed he had provided 'a combination that not only will be a credit to our association but a credit to Australia. I want to show the people of Sydney', he went on, 'that we have a band here equal to any in any part of the world.'[70]

Brass bands and the Musicians Union also clashed on the question of engagements being taken by amateurs (with paid jobs elsewhere) which would otherwise have gone to professionals. The Musicians Union was especially suspicious of bands composed of secure, well-paid employees from the railways, tramways, police, or post office, and tried on several occasions to persuade the managers of these public bodies to stop their men taking engagements, even when they gave their services free, if 'there was any probability of the engagement of professional musicians'.[71] Likewise, the Musicians Union protested vigorously when Sydney's municipal authorities engaged amateur

---

[68] The Minutes of the Professional Musicians Union, Sydney branch, are in ANU/ABL. See meeting of 13 June 1901, (T7/1/2).

[69] *Sydney Morning Herald* (3 Oct. 1904).

[70] Secretary's report to the AGM of the Professional Musicians Union, 15 Aug. 1904 (ANU/ABL, T7/1 /4).

[71] See e.g. minutes of the meetings of 28 Mar. 1901 (ANU/ABL T7/1/2); 16, 23, and 30 Jan. 1906 (T7/1/4); and 27 Oct. 1913 (T7/1/5).

bands for the parks at cheap rates. These issues became particularly contentious in the late 1920s and early 1930s, when professional musicians suffered both from the effects of the general recession and from diminishing employment prospects as silent films gave way to 'talkies'. Once again, in the interests of its unemployed members, the union reasserted its claims for priority in Eight Hours Day playing and park engagements, and reactivated the Professional Musicians Band. Brass band enthusiasts, in turn, ridiculed the inflated pretensions of the professionals who, in any case, were quite incapable of raising an all-brass ensemble, given their particular membership. As one disgruntled observer of the 1929 Eight Hours parade wrote:

What a difference there is now in the playing of the bands from that of some years back when the amateur bands held sway. At that time bands could be heard some distance off, but not today . . . The professional musicians had six bands present, and none of them except the last one in the procession could be heard until almost on top of you. The amateur bands which took part made all the difference . . . One could easily pick out the bands which compete in marching competitions.[72]

Nor was the difference simply one of the loudness of the playing or the smartness of the turn-out. As the Professional Musicians Band committee itself admitted, it was also a matter of musical quality, because there was clearly a conflict of priorities between fielding the best band possible, and fielding one which gave employment to otherwise out-of-work musicians. In January 1931, the committee agreed that 'things musically in the band were not up to standard at some important engagements' and that 'the best men for the best jobs was advisable at all times'. One telling argument advanced in the discussion on this occasion was that within the next few weeks 'a monster band contest will be held, and a great number of visiting bandsmen from different states would be in Sydney, and would no doubt be present at the band's performances'.[73] Although rather oblique, there surely could be no finer compliment to the high standard of musicianship attained by the leading Australasian brass bands in the heyday of the movement.

CONCLUSION

As this chapter has made clear, historians who have recently begun to take an interest in the brass band movement in Australia and New Zealand have a lengthy agenda in front of them. Certain central issues—for example, the number and types of bands, and their changing geographical distribution and social composition—call for detailed examination. There is room for a definitive history of contesting and of the band associations which controlled

[72] *Australasian Band and Orchestra News*, 25 (Oct. 1929), 11.
[73] Musicians Union of Australia, Sydney Branch. Minutes of the Professional Musicians Band (ANU/ABL T7/6/1, meeting of 5 Jan. 1931).

it. The ways in which the movement has adapted to a smaller role in the music making of the two countries since the Second World War—a subject ignored in the present chapter—deserves to be explored. And more biographies of the movement's leading figures—increasingly, native-born rather than immigrant —need to be undertaken. Whilst properly focused histories of individual bands, obscure as well as famous, can be enlightening, a full appreciation of 'the big picture' will probably require a series of comprehensive regional studies of all these matters. Some of the source materials which should prove useful in tackling this agenda have been indicated earlier: but there is one more which should not be overlooked. At the end of the century which has witnessed the rise and decline (but not the extinction) of the brass band, there must still be dozens of ex-bandsmen in both Australia and New Zealand whose memories stretch back to the 1930s, and hundreds more who were active in the 1940s and 1950s. It is still both pertinent and possible for students of the recent history of mass leisure and popular culture to ask 'what was it like?' and 'why did you do it?'. The techniques of oral history, used with intelligence and discrimination, still offer the best chance of finding the answers.

7

Building a Repertoire:
Original Compositions for the
British Brass Band, 1913–1998

PAUL HINDMARSH

THE CONTEXT

In a typically provocative talk broadcast on BBC Radio 3 in 1972, the composer Robert Simpson[1] called into question the way in which musical commentators and composers have used words like 'progress' or 'advance' when charting the paths which 'serious' composition has taken during the twentieth century. If we consider the composing of music to have progressed or advanced, Simpson argues, are we to regard Wagner's powers of musical thought as superior to Beethoven's, or to consider Beethoven more musically intelligent than Mozart, simply because the style and structures they employed have developed and changed? In Simpson's view, creative powers and musical intelligence should not be confused with mode of address or changing fashion—concepts which are equally pertinent to any overview of the contribution made by composers writing for the brass band in the twentieth century.

I am especially grateful to Philip Maund, of Rosehill Music, whose researches in the archive of the *British Bandsman* provided much of the important background to the first part of this chapter. The recollections of E. Wulstan Atkins, Geoffrey Brand, Bram Gay, and Roy Newsome have provided me with valuable contextual information upon which to make musical judgements. My thanks are extended to them, and also to the BBC Written Archives, Caversham, and to the John Ireland Trust.

[1] Robert Simpson (1922–97), composer, writer, and broadcaster.

While the brass band movement has been a fruitful area of investigation for social historians and biographers, the music which brass bands play has not received an equal measure of critical commentary. Although the appetite for new work is undiminished, little consideration has been given to its cultural context or perspective. Social, often emotional, values, have provided the framework for musical judgements: how great the technical challenge; how enjoyable the hours of preparation for the performance; how successful the work in competition; how enthusiastic the audience's response—these are the common yardsticks by which band music has been appreciated. However, in developing a critique of artistic or musical value, other criteria are more revealing: how a work came to be written; how well it fulfils its function; how it fits into the wider context of the century's 'art' music; the quality, truth, or integrity of the ideas. It is also possible to observe in the evolving brass band repertoire a progression or advancement of musical thought and technical ambition. This has been fuelled by the competitive spirit that lies at the heart of so much brass band performance.

1913: THE FIRST ORIGINAL TEST PIECE

In September 1913, over 100,000 people packed into the Crystal Palace pleasure gardens to hear over 100 bands, whose members had travelled from all parts of the country to compete for five trophies in the thirteenth National Brass Band Festival.[2] The success of the Nationals had been engineered, through a potent mixture of enthusiasm, entrepreneurial zeal, and sound business acumen, by John Henry Iles,[3] a self-confessed convert to the brass band cause. He was won over to banding in 1898, when he witnessed the spectacle of the thousands who gathered each year at Belle Vue, Manchester, to hear mainly northern bands compete for what is now the British Open Championship. He bought up two major promotional tools, the band music publisher, R. Smith & Co., and the weekly paper, the *British Bandsman*, and set about expanding his influence within the band movement.

The National Festival became his flagship. In addition, he developed graded area qualifying contests, and used famous bands like Besses o' th' Barn, with their legendary conductor Alexander Owen (1851–1920) to promote the brass band and its music at home and abroad. The prospects for the brass band publisher had never been better, with a buoyant market for marches, solos, popular arrangements, and selections, many sold in graded journals. Providing arrangements for use as test pieces became Iles's responsibility. Arrangers like Lieut. Charles Godfrey and J. Ord Hume turned out annual operatic selections with traditional ingredients and a routine formula: tutti

---

[2] The National Brass Band Festival or Championships were established in 1900.
[3] John Henry Iles (1871–1951).

orchestral or choral numbers from an opera, interspersed with suitable solo or ensemble numbers arranged for the principal soloists, the whole selection punctuated by operatic cadenzas. Little attention was paid to the subtleties of structure or proportion, and because the ingredients and style were familiar, it did not matter whether the music was well known or not. Some choices, like *Moses in Egypt* by Rossini (1897, Belle Vue Contest), or *Joseph and his Brothers* by Méhul (1914, National Championship), were decidedly obscure.

However, Iles and his editor, Herbert Whiteley,[4] were aware of the commercial and artistic advantages of developing an original contesting repertoire. As the brass band historian J. H. Elliot observed in 1933, 'As long as the all-brass ensemble was confined to arrangements . . . it was employing a foreign tongue, while its own rich and resourceful language remained undeveloped—indeed largely unsuspected'.[5] Whiteley sought to enlist reputable 'classical' composers for the flagship contests. There was a small army of possible candidates emerging from the Royal College of Music and the Royal Academy, but writing for the amateur brass band, with its idiosyncrasies of instrumentation, transposition, and scoring, was outside their experience. Herbert Whiteley made many pleas for 'better' music to be composed for the brass band. The most significant of these appeared on the front page of the *British Bandsman* in May 1913:

Practically the whole of the *best* music written during the last fifty years is a closed book to brass bands. This fact alone, in our opinion, justifies the suggestion that reform should come *from within* . . . Modern music is often made prohibitive owing to the Copyright Laws, and the high royalty fees demanded . . . for anyone to issue a selection from certain works . . . one of the solutions is to commission living composers of merit to write for the brass band. The first step in this direction will be made at the Crystal Palace contest next September, when a modern work, specially written . . . will be the test-piece in the Championship Section. In our opinion this will be the first serious attempt to lift brass band journals out of the rut . . . We wish to see our brass bands take their right place in the musical life of the country, and to stop the taunts which are continually flung at them by musicians who know what they are talking about.[6]

Only one composer took Whiteley's call for 'better' music seriously. He was Percy Fletcher (1880–1932), a conductor and composer, significantly, of light music, ballads, salon pieces, and theatre music. It was his tone poem *Labour and Love* with which Whiteley was impressed, and which he persuaded Iles to use for the 1913 event. The performances of *Labour and Love* were a landmark in the history of brass band music. All the music was original, but, having previously been to a Crystal Palace event, he made sure that there was

---

[4] Herbert Whiteley was the editor of the *British Bandsman*, 1906–30. In the 1890s, he was organist at Saddleworth Parish Church, near Oldham, from where he conducted correspondence courses in harmony and counterpoint.

[5] J. F. Russell and J. H. Elliott, *The Brass Band Movement* (London: J. M. Dent & Sons, 1936).

[6] *British Bandsman*, 586 (24 May 1913).

Ex. 4*a*. Percy Fletcher, *Labour and Love*: principal subject (fig. 1, bars 1–4)

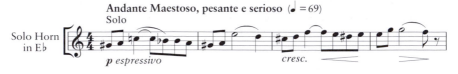

Ex. 4*b*. Percy Fletcher, *Labour and Love*: first episode (Allegro agitato, bars 1–4)

Ex. 4*c*. Percy Fletcher, *Labour and Love*: second episode
(Andante patetico, bars 11–14)

Ex. 4*d*. Percy Fletcher, *Labour and Love*: fourth episode
(Andante molto expressivo, bars 3–6)

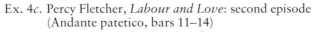

nothing in the style or structure that would not be understood. He shaped it like an operatic selection. The dramatic rhetoric of the fast music, the operatic character of the cornet and euphonium solos, and the recitatives for horn and for trombone, would have held no musical fears for the competing bandsmen. He gave his themes a measure of coherence by constructing them from a single rising motif (see Ex. 4*a*–*d*). He also included a narrative programme, deemed an essential ingredient to help the largely untutored bandsmen characterize the music. Fletcher's 'plot' advocated contentment through honest hard work and the redemptive power of love.

Labour and Love was specially composed music of some substance, which was available to *all* bands. It was not simply part of a local 'bespoke' repertoire like the *Tydfil Overture* of Joseph Parry,[7] or the little test pieces which Sibelius composed early in his career.[8] It stands like a solitary beacon in the writing for brass band in the early twentieth century, since the National Festival was suspended for the duration of the First World War.

1914–1928: New Composers for Crystal Palace and Belle Vue

Towards the end of his life, Whiteley confided to Elgar's daughter, Carice, that he had first written to the great man about composing for brass band in 1918, and that Elgar was 'the first composer to give me any encouragement in my plan of improving the outlook of brass bands and their music'.[9] However, after the First World War, and the subsequent death of his wife, Alice, Elgar seemed to have had little appetite for composing anything himself.

Another episodic tone poem, *Coriolanus*, originally composed for the 1914 event, was pressed into service when the Festival resumed in 1920. Its composer was Cyril Jenkins (1884–1978), who had been one of the lesser lights in Sir Charles Stanford's composition class at the Royal College of Music. Jenkins's next effort, *Life Divine* (1921), was a more severe technical challenge.[10] He tested every player, not just the four or five soloists, contriving to 'shoe-horn' showy trills, scales, and runs, as well as sentimental melodies and fanfares, in a sonata form. While the piece is energetic, exciting, and remains popular, its rhetoric sounds empty, and its phrasing is four-square and repetitive —a pale imitation of Rimsky-Korsakov and Liszt at their most bombastic.

Henry Geehl (1881–1961) and Hubert Bath (1883–1945), Whiteley's next converts to the brass band cause, both built solid reputations in the musical theatre. Geehl's song, 'For you alone', was a popular hit for Caruso. Bath achieved some success with two early, one-act, light operas, and was for many years Director of Music for the London Parks. He called his suite *Freedom*, Brass Band Symphony No. 1 (1922), and he gave it an uplifting programme about the 'Joy', 'Love', and 'Freedom' of the great outdoors. However, it is neither symphonic, nor especially evocative. The invention is more suited

---

[7] Joseph Parry (1841–1903), composer of operas, oratorios, cantatas, hymns, and songs. His *Tydfil Overture* was the first original work of substance for brass band. Parry is best remembered for his hymn tunes, among them the tune *Aberystwyth*.

[8] Jean Sibelius (1865–1957) composed a series of works for seven-part brass ensemble without trombones—the usual ensemble in Finland at the end of the 19th cent. He spent many summers in the resort of Loviisa, where the horn player Christian Haupt conducted the local band. He had composed an Allegro for brass in 1889 for a competition. An Overture in F minor and a *Petite Suite* were written for the Loviisa band between 1889 and 1891. In 1898 he composed a short tone poem, *Tiera*, for eight-part brass band and percussion.

[9] Arthur R. Taylor, *Labour and Love: An Oral History of the Brass Band Movement* (London: Elm Tree, 1983), 66.

[10] Jenkins's original title, *A Comedy of Errors*, was thought inappropriate by Whiteley.

to the operetta stage. In this context, it is rather overdressed in technical elaboration. Geehl's concert overture, *Oliver Cromwell* (1923), is a much more 'thoroughbred' work. His model was the Liszt symphonic poem, and there are direct comparisons of idiom and technique to be made with the orchestral works of contemporaries like Sir Granville Bantock (1868–1946) and Joseph Holbrooke (1878–1958).[11] *Oliver Cromwell* makes strenuous demands on the stamina of the whole band. Geehl exploits a range of dynamics and organ-like textures that matched those in Alexander Owen's grand selections from Wagner, which were still part of the unpublished repertoire of Besses o' th' Barn. Yet *Oliver Cromwell* has never been a popular test piece like *Life Divine*. It provides few opportunities for the stars of the band to demonstrate either their agility or their interpretation of a memorable tune. However, as a creative statement, its detailed thematic working and contrapuntal interest set the standard for a whole generation of brass band specialists, like Denis Wright (1895–1967), who modelled the form of his prize-winning test piece *Joan of Arc* (1925, Crystal Palace) on it.

Geehl continued to provide contest music for bands of all abilities, but he was never as inventive again, being content instead to follow conventional practice. He exploited the medium with greater freedom in his concert music, particularly in two works, a poignant *Threnody* (1952), composed in memory of Fred Mortimer, the inspirational leader of the Fodens Band,[12] and a touching, three-movement symphonic ode, *Normandy* (1945), composed for the first National Championship gala concert after the Second World War. This is unpretentious, heart-felt music, with a central elegy composed in memory of the composer's own son, who was a war victim, and a finale entirely founded on a repeated 'bell theme'— an ingenious formal conceit, which Geehl brings off with great confidence (Ex. 5).

It was the First World War—and its devastating effect on the brass band community—that provided the musical impulse for Percy Fletcher's *Epic Symphony* (1926, Crystal Palace). Fletcher used the ingredients and conventions of contesting to produce a work of character and technical sophistication. He turned the cadenzas and athletic solos into a prelude, called 'Recitare', comprising contrasting fanfares and recitatives. The central elegy, written as a musical war memorial, has an Elgarian breadth and poignancy about it. The gently undulating sighs of the horns, supported by the soft tread of the basses, make an especially haunting impression. Those same horns

---

[11] Sir Granville Bantock (1868–1946) was a great encourager of amateur music making, especially brass bands. He was the principal of the Birmingham and Midland Institute School of Music, 1900–34, and Professor of Music at Birmingham University, 1908–30. His first brass band work, *Festival March*, dates from 1914. His two best contest pieces were *Prometheus Unbound* and *Orion*.

[12] Geehl's *Threnody* remains unpublished. The autograph score and a set of parts is held in the library of the Foden (Courtois) Band.

Ex. 5. Henry Geehl, *Normandy*

No.3 (Finale) LIBERATION

NB The Bells must provide a quiet background, therefore follow the marks of expression carefully.

Ex. 5. (cont.)

become like distant trumpets at the start of the 'Heroic March'. This is a spirited amalgam of patriotic Elgar and Eric Coates, with an unexpected and very English-sounding chorale at its climax.

In 1925, Manchester's Belle Vue was purchased by a business syndicate that included John Henry Iles, who became its managing director, thereby achieving a controlling interest in both flagship festivals of the brass band year. It was no coincidence that, in 1926, an originally composed work was played by the bands competing in the pleasure gardens of Manchester as well as London. Iles and Whiteley may have considered that the northern audience was not ready for the musical adventures of a Percy Fletcher, because the series of Shakespearian tone poems commissioned from Dr Thomas Keighley[13] were a retreat to the style of the operatic selection. With one notable exception, in 1934, this episodic formula persisted in Manchester throughout the 1930s. The formulaic strait-jacket inhibited even the most creative minds. Granville Bantock found it impossible to make anything coherent for the 1930 contest out of his orchestral rhapsody, *Lalla Rookh*. The result, his *Oriental Rhapsody*, bears the scars of his labours.[14] The attractive invention in Joseph Holbrooke's *Clive of India* (1939) sounds cramped and underdeveloped.

1928–1936: THE FIRST HARVEST

All those Belle Vue works pale into insignificance beside the music which Whiteley and, after his retirement in 1930, Sam Cope[15] were eventually able to wrest from the distinguished quartet of Gustav Holst, Elgar, John Ireland and Herbert Howells. There were those in 1928 who wondered why Holst (1874–1934) took the trouble to write for amateurs and schoolchildren. As far as Holst was concerned, there was no trouble about it. He dedicated much of his time to teaching at St Paul's Girls' School and at Morley College, in London. Imogen Holst recalled that,

Propaganda in any form was always distasteful to him, but the one thing that would rouse him to indulge in it himself was the need of better music for brass bands. It was difficult enough to persuade bandmasters that 'selections' were things to be avoided.

[13] Dr Thomas Keighley (1869–1935) was born in Stalybridge, Cheshire, and worked in the cotton mills before becoming a professional musician. He taught organ and composition at the Royal Manchester College of Music, and composed six test pieces, four Shakespearian tone poems, a symphonic rhapsody *The Crusaders* (1932), and *A Northern Rhapsody* (1935).

[14] There are also two substantial concert works deserving of revival, an evocative tone poem, *Land of the Ever Young*, and a twelve-minute concert overture, *King Lear*, composed in 1932 for the Callender's Cable Works Band from Erith, Surrey, then the most regular broadcasting band in the south-east of England. The manuscript of *King Lear* was rediscovered in 1997 in the library of the Haydock Band, Lancashire, which acquired the library of the Callender's Band when it folded. Also in this significant collection are unpublished marches by Percy Fletcher and Alan Bush.

[15] Samuel Cope (1856–1947) was the founding editor of the *British Bandsman*, and an advocate in the 1890s of a fair adjudication procedure, without intimidation and threat of disruption.

But it was still more difficult to try to persuade composers that brass bands were *not* things to be avoided.[16]

So he led by example, and others were soon to follow.

Holst was a great walker, especially in rugged, bracing landscapes like the North York Moors, which are said to have inspired the 'Scherzo', 'Nocturne' and 'March' that comprise *A Moorside Suite*. This work, which was scored by Henry Geehl, presented music for the brass band in a fresh and individual way. The writing is clear, the musical gestures free of empty rhetoric. His primary concerns were musical, not technical, and, unfettered by the traditional function of a test piece, he produced a work whose considerable difficulties, such as the whispered chorale of the 'Nocturne', rise naturally out of the compositional process. The idiom was light-years away from the familiar brand of romantic chromaticism. For the first time, the brass band was playing original tunes founded on modality rather than diatonic harmony: its origins were in folk song, and it unfolded entirely without contrivance.

The musical aspirations of bands and conductors were enhanced by the process of mastering *A Moorside Suite*. 'I listened to musicians conducted by musicians', was Holst's verdict, after the contest (29 September 1928).[17] The signal went out to other composers that it was perfectly possible to write imaginatively for the medium, without compromising style or expression. J. H. Elliot records that during rehearsals for a 1933 concert in which Holst conducted the Carlisle St Stephen's Band, he noted his 'deep concern for the welfare of the movement. It is no secret that his untimely death [in 1934] prevented some ambitious "missionary" schemes from maturing.'[18]

Securing the services of the Master of the King's Music, Sir Edward Elgar (1857–1934), for the 1930 Festival set the seal on Herbert Whiteley's 'missionary' career. Whiteley had been trying to persuade Elgar to write a work for the Crystal Palace Championship for many years. In 1930 his financial offer was considerable, and Elgar, who was never a wealthy man, did not refuse. On 27 September, George Bernard Shaw was among the crowd that flocked to the Crystal Palace to hear the work which his great friend had just dedicated to him—the *Severn Suite* (Op. 87). He was very impressed: 'The scoring is, as usual, infallible. You should have heard the pleasant oboe quality of the muted flugel horn, picking up after the cornets. Nobody would have guessed from looking at the score and thinking of the thing as a Toccata for brass band, how beautiful and serious the work is as abstract music.'[19]

---

[16] Imogen Holst, *The Music of Gustav Holst*, 2nd edn. (London: Oxford University Press, 1968).

[17] Letter to Whiteley, quoted in Imogen Holst, *A Thematic Catalogue of Gustav Holst's Music* (London: Faber, 1974), 172.

[18] Russell and Elliott, *The Brass Band Movement*.

[19] Letter from George Bernard Shaw to Elgar, quoted in Jerrold Northrop Moore, *Sir Edward Elgar: A Creative Life* (London: Oxford University Press, 1987).

The *Severn Suite* has been a problematic work. In brass band circles, it has been thought that, because Elgar assembled much of the music from earlier sketches, he was not genuinely enthusiastic about the project. But it is clear from what he said to friends like Shaw and his godson Wulstan Atkins[20] that Elgar was very fond of the work, especially the slow 'Fugue', which he had sketched in 1923. By 1930, Elgar was in his early seventies, with over fifty years of composing experience behind him. His notebooks were full of unused ideas. Inspiration and composition were two distinct processes for him, and he never thought twice about appropriating ideas intended for one project to another if it suited his purpose.[21] The noble 'Introduction' and the 'Toccata' were new and first-rate Elgar. The 'Minuet', which is less distinguished, was based on wind quintets composed fifty-one years earlier. The suite was edited for the publisher, R. Smith, by Henry Geehl, whose assertion that he had scored the work from Elgar's sketches further diminished its stature:

During the time I was arranging Elgar's *Severn Suite*, I was in continuous consultation with the composer, who provided me with a very sketchy piano part with figured bass and a kind of skeleton orchestral score, mostly in two or three parts, with an indication of the sort of counterpoint he desired me to add; the rest of the score he left to my discretion.[22]

That Geehl made the military band score is well documented, but the discovery of Elgar's full score in Wulstan Atkins's manuscript collection confirms that Geehl's role was not as extensive as he asserted. The skeleton score to which he refers is actually a complete draft full score in C, with all parts complete, and the tenor and bass instruments in bass clef. Bram Gay, General Editor of band music for Novello & Co., prepared a performing edition faithful to Elgar's original for the 1996 Open Championship, Manchester. He also offered practical alternatives to the various problems of compass and range which both he and Geehl have acknowledged in Elgar's original. Geehl's score was also in C major. However, the work was published in a sounding B♭ (that is, written in C major for the B♭ transposing instruments), and with many notational errors. Who made the decision to transpose the music down a tone is not clear. It may have been Geehl, who recalls many difficulties in persuading the composer to make his score more practical. There may, in fact, have been good reasons why it was done. It makes some of Elgar's cornet writing easier to bring off. Also, because bands of that time were constructed in high pitch, over a quarter of a tone higher than orchestral brass, publishing a score in Elgar's desired key would raise the sounding pitch well above C major. The

[20] E. Wulstan Atkins (b. 1904): reference in conversation with the author, during production for BBC Radio 3 of 'Elgar's Final Enigma', a feature on the Symphony No. 3, broadcast 15 Feb. 1998.
[21] All three of Elgar's symphonies were composed in this fashion. Each one includes ideas written down sometimes many years before they were used.
[22] From a memoir by Henry Geehl, quoted in Moore, *Sir Edward Elgar*, 784.

slightly 'bright' B♭ major may have been a compromise. However, it is clear from the orchestral score which Elgar made soon afterwards, that a majestic C major was what he wanted.

The two contributions of John Ireland (1879–1962) to this emergent repertoire are arguably the most personal of the decade, and also the most unexpected. He was a sensitive and solitary composer. Unlike Holst, Howells, or Bantock, he did not involve himself in amateur or community music making. Ireland was essentially a musical miniaturist, a writer of refined, often exotically coloured, instrumental chamber works, and haunting, nostalgic songs. Epic subject-matter and extrovert rhetoric—the popular ingredients of the brass band *lingua franca*—were not part of Ireland's natural language. Yet in the range of invention and refinement of musical argument displayed in *A Downland Suite* (1932, Crystal Palace) and *A Comedy Overture* (1934, Crystal Palace), he produced worthy successors to *A Moorside Suite*. His friend and biographer, John Longmire,[23] felt that 'probably no native composer conveyed the loveliness of his own countryside' like Ireland, who seems to have enshrined his love of the Sussex Downs in *A Downland Suite*. At this time, too, Ireland was very close to a young pianist and composer, his pupil Helen Perkin.[24] She accompanied him on many of his trips from Chelsea to his country retreat on the Downs. He described her as 'so beautiful, so young, so talented', and she inspired a number of his works, including the Piano Concerto and the lyrical moments of the suite. The music of this substantial work traverses a wide expressive and technical landscape, from the energy of the 'Prelude', to the touching eloquence of the 'Elegy', the wistful elegance of the 'Minuet' and the windswept final 'Rondo'. Whatever plans he ultimately had for the music—he reworked three of the movements for strings some years later—it is beautifully conceived for the brass medium. Ireland dedicated the work to his friend Kenneth Wright,[25] who did so much to stimulate his interest in the medium. The full scores of this work and his next were prepared by Frank Wright.

Ireland was not always comfortable working in extended forms, but in *A Comedy Overture* he achieved one of his most successful balances between the demands of symphonic form and the immediate appeal of his great melodic

---

[23] John Longmire, *John Ireland: Portrait of a Friend* (London, 1969), 28.

[24] Helen Perkin (1909–97), pianist and composer, and a composition pupil of John Ireland. He wrote his Piano Concerto for her. Perkin was encouraged to write for the brass band by John Ireland. Two of her works were used as test pieces at the Belle Vue Championship, *Carnival* (1957), and *Island Heritage* (1962).

[25] Kenneth Wright (1899–1975) was born in East Tuddenham, Norfolk, studied music at Sheffield University, and became the first director of the BBC's Manchester station in 1922. He was personal assistant to Sir Adrian Boult (1930–7). During that time he was responsible for bringing Denis Wright into the BBC Music Division. He composed for brass and military bands, as well as light orchestra. His work *Pride of Race* was composed for the 1935 National Championships.

gifts. It is a portrayal in music of a busy urban landscape—London. The four-note 'Piccadilly' motif was recalled from a bus conductor's cry. The central slow section, with its chromatic harmonies and sighing lyrical phrases, is a romantic portrait of another close friend, Percy Bentham. When Ireland came to prepare the version for orchestra in 1936, he elaborated the harmonies and textures a good deal, on the advice of another friend from the BBC, Julian Herbage, and renamed it *A London Overture*.

In September 1934, Belle Vue's conservative tendency was broken with the emergence of the most demanding of this group of celebrated works: *Pageantry*, a suite by Herbert Howells (1892–1983). Its ceremonial subjects—fanfares in 'King's Herald', solemn melody in 'Cortège', and the virtuosic tilting in 'Jousts'—are ideally suited to the brass band. The music presents a formidable test of ability, but its technical demands spring directly from the musical language, which is founded on English modality and an individual reinter-pretation of Tudor polyphony. The profusion of rhythmic and textural detail is brought to life with the flair of a colourful orchestrator and the skill of an accomplished organist. In 1937, Howells also recast 'King's Herald' for orchestra with organ. He added further layers of textural and harmonic detail, transforming it into a glittering fanfare prelude for the Coronation of George VI.

There is a fine distinction to be made between music like that of Ireland and Howells, which expresses its creator's ideas *through* the brass band medium, and music written *for* the band, with preconceptions of the kind of music which suits the medium and its amateur players. Writing in 1936, just before his short suite *Kenilworth* was played at the National Festival (1936), its com-poser, Arthur Bliss, remarked, 'I have always thought that the true home of brass bands is in the open air, where their power of conveying ceremony and pageantry, brilliant or solemn, is most finely felt.'[26] Bliss's experience of brass bands was limited, and *Kenilworth* lacks the individuality of *Pageantry*. The music is much closer to and probably modelled on Fletcher's *Epic Symphony*, than Bliss's more personal works like the ballet *Checkmate*, also from 1936. It describes Queen Elizabeth I's visit to Kenilworth Castle. Fanfares and cadenzas herald her arrival. A masque is presented in her honour—a graceful, balletic aria. A brilliant march brings her visit to a festive conclusion.

In his powerful, symphonic prelude, *Prometheus Unbound* (1933, Crystal Palace), Granville Bantock integrated the specific demands of the test piece into a single span, whose late romantic gestures and fluid musical argument made it perhaps the single most important influence on the rising generation of brass band composers, Eric Ball in particular. Its reflective, rather than triumphant, ending was innovative in this context, and points perhaps to the work's real purpose. In 1936 it became the orchestral prelude to a substantial choral work.

---

[26] Sir Arthur Bliss, *As I Remember* (London: Faber, 1970).

Bandsmen of the 1930s were not always impressed by the musical adventures of these composers. The repertoire at concerts was predominantly taken from tried and tested selections. 'There were those who thought that Elgar, Holst and Ireland contained too many wrong notes.'[27] This handful of original works hardly constitutes a repertoire in itself. That the composers of the best of them made versions for strings or full orchestra is testimony to the value they placed on their work. That they remain the cornerstones of the brass band concert and contest repertoire is testimony to their enduring quality, and to the advances in musical expectation and understanding that have followed in their wake. At the time, these works were a spur to a number of distinguished musicians to work towards a distinctive core of original music for all brass band occasions—for the concert hall, for the grander 'gala' festival, for worship in the Salvation Army, as well as for the contest stage.

Music for Concert Hall and Citadel

Of all the music which bands play, it is the march and the hymn tune which have traditionally provided its distinctive character. The heyday of the contest march, a genre unique to the brass band, was during the first quarter of the twentieth century. Its undisputed kings were William Rimmer (1862–1936), cornet virtuoso, conductor, arranger, and composer of well over 100 marches, and his near contemporary James Ord Hume, military musician, arranger, and composer of over eighty marches. Rimmer and Ord Hume, together with their pupils and imitators like George Allen (1864–1931) and Shipley Douglas (1868–1920), were able to conjure up music of technical complexity, dynamic and rhythmic detail, and melodic variety out of the rigid conventions and structural formulae of the military march. Contest marches such as Rimmer's *The Cossack* (1904) or Ord Hume's *Brilliant* (1901) remain stiff challenges for any band. The range of the melodic invention and the level of textural and contrapuntal detail in *The Wizard* by George Allen or *Mephistopheles* by Shipley Douglas have more in common with a light opera overture than a traditional road march. The contest marches composed between the 1890s and the 1920s comprise a rich and substantial body of work, which, apart from a few enduring favourites, awaits rediscovery and re-evaluation.[28]

The building of a core repertoire for bands of all sizes and standards was spearheaded by two composers, Denis Wright and Eric Ball (1903–89). Born

[27] Taylor, *Labour and Love*, 38. Among the portions of the R. Smith archive, sold off in 1996, were several short score manuscripts by Havergal Brian (1877–1974). These included a number of transcriptions and one original work from 1930, a nine-minute symphonic poem, *The Battle Song*. The score of this demanding and musically adventurous work was purchased by the Havergal Brian Society. A performing version has been made by composer John Pickard.

[28] The most prolific publishers of marches were R. Smith & Co., Richardson & Sons, Boosey & Hawkes, and Wright & Round. Archive copies are available from R. Smith and Wright & Round. The Doyen Centre, Vulcan Street, Oldham, houses a substantial reference collection of marches.

Ex. 6*a*. Eric Ball, *Resurgam*: 'Faith' motif (opening bars)

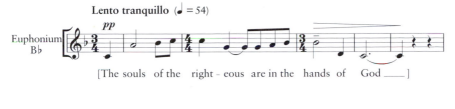

[The souls of the right - eous are in the hands of God ____]

Ex. 6*b*. Eric Ball, *Resurgam*: Adagio lamentoso

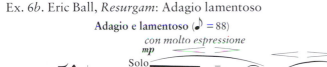

[Death took my love a-way]

into a Salvationist family from Bristol, Ball became an accomplished pianist and organist, and taught himself to compose. Denis Wright did not come from a brass band background. He was a contemporary of Arthur Bliss at the Royal College of Music, and one of the many young talents to come into contact with the most influential teacher of the time, Sir Charles Stanford. The creative ambitions of both Wright and Ball grew from their love of the classical traditions; and by studying how composers like Geehl, Bantock, and Holst wrote for brass band, they exploited the richness of the brass medium and set the standard for a generation of brass specialists to come.

Eric Ball's creativity was an expression of his deep Christian faith, and his inspiration was rooted in song. Significantly, he wrote a greater number of anthems and sacred songs than band pieces. From a grounding in hymnology, classical *Lieder*, and romantic ballads, he responded to the meaning and character of a text with a refined sensibility. And it is this, rather than any particular originality of idiom, that distinguishes his achievement from other brass band composers of the time. The themes of his best-known work *Resurgam* ('I shall rise again'), for example, owe their range and character to the words Ball associated with them (Ex. 6*a* and *b*). Christian preoccupations with eternal life and a spiritual communion with God through life and in death, underpin Eric Ball's best original music, including *Resurgam* (1950), *The Eternal Presence* (1966), *A Song of Courage* (1962), and the neo-classical suite *Festival Music* (1956):

Resurgam is the best of me—that, and a Salvation Army piece called *The Eternal Presence*. I still like *Journey into Freedom*—I think that has a certain philosophy behind it. Although, looking at the whole thing in another way, the piece that gets played most is *Indian Summer*—lots of school bands play that, and I get more royalties from that than anything else. My music is a bit old fashioned—back in the romantic era. Elgar, Vaughan Williams, Sibelius, that was about as advanced as I got. As a young man, I soaked myself in Mozart, Beethoven, Schubert. Elgar was probably the strongest influence.[29]

Ball described his music as derivative, but as his friend Robert Simpson once reminded him:

The very greatest composers were 'derivative'. Bach studied all his precursors and often copied out their works. Beethoven derived from his musical fathers. The real artist uses what he finds—he doesn't try to start from nowhere. Eric's work had its own stamp, the result of his ability to make fresh use of what he knew. His originality lay in being innocently himself.

I remember Eric as mentor (in my youth), brilliant musician, humane man—an unforgettable combination of qualities.[30]

During the 1930s and early 1940s, Eric Ball served the Salvation Army as a full-time officer. He was a perceptive and influential music editor for Salvationist Publishing and Supplies (S.P.&S.) Ltd. Recordings by his S.P.&S. Band are testimony to his skills as a band trainer and musicianly interpreter. The S.P.&S. Band was founded in 1928, as a means of demonstrating the possibilities of the new *Second Series Band Journal*. Ball had seventeen members at his disposal to begin with, but by 1931 it had grown into a standard line-up used by contesting bands—twenty-five players—and was playing the most ambitious Salvationist music of the time. When Ball became bandmaster of the 'rival' band, the International Staff Band, in 1939, the S.P.&S. Band folded. Ball's exploration of the world of spiritualism forced his resignation from full-time Salvationist work in 1942. The wider brass band fraternity was then able to benefit from his musical and personal influence, through his conducting and his long associations with R. Smith & Co. and the *British Bandsman*.

Both Denis Wright and Eric Ball became prolific providers of well-crafted, accessible music—light and serious—for bands of all abilities. 'It's a real challenge to write for school bands and lower section bands. It's difficult to write music that's effective, but isn't horrendously difficult to play.'[31] The best of Eric Ball's music has found a permanent place in the band repertoire, but it is Denis Wright's skill as an arranger, rather than as a composer, that has stood the test of time most strongly. His lasting influence on the musical ambitions of generations of young brass players is enshrined in the National Youth Brass Band of Great Britain, which he established in 1952.

The full extent of the influence which the Salvation Army has exerted on the musical life of Britain has yet to be documented (see Chapter 5). In the brass

---

[29] Taylor, *Labour and Love*, 147.
[30] Forward to Cooke, *Eric Ball: The Man and his Music* (Baldock: Egon, 1991), 7.
[31] Taylor, *Labour and Love*, 146.

band world, the Salvation Army has produced generations of musicians and composers for whom musical expression rather than technical display comes first. Salvationist brass music is intended to be spiritually uplifting as well as musically satisfying. Obligatory references, in every work, to hymns or sacred songs might be regarded as a limitation for composers with real artistic ambition. However, the richness and diversity of Salvationist music from the twentieth century would indicate the reverse. Until 1992, the reams of band music published by the S.P.&S. remained the Army's exclusive property. Now that access to that music is unrestricted, a clearer picture is emerging of its significance in the continuity of the developing repertoire. Many of the most skilled and innovative brass band composers of the second half of the twentieth century, most acknowledging the example of Eric Ball, have emerged from the Salvationist environment—composers such as Sir Dean Goffin (1916–83), Wilfred Heaton (b. 1918), Ray Steadman-Allen (b. 1922), and Edward Gregson (b. 1945). Robert Simpson (1922–97) and Elgar Howarth (b. 1935) also have family roots in Salvation Army traditions.

1939–1960: YEARS OF CONSOLIDATION

The golden years of the 1930s were followed by twenty years when innovation in contest music flagged. The strongest musical developments took place in the concert halls, on the radio, and in the Salvation Army. After the ravages of the Second World War, these were years of consolidation and rebuilding. It was more important for the leaders of the banding community to renew interest and aspiration. It was almost like starting again. The BBC, with Denis Wright and then Harry Mortimer supervising broadcasts, was hugely influential in keeping the brass band sound in the public ear. The massed band concert with celebrity conductors became popular. But with the notable exceptions of Denis Wright—Cornet Concerto (1942); *Overture for an Epic Occasion* (1945); *Tam O'Shanter's Ride* (1955)—and Eric Ball, using his craftsman's skill to provide a whole string of test pieces, creative work of substance was developing, largely unnoticed, within Salvation Army citadels.

Sir Dean Goffin, born in New Zealand, possessed a genuine contrapuntal gift. Beethoven, Mozart, and especially Bach and Schubert were his musical idols. He was one of the first Salvationist musicians to benefit from a university education. When he used titles like 'rhapsody', as in his two most extended compositions, he was not implying a loose, episodic construction, but simply indicating that these were abstract compositions, for which titles like 'symphony' or 'sonata', with all their implications for the structure of a piece, were not appropriate. Goffin sketched his three-movement *Rhapsody in Brass* in 1942, during war service in North Africa. There is a classical poise and proportion about the form. It is conceived on a similar scale to a divertimento by Mozart. A subtle use of modal harmony and counterpoint continues the line of musical thought from Holst and Howells. An elegantly shaped modal melody is also the foundation for his finest work, *Rhapsodic Variations—My Strength, My Tower* (published in 1961). Variation Four, a passacaglia, reveals Goffin's contrapuntal imagination at its most resourceful, with all manner of devices displayed. On entering the full-time ministry of the Salvation Army in the 1950s, Goffin dedicated his skills to its music and worship. Sacred words were contrived to fit the theme of the Variations, to make it suitable for performance and publication by the Salvation Army. The 1950s was also the decade when the names of Wilfred Heaton and particularly Ray Steadman-Allen were beginning to appear more frequently in Salvationist band journals.[32]

The musical ethos of the Salvation Army is founded upon the expressive power of music. There were no rules about numbers of players, and no requirements for technical display other than those demanded by the music. And this expressive dimension is what attracted the octogenarian Ralph Vaughan Williams (1872–1958) to the sound of the International Staff Band of the Salvation Army. He had composed for brass band before (Overture, *Henry V*, 1936), but without any great personal enthusiasm. In 1954, he turned three of his Preludes for organ into *Preludes on Three Welsh Hymn Tunes* for brass band, scored with the expert help of Philip Catelinet.[33] Three years later came the concise and sprightly *Variations for Brass Band* (1957, National Championships, Royal Albert Hall). Vaughan Williams was the first English master of modal melody and counterpoint in the twentieth century. He loved English hymnody. He admired the rich, organ-like sounds of the deep brass, and he was also a life-long supporter of amateur music. How appropriate then, that his penultimate work should be for brass band, adding his unique voice to the achievements of his friends and imitators like Holst and Howells.

The idea of writing variations on an original theme as a brass band test piece was both innovative and influential. The *air varié* solo has remained one of the most popular genres in the band concert repertoire—a rich and continuing seam of invention and display, with its roots in the genre made famous by virtuosos and composers like Paganini and Liszt. There are sound practical

[32] There are four graded Salvationist band journals: 'Festival Series', including the most ambitious and musically demanding material; 'General Series', comprising marches, selections, and arrangements for worship; 'Second (subsequently 'Triumph') Series', embracing music for worship for small or youth bands; 'Unity Series' was a shorter run journal of simple music in five parts for adult or young people's groups.

[33] Philip Catelinet (1910–95), tuba player, arranger, and composer. He was a life-long friend of Eric Ball, and his colleague during the 1930s in the Music Editorial Department of the Salvation Army. He arranged or composed almost 200 pieces for brass band, but left full-time Salvation Army service to become a professional tuba player. He played in the Philharmonia and London Symphony Orchestras. Vaughan Williams composed his Tuba Concerto for him. In the 1960s he was Professor of Brass at the Carnegie-Melon University, Pittsburgh.

reasons why even major works for brass band—until then, largely suites, tone poems, and overtures—tend to be between ten and twenty minutes in length, not least reasons of stamina. Writing variations allows for maximum variety of texture and character, and a musical assembly of the familiar test-piece conventions, within a concise structure. The long list of variations composed in the wake of the Vaughan Williams piece began the following year. Perhaps inspired by his teacher's example, Edmund Rubbra (1901–86) added his gentle musical voice to this growing body of original music, with another set of variations on a little piano piece of his own, *The Shining River*. Although Rubbra was helped in the idiosyncrasies of scoring by Frank Wright,[34] the sound-world, with its emphasis on the horns and flugel horn, is highly personal. *The Shining River* is an undemonstrative work, the antithesis of the traditional test piece, and for that reason has not been played as much as the quality of its invention deserves. Rubbra gave the variations evocative titles: 'First Dance', 'Cradle Song', 'Pageant', 'Ostinato', 'Second Dance', and 'Lament'.

THE ART OF THE ARRANGER

The arranger has played a significant role in the evolution of the repertoire and sound of the brass band. Arranging for band is a highly specialized business, given its idiosyncratic instrumentation and transposition system (all instruments except the bass trombone are transposed to B♭ or E♭, and are written in treble clef, irrespective of compass). The skill with which arrangers manipulate the band—their choice of instruments, the range of colour, the level of individual exposure—has become a barometer of technical accomplishment. The music which is arranged reflects the current tastes and fashions.

   The advent of music by Holst and Elgar did little to change what the majority of bands played on the bandstand. Raising the musical consciousness of bands was a matter of persistent education and exposure, not of an occasional masterpiece. This was recognized by Holst, and by others such as Eric Ball and Denis Wright in the 1930s. Wright, in particular, set about the educative process with purpose. He brought a fresh vision and integrity to the brass band arrangement, favouring whole works, large and small, classical and popular, rather than bits and snippets from the musical theatre. Wright's biographer, Roy Newsome,[35] refers to 1,000 arrangements and transcriptions, of which seventy-eight were selections from shows and light opera.[36] Brahms's

---

[34] Frank Wright (1901–70). Born in Ballarat, Victoria, Australia, Wright was a baritone singer and cornet player in the early part of his career. He came to Britain in 1934, and eventually became Director of Music for the London County Council. He was much in demand for his skills as a brass band arranger. He also taught at the Guildhall School of Music.

[35] Roy Newsome, *Doctor Denis: The Life and Times of Dr Denis Wright* (Baldock: Egon, 1995).

[36] Arrangements from the catalogue of Chappell & Co., for whom Denis Wright was general music editor.

Academic Festival Overture and *Tragic Overture* are the pinnacle, but there are also miniatures by Schubert, Elgar, and Percy Grainger, among others. Eric Ball was less productive in this field, preferring to transcribe the works for which he felt a personal affinity. His illuminating transcriptions of works like Elgar's *Enigma Variations* and Bliss's *Checkmate* took the art of brass band arranging on to a higher recreative plane, where translating the character of the composer's orchestral sound into the band's terms was more important than simply making the notes available to brass band players.

Arranging an orchestral work for band is as much an exercise of pruning and revoicing as it is of literal transcription. During the fallow decades after the Second World War, the test-piece transcriptions by Frank Wright opened new technical horizons. His method of setting a technical challenge was to leave out as little of the original information as possible. The choice of work was also crucial, and his inclination was towards an orchestral show-piece, or an overture with powerful dramatic effects. Wagner's *Mastersingers* Overture, Verdi's *Force of Destiny* Overture, Berlioz's *Judges of the Secret Court*, Bantock's overture *The Frogs*, and especially Lalo's overture *Le Roi d'Ys*, are the most effective and challenging. Frank Wright also lent his skills to composers who did not have first-hand experience of scoring for brass band, just as Henry Geehl had done for Holst and, perhaps, Elgar. He prepared full scores for Rubbra, for Edric Cundell (*Blackfriars*, 1955), for William Alwyn (*The Moor of Venice*, 1958), and for the second brass band works of Howells (his masterly *Three Figures*, 1960) and Bliss (*The Belmont Variations*, 1963).

Frank Wright thought of the band as a brass orchestra. Taking up the challenge of recreating orchestral music in terms of the band—adding a recreative dimension to the arranger's art—has been the chief concern of those that followed him. Arrangers with many years of experience as orchestral trumpeters —Bram Gay, Ray Farr, Elgar Howarth, Howard Snell—have uncovered hitherto unimagined layers of colour within the band. Elgar Howarth's monumental transcription of Mussorgsky's *Pictures at an Exhibition* (first for the Philip Jones Brass Ensemble, then for Grimethorpe Colliery) reaches levels of sophistication and subtlety comparable to Ravel's orchestral version. It was the idea of pitting his arranger's skill against those of a master of the orchestra like Ravel, that led Howard Snell to recreate the second suite from *Daphnis and Chloé* for brass, and to tackle the ultimate in orchestral extravagance, *The Pines of Rome* and *Roman Festivals* by Respighi—a *tour de force* of orchestration and reorchestration. Less demanding to play, but equally effective are Snell's versions of Shostakovich film music, like *Folk Festival* from *The Gadfly*.

Ray Farr is equally inventive in his transcriptions of orchestral showpieces —for example, Malcolm Arnold's *English Dances*, and the finale from Stravinsky's ballet *The Firebird*; but it is his scintillating arrangements from the commercial world of the cinema and musical theatre that have highlighted the greatest change in brass band music, and consequently in expectations of the sound of the brass band. Farr and many other skilled arrangers were no longer taking their cues from opera or operetta, or even light orchestral music, but from music which had become part of contemporary experience.

1960–1970: Revolutions in Sound

Until the 1960s, brass band music remained largely untouched by the onward march of musical modernism. The musical legacies of Bartók, Stravinsky, Schoenberg, and the Second Viennese School, were beginning to take hold of the generation of classically trained composers. Of much more consequence for the mass of the band movement was the impact of the revolution in the sound of popular music. The highly rhythmical and sharply etched music of the modern dance orchestra, the big band, and especially the cinema began to transform the manner in which brass bands delivered their music, just as operatic styles had dominated the band sound of earlier generations. Tuned percussion was becoming more common (in the twentieth century, drums of any kind were to remain absent from the contest stage until the 1970s). A wider range of muted effects—not just with cornets and trombones—helped to make the band sound more colourful. Organ-like, homogeneous scoring was no longer the only way to write for brass band. This new approach to sound was realized by arrangers and composers alike.

Gilbert Vinter (1909–69), a distinguished voice from the world of light music, was convinced that inside the brass band monochrome was a palette of brilliant colour, and he experimented constantly in the attempt to uncover it, using all his skills as a composer and orchestrator of light music. For many years, he was the Musical Director of the BBC Midland Light Orchestra, in Birmingham. He became involved with brass bands in 1960, and for the remaining years of his life produced a steady stream of concert music and test pieces, beginning with the elaborately scored and much played suite, *Salute to Youth* (1961). Band musicians point to innovative, and much imitated, moments like the passage in *James Cook—Circumnavigator* (1969), where the four bass players are exposed in a solo quartet; or his use of non-functional, often astringent, harmonic effects, like the angular melodies in *Variations on a Ninth* (1964), or the exposed, clashing seconds in *Triumphant Rhapsody* (1965). But it is the variety of harmonic colour, the syncopated rhythms, and the range of instrumental effects, allied to the organic strength of the structure, in *Spectrum* (1969), that have made perhaps the strongest, most lasting impression. In other works, like the popular *Variations on a Ninth*, he manipulated his material in manner that was craftsman-like, but sometimes too facile.

It was those who came after Vinter who enriched with more rigorous musical argument the range of colour and virtuosity that he showed to be possible. Investing an accessible musical style with seriousness of purpose and a professional quality of craftsmanship has given an enduring life to substantial portions of 'lighter' band music, which in past generations would have been the victim of changing tastes. The polished, imaginative scores of Gordon Langford (b. 1930), Goff Richards (b. 1944), and Gareth Wood (b. 1950), for example, have breathed life into familiar patterns and gestures.

The challenge of producing ever more searching tests of virtuosity has been met head on by the prolific Philip Sparke (b. 1951). His musical language is accessible, and direct—embodying the traditional values of popular brass band music, enlivened by the style and polish of jazz, of the cinema, and of Americans like Leonard Bernstein and Aaron Copland. What distinguishes the best of his music from much of the music written in the updated *lingua franca* of brass bands is the virtuoso compositional technique he displays. The ingredients which make works like the energetic suite *The Year of the Dragon* (1984, commissioned by the Cory Band), the Ravel-inspired *Harmoniemusik* (1986, National test), and the elaborate *Variations on an Enigma* (1988, Desford Colliery commission) so successful, are immediate and direct— the elaborate and vital invention, the excitement of the music's energy and power. It is all too easy to underestimate the skills which created them. The closing pages of *Variations on an Enigma*, for example, are a *tour de force* of contrapuntal ingenuity; a gesture of admiration, perhaps, from one brass band composer to another, Wilfred Heaton, part of whose *Contest Music* forms the enigmatic theme. Sparke describes his work *Between the Moon and Mexico* (1988, National Championships) as more spontaneous in inspiration and construction.

TRADITIONS RENEWED

The final third of the century witnessed an unprecedented blossoming of the band repertoire on all fronts. New stylistic paths opened up—light and jazz-inspired arrangements, substantial concert work, symphonies, concertos, scintillating virtuoso scores. Refinements in instrument technology increased dynamic power. Conversion to 'low' pitch ended decades of isolation from other instrumental forms. It was no longer a problem for the brass band to play with organ or piano, for example. Ray Steadman-Allen was one of the first specialists to take advantage of this new creative opportunity, in his work for solo piano and brass band (whose members are also required to sing), *Christ is the Answer* (1965). Some years later, he wrote an exhilarating set of symphonic variations on the splendid tune 'Moscow', for fanfare trumpets, brass band, and the organ of the Royal Albert Hall, entitled *Chorales and Tangents*.[37] One of Edward Gregson's earliest works, *Concertante* (1966),

---

[37] Unpublished, and only one performance up to 1998.

was also composed for piano and band. Musically speaking, it could be argued that the brass band had come of age. There was now an expanding market for commissions from all quarters: from individual bands, from the emerging star soloists, those who had matured through the evolving band movement, as well as from the prestigious competitions and music festivals.

The Scottish Amateur Music Association, for example, initiated a commissioning policy for their youth band. Included among the works were *Little Suite No. 1* (1963) by Malcolm Arnold, a Suite (1964) by Alan Rawsthorne, *Music for a Brass Band* (1965) by Martin Dalby (b. 1941), *Variations* (1966) by Thea Musgrave (b. 1928)—which was the first non-tonal work to be published for band—*Sinfonietta* (1967) by Thomas Wilson (b. 1928), and *Divertimento* (1968) by Bryan Kelly (b. 1934). All these composers came from the wider 'art' music traditions: Martin Dalby, at that time still a student at the Royal College of Music; Thea Musgrave, one of the country's most distinguished international composers; Thomas Wilson, already well-established on the Scottish scene with his orchestral and chamber music. He composed his *Sinfonietta* at a time when his mature style was beginning to emerge. The pithy, fourth-based motifs and uncompromising harmonic style stem from his admiration of the music of Bartók and Hindemith. Dalby's suite apart, the complexity of these works is such that they have remained on the fringes of the youth band repertoire, although they have been taken up by many adult bands. However, the two *Little Suites* which Sir Malcolm Arnold composed in the mid-1960s have become pillars of the youth band repertoire. (His *Fantasy* of 1974 provided championship bands with a more virtuosic slice of his witty and often darkly sardonic style.)

In 1971, a fresh name was added to the list of National Championship composers. Robert Simpson was a much-respected symphonic composer and a provocative writer on music. He was born into a Salvationist family, and played in brass bands as a boy. As might be expected from the trenchant views highlighted at the start of the chapter, Simpson held traditional, classical opinions about the composition of music. Beethoven, Sibelius, and Carl Nielsen were the composers to whom he felt closest, and this is reflected in all his music, including fifteen string quartets, eleven symphonies, and five works for brass band. The commission to write for brass band came about through the recommendation of his friend, Eric Ball, to whom the resulting work, *Energy*, was dedicated. Organic growth and momentum are the terms that best convey the character of the music, and he describes *Energy* as a composed accelerando. As he once wrote, the brass band 'is like a living organ. You can write wonderful counterpoint for brass band. It's a marvellous instrument when it's handled imaginatively'.[38] This symphonic study opened ears to new ways of writing symphonically for the medium.

[38] Quoted in CD note by Matthew Taylor for Hyperion CDA66449.

A year later, Thomas Wilson revealed to the band movement another equally valid but very different way of constructing a substantial musical work—one that he was exploring in his orchestral and chamber music. His concern in *Refrains and Cadenzas* (1972) is with the juxtaposition of opposites: chordal chorales with free-flowing melodies, dramatic tuttis with exposed chamber-like writing. The music does not develop organically, but through the cumulative effect of musical contrast. *Refrains and Cadenzas* was composed for Black Dyke Mills Band to play at the Cheltenham International Festival (another sign perhaps that the artistic potential of the brass band was being recognized).

At much the same time, the economy and precision with which Wilson and Simpson constructed their brass band scores found an echo in the work which Wilfred Heaton composed for the 1973 National Brass Band Championships, *Contest Music*. Uppermost in Heaton's mind was not the display of technical tricks with hundreds of notes, but the unfolding of a classically proportioned musical argument. There are moments of wit and humour, expressive melody, and vibrant 'big-band' rhythm, all treated with classical control and discipline. The first movement in particular is finely balanced and proportioned. Every note has a defined place in the musical argument. A comparison of the second subject material as it appears in the exposition, and, inverted, in the reprise, is one of many examples of the control he exerts over his material (Ex. 7*a* and *b*). *Contest Music* was commissioned by the new promoter of the

Ex. 7*a*. Wilfred Heaton, *Contest Music*, second subject: exposition

Ex. 7*b*. Wilfred Heaton, *Contest Music*, second subject: recapitulation

Nationals, Geoffrey Brand (b. 1926). Brand, like Heaton and Simpson, came from Salvationist stock. He worked closely with brass and military bands as a BBC producer (1955–68), before turning, with great success, to conducting and publishing. Many were disappointed, not least the composer and promoter, that due to the strict timetable enforced by the live radio transmission of the results, *Contest Music* was too long for twenty-four bands to play in the time available. The work's undoubted quality was not exposed publicly for another twelve years. Only since then has Heaton's innovative contribution to brass music begun to be fully appreciated. He has written substantial concertos for cornet and for trombone, a highly charged, Walton-inspired *Partita* (1947, revised 1984), and a number of sharply etched Salvationist works—*Toccata*, *Glory glory*[39], and *Victory for Me* being the most typical.

In describing his music, Heaton often talks about 'keeping emotion—out of date—in check'.[40] He is referring not to an emotional quality that might arise naturally from his music, but to his dislike of sentimental melody, a view which Edward Gregson would endorse: 'I can't stand the sentimental in music; my kind of emotion is Brahms or Mahler. My influences as a composer are Bartók, Stravinsky, Hindemith, and I feel a strong affinity with Vaughan Williams and Walton.'[41] Principal of the Royal Northern College of Music since 1996, Gregson is another composer whose musical aspirations were nurtured in the Salvation Army. He was just 21 and learning his craft, when Geoffrey Brand invited him to write under contract for R. Smith & Co. Sixteen pieces followed in seven years. Some were for contests, like *Essay* and *The Plantagenets*, others, like *Partita* and *Patterns*, were commissioned by youth bands. Writing to order taught him to be economical, and 'never to write notes that were not absolutely part of the intended texture'.[42] Gregson is unique among composers for the brass band in having forged a distinguished creative career in the wider musical world from a grounding in brass composition. In recent years, he has resisted the temptation to become 'type-cast', and has perhaps displayed greater creative freedom and originality in his orchestral music, like the Trumpet and Clarinet Concertos. There are three major works for brass band, in which he has extended the boundaries of test-piece composition, especially in the rigour of their construction and the range of percussion effects he calls for. The Vinter-inspired *Connotations* (originally to be called 'Variations in a Fourth') uses a taut framework of symphonic variations. *Dances and Arias* (1984) is the most concentrated and stylistically adventurous of the three. Its chorale theme and episodic structure bear some comparisons with Thomas Wilson's *Refrains and Cadenzas*. *Of Men and*

---

[39] Commissioned by Regent Hall Band of the Salvation Army, unpublished.
[40] Recalled in interview by Howard Snell, 'Portraits in Brass', BBC Radio 3, 1992, produced by Paul Hindmarsh.
[41] Eric Ball, 'The Music of Edward Gregson', *Sounding Brass*, 6/3 (Oct. 1977), 98.
[42] Ball, 'The Music of Edward Gregson'.

Mountains (1991) is the most expansive of gesture and atmospheric in colour, inspired perhaps by the example, if not the manner, of John McCabe's *Cloudcatcher Fells*.

Geoffrey Brand was also among those to encourage George Lloyd (1913–98), composer of five major works including *Royal Parks* (1985), *Diversion on a Bass Theme* (1986), and *English Heritage* (1988), and Joseph Horovitz (b. 1926), whose works for band include *Sinfonietta* (1971), three concertos, *Ballet for Band* (1984), and *Theme and Co-operation* (1994). Their contributions are distinguished by traditional values of structural integrity, allied to an ability, all too rare these days, of imbuing a simple melody with character and expression. Horovitz's observation that his lyrical Euphonium Concerto (1972, National Gala) was 'guided by the kindly hand of the Goddess of Tonality—long may she prosper',[43] might well apply to them both.

The composer and pianist, John McCabe (b. 1939), first encountered the brass band in the 1960s, through the horn player, Ifor James, then Musical Director of Besses o' th' Barn. McCabe found the band's playing 'staggeringly good . . . there's an enormous wealth of technique and abundant good musicianship'.[44] He was sufficiently impressed to accept a commission, and *Images* (1967) was the result. When he came to write *Cloudcatcher Fells* (1985, National Championships), the third of his five brass band works, he knew much more about the complex inner workings of the medium, and he exploited the sound-world with unrivalled resourcefulness, giving to each player an individual part, and thinking of the whole as an orchestra of distinct sounds. 'You might lose the highest register,' he has observed, 'but the band has a tremendous variety of tone colours, with or without mutes.'[45] All of McCabe's most characteristic compositions have been inspired by landscapes—of the desert, of ice, of fire. *Cloudcatcher Fells* is one of his most personal. As a child, he spent three months in Patterdale (the Lake District), and he describes Angle Tarn, so evocatively portrayed in the middle of the work, as 'his favourite place in the world'. The music is not simply illustrative. The mountain and lakeland associations are reflected in the structure of the music, on both the small and the large scale, from the undulating shape of the main theme (Ex. 8) to the final sequence of variations, which follows one of the famous walks from Angle Tarn, up Grisedale Brow, and across Striding Edge, to reveal the majestic peak of Helvellyn. The variation form has been fertile ground for so many of the important brass band scores since Vaughan Williams's *Variations* of 1957. *Cloudcatcher Fells*, with its synthesis of musical logic, technical challenge, evocative content, and personal association, is one of the finest examples.

---

[43] From the composer's programme note, Novello & Co.
[44] John McCabe, 'Portraits in Brass', BBC Radio 3, 1992, produced by Paul Hindmarsh.
[45] McCabe, 'Portraits in Brass', 1992.

Ex. 8. John McCabe, *Cloudcatcher Fells*, opening bars

New Horizons

At the 1975 Open Championship in Belle Vue, the commissioned piece was another set of innovative variations. The composer was Elgar Howarth, and the piece was *Fireworks*, a series of variations modelled on Benjamin Britten's *Young Person's Guide to the Orchestra*, with optional narrator. It proved to be a momentous occasion. The musical style was unfamiliar; as Eric Ball recalled, '*Fireworks* was fun, but many bandsmen weren't prepared for it. If they'd listened to Prokofiev, Shostakovich, they wouldn't have thought it strange in any way. It has a sort of sardonic wit, which I liked enormously— a sort of French sparkle to it.'[46] Extraordinary demands were also made on the percussion section, which had only just been admitted to the contesting arena. Howarth was brought up in a banding household. His father, Oliver Howarth, was a passionate enthusiast of opera, brass bands, and hymn tunes. As boys, Elgar and his brother, Stanford, played cornet and trombone in his father's Barton Hall Works Band, in Eccles, Lancashire. However, the music he encountered at Manchester University in the 1950s, by composers like Hindemith, Stravinsky, and Schoenberg, was a revelation, and, as first a trumpeter and then a conductor, he has gone on to specialize in opera and in contemporary music. He also remained committed to the brass band cause, and part of his crusade is 'to try to show people interested in bands what other possibilities exist as well as what is good in the mainstream'.[47] In particular, he used a long association with Grimethorpe Colliery Band to reveal the range of what it is possible for a band to achieve, from entertaining *jeux d'esprit* designed to bring the house down,[48] to wonderfully resourceful pastiches. The intensely moving *In Memoriam RK* was composed as a tribute to the Austrian conductor Rudolph Kempe, in the style of Mahler and Richard Strauss. *The Bandsman's Tale*, a witty parody of Stravinsky's *A Soldier's Tale*, uses William Booth's Salvationist hymn 'O Boundless Salvation' as its theme. Howarth has also composed a number of musically demanding works,

[46] Elgar Howarth, 'Portraits in Brass', BBC Radio 3, 1992, produced by Paul Hindmarsh.
[47] Taylor, *Labour and Love*, 201.
[48] Many of these short works were composed or arranged for the TV series, 'Granada Band of the Year', under the pseudonym W. Hogarth Lear.

with strong personal associations. The Messiaen-inspired threnody, *Ascendit in Coeli*, was composed in memory of his father, 'who loved hymn tunes'. *Songs for BL* (1995, BBC commission), is a series of evocative family portraits. *Hymns at Heaven's Gate* (1997, commissioned jointly by the Norwegian, Dutch, and Swiss Band Federations) juxtaposes virtuoso fanfares and poignant melody as a tribute to Harry Mortimer, and reuses parts of *Ascendit in Coeli*.

Reconciling his love of the brass band tradition with his modernist, reforming crusade, has not been without its controversies. During the 1970s, Howarth created in Grimethorpe a band which achieved a reputation in the wider musical world for its adventurous spirit. He encouraged fine composers without experience of bands to write substantial work. Notably, these included Sir Harrison Birtwistle, whose *Grimethorpe Aria* has been followed by an even more challenging and complex sequel, *Salford Toccata*. Hans Werner Henze's *Ragtimes and Habaneras* is hugely entertaining. George Benjamin's evocative and accomplished work *Altitude* was composed in 1977, when he was still in his teens. Anthony Payne's uncompromising *Fire on Whaleness* is an essay in atonality for brass band. Derek Bourgeois composed four technically demanding concertos for band in the 1970s. With Elgar Howarth's help, Sir William Walton rescored a short C. B. Cochran revue ballet from 1936, *The First Shoot*. Without any preconceptions about what brass band players were traditionally capable of doing, all these composers created some startlingly novel, sometimes electrifying sounds, particularly Henze and Bourgeois, the latter going on to write shorter, but equally effective works for competition and concert, including *Blitz*, *Diversions*, and *The Forest of Dean* (variations on a theme by his teacher, Herbert Howells).

The idioms of popular music, very different from those used by Henze and Walton, were employed by Sir Michael Tippett (1905–97) in his only work for brass band, *Festal Brass with Blues*. It was a commission from the Hong Kong Festival, and was premièred there in 1984 by the Williams Fairey Engineering Band, conducted by Howard Williams. It is a single movement, and could be described as a fantasy on themes from his Third Symphony. In the second part of the Symphony, Tippett produced an ironic vocal blues commentary on Schiller's 'Ode to Joy' and Beethoven's setting of it in his Ninth Symphony. In *Festal Brass with Blues*, Tippett builds up a festive interplay of ideas, exploiting antiphonal contrasts between different sections of the band, until a quotation of the dissonant opening of Beethoven's choral finale leads to a transcription of the first, slow blues, featuring the flugel horn, as it does in the Symphony, with solo cornet taking the vocal line. *Festal Brass with Blues* is one of the most accessible of Tippett's late works, and the only opportunity for brass band musicians to play an original work in his unique style.

Extended instrumental techniques or 'modern' methods of notation formed a small but significant part of the band repertoire of the last quarter of the century. Elgar Howarth's *Five Pieces for Spielberg*, in which he adopts a

Lutosławskian semi-aleatoric manner, create a somewhat elusive impression in performance. A touching elegy for Harry Mortimer, *Shadow Songs* (1991), composed for Besses o' th' Barn Band by Philip Wilby (b. 1949), uses the same techniques, but in a more tangible way, employing modal melodies and the hymn tune 'Abide with Me'. In 1994, Wilby was commissioned by the National Youth Brass Band of Great Britain to write a work which included an element of live electronics. The result was a powerful sinfonia, based on a fragment of Herbert Howells's anthem, 'Like as the hart', entitled *Dance before the Lord*, involving live, computer-manipulated sounds, organ, and a large brass band, with off-stage soloists. The systematic use of live, electronic delay in Tim Souster's *Echoes*, commissioned for Besses o' th' Barn in 1990, is an integral part of the pulse and texture of the music. Paul Patterson's *Cataclysm* (1975) makes extensive use of aleatoric notation and chance episodes. It was commissioned by the National Youth Brass Band during the tenure as Musical Adviser of Arthur Butterworth (b. 1923), whose own contribution to the brass band movement, first as a player with Besses, and then as a composer with an individual 'northern' voice, has been considerable. He readily acknowledges the influences of Sibelius and the landscape and legend of Northern Europe on his music, in works like the powerful symphonic study, *Odin* (1986, commissioned by the Black Dyke Mills Band). In 1989, the National Youth Brass Band under its Musical Director, Roy Newsome, initiated an enterprising commissioning policy, which introduced Philip Wilby to the medium.

New horizons came into view for the Salvationist composer and arranger Ray Steadman-Allen, when he retired from full-time service in the mid 1980s, and added to his substantial output a number of wholly original works. Throughout his creative life, he has composed using borrowed material—largely songs and hymns—sometimes with considerable sophistication. His list of published work runs into several hundred pieces, but there is a smaller number of key works which reveal how he has reconciled the demands of the Salvationist ethos and his own adventurous creative instincts: *The Holy War* from the 1960s, *On Ratcliff Highway* from the 1970s, and *The Lord is King* from the 1980s. His music is vibrant and often quixotic in mood, manipulating the given material as though it were his own, stretching the conventions of tonal melody and harmony to their limit through abrupt changes in mood, texture, and pace. In his 'post-retirement' contest works he simply applies the same techniques, inventing his own tunes and working with them in the same way. Significantly perhaps, the most successful of them, *Hymn at Sunrise* (1996, All England Masters), is based on the famous canon by Thomas Tallis.

VIEWS OF THE PAST

Because composing for the brass band largely is a twentieth-century phenomenon, the band movement has been concerned more with 'progress'—with what is new and current—than with developing a perspective on its musical past. However, as the repertoire has grown in volume and range, so a number of composers have begun to recognize a creative potential in drawing inspiration from the musical traditions out of which brass band music has evolved.

In the early 1980s, for example, Robin Holloway (b. 1943) drew on the idioms of pre-1920s popular music to help him create a poignant mix of tragedy and nostalgia in his two *War Memorials*, *Men Marching* and *From Hills and Valleys*, commissioned by the Yorkshire Imperial Band. Ray Steadman-Allen created an Ivesian kaleidoscope of popular Victorian hymns and song to convey the pioneering spirit of the early Salvation Army bands in *On Ratcliff Highway* (1978). Michael Ball (b. 1948) appropriated the idioms and conventions of the pioneering test pieces and contest marches to evoke the spirit of the old Belle Vue and Saddleworth contests in *Whitsun Wakes* (1997). Following on from the success of his first 'all-American' work, *Frontier!* (1986, Open Championship), this score was used for the 1997 Open, and led to several earlier works being adopted by other contests: the Shakespeare-inspired *Midsummer Music* (1992, commissioned by Besses o' th' Barn) for the 1998 National First Section Finals, and *Chaucer's Tunes* (1994) for the 1999 National Youth Brass Band Championship (Open Section).

Philip Wilby has embraced a view of the musical past of the band movement with perhaps the greatest sense of purpose. He has strong convictions about the place and purpose of the composer. Composing is for Wilby 'an act of worship',[49] an expression, as it is for Eric Ball, of his Christian faith. Indeed, the spiritual background to his first band piece, *The New Jerusalem* (1989), also underlies Eric Ball's tone poem, *The Eternal Presence*. Wilby is especially conscious of the context and tradition of the music he writes. Mediating between past and present, personal expression and musical function, enables him to write music which amateur performers and non-specialist audiences can enjoy, without compromising his own musical integrity. *Paganini Variations* (1991, BBC commission), for example, is full of characteristic layers of invention—virtuoso display and romantic melody. These much used 'test-piece' ingredients become part of the symbolism of the music. By taking the listener on a journey from Paganini's style, through Brahms, Wagner, even Britten, to the 1990s, Wilby reveals the brass band as the inheritor of a living virtuoso tradition. In *Masquerade* (1993, Open Championship), based on Verdi's *Falstaff*, he takes the concept of the operatic 'pot-pourri' to unparalleled heights of elaborate display and dramatic characterization.

The layers of symbols and associations underpinning *Revelation* (*Symphony for Double Brass after Purcell*), of 1995, are almost as complex as

---

[49] A quotation from the American poet Mark Jarman, whose *Unholy Sonnets* Wilby set for tenor and brass band in 1995. The first performance was given at the 1996 BBC Festival of Brass by Martin Hindmarsh (tenor), and the Grimethorpe Colliery Band, conducted by Peter Parkes.

the music itself. Wilby describes it as a 'tribute to Purcell's music and the ornate and confident spirit of his age'.[50] Purcell's 'Three parts on a ground' provides the musical content for virtuoso variations and fugues. John Donne's paraphrase from Revelation 7, provides the basis of the symbolism. Wilby instructs soloists and groups from within the band to leave their seats to play their solo and concertante passages as a physical symbol of the last trumpet sounding 'At the round earth's imagined corners'. The idea of small groups set against the full band is borrowed from the baroque concerto grosso. The concept of double or antiphonal choirs has its roots in the sixteenth century and the brass music of Giovanni Gabrieli. After a procession of canons, fugues, variations, and cadenzas, Purcell's melodies are given a nostalgic, sentimental treatment by duetting euphoniums. The music comes to an exultant, affirmative climax as if on the 'Day of Judgement'.

Among the other postmodernist composers writing for brass band, Nigel Clarke (b. 1960) has also sought inspiration from the past. Clarke has composed a series of substantial works for the Black Dyke Mills Band. He was appointed composer-in-residence in 1991. His fifth brass band work, *Mechanical Ballet* (1998), takes as its starting-point the industrial heritage of the British brass band, in, to quote the composer's note, 'a post-minimalist exploration of the relentless and irregular rhythm of the mechanical factory'.

BRASS BANDS AND THE CONSERVATOIRES

The establishment of a full-time music degree course in Brass Band Musicianship, at what is now the University of Salford, in the 1970s, created new opportunities for greater professional participation in what had been until then a largely amateur musical world. During the 1980s and 1990s further degree or diploma courses were started in the University of Huddersfield and at the Royal Northern College of Music. All the British conservatoires of music include a brass band as one of their performing ensembles. Leading bands like Black Dyke, Grimethorpe, and Williams Fairey also established close relationships with the leading music colleges, thus providing a fresh and increasingly valuable platform for the performance of new and original work for the medium.

Sir Harrison Birtwistle's formidably difficult *Salford Toccata* was written for the Salford University Brass Band. During the 1990s composers like Edward Gregson, Elgar Howarth, and Nigel Clarke, and conductors like James Gourlay, Howard Snell, and James Watson, devoted increasing amounts of time and energy to fostering the professional dimension within the band movement.

---

[50] From the composer's programme note, Novello & Co.

Brass Bands and Broadcasting

From July 1936, when Denis Wright was invited by Kenneth Wright to join the BBC's Music Division as Programme Organiser for a new brass band section, the BBC has served both as a barometer of current tastes and as a significant patron of new work. The heyday of band broadcasts was during the Second World War, when brass and military music performed a valuable national service. In 1940, for example, there was a brass band broadcast three or four times a week. There were also five weekly broadcasts by military bands—two by Service bands, and three from the BBC Military Band.

When, in April 1942, Denis Wright moved on to become the Assistant Music Director of the Overseas Service, his place was taken by Harry Mortimer.[51] As Supervisor of Brass and Military Band Programmes for the BBC, Mortimer brought all his years of experience from working with bands and from his time as a professional orchestral trumpeter to bear on the post. The first part of his tenure coincided with the years of rebuilding after the war, and of his greatest success as a contest conductor. He widened the range of coverage, including parts of major events like the National Championships and Gala concerts. All of these broadcasts were transmitted on the BBC's Light Programme (now Radio 2). When he retired, the baton passed to Geoffrey Brand in London, and to other regional centres, principally Manchester, with an editorial brief to reflect the range of brass band performance throughout the country. Since 1994, the flagship programme, *Listen to the Band*, one of the most popular programmes on the network, has been produced in Birmingham by the Specialist Music Department. It continues to serve the brass band audience with a diet of entertaining, populist repertoire in weekly half-hour programmes, complemented by programmes on some BBC local radio stations.

Brass bands have not attracted as much sustained interest on television. During the 1970s, Granada Television produced an entertainment competition, the 'Granada Band of the Year'. In the early 1980s, the Manchester-based television producer, Gerald Harrison, established a similarly gladiatorial contest for BBC2. These two series have spawned a new competitive genre, the entertainment contest, where marks are given for entertainment value and programme content, as well as for the standard of execution.

The commitment to the performance of original repertoire was reflected in the long-running *Bandstand* series, broadcast on the BBC Music Programme (now Radio 3). It was an unfortunate title in many ways, since it suggested music of an outdoor kind. Nevertheless, it brought the burgeoning repertoire

[51] There was a general shift of management posts in the BBC Music Division. In 1942, Denis Wright moved to the Overseas Service as Assistant to its new Director, Kenneth Wright. The previous Assistant, Arthur Bliss, was promoted to Head of the Music Division.

of new and challenging music to a wider audience. It was through *Bandstand*, for example, that the music of Wilfred Heaton was first appreciated. The BBC continued to commission new work, including *Royal Parks* (1985, European Championships) from George Lloyd (1913–98), *Flowers of the Forest* (1990, National Youth Brass Band) from Sir Richard Rodney Bennett (b. 1936), and *Chi* (1993, National Youth Brass Band) from Gary Carpenter (b. 1951). The appetite for new music in the brass band of the late twentieth century is undiminished. Many outstanding composers have come to value the commitment that bands of all levels give to the preparation of innovative work.

In 1989, when the *Bandstand* programme came to an end, the Controller of Radio 3 at that time, Sir John Drummond, requested a new format, which would aim at a higher artistic profile and greater editorial consistency. The BBC Festival of Brass was devised to provide that concentrated focus, with the finest bands playing the best music. During its eight-year run, the Festival brought several young composers of brass music to a wider audience, notably the prolific composer and arranger Peter Graham (b. 1958); composers Nigel Clarke and Martin Ellerby (b. 1957), whose spectacular Euphonium Concertos were given their broadcast premières by Robert Childs and Steven Mead; John Pickard (b. 1963); and Robin Walker (b. 1953), whose evocative study *Miners* was premièred by the ex-miners of Grimethorpe Colliery. The BBC also commissioned fifteen new works for the series. Some were designed to attract the brightest young composers to the medium, like Judith Bingham (*Four Minute Mile, Prague*), Philip Grange (*Lowry Dreamscape*), and David Sawer (*Hell-noise*). Others were commissioned to bridge the gap between contest and concert music: David Bedford (*Toccata for Tristan*), Philip Wilby (*Paganini Variations*), Elgar Howarth (*Songs for BL*), and Michael Ball (*Whitsun Wakes*).

In 1998, the evolving music policy of Radio 3 left no room for a regular brass band series on this scale, although brass band music continues to be heard. Over the last thirty years, the musical outlook, social context, and artistic aspirations of bands at all levels have been transformed. The British brass band has continued to be one of Britain's distinctive musical exports, and the BBC has achieved more in raising public awareness of the remarkable quality and range of the brass band and its music than any other single organization.

8

Aspects of Performance Practices: The Brass Band and its Influence on Other Brass-Playing Styles

Trevor Herbert and John Wallace

There has been little systematic research into the performance practices of brass bands. Anyone wishing to undertake a comprehensive study of the subject (and this chapter has no pretensions to pass as such) would find it difficult. Not only are there comparatively few sources for performance practices in the past dating from before the twentieth century, primarily because performance practices and styles have been communicated through largely aural, rather than written, means; but also, the richest vein of source materials pertains to the very best brass bands, and this group is but a tiny part of the mass practice of brass banding.

In this chapter, through a limited number of textual and oral sources and recordings, we examine some of the performance practices of bands and players for which such sources exist. We also suggest what the main strands of influence have been on professional brass playing in Britain. The names of the greatest bands—Black Dyke, Cyfarthfa, Foden's, Besses o' th' Barn, Grimethorpe, and so on—are prominent in this story. For each one of these bands, there have been hundreds—perhaps even thousands—that eked out a modest existence, perhaps occasionally attempting to run through one of the great contest test pieces, before resorting to the plethora of pieces which are written in a safely predictable tessitura and which present no special challenges to technique or musicianship. Algernon Rose pointed out in the late nineteenth century that such bands littered every corner of Britain, and it is likely that they still do in

Figure 8.1. The Black Dyke Mills Band, photographed at Durham Cathedral in 1998. The conductor is James Watson.

the late twentieth century. To this group can be added Salvationist bands, the majority of which have never shared the ambitions of the best secular bands. These less ambitious bands have had as important a function within their own communities as have the more august members of the species in theirs—possibly more so, as the better bands perceive themselves as players on a wider cultural and media stage. But to attempt an ethnography of all types of brass band would be difficult and probably fruitless. The reality is that since contesting began as a spectacle of mass entertainment, the brass band idiom has been defined by the greatest secular bands and the finest of their players. It is to these mentors that the movement has looked to define matters of technique, repertoire, and style, and its interaction with wider spheres of musical activity.

We have looked at the development of the brass band idiom in terms of three loosely and somewhat crudely defined periods. The first takes in the period between the discernible advent of brass bands as a mass activity—the late 1840s—and the second decade of the twentieth century. The Victorian period is an important time, not least because it witnessed the formation of the standard brass band instrumentation, and the beginning of the modern contest movement and the administrative structures which support it.

The 1920s is a good place to start looking at a new phase, which lasted until about the end of the 1960s. The social fracture caused by the First World War had its effects on brass bands, but there were other more positive changes: the idiomatic contest repertoire developed with new rapidity from the 1920s, and also during this period, brass bands became something of a focus for gramophone recording companies. Though some have referred to the last thirty years of the nineteenth century as 'the golden age' of the brass band movement, and drawn this epithet from the fact that (as far as we know) it was the time when the greatest number of brass bands were in existence, there is a good case for seeing the period between the 1920s and the 1960s as the period when the brass band idiom was, as far as style is concerned, most standardized and stable, and when bands were dealing most earnestly with a commonly shared, sophisticated, idiomatic repertoire. It was in this period, too, that radio broadcasting and gramophone records became widely available, and made the sound of brass bands popular throughout the country and beyond—perhaps to a yet greater extent than in the period when bands relied on 'live' audiences.[1] Throughout this time, needless to say, contesting was as popular as ever, and the musical and stylistic features generated by the contesting ethos were all-pervading.

From the 1960s and 1970s, there were a number of important developments which suggest to us that this should be seen as a separate phase. These changes, as we discuss below, were brought about by a number of events and trends occurring in rapid succession. The change to the standard A440 pitch, and the subsequent shift to new, wider bore instruments, marked the beginning of this process, but there were other elements at work: the rise of a small group of imaginative and sophisticated conductors, the appearance of a more radical repertoire, a new type of interchange between brass bands and mainstream art music, and, one suspects, other influences too, which came from a wider set of social and cultural sources.

THE NINETEENTH CENTURY

It is hard to distinguish a time before the last two or three decades of the nineteenth century when assumptions about a single brass band idiom can be made. The reality appears to be that for the first thirty or so years of the Victorian era, there were as many instrumental formulations, as many stylistic idiosyncrasies, as there were bands.

The printed journals, the most widely consumed music for brass bands in the Victorian period, were deliberately aimed at, and designed for, a market which was diverse rather than standardized. The music was arranged so that it could be played on a wide variety of different combinations of instruments.

---

[1] For a chronological catalogue of brass band recordings in this period, see Frank Andrews, *Brass Band Cylinder and Non-Microgroove Disc Recordings 1903–1960* (Winchester: Piccolo Press, 1997).

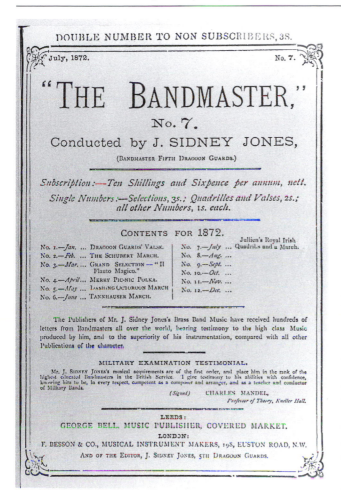

Figure 8.2. *The Bandmaster* journal was typical of its kind, and was edited by one of the leading military bandmasters of his day. The music contained in the journal was undemanding and contained parts which could fit bands of various instrumentations.

The repertoires offered in these journals—even though some publications made greater demands on players than others—provide no really telling evidence about playing styles and techniques. We do not know whether journal music reflects the limits of the technical ability of early players, something beyond their ability, or something considerably short of it.

Hand-written music, however, is different; it is a more intimate, bespoke testimony of the musical behaviour of particular players at a particular time. Though some 'Professors of Music' were advertising their services as arrangers of music for bands, the hand-written music which survives in small manuscript collections across the country is usually in the hand of a bandmaster or a band copyist. It is virtually certain that where such music existed, it represented the main staple of the repertoire of the band in question. It also

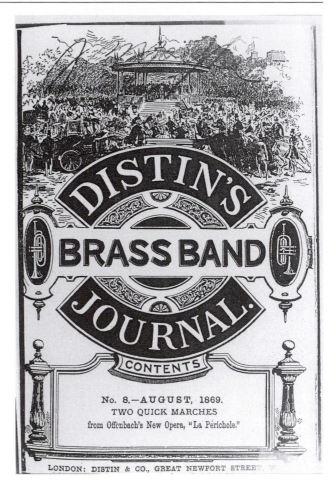

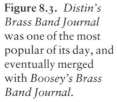

Figure 8.3. *Distin's Brass Band Journal* was one of the most popular of its day, and eventually merged with *Boosey's Brass Band Journal*.

indicates not just the titles in a band's repertoire, but, to a significant extent, the technical ability of its players. Bandmasters would not have arranged music so that it was beyond the capabilities of their players, but they would have done their best to exhibit the outer limits of their techniques.

The surviving manuscript sources for Victorian bands (and they are but a tiny morsel of the total quantity which must have existed) show a number of similarities, and in some respects these repertoires reflect predilections which are apparent in broader aspects of working-class music culture. The two most prominent similarities are, first, the predominance of operatic transcriptions, dance music, and functional pieces such as marches, hymns, and anthems; and secondly, a gradual change from instrumentations which follow no set pattern, towards a more standard, coherent line-up based on cornets, trombones, and saxhorns. Few brass bands included trumpets or french horns. A clarinet might occasionally be included in the line-up (one was still present in the Besses o' th' Barn Band in 1860), but clarinets were rarely found in brass bands after that date.

The repertoire of the Besses o' th' Barn Band, which dates from the 1880s, and that of the Cyfarthfa Band, which dates from some time after 1850, are the two largest and most revealing hand-written virtuoso repertoires to survive virtually intact.[2] The Besses o' th' Barn repertoire was crafted and arranged by Alexander Owen, and the band library contains some of the operatic transcriptions by Owen and John Gladney. Six sets of the Cyfarthfa band books survive in a total of 105 part books: each set is cumulative. Even this large collection is only part of what is known to have been a much larger repertoire. The music played in the 1840s, when the band was in its early years, is lost. The pieces that survive can be dated no earlier than the mid-1850s. The collection is exceptional because it provides the largest coherent sample of surviving Victorian brass band music from such an early date. The repertoire can be categorized into three groups: dance music (quadrilles, polkas, and waltzes are the most popular); transcriptions of art music (the most popular source is Italian opera); and miscellaneous religious and secular pieces that were of local interest (Welsh airs and so on).

Both the Cyfarthfa and the Besses repertoires were played by bands which were especially virtuoso, so they can hardly be taken as typical. But the music does allow us to draw some conclusions about the performance practices of the best brass bands of the century. The Cyfarthfa Band material has had the greater amount of scrutiny and experimentation.[3] The band used a mixture of keyed and valve instruments until well into the 1860s. The valve instruments which were eventually bought by the band's owner, Robert Thompson Crawshay, were, in the main, Viennese instruments with rotary valves. It is hard to determine why instruments with the Sax design of piston valves were not favoured, but one might speculate that the ostentatious Crawshay wanted to equip his band with instruments that distinguished it from others in the emerging amateur brass band movement. There are no other cases of large-scale British bands using a predominance of rotary valve instruments.

---

[2] For the Cyfarthfa repertoire see Trevor Herbert, 'The Repertory of a Victorian Provincial Brass Band', *Popular Music*, 9/1 (1990), 117–32; and 'The Reconstruction of Nineteenth-Century Band Repertory: Towards a Protocol', in S. Carter (ed.), *Perspectives in Brass Scholarship: Proceedings of the International Historic Brass Symposium, Amherst, 1995* (Stuyvesant, NY: Pendragon Press, 1997), 193–222. There is no comprehensive annotated catalogue of the Besses o' th' Barn library, but handlists of this and other band libraries are given in the appendices to Roy Newsome, *Brass Roots: A Hundred Years of Brass Bands and their Music, 1836–1936* (Aldershot: Ashgate, 1998).

[3] A reconstruction of this repertoire has been recorded on period instruments by the Wallace Collection, under the title *The Origin of the Species: Virtuoso Victorian Brass Music from Cyfarthfa Castle, Wales*, Nimbus NI5470.

The Cyfarthfa manuscripts show the players to have had rounded techniques in which a very broad dynamic and expressive range, and the capacity to perform lyrical lines over a wide tessitura, were commonplace. It also shows them to have been capable of intricate ensemble playing (the bandmaster and arranger explored a wide range of textures) and to have possessed playing skills which were diverse and sophisticated. Indeed, the technical demands made of the Cyfarthfa players comfortably outstrip anything found in the brass orchestral writing contemporaneous with it. It is not just that there are occasional passages which test the players; it is that there is apparently an underlying assumption upon the part of the arrangers of this music that the players could play almost anything which was placed before them, provided it was within a given range.

This assumption is also evident in the Besses repertoire. Like the Cyfarthfa conductor, George Livesey, Alexander Owen knew brass instruments and their idioms intimately.[4] Both were cornet players. Yet both men persistently wrote uncompromisingly difficult passages for their players. These two important repertoires provide us with the first generalization that one can make about the development of brass band technique as against orchestral brass technique in the nineteenth century. Whereas the composers of orchestral brass parts (particularly those in the German-speaking countries[5]) wrote for brass instruments in a well-established and largely conservative idiom, brass band arrangers either ignored or were oblivious to such matters, and were guided only by the practical considerations of getting twenty or more brass players to substitute for—perhaps even provide a passable imitation of—the ensemble for which the music was originally written: usually a full symphony orchestra.

Orchestral brass players and brass band players had fundamentally different experiences in their encounter with new repertoire in the mid-Victorian period. Orchestral brass players found themselves playing music which usually required only incremental extensions of the technical idioms fashioned by classical and early romantic composers. The cotton workers of Lancashire and the iron smelters of South Wales probably had little sense of this aspect of the history of music or its practices. Their understanding of repertoire and style was contemporary: they appear to have had a relationship with music and its associated technical and stylistic challenges which was pragmatic and instinctive. They did not engage with, or attempt to adhere to, continuities of

---

[4] Both players made reputations as cornet players before becoming conductors. Livesey, like his father, was a theatre player before he moved to Merthyr. Alexander Owen played in a militia band.

[5] The distinction is important. Many German composers (before Wagner) were conservative in their writing for brass. On the other hand, Berlioz was more experimental. Verdi's orchestral writing needs special consideration, particularly in respect of the use of valve trombones and *cimbasso* in Italian theatres.

technique or idiom, because they were probably unaware of such continuities. Indeed, it is possible that there was effectively no *influential* prehistory upon which amateur brass players built their styles in the nineteenth century. It may be that earlier forms of music making—church bands and the like—gave these brass band players their first experience of instrumental music. But did this experience have such substance that it infiltrated the consciousness of players with the ingredients of idiom and style? If it did, it must have been a minor influence, for the repertoire which confronted brass band players was of an entirely different order than had previously been encountered by amateurs. The most important influence on the euphonium and ophicleide idiom in the mid-century may well have been the cello and bassoon writing in the operas of Verdi and Rossini. Similarly, cornet players were (perhaps unknown to them) imitating the figurations and phrases idiomatic to violins, oboes, clarinets, and flutes.

A second generalization which one can make about mid-Victorian brass bands has been made in Chapter 1, but bears repetition in this context. It concerns the relative importance of valve as against keyed brass instruments in respect of the growth of an increasingly complex repertoire. The advent and wide availability of piston valve instruments led to the mass popularity of brass bands as a participatory musical activity, and probably meant that players became efficient faster than most would have done on keyed instruments. This does not mean, however, that players on keyed instruments were not virtuoso; indeed, it is evident that some of the most technically complex passages to have survived were written for keyed instrument players. When valve instruments became widely available in the 1840s, the best brass players were the most well-established ones, and the majority of these were keyed instrument players. They had no reason to take up valve instruments when their techniques were so advanced on their existing instruments. This was certainly true of ophicleide players, because, leaving aside the serpent, which has a comparatively weak currency as an art-music instrument, there was no other lip-vibrated bass instrument of that range on which very fast chromatic passages could be played.[6] The ophicleide parts in the Cyfarthfa repertory provide conclusive proof in this regard (see Ex. 9).

A third generalization about brass bands in the Victorian era is that, from the late 1860s onwards, the most important influences on the idiom were the more successful 'mentor' or 'crack' bands. This period saw the beginning of the process of standardization—a process which worked mainly through imitation. The focus for imitation was a relatively small number of bands

---

[6] The trombone appears not have been a virtuoso instrument among amateurs in Britain in the 19th cent. Indeed, the writing for trombones in manuscript collections such as those connected with the Cyfarthfa players, gives the impression that trombone players were not expected to adopt an idiom notably different from that written for the orchestral instrument.

Ex. 9. A section of the ophicleide part (in bass clef) of an arrangement of Wagner's 'The Rhine Daughters', from the Cyfarthfa band books.

conducted by the northern triumvirate of Gladney, Swift, and Owen. By the 1870s, many brass bands recognized, and to an extent, shared, a common style, which did not include virtuosity as a necessary prerequisite. This applied equally to the best and biggest bands and to the smaller, more modestly talented of them. The idiom was characterized by two broad parameters which were to persist as the key identifiers of the British brass band idiom: first, the homogeneity of its sound; and secondly, the primacy of 'discipline' in its musical practices. From the time that such writings first appear, journalism about brass bands refers to the 'organ-like' sound as the ideal band sonority. The same sources unproblematically refer to playing techniques in terms of right and wrong, good and bad, correct and incorrect. There were no issues of fashion and experiment; all was distilled into matters of authenticity.

The most crystallizing factor as regards the movement towards uniformity must have been the standardization of instrumentation which was very similar to the instrumentation of the twentieth-century brass band by 1890. Also evident by this time was the practice, which was to endure, of writing all but one of the parts in the treble clef. This idiosyncrasy was intended to be pragmatic and didactic. However, it was not originally ubiquitous, though some journal music was published in multiple parts (for different clefs and transpositions), the manuscript part books which survive from earlier in the century often show parts in the orthodox transposition pitch and clef.[7]

The instrumentation recommended by Wright and Round in the late 1880s as 'A full brass band, as per all the best contesting bands' was similar but not identical to the twentieth-century format:

1 E♭ Soprano Cornet	2 B♭ Baritones 1st and 2nd
3 B♭ Cornets	2 B♭ Trombones 1st and 2nd
2 B♭ Repiano Cornets	1 G Trombone
1 Second Cornet	2 B♭ Euphoniums
1 Third Cornet	2 E♭ Bombardons
1 B♭ Flugel 1st	1 B♭ Bass (medium size)

---

[7] The treble clef is used for all instruments except the bass trombone (which is written in bass clef—a tradition usually regarded as a legacy from the early days of banding, though early sources often show all bass parts in bass clef). This odd convention is attributed, not entirely convincingly, to the didactic advantages of having all instruments (except one!) understanding a common denomination of note recognition. This has little practical advantage in terms of the sounds they produce, because if all the treble clef instruments were to be asked to play, for example, a C, they would not produce the same note, since six of the instruments are in E♭ and the others in B♭. However, the system has practical and didactic advantages, because a player schooled on any treble clef instrument would be able to read and play any other treble clef part in the band without difficulty. A bass trombone player reads and understands notation in the same way as his/her orchestral counterparts: the music is written out and sounds in concert pitch in the bass clef, but a tenor trombone player confronted with a tenor clef part (as sometimes they are) would mentally subtract two flats from the key signature or raise it by a tone (an E♭ signature becomes F, an F signature becomes G, and so on), and play it as if it were in treble clef and transposed down one octave.

1 B♭ Flugel 2nd	1 BB♭ Bass (monstre)
3 E♭ Horns 1st 2nd 3rd	Drums *ad libatum* [*sic*]

Wright and Round also advocate a set instrumentation for 'a smaller band':

1 E♭ Soprano Cornet	2 B♭ Baritones
2 B♭ Solo Cornets	2 B♭ Trombones
1 B♭ Repiano Cornet	1 B♭ Euphonium
1 B♭ 2nd Cornet	1 E♭ Bombardon
1 B♭ 3rd Cornet	1 B♭ Bass (medium size)
2 E♭ Horns	Drums *ad libatum* [*sic*]

The authors add the note: 'It is not advisable to have a smaller band than this.'[8]

The move towards standardization and the authoritative influence of a small group of leading conductors intensified the feeling that there was a common idiom in the brass band world, and the pursuit of excellence within this idiom by contesting bands gave rise to what was probably an improved general standard of playing. Players in the later nineteenth century were no better technically than the Cyfarthfa players had been thirty years earlier, but such high standards of virtuosity were more widespread by that time, and the performance of startlingly impressive configurations, employing deft manipulations of the valves and the tongue, were commonplace. Though different types of tonguing have existed since at least the sixteenth century, the combination of single-, double-, and triple-tonguing within single figures and phrases had never before been used so prolifically. Such figurations were to become something of a generic feature in *airs variés*. The *air varié* was a solo instrumental form with band or piano accompaniment (see Ex. 10 and Ex. 11). It is essentially a theme-and-variation form in which the variations are often separated by a *ritornello*-type tutti passage played by the accompanying band (or pianist). The individual variations focus on different features of technique—single-tonguing, slurring, high and low extremes of the range, and so on. Many such solos also carried at least one cadenza. Predictably, there were soon *air varié* contests for solo players.

Almost all knowledgeable late Victorian writers who express a view about the brass band, and also subsequent writers, emphasize the need for it to have a good 'tone'. It is difficult to define exactly what was considered good

Ex. 10. This piece and Ex. 11 are typical examples of *air varié* solos, and show figurations which are especially idiomatic of brass band valve instruments. 'Keel Row' is from a compilation published by Wright & Round, in a collection called *The Cornettist*.

---

[8] *Wright and Round's Amateur Band Teacher's Guide and Bandsman's Adviser* (Liverpool: Wright & Round, 1889), 3.

N.º 15. AIR VARIED. "KEEL ROW." T. H. WRIGHT.

JENNY JONES.

GEO. FRED BIRKENSHAW

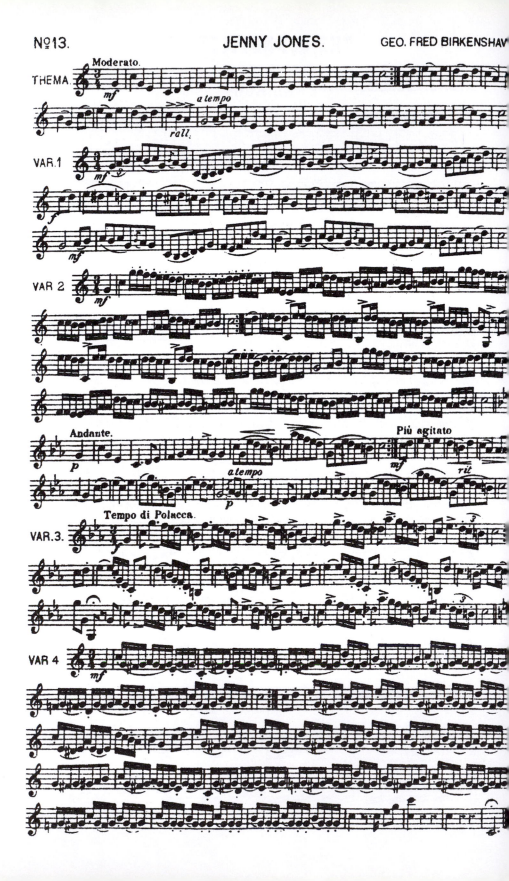

tone, but words such as 'full', 'sweet', 'musical', and 'pure' abound. However, what seems undeniably to be the case is that perceptions of tone rest on the ability of any one player to blend his sound with that of others. Thus, even in the nineteenth century, the idea of homogeneity seems to have been widely accepted. Besses o' th' Barn played several hymn and psalm tunes from memory at the start of every rehearsal and prior to any contest, and this was taken to be the basis of a correct technique for acquiring a good sound. One can only guess the extent to which vibrato was employed by brass band players before the turn of the century. It seems unthinkable that it was not used, but its constant presence as a standard, distinguishing feature of the homogeneous brass band sonority in the twentieth century may not have been so evident in the nineteenth century. The earliest recordings of brass bands (which date from the turn of the century) do not provide totally reliable clues; the recording quality is not always good, and primitive early recording techniques, which relied on players using strong articulations and straight sustained notes so as to make an imprint on the wax cylinders, may often have led to players adjust their normal techniques. However, early recordings of the American brass virtuosi, Herbert C. Clarke, the cornetist, and Arthur Pryor, the great trombone player, suggest that they used vibrato discriminatingly.[9] Such an approach, where vibrato is used only sparingly, for very special expressive purposes, would be in keeping with evidence of its use in mainstream art music, but whether such discrimination filtered through to brass bands is not known. It seems likely, however, that vibrato was not such a ubiquitous feature of the brass band sound in the nineteenth century as it was to become in the twentieth. By the end of the nineteenth century, even the Salvation Army had a view on the matter. Richard Slater, the most influential voice on music in the Salvation Army as a whole, and a musician of considerable knowledge and sophistication, emphasized that each Salvationist band should have a tone of 'quite distinguished character . . . What is aimed at is a tone full, free, rich, flexible'. On the question of vibrato—or 'tremolo', as he preferred to call it—he is specific: 'There are certain ways of rendering which would be appropriate in a soloist that would be altogether out of place in the efforts of a band, as in tremolo effects, as of great emotion, as well as increasing or slackening the time.'[10]

Ex. 11. 'Jenny Jones' was published in *Wright & Round's Second Bandsman's Holiday*.

---

[9] The playing of Clarke and Pryor can be heard on two recordings in the Crystal Records Historical Series, *Cornet soloist of the Sousa Band: Herbert L. Clarke*, Crystal Records CD450, and *Arthur Pryor: Trombone soloist of the Sousa Band*, Crystal Records CD451.

[10] Salvation Army International Heritage Centre London (SAIHC), Richard Slater file. This article on the subject of 'Expression' was published in the *Musical Salvationist* (July 1898).

The Twentieth Century (1914–c.1970)

Between the end of the First World War and the late 1960s, the main structural features of the brass band movement remained constant despite the pressure and competition which came from other forms of leisure: there were no changes in instrument designs which were so significant that they impacted greatly on the sound that brass bands made. The contesting structure remained solid, and though there were changes in the sponsorship and organization of brass band contests, there was not a fundamental change in the way they were judged or the qualities which were looked for in champions. An elderly man listening to a brass band contest in the 1960s—marking his own card, being his own adjudicator—would have summoned up more or less the same set of value-judgements as he had used half a century earlier to pick his winner. Terms like 'good tone', 'neat ensemble', 'no cracked notes', 'good balance', and 'good intonation' applied throughout this period.

It is not just that the broad meanings conveyed by such terms were always applicable—it is that the underlying values and the systems which sustained them remained almost intact. In the 1920s, in a series of articles entitled 'Common Faults of Bands', 'Pioneer', the *British Bandsman*'s columnist, listed the categories 'under which the majority of bands lose points': 'tone, tune, precision, balance, intonation, rhythm, technique, style, tempi, phrasing, expression, and general interpretation'.[11] The *British Bandsman*'s hapless readers might well have pondered how many more possibilities there could have been. Four decades later, the same paper carried a description of the criteria recognized by the conductor, Alex Mortimer, as appropriate for adjudicators when judging band contests, which was almost a synopsis of the same article, reminding readers of 'those essential qualities, tuning, tonal control, dynamic contrast, internal balance and clarity of detail'.[12]

From this it can be gathered that changes to the idiom of the brass band during this period were almost imperceptible. Many brass bands were distinctive, even great. But none were blatantly radical—none kicked against tradition sufficiently strongly to be a maverick or to create a watershed in the brass band idiom. The reason for this continuity is obvious: the contest remained the focus of the brass band world, and the culture of contesting bred conformity. Even the embarkation of the St Hilda's Band into 'professionalism' did not cause it to develop an especially new style. Orthodoxies also remained intact because of other significant factors: there were several key individuals who exerted a special influence on the movement as a whole, and there was a continued trend towards 'nationalization' as opposed to regionalism (a trend which was to be fashioned mainly through the emergence of electronic media, but which was already in place through centrally focused band magazines).

[11] *British Bandsman* (13 Nov. 1920).   [12] *British Bandsman* (11 June 1960), 4.

This does not mean that there was no change to the idiom of the brass band in the first half of the twentieth century, or to the culture of playing that its devotees adopted. But the first and most important feature of this change is the slowness and subtlety of the process. This could be described as the triumph of conservatism over progress. It is equally wrong, however, to cast the idiom of the brass band in this period as a mere sound relic. Indeed, the most interesting feature of this story is the extent to which a cast-iron orthodoxy accommodated any degree of difference and individuality. Such individualities and differences did occur, and the main stimulant for them came from challenges posed by the development of the idiomatic repertory—a topic which is covered elsewhere in this book—and the influence of individual players and conductors in the leading bands. The most prominent soloists, especially cornet players, have been particularly important in this respect.

This period saw the migration of some of the best brass band players to the mainstream of British music (into both art music and various denominations of popular music: dance bands, theatre orchestras, and professional military bands). This migration was not debilitating, because, though it troubled some commentators (see Chapter 2), and provided a seductive alternative to young potential bandsmen, it neither deprived the brass band world of all its best talent, nor entirely stemmed the flow of new, young, outstanding players. Indeed, as we explain below, some players experienced little difficulty in playing in brass bands and simultaneously conducting the life of a professional musician.

The causes of the migration are partly rooted in social changes which promoted the inclination, need, and ambition of working-class people to seek a better, more prosperous, amenable, and potentially exciting life in music. But there was also a commensurate growth in opportunity. The musical profession was still buoyant, and brass instruments figured in almost every species of music making—military bands, dance bands, orchestras, theatre bands—which was in the ascendancy.[13]

Furthermore, there were artistic trends which favoured brass *band* players. Before the turn of the century, the brass parts in the canonical orchestral repertoire[14] held little in the way of challenges for most mainstream orchestral players—a body of men whose tutelage followed predictable patterns of conservatoire and military training. This was to change rapidly when a procession of composers, many using expansionist and radical musical languages, started

[13] See C. Ehrlich, *The Music Profession in Britain since the Eighteenth Century* (Oxford: Clarendon Press, 1985), ch. 9.

[14] Composers of opera have frequently imposed greater demands on brass players than have symphonists. Italian opera composers (who frequently wrote for valve trombones) were often fairly free in their writing idioms, and employed trumpets and cornets in lyrical solos. For a discussion of the development of brass writing in the 19th and 20th cents. see Simon Wills, 'Brass in the Modern Orchestra', ch. 12 in Trevor Herbert and John Wallace (eds.), *The Cambridge Companion to Brass Instruments* (Cambridge: Cambridge University Press, 1997), 157–76. Other chapters in the same book deal with the development of brass idioms since the start of the 19th cent.

writing brass parts which were to redefine the idiom of brass instruments. Signals were evident in the writing of Russian and Austro-German composers in the later nineteenth century, but those based in Vienna and Paris in the opening decades of the twentieth century were of a yet different order.[15]

Evidence of migration and its impact on the infrastructure of the music profession is hinted at in the extent to which brass band players started to engage with formal systems of musical education. It was not just that students who passed through the rarefied portals of the Royal Academy, the Royal College, and the Guildhall School were from the brass band practice rooms, but that when they got inside, they encountered teachers who were themselves products of that same tradition. The case of the Royal Academy of Music provides a neat example. Jesse Stamp (certainly a military band player, and probably a brass band product) was appointed trombone professor in 1925, and remained there until 1932. Harry Barlow of Besses o' th' Barn was tuba professor from 1931 until his death in 1932; and from 1938–56, the trumpet professor was George Eskdale (St Hilda's). Subsequent former brass band players to teach there include Harold Nash (Parc and Dare), Ian Bousfield (Yorkshire Imperial Metals), William Overton (Salvation Army), and John Wallace (Tullis Russell Mills). Even the distinguished french horn player, Ifor James, originated as a cornet player with Carlisle St Stephen's Band.

The dissemination of aspects of the brass band style to wider areas of music did little to change the prevailing stylistic patterns within the brass band movement itself. Indeed the existence of a strong contesting structure, mediated by contest adjudicators who were themselves the leading conductors of the day, ensured such continuities; and in any case, irrespective of novel demands which new works imposed, the contest test piece, the genre which offered composers the most substantial opportunity for musical expression, was developed to serve and sustain the prevailing orthodoxy, rather than to change it.

At the start of the twentieth century, books such as *Wright and Round's Amateur Band Teacher's Guide and Bandsman's Adviser*, subtitled 'A Synthesis of the Systems on which the celebrated Prize Bands of Lancashire and Yorkshire are Taught',[16] were still in circulation, offering readers a host

[15] Wagner expanded the brass section. Mahler and Richard Strauss stretched technical demands beyond previously perceived limitations. The composers of the Second Viennese School consolidated these advances. Tchaikovsky introduced virtuoso cornet solos into his ballet music with the 'Neapolitan Dance' in *Swan Lake* (1875–6). Rimsky-Korsakov and Stravinsky extended virtuoso use of brass yet further. Composers of the Les Six group, most notably Milhaud and Poulenc, employed jazz-influenced, idiomatic traits. Many such developments in orchestral repertoire stretched 'traditional' orchestral players to the limit of their techniques and endurance—but to brass band cornet players, schooled in operatic transcriptions and *air varié* solos, the tests posed in works such as Stravinsky's *Petrushka* (1910–11) and *Pulcinella* (1919–20) were as meat and drink.

[16] Published by Wright & Round in 1889, though the imprint is undated. Most of the book is a compilation of articles previously published in the *Brass Band News*.

of systematically presented tips on matters of musical ensemble, individual technique, and music theory, with a sprinkling of behavioural ethics thrown in for good measure. Such books, which, like many other popular Victorian manuals, had previously been released in serial form, enshrined values which a widely dispersed population of bandsmen could use as points of reference. They presented their message in terms which often drew analogies with social behaviour. For example, the section on 'Articulation-Tonguing' begins, 'By clear articulation, when applied to speech, we mean a clear spoken person— a person who speaks distinctly . . . If a man's speech is thick and confused he will have difficulty in making himself intelligible.'[17]

Evidence from contest adjudications, together with the abundant advice that was being served to aspiring brass bands in magazines such as the *Brass Band News* and the *British Bandsman*, makes it clear that there were three primary values to which every brass band was encouraged to subscribe and aspire. The first was musical discipline, and in particular, that aspect of discipline which makes for precision. 'Precision, in a musical sense, means playing exactly together . . . this is well expressed by the phrase "the band plays like one man."'[18] Precision of rhythm, articulation, and ensemble are easy to understand, because they can almost always be described in such temporal or durational terms. But it is not unusual to encounter more subtle and complex meanings in the framework of musical 'discipline'. Within such terminology, the phrase 'internal balance' has high currency. It refers to the balance and homogeneity of those alto and tenor instruments—usually horns, baritones, trombones, euphoniums, and the lower cornet parts—which are assumed to be the warm core of the traditional brass band sound.

The second value is the assumption that slower solo passages are always vehicles for lyrical expression. There is little evidence of coolness and deadpan objectivity having much currency. The abundant—even excessive—use of vibrato may well have derived from the need that brass band players appear to have felt to express melodic lines in terms which are self-consciously lyrical, rather than emotionally detached. Harry Mortimer claimed that it was through his 'wonderful' encounter with the Hallé Orchestra that he learnt 'not to be afraid of emotion in music. Extract it to the last ounce. It will never topple over to sentimentality as long as you concentrate on giving the music full rein.'[19] It is, however, doubtful whether the Hallé Orchestra under Hamilton Harty had much to teach Mortimer about lyricism or expression.

The third value of the brass band style as it developed in this period is a particular type of idiomatic virtuosity, in which certain features of brass technique, most notably the capacity to play fast passages—especially in mixed figurations of single-, double-, and triple-tonguing, together with scalic runs

---

[17] Ibid. 17.   [18] Ibid. 22.
[19] Harry Mortimer, *Harry Mortimer on Brass* (Sherborne: Alphabooks, 1981), 74.

in different types of articulation—is especially cherished. Performance techniques which are valued in other schools of virtuoso brass playing are less important to brass band players, such as the ability to play in long passages in the extremities of the tessitura, to play widely separated intervals in quick succession, and to employ so-called 'special effects'. This interpretation of the virtuoso ideal is yet another example of how technique and repertoire—here mainly in the shape of the *air varié* genre—followed a predictable path, in which the idiom of the instrument was served by a largely unspoken consensus between composers and players.

Values such as these gained currency because there were players and conductors who subscribed to them unquestioningly, and who were able to demonstrate what they believed to be their inherent truths in performances of unequivocal brilliance. Such players displayed a level of virtuosity which impressed everyone except those hopelessly prejudiced against the brass band sound. Nowhere were these values acted out more consistently, with greater passion, and with such influence, than in the domain occupied by the Mortimer family, the most influential and visible focus for brass bands in the UK for whole of the period between the Great War and the 1960s. Harry (1902–92), his father Fred (1879–1953), and his brothers Alex (1904–75, also an influential euphonium player) and Rex (b. 1911), created a powerful nucleus for the movement. Their example became widely admired and imitated. The importance of the Mortimers was not just that each member of the family was successful; it was that their success manifested itself widely and powerfully in traditional media such as contests, and also in newer forms of dissemination such as recording and broadcasting.

Harry Mortimer was probably the first brass band soloist to gain national fame outside the brass band world by exploiting what was seen as the archetypal brass band style. This can largely be put down to the impact of his recordings. He never repudiated this style, even though he became first trumpet of the Hallé Orchestra (1926–30), the Royal Liverpool Philharmonic (1930–4), the BBC Northern (1935–42), and, for a short time, the Philharmonia (1945), positions which he managed to combine with many other enterprises.[20] The bands with which his family became associated—Foden Motor Works Band and the Fairey Aviation Works Band in particular—were probably the most frequently imitated stereotype. The recorded legacy largely bears this out. Foden Motor Works was by far the most recorded band before the 1950s.

A 1930 recording of *Shylock*, Thomas Lear's 'Polka brillante', by Harry Mortimer with Fred Mortimer conducting the Foden Motor Works

---

[20] Mortimer, *Mortimer on Brass*. Harry Mortimer continued to rehearse and perform with Foden's Band for most of the time that he was with the Hallé Orchestra.

Figure 8.4. The great cornet virtuosi, Jack Mackintosh and Harry Mortimer (from left to right) known ubiquitously as 'Mack & Mort'.

Band, provides a particularly revealing illustration of the performance technique which became widely imitated. Articulations are clearly enunciated, and in slower phrases he uses a 'bell-chime' start to each note. This was something of a feature of Mortimer's playing: notes are given a subtle accent, followed by an equally subtle diminuendo. In addition, phrases are lucidly shaped, and the speed of the vibrato is varied. Tonguing configurations—single, double, and triple—are executed with precision, and the entire performance is characterized by fastidious neatness and clarity.

There were other important contemporaries of Harry Mortimer, but perhaps the best known was Jack Mackintosh (1891–1979). Mackintosh was of a modest, retiring disposition, particularly in comparison to the exuberant Mortimer, but paradoxically, he had a more outrageously virtuosic and extrovert performance style. Mortimer and Mackintosh were considered sufficiently eminent for recording companies to invest in full orchestral accompaniments for some of their solo recordings. Harry Mortimer's composition, *Mack and Mort*, recorded in 1933, became one of the most popular brass duets.

Both Mackintosh and Mortimer employed a relaxed, playful approach to tempi—a feature which became rarer among cornet soloists as the century progressed. Much of their playing is outside a strict tempo. At the end of the *Mack and Mort* duet, Jack Mackintosh improvises a very short snatch of one of his 'cowboy cadenzas'. The 'cowboy cadenza' was a trademark flourish often employed by Mackintosh, in which he played a succession of dazzlingly

Ex. 12 Jack Mackintosh's 'cowboy' cadenzas.

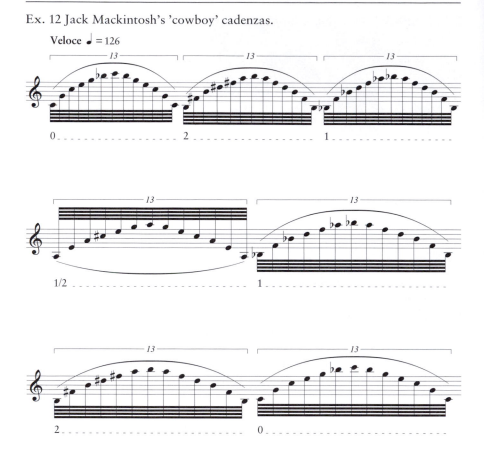

rapid, slurred harmonic series reminiscent of glissandi (see Ex. 12). This device points to one of the reasons for Mackintosh's exceptional stamina, evident in all his recordings—the use of lip flexibilities in his practice. Although present in rudimentary form in Arban's *Grande méthode complète*,[21] lip flexibilities had been extended in the popular American methods like *Eby's Complete Scientific Method for Cornet and Trumpet*, which had appeared and become widely available in 1926. Mackintosh also blows very hard and powerfully in many of his recordings. This robust approach can be heard in his 1932 recordings of *Il Bacio* and *Carnival of Venice*,[22] and belies later polarizing assumptions about the essential nature of the cornet being *merely* lyrical, as opposed to the more strident tone of the trumpet.

[21] J.-B. Arban, *Grande méthode complète pour cornet à pistons et de saxhorn* (Paris, 1864).
[22] Columbia, recorded 14/4/32, issued 7/32; number DX.358, matrix CAX 6379-1, 6380-1.

Ex. 13. Basil Windsor, *Alpine Echoes*

Ex. 14. Grand March from Verdi's *Aida*.

The Mortimer/Mackintosh partnership influenced the playing of species of figurations too. A rhythmic fingerprint typical of them can be found in their reluctance to play groups of upbeat notes in mechanical tempo. A phrase from Basil Windsor's *Alpine Echoes*,[23] recorded by Mackintosh in 1928, demonstrates this (see Ex. 13).

Recordings from this period provide evidence of players using a device whereby rhythms are sprung over a long tactus, rather than being accurately and mechanically subdivided, which became the norm by the latter part of the century. The St Hilda's Professional Band's recorded performance in 1930 of Verdi's *Grand March from Aida*,[24] as well as being played with an exciting continuous feel of accelerando, shows the second theme being played as in Ex. 14, the dotted rhythms *inègale* in all but name.

Neither Harry Mortimer nor Jack Mackintosh wrote cornet instruction books. This could be regarded as surprising, given that the imprimaturs of such star players would have found a ready market. Indeed one of the most surprising features of instructional literature for brass players is the chronic paucity of home-produced didactic publications. The most popular didactic manuals to come out of, and be consumed in, the brass band world were probably Wright and Round's series of brass instrument 'tutors'. These books were uninspiring, unimaginative, and displayed an almost total indifference to the distinctions between individual instruments of the band. Most of the exercises are identical, irrespective of which instrument the book is ostensibly written for.

[23] Regal, recorded 30/9/28, issued 1/29; number G.9227, matrix WA7913-3, with Harton Colliery Band, conductor Ernest Thorpe.

[24] Regal, recorded 15/9/30, issued 12/30; number MR.199, matrix WAR 317-1.

Foreign instruction manuals which espoused more systematic approaches to playing technique appear to have been widely consumed by British brass band players. However, the methods which were put forward in them had little impact on brass band style. This can almost certainly be accounted for by the nature of didactic communication within brass bands—a feature of the culture of the brass band which it is important to understand. The most influential mediation comes through the conductor or bandmaster, and the process of learning is primarily aural rather than literary, and communal rather than individual (brass band players speak literally when they refer to band *practice* rather than band *rehearsal*).

It is probably safe to assume that it was the musical exercises contained in foreign *méthodes* which provided the interest for brass band players, rather than the commentary which contextualized those exercises. The Arban method—which is probably the most influential trumpet/cornet method—was produced by a professor at the Paris Conservatoire, as was the trombone method of André Lafosse. The Lafosse was often seen as the advanced treatise for trombone which succeeded the *Complete Method* of Otto Langey, published by Boosey and Hawkes.[25] Ironically enough, Langey's book, which was also published for other instruments, was given an extra breath of life when it was revised and extended by the trumpeter Ernest Hall, who, though from the north of England and one of the greatest trumpeters of the century, had never had strong associations with brass bands.

The one instructional book which appears to have had a genuine influence was by an American, Walter M. Eby. From the late 1920s, Eby placed adverts in the *British Bandsman* for *Eby's Complete Scientific Method for Cornet and Trumpet*, in which he advocated his 'no-' or 'non-pressure method'.[26] The so-called no- or non-pressure method may have been the only basic new approach to playing to have taken root in the brass band movement which did not originate within it. Its attraction was that it did not influence style, but did (in theory, at least) improve the endurance levels of players—two features which found happy accord with traditional bandsmen. Not all players adopted this method, but those who did (especially cornet and trombone players) found that they could master another aspect of technique—the ability to play effortlessly in the very high, 'screaming' register of their instrument. This facility was almost entirely redundant for the brass band repertoire, but

[25] A. Lafosse, *Méthode complète de trombone à coulisse*, 2 vols. (Paris: Éditions Musicales Alphonse Leduc, n.d.); O. Langey, *Complete Method for Trombone* (London: Boosey & Hawkes, n.d.).

[26] *Eby's Complete Scientific Method for Cornet and Trumpet*, containing his 'No-Pressure Method' was first published in 1926 (Buffalo, NY: Virtuoso Music School), and sold mainly through mail order directly from his 'Virtuoso Music School' in Buffalo. See e.g. *British Bandsman* (22 Feb. 1930), 10.

in the world of jazz and big bands it was highly prized. Thus the brass band world made its contribution to the dance band era.

George Swift of St Hilda's Band was one of the first brass band players to make an impact as a trumpet soloist in the burgeoning British jazz and light music scene. He became a British counterpart to the American trumpeter, Harry James. He commanded an astonishing range: for example, in an arrangement of violinist/composer Pablo Sarasate's *Zigeunerweisen*, and in Alec Templeton's *Sonia*,[27] his cadential flourishes take the B♭ trumpet range up to A_6 and down to F_3.

The development of such techniques was especially relevant because, during the post-war era, young brass band players continued to break into opportunities in the rapidly expanding world of professional music, both 'light' and 'classical', often after a period with one of the army bands. A typical example is that of three young cornet-playing contemporaries in the immediate post-war era, known popularly in London brass-playing circles as 'The Three Musketeers'.[28] All three came from brass band backgrounds: Eric Bravington went to the London Philharmonic as principal trumpet before becoming the orchestra's Managing Director; Cliff Haines (b. 1921) became trumpet soloist in Ted Heath's band; and Bram Wiggins went to the London Symphony Orchestra as George Eskdale's second trumpet. Other brass band and Salvationist players who dominated the London session studios were the trumpeters, Stan Roderick, Bert Ezzard, Greg Bowen, Tommy McQuater, Johnny McLeavy, and Derek Watkins, and the trombonists, Don Lusher, George Chisholm, and Cliff Hardy.

Many players remained in brass bands, however, and a consistent tradition continued into the 1960s. Black Dyke's remarkable legacy of cornet players, which has included John Paley, Harold Pinches, Harold Jackson, Willie Lang, Maurice Murphy, and Phillip McCann, was matched by players of equal stature in newer bands: Derek Garside (CWS Manchester), John Berryman (GUS Footwear), John Dickenson (Morris Motors), and Willie Barr (Scottish CWS). It was always the cornet players whose stellar talents shone most brightly, but Bert Sullivan of Gwauncaegurwen and latterly Munn and Felton's, and Lyndon Baglyn (CWS Manchester and later Stanshawe) acquired reputations as euphonium players. Gordon Higginbottom, another Black Dyke player, became probably the first tenor horn player to obtain national celebrity within the brass band world. Some of these players joined forces in occasional professional groups such as James Shepherd's Versatile Brass, an ensemble of virtuoso brass players.

---

[27] Parlophone, recorded 15/10/36, issued 12/36; number F.613, matrix CE7889-1, CE7890-1.

[28] The authors are indebted to Cliff Haines and Philip Jones for this information.

THE 1960S AND BEYOND

The introduction of standard pitch by the brass band movement and the Salvation Army in 1964 came about because it was no longer feasible for manufacturers—especially Boosey & Hawkes, the main producer of band instruments—to manufacture instruments in more than one pitch standard. By that time, the Salvation Army instrument factory at St Albans was operating at a much lower strength than it had done earlier in the century, and many Salvationists played instruments manufactured elsewhere. The St Albans factory was already losing money and causing concern to Army leaders; it closed in 1972 (see Chapter 5).

The change to the lower pitch instruments caused financial hardship to many bands, but paradoxically, this was mitigated by a renewed sense of purpose, as some bands worked, through concerts and other fund-raising events (as well as aligning themselves to a new breed of sponsors), to raise capital for instruments. It was widely assumed that the practice of extending tuning slides or inserting additional tube lengths at other points in the sounding length would put instruments into the new standard pitch. The expediency of extending the tubing of a sharp-pitch instrument may have nominally changed the pitch, but in so doing, the playing characteristics changed, and the best players felt the effects instinctively and were disturbed by it. Whereas the use of high pitch limited the choice of instruments which brass band players could use—for example, no American makers manufactured high-pitch instruments—the shift to the lower, internationally used pitch standard, swept away such restrictions. Many players bought new instruments, and the tendency was to buy instruments with a wider bore. The most marked change was probably in respect of the trombone. There was already a trend towards medium-bore instruments, but by the mid-1960s, almost all British orchestral trombone players were using wide-bore American instruments. The most favoured was a particular model (known by the model codes 8H and 88H) made by C. G. Conn of Elkhart, Indiana. Many brass band players followed this trend and bought wide-bore American instruments. The old-fashioned bass trombone in G died out almost entirely, in favour of a yet wider bore instrument in B♭ with an F trigger attachment which allowed it to play effectively in the lower range of the instrument. The last sighting of the G trombone in the hands of a regular symphony orchestra player was allegedly in the BBC Welsh Orchestra at about this time. Though some die-hard brass band bass trombone players continued with the older type of instrument, it soon became virtually obsolete. The effect of a group of three trombones playing in a brass band with a new type of sonority had a fundamental and influential effect on the rest of the band. American manufacturers were to have a sustained influence on brass playing in Britain, even though British manufacturers produced impressive new designs.[29]

The result of the shift to wider bore instruments was a change in the sonority of the brass band. However, this was not as acute and definitive as one might expect. The instruments had changed, but the musical culture of the brass band had not. These changes, perhaps the most momentous since the end of the nineteenth century, came as a new breed of conductors was becoming involved with the brass band movement, and it was the combination of the new instruments and the impact of the influence of these performers which was to affect, if not irrevocably revolutionize, the brass band movement.

The most influential conductors were Elgar Howarth, Howard Snell, and James Watson. All three were highly respected trumpeters with major London symphony orchestras, who had been introduced to music in the brass band. Howarth was also a composer and a gifted conductor of avant-garde music, who had been part of the so-called Manchester group. They were all brilliant musicians, technically outstanding as conductors, and they were thoroughly familiar with the idiom of brass instruments, the latest techniques, and the most advanced aspects of brass repertoires in mainstream music.

Prior to the involvement of Howarth, Snell, and Watson, brass bands were conducted either by conductors nurtured in the brass band movement, many of them excellent and imaginative musicians, or by other 'professional conductors' who advertised their services in the classified columns of magazines such as the *British Bandsman*. Professional conductors came from a variety of backgrounds. Roy Newsome, a long-time director of the Black Dyke Mills Band, was a university-educated musician and a skilled keyboard player, with deep roots in the brass band movement. Others such as the Mortimers, James Scott, and Derek Broadbent developed their reputations almost exclusively within the brass band movement. However, a significant category of conductors was made up of those who came from a career as high-ranking musicians in the army. Such musicians found employment in retirement from military service as brass band conductors. One of the first to make a really significant musical impact was Major George Willcocks, who conducted memorable contest performances with the Black Dyke Mills Band. Others included Arthur Kenney, who was largely responsible for the ascendancy of the Cory Band in the 1970s. But the most successful was Peter Parkes, who had multiple successes in national contests with bands including Black Dyke. These conductors

---

[29] The C. G. Conn company was founded in Elkhart, Ind. in 1879, though Conn was active as a maker earlier in that decade. It has been the most successful and influential US maker. F. E. Olds founded his company in 1908. Olds was a trombone player like Frank Holton, who was bass trombonist with Sousa's Band. The King company was founded after the Second World War. See William Waterhouse (ed.), *The New Langwill Index* (London: Tony Bingham, 1993).

were sophisticated and methodical in their approach, and possessed the type of commanding presence which many bands found easy to respect.

The importance of Howarth, Snell, and Watson in comparison with other band conductors of their time is that they acted as catalysts for change, and the change was radical. Howarth was the first, and perhaps the most important, influence. In 1973, he left the Royal Philharmonic Orchestra in order to devote his time to a wider range of activities. He was already the first trumpet player with the Philip Jones Brass Ensemble. He started conducting the Grimethorpe Colliery Band. Though Howarth conducted Grimethorpe successfully at contests, he did not have a special interest in contesting; his main interest was in style, technique, and repertoire. He was influential in the commissioning of new works from Hans Werner Henze and Harrison Birtwistle, and his own compositions and arrangements were also fresh and radical.

Performance styles are difficult to analyse in all but impressionistic terms. Though it is fairly easy to explain the influences on the brass band idiom because it is so fixed, the way that it has itself influenced wider spheres of British brass playing and writing is more taxing to define. Orchestral brass performance practices are heavily influenced by factors found within the continuum of the European art-music tradition, and also by other trends from the USA, which, by the second decade of the twentieth century, were of more than minor importance. But the influence of brass bands on British brass playing in general—and on aspects of the compositional style of British composers— is not insignificant. The writing of composers such as Elgar, Bliss, Walton, Maxwell Davies, and Birtwistle bears witness to this. It is not that the work of such composers is directly imitative of the brass band sound or technique, but that its stylistic language is replete with assumptions about the idiom of brass instruments.

The fact that most British brass players adopt a similar style can in part be attributed to the sheer geographical proximity of brass bands and players, and the ease of communication between them. The style of brass playing in the UK has been comparatively free of stylistic divergences, many elements of this style deriving directly or indirectly from the influence of the brass band tradition and its inherent values. Of course, brass players who have had no major engagement with the brass band world have played their part in the shaping of style too. The list of such players is formidable. It includes Ernest Hall, whose career spanned the first half of the century; Crispian Steele-Perkins and Michael Laird who pioneered the revival of the 'natural trumpet'; David Mason, whose considerable achievements as an orchestral player are eclipsed by the fame of his performance of the trumpet solo in the Beatles' 'Penny Lane'; and the trombone players, Arthur Wilson and Dennis Wick, who, from their playing and teaching positions at the Philharmonia Orchestra and Royal College, and London Symphony Orchestra and Guildhall School respectively, have influenced most of the top professional trombone players who have emerged since the 1960s. But these players were part of an alchemy in which the influence of band players was the major ingredient.

Another formidable influence in the last forty years of the century has been the Philip Jones Brass Ensemble. It achieved world fame, and many see it as the brass ensemble which did most to develop that medium and its repertoire. It was made up of some of the finest London orchestral players, but most members of that distinguished group were products of brass bands.

Brass bands nurtured techniques which were, in some respects, more advanced than those required in the canonical orchestral repertoire. They also nurtured a form of playing which is based on instinct and intuition rather than study and contemplation. This is doubtless a result of the pre-eminence of aurality and imitation in processes of learning in the brass band world. Maurice Murphy, who, following in the footsteps of Willie Lang, made the transition from the Black Dyke Mills Band to the London Symphony Orchestra, via Manchester orchestras, offers a neat, if atypical illustration of this phenomenon, in his description of how he coped with the complexities of transposition when he first joined a symphony orchestra: 'I don't know anything about theory or the rudiments of music and I'm not interested in scales and how many sharps or flats a piece is in. They are just all notes, and I transpose note for note by ear. When I first started I used to listen if anyone else had the same figure and then play it by ear, I picked up a lot of transposition from that.'[30]

Such an attitude would be viewed with incredulity in the USA, where instrumental instruction is largely based on the analysis of technique rather than on repertoire, and where literature with titles such as 'Diagnosing embouchure problems', 'Understanding breath technique', 'A search for better intonation', and 'Development of physical aspects of brass playing' often forms the basis of didactic methods. But Murphy's lineage is robust and its proponents so numerous that this aspect of the British musical character shows no signs of being imminently in danger of disappearing.

[30] *Sounding Brass*, 7/2 (1978), 56.

Prices of Brass Band Instruments Extracted from Manufacturers' Advertising Material

D'ALMAINE & CO., LONDON, 1839

Clarionet
  with five keys   £1 1s. 0d. to £3 3s. 0d.
  with thirteen keys   £3 0s. 0d. to £5 10s. 0d.
Cornopean or cornet à piston
  with two valves   £4 4s. 0d. to £7 7s. 0d.
  with three valves   £5 12s. 6d. to £8 8s. 0d.
Bugle
  with six keys   £1 15s. 0d. to £2 5s. 0d.
  with eight roller keys   £5 10s. 0d. to £6 10s. 0d.
French horn
  with four crooks   £4 4s. 0d.
  with ten crooks   £9 0s. 0d.
Alto slide trombone   £2 5s. 0d. to £4 15s. 0d.
Tenor slide trombone   £2 10s. 0d. to £4 18s. 0d.
Bass slide trombone   £3 0s. 0d. to £5 17s. 6d.
Valve trombone   £12 12s. 0d. to £15 15s. 0d.
Ophicleide
  with nine keys   £7 10s. 0d. to £15 15s. 0d.
  with eleven keys   £9 9s. 0d. to £16 16s. 0d.
  with patent valve stops   £18 0s. 0d. to £21 0s. 0d.
Serpent
  with three keys   £5 15s. 0d. to £7 0s. 0d.
  with five keys   £6 12s. 0d. to £7 17s. 6d.
Bass horn with four keys   £6 6s. 0d. to £7 10s. 0d.
Side drum
  wood   £2 12s. 6d. upwards
  brass   £4 10s. 0d. upwards
Bass drum
  24″   £5 17s. 6d. upwards
  30″   £8 5s. 0d. upwards

The cheaper bugles and bass horns are in brass, the more expensive in copper.

Source: H. Edmund Poole, 'A Catalogue of Musical Instruments Offered for Sale in 1839 by D'Almaine & Co., 20 Soho Square', *Galpin Society Journal*, 35 (1982), 2–36.

JAMES JORDAN, LIVERPOOL, 1851

Instrument	Good quality	Best quality
Clarionet, B, C, E♭ or F		
6 key'd	£1 1s. 0d.	£2 0s. 0d.
13 key'd	£2 2s. 0d.	£5 5s. 0d.
Cornopean with transposing slide	£3 0s. 0d.	£6 0s. 0d.
Cornopean with crooks	£4 0s. 0d.	£7 0s. 0d.
Cornopean, best german silver	£10 0s. 0d.	£20 0s. 0d.
Valve trumpet	£3 3s. 0d.	£8 8s. 0d.
Valve horns	£6 6s. 0d.	£12 12s. 0d.
Soprano Sax horn in E♭, D, & D♭	£3 0s. 0d.	£6 0s. 0d.
Treble Sax horn in B♭ & A♭	£3 10s. 0d.	£6 10s. 0d.
Alto Sax horn in F	£4 0s. 0d.	£7 0s. 0d.
Tenor Sax horn in E♭, D, or D♭	£4 10s. 0d.	£7 10s. 0d.
Barytone Sax horn in C or B	£5 10s. 0d.	£9 0s. 0d.
Clavicor	£4 14s. 6d.	£10 0s. 0d.
Alto slide trombone	£1 5s. 0d.	£2 10s. 0d.
Tenor slide trombone	£1 10s. 0d.	£4 4s. 0d.
Bass slide trombone	£2 0s. 0d.	£5 5s. 0d.
Alto valve trombone in F	£3 3s. 0d.	£7 7s. 0d.
Tenor valve trombone in C or B♭	£4 4s. 0d.	£8 8s. 0d.
Bass valve trombone in G or F	£4 14s. 6d.	£9 9s. 0d.
Bassetto Sax horn in D♭ or C	£6 0s. 0d.	£10 0s. 0d.
Basso Sax horn in B♭ or A	£7 0s. 0d.	£12 0s. 0d.
Contrabass saxhorn in F, E♭ or C	£10 0s. 0d.	£16 0s. 0d.
Bombardone	£10 10s. 0d.	£16 16s. 0d.
Key'd ophicleide	£5 5s. 0d.	£10 10s. 0d.
Key'd serpent	£7 7s. 0d.	£14 14s. 0d.
Side drum		
wood shell	£1 10s. 0d.	£3 3s. 0d.
brass shell	£2 10s. 0d.	£4 4s. 0d.
Bass drum	£4 4s. 0d.	£9 9s. 0d.

Source: James Jordan's pricelist, in Peter and Ann Mactaggart (eds.), *Musical Instruments in the 1851 Exhibition* (Welwyn: Mac & Me, 1986), 107–8.

HENRY DISTIN, LONDON, 1857

Brass piccolo clarionet in A♭	£7 7s. 0d., electro-plated £9 9s. 0d.
Brass clarionet in E♭	£7 7s. 0d., electro-plated £9 9s. 0d.
Piccolino soprano in A♭ with 4 rotary cylinders	£10 10s. 0d.
Piccolo soprano in E♭ with crooks for D and D♭, 3 rotary cylinders	£10 10s. 0d.
Piccolo soprano cornet in E♭ with crooks for D and D♭, 3 pistons	£7 7s. 0d.
Distin's New Cornet, crooks from B♭ to G	£8 8s. 0d.
Distin's Military Cornet, crooks from B♭ to G	£8 8s. 0d.

Portable alto chromatic horn in B♭ with crooks for A and A♭	£9 9s. 0d.
Alto flügel horn, 3 rotary cylinders, in B♭	£10 10s. 0d.
Tenor flügel horn, 3 rotary cylinders, in F	£11 11s. 0d.
Tenor chromatic horn in E♭ with slide crooks for D and D♭, 3 pistons	£11 0s. 0d.
Baritone tuba in B♭, 3 pistons (also called 'Alt-Horn')	£11 11s. 0d.
Trumpet in E♭ with crooks for D and D♭, 3 pistons	£9 9s. 0d.
Alto slide trombone in F or E♭	£6 10s. 0d.
Tenor slide trombone in C or B♭	£7 7s. 0d.
Bass slide trombone in G or F	£8 8s. 0d.
Alto piston trombone in F or E♭, 3 pistons, bell forward	£11 11s. 0d.
Tenor piston trombone in C or B♭, 3 pistons, bell forward	£11 11s. 0d.
Bass piston trombone in G or F, 3 pistons, bell upwards	£11 11s. 0d.
Bass piston trombone in G, 3 pistons, bell forwards	£11 11s. 0d.
Bass euphonion in B♭, 4 rotary cylinders (known as the 'Sommerophone')	£16 16s. 0d.
Bass tuba in B♭, 4 pistons	£14 14s. 0d.
Contrabass in E♭, 3 pistons (also called 'Bombardone')	£15 15s. 0d.
Contrabass in E♭, 4 pistons (also called 'Bombardone')	£17 17s. 0d.
Contrabass in E♭, 4 rotary cylinders (also called 'Bombardone')	£20 0s. 0d.
Patent side drum, brass, with strap and sticks	£5 10s. 0d.
Bass drum, largest size, with sticks	£12 12s. 0d.
Pair cymbals	£6 6s. 0d.

Source: *Complete Catalogue of Military Musical Instruments, &c., &c. Manufactured by Henry Distin . . . London*: Published by Henry Distin . . . 1857. National Library of Scotland (Pressmark 3.1399).

BOOSEY & CO. TRADING AS DISTIN & CO., C.1873

After Henry Distin had sold the business to Boosey & Co.

	Ordinary	Equisonant pistons
Imported (French) cornet in B♭	£1 5s.	
New model cornet in B♭	£3 3s. ('The cheapest English cornet manufactured')	
New model cornet in B♭	£4 4s.	

Soprano saxhorn in E♭ and D♭	£2 os.	
Soprano cornet-a-pistons	£3 5s.	£4 10s.
Alto saxhorn or flugel horn	£3 10s.	£4 10s.
Tenor horn in F or E♭	£4 os.	£5 os.
Baritone in C or B♭	£4 10s.	£5 10s.
Alto slide trombone in E♭	£2 os.	
Tenor slide trombone in C or B♭	£3 os.	
Bass slide trombone in G or F	£4 os.	£4 os.
Euphonion or bass saxhorn		
in C or B♭ three valves	£5 10s.	£7 os.
in C or B♭ four valves	£6 10s.	£8 10s.
Contrabass saxhorn or Bombardon		
in F or E♭ three valves	£6 10s.	£8 10s.
in F or E♭ four valves	£7 10s.	£9 10s.
in BB♭ three valves	£8 10s.	£10 10s.
Monstre champion circular bass		
in E♭ three valves	£12 os.	£14 os.
in BB♭, three valves	£13 os.	£15 os.
Side drum, rope and tug, 14″		
wood shell	£2 os.	
brass shell	£2 10s. to £4 10s.	
Bass drum		
28″ diameter	£6 15s.	
32″ diameter	£8 10s.	

Valve trombones priced at £1. os. more than the slide trombones (£2. 10s. more for Equisonant pistons).

P. Robinson trading as J. Higham, 1889

	Cheapest	Patent clear-bore
Soprano cornet in E♭	£2 12s.	£6 10s.
Cornet in B♭	£3 os.	£7 os.
Flugel horn in B♭	£3 3s.	£7 os.
Alto or tenor in E♭	£3 12s.	£7 10s.
Baritone in B♭	£4 10s.	£8 os.
Tenor slide trombone in B♭	£2 2s.	
Bass slide trombone in G	£2 12s.	
Euphonion, bass		
in B♭ three valves	£5 5s.	£9 10s.
in B♭ four valves	£6 10s.	£11 os.
Bombardon		
in E♭ three valves	£7 10s.	£11 11s.
in E♭ four valves	£7 10s.	£14 os.
in B♭ three valves	£11 11s.	
Circular bombardon, over shoulder		
in E♭ three valves	£12 12s.	£16 16s.
in B♭, three valves	£14 10s.	£18 18s.

Side drum, brass shell
    with cord and braces   £2 10s. upwards
    with six tuning screws   £3 10s.
Bass drum   £6 6s. upwards

Silver-plating charged extra, ranging from £2. 0s. for a soprano cornet to £12. 0s. for a circular bombardon in B♭.

Source: Joseph Higham, catalogue, 1889; in 1990 in the possession of Howard Higham Robinson, Esq., Bradford, a descendent of Peter Robinson, the proprietor of the firm at that time.

BESSON & CO., c.1913

	Ordinary	Enharmonic valves
E♭ Soprano	£4 4s.	
B♭ Cornet		
'School' Model	£3 10s.	
'Class A'	£9 9s.	£12 12s.
Echo cornet	£14 14s.	
Flugel Horn 'Class A'	£8 8s.	£11 11s.
E♭ Tenor Horn 'Class A'	£9 9s.	£12 12s.
B♭ Baritone 'Class A' 3 valves	£11 11s.	£14 14s.
B♭ Tenor Trombone 'Class A'	£7 7s.	
G Bass Trombone 'Class A'	£8 8s.	
B♭ Euphonion		
3 valves 'Class A'	£12 12s.	£15 15s.
4 valves 'Class A'	£14 14s.	£18 18s.
5 valves 'Class A'	£16 16s.	
E♭ Bombardon		
3 valves 'Class A'	£15 15s.	£19 19s.
4 valves 'Class A'	£18 18s.	£24 0s.
B♭ Bombardon		
3 valves 'Class A'	£20 0s.	£25 4s.
BB♭ Bombardon (Monster)		
3 valves 'Class A'	£26 0s.	£31 0s.
Side drum		
Guards pattern	£3 3s. to £7 7s.	
Cheese pattern	£2 10s. to £6 6s.	
Bass drum 32″ × 20½″	£7 7s. to £12 12s.	

Silver-plating extra: cornets £2. 2s. 6d., tenor trombones £3 0s. 0d., Monster BB♭ bombardon £12. 10s. 0d. typical. 'Class C' instruments (guaranteed 6 years) priced at half that of 'Class A' (guaranteed 10 years).

Source: Arnold Myers's collection.

HAWKES & SON, 1927

Cornet in B♭	
'Excelsior' Model	£6 15s. 0d.
'Clippertone' Model	£8 12s. 6d.
Tenor Saxhorn in E♭	£9 7s. 6d.
B♭ Baritone (or Althorn)	
'Excelsior' Sonorous Model	£12 7s. 6d.
B♭ Tenor slide trombone	
'Artist's Perfected' Model	£7 17s. 6d.
G Bass slide trombone	
'Artist's Perfected' Model	£9 7s. 6d.
B♭ Euphonium	
3 valves 'Excelsior' Model	£12 15s. 0d.
4 valves 'Excelsior' Model	£15 15s. 0d.
4 valves Compensating	£19 13s. 9d.
4 valves Dictor Model	£18 15s. 0d.
E♭ Bass 'Excelsior' Model	£17 12s. 6d.
EE♭ Bass, monster bore	
3 valves	£27 0s. 0d.
4 valves	£32 5s. 0d.
BB♭ Bass, monster bore,	
3 valves	£33 0s. 0d.
Side drum, narrow pattern	£5 5s. 0d. to £8 13s. 3d.
Bass drum, 32″ diameter	£13 2s. 6d.

Silver-plating charged extra, ranging from £2. 3s. 2d. for a cornet to £13. 4s. 0d. for a monster bore BB♭ bass.

Source: Arnold Myers's collection.

The Salvation Army

GENERAL WILLIAM BOOTH'S FIRST ORDER FOR SALVATION ARMY BANDS, PUBLISHED IN THE *WAR CRY* (27 MARCH 1880)

Psalm xcviii. 6.—'With trumpets and sound of cornet, make,' etc.
Psalm cl. 4.—'Praise him with the timbrel,' etc.
Isaiah xxxviii. 20.—'The Lord was ready to save me; therefore we will sing my songs to the stringed instruments.'

Whereas, during the late Welsh and Cornish Councils, and before that time at Plymouth, Nottingham and elsewhere, we have proved the great utility of musical instruments in attracting crowds to our open-air and indoor meetings, we do here express our desire that as many of our Officers and Soldiers generally, male or female, as have the ability for so doing, learn to play on some suitable instrument.

And as in many instances the obtaining of an instrument is a difficulty, we shall be glad if any friends who may have such instruments lying idle will consecrate them to this service, and send them to Headquarters. This includes violins, bass viols, concertinas, cornets or any brass instruments, drums or anything else that will make a pleasant sound for the Lord.

William Booth, General

Headquarters
272 Whitechapel Road
London, E.

NUMBER OF BANDSMEN BY YEAR

The Salvation Army *Year Book* has been published annually since 1906 with the exceptions of 1909, 1911 and 1912. Each publication has contained a section on international statistics, and the total number of band players has always been declared. The methods used to count these players is far from clear, so even though they might provide an interesting profile of trends, they should be treated with some caution. It is safe to assume that the figures were compiled from the reports of corps and territories but the accuracy of such reports is impossible to test. Some sudden shifts are especially baffling. For example, the increase in youth band members from 12,807 in 1979 to 26,967 in 1980 does not have an obvious explanation; nor does the apparently huge increase in senior band players between 1991 and 1992.

Most sets of figures pertain to a census point, which occurred at some time in the year previous to the publication in question. The 1914 and 1915 *Year Books* declare a census point of June the previous year. Between 1916 and 1927 the census point was December two years previous (for example the 1928 *Year Book* uses figures gathered in December 1926). The census date is not declared between 1930 and 1950. From 1951 the *Year Book* once again declares figures as at the year ending two years previous. In 1981 a census date of 1 January the previous year was adopted. The 1995 and 1996 statistics are based on information collected a full two years previous to publication.

TABLE 4. Statistics of Salvation Army Bandsmen, 1878–1998

Year of publication	Senior band players[a]	Junior or youth band members	Territories where S. Army was operational[b]
1906	18,507		
1907	19,498		53
1908	19,683		54
1909			
1910	21,681		56
1911			
1912[c]	23,313	2,553	
1913	25,537		58
1914	23,313	2,553	58
1915	23,994	3,970	58
1916	24,406	3,742	60
1917	24,405	4,218	63
1918	24,477	4,270	63
1919	24,477	4,270	63
1920	25,626	5,763	66
1921	26,181	6,417	70
1922	26,017	7,419	73
1923	27,522	8,782	76
1924	28,908	9,282	79
1925	30,182	10,256	79
1926	30,921	10,450	81
1927	32,412	11,059	82
1928	33,297	9,589	82
1929	34,901	8,858	83
1930	35,323	9,741	82
1931	34,747	10,082	82
1932	34,544	10,130	83
1933	34,394	10,035	84
1934	35,065	10,957	86
1935	35,910	12,065	88
1936	36,867	12,842	88

Table 4. (*cont'd*)

Year of publication	Senior band players[a]	Junior or youth band members	Territories where S. Army was operational[b]
1937[d]	36,867	12,842	90
1938	38,036	13,293	95
1939	38,036	13,293	97
1940	38,335	12,179	97
1941[e]			97
1942			
1943			
1944			
1945	39,116	11,458	
1946	39,082	12,090	
1947	39,173	12,382	
1948	39,235	12,458	
1949	35,647	10,801	94
1950	34,962	11,632	92
1951	34,593	11,937	89
1952	34,795	12,935	89
1953	35,137	13,416	89
1954	35,268	13,778	85
1955	35,524	13,959	85
1956	36,076	13,769	85
1957	36,389	14,729	85
1958	36,233	14,973	86
1959	37,444	15,212	86
1960	38,040	16,230	86
1961	38,336	16,395	86
1962	37,435	16,603	86
1963	38,755	16,658	86
1964	45,554	15,029	71
1965	39,474	15,245	69
1966	39,260	15,767	70
1967	39,417	13,283	70
1968	39,389	13,546	70
1969	39,517	12,634	71
1970	39,772	12,701	71
1971	38,714	12,791	74
1972	33,203	12,853	77
1973	37,253	13,479	79
1974	37,333	13,770	81
1975	41,044	14,449	82
1976	41,719	13,940	82

TABLE 4. *(cont'd)*

Year of publication	Senior band players[a]	Junior or youth band members	Territories where S. Army was operational[b]
1977	39,663	12,218	82
1978	40,030	12,825	82
1979	42,035	12,807	83
1980	41,333	26,967	83
1981	41,481	27,161	86
1982	42,401	26,861	86
1983	43,521	26,829	85
1984	43,968	27,311	84
1985	44,244	28,350	84
1986	43,987	28,018	86
1987	41,474	20,346	89
1988[f]	36,865	25,493	89
1989	40,347	27,902	90
1990	41,998	31,681	91
1991	48,986	33,433	93
1992	60,240	24,458	93
1993	52,791	19,142	94
1994	52,791	19,142	98
1995	39,838	11,020	100
1996[g]	25,041	11,124	101
1997	25,166	11,271	103
1998	25,183	11,763	103

[a] Until 1914 numbers are given only for 'Bandsmen'. From 1914 the compilers distinguished between 'Senior Bandsmen' and 'Junior Bandsmen' ('Members of young people's bands' from 1916).

[b] This category was described as 'Countries, Colonies and Dependencies' in 1906, 'Countries and colonies' in 1907–66, 'Countries' in 1967–89, and 'Countries and other territories' since 1990. The sudden decrease in the number of territories declared in 1964 is accounted for by Federation and revisions (see 1964 *Year Book*, p. 45).

[c] These figures were published in the 1930 *Year Book* (for the purpose of illustrating growth in the Army's membership) and are spurious.

[d] These are the figures for 1936. The explanation was that detailed information could be found in the statistics for individual countries.

[e] Because of the war, numbers given in 1941–4 for senior and youth band players were those from the 1940 *Year Book* (gathered in Dec. 1938). In 1942–9 no figures were published for the number of countries in which the Army was active.

[f] The 1988 *Year Book* announced a new system for calculating statistics which was based on 'definitive IHQ records' (see 1940 *Year Book*, p. 86).

[g] In 1996 two additional new categories were introduced. Numbers recorded for 'Other musical groups' were 17,686 (1996) and 19,028 (1997) and for 'Other young people's musical groups' 21,011 (1996) and 39,164 (1997).

BANDMASTERS OF THE INTERNATIONAL STAFF BAND OF THE SALVATION ARMY

Harry Appleby (director of 'all staff bands')	1891–4
Frederick Fry	1891–2
Jabez Lyne	1893–4
Caleb Burgess	1894
George Mitchell	1894–1920
George Fuller	1923–42
Eric Ball	1942–4
William Stewart	1944–7
Bernard Adams	1947–75
Ray Bowes	1975–90
Robert Redhead	1990–4
Stephen Cobb	1994–

EDITORS-IN-CHIEF OF THE INTERNATIONAL MUSIC EDITORIAL DEPARTMENT OF THE SALVATION ARMY

Frederick Fry	1881–3
Richard Slater	1883–1913
Arthur Goldsmith (with F. Hawkes)	1913–21
Frederick Hawkes	1913–36
Bramwell Coles	1936–52
Albert Jakeway	1952–8
Charles Skinner	1958–67
Ray Steadman-Allen	1967–80
Ray Bowes	1980–90
Robert Redhead	1990–2
Trevor Davis	1992–4
Richard Phillips	1994–

Appendix 3

Contest Rules

1860 Peel Park, Bradford, Contest

These regulations are shown in facsimile in Fig. 1.6.

Crystal Palace Band Contest, September 1902

1. This great Musical Festival and Contest is restricted to Amateur Brass Bands of not more than 24 players in each band. Any performer who, within six months of the date of close of the entries, has been engaged as a regular member of the bands of any theatre or other public place of amusement, or resort, will be considered professional, and therefore ineligible to compete. Every performer must be in a position to prove that he is in some business or profession from which he derives his chief income, apart from the playing of music.

2. The bands competing at this Festival will be divided into four sections:–
   First Section—For the One Thousand Guinea Cup.
   Second Section—For bands wishing to be eligible to compete in the first section next year.
   Third Section—Limited to bands who have not won a cash prize exceeding £15. in value.
   Fourth Section—Limited to bands who have not won a cash prize exceeding £6. in value.

3. All the above sections are open to bands of Great Britain and the Colonies.

4. All the players must be bona fide members of the bands in which they are entered, and each player must have been enrolled as a member of such a band at least three months prior to the day of the contest. No member will be allowed to play with more than one band, and if found playing with two bands, both bands will be disqualified.

5. Every member of the bands must be resident in the town or within a distance of four miles, or thereabouts, of the town from which the band is entered. Special remark must be made, and special permission obtained from the Contest Director, at the time of entry, before any member, whose residence is more than four miles distant, will be allowed to play.

6. Each band must play the test piece selected which will be sent free to each band competing at least six clear weeks prior to the day of Contest. No rearrangement of the music will be allowed.

7. No valve trombones or drums will be allowed.

8. Each band to send the name by which it is known, together with the names of every performer, instrument, conductor and secretary, accompanied by an entrance fee of £1 1s. for the first section and 10s./6d. for other sections. The entry fee and entry forms for first section bands containing the above particulars to be forwarded to the Contest Director, Crystal Palace, London S.E., not later than August 23, 3rd and 4th sections close on August 30.

    It is particularly requested that early application be made. No performer will be allowed to play during the contest except upon the instrument entered opposite his name in the entry form.

9. The order of playing to be balloted for in front of the Great Orchestra, Crystal Palace, at 11.30 o'clock. All bands will be balloted for whether present or not. Any band failing to be ready within five minutes to take its place as drawn will be disqualified. Representatives from each band will be expected to be present at the ballot and elect supervision committees for each section.

10. The Contest for first section bands will start sharp at 12 o'clock in the Concert Room as usual. The second, third and fourth sections will start playing at the same time, at stands provided at convenient places in the grounds (that is to say, in the open).

11. The Contest Director will have power to decide any dispute that may arise in connection with the Contest, and his decision will be absolutely final. The decision of the various Adjudicators to be final, and from such decisions there will be no appeal, except where a band is disqualified for an infringement of the rules. Where a prize is withheld for a breach of the rules, such prize will be given to the next in order of merit. All cash prizes will be paid on the day of the Contest.

12. If any band wish to lay an objection against another band the sum of one guinea must be deposited, at the same time such band must enter the protest in writing to the Contest Director, and such protest must be lodged in his hands or at the General Manager's Office within half-an-hour of the finish of the performance of the band objected to. Should the objection not be sustained the deposit will be estreated but if proved genuine the deposit money will be returned.

13. No objection will be entertained as to a performer being a professional or being otherwise ineligible (except in connection with the playing of the music on the day as provided in the Rules), unless full particulars are forwarded at least one week previous to the Contest.

14. Bands winning first prize in sections for which a Trophy is provided before receiving possession of the same must conform with the usual regulations which have been provided by the Crystal Palace Company to ensure the safe custody and return during the period of holdership by the band.

15. In order to ensure fairness to all, no band will be allowed to rehearse on the day of the contest owing to the large number of bands competing. This rule will be rigidly enforced. Any band infringing it will be disqualified.

16. A conductor, professional or amateur may act for more than one band, in either of the first, third and fourth sections, but will not be allowed to play in any band. In the second section only the resident bandmasters will be allowed to conduct, no man conducting more than one band.

17. Each band of the first section must appear in uniform. For the other sections it is optional.

18. Admission tickets to the Palace to the number of twenty-six will be forwarded to each competing band, and on no account can a bandsman enter the grounds without a ticket or payment of the usual entrance fee. Bands can obtain railway tickets at special low rates from London to the Palace by applying to the Contest Director.

19. Any band infringing any of these rules is liable to disqualification.

20. The Contest Director reserves the right to add to or amend either of these rules, each band being advised of such alterations or additions, at least fourteen days previous to the contest.

BELLE VUE, SEPTEMBER 1907

1. In the event of any band winning first prize three years in succession, every man will be awarded a gold medal and not allowed to compete the following year.

2. Every member of the band must be resident in the town, or within a distance of four miles, or thereabouts.

3. A player entered and playing at the July contest will not be allowed to play with another band at the September contest.

4. A professional may be engaged as conductor and may conduct more than one band, but will not be able to play in any band.

5. The number of competing bands will be limited to twenty.

6. The number of members in each band will be limited to twenty four.

7. No member will be allowed to play an instrument other than the one on which he is registered.

8. All players must have been members for more than three months.

9. Any member, who within six months of the date of the close of entries, has played regularly with a professional orchestra, will be considered a professional.

10. Every performer must be in a position to prove that he derives his chief income apart from playing music.

11. Preference will be given to bands who have gained a prize at the September Belle Vue contest in the past two years, or the July Contest this year.

12. The test piece must not be played in public prior to the contest.

13. Only slide trombones are allowed.

NATIONAL BRASS BAND CHAMPIONSHIPS OF GREAT BRITAIN
Rules issued 1 January 1989

Definitions

1. These rules regulate the National Brass Bands Championships of Great Britain.

2. In these Rules the expressions listed shall have the following meanings:

'Boosey & Hawkes'	means Boosey & Hawkes Band Festivals Limited, a limited company whose registered office is at 295 Regent Street, London W1R 8JH;
'Championships'	means the National Brass Band Championships of Great Britain;
'Contest Management'	means Boosey & Hawkes in respect of the Finals and the Regional Committees in respect of the Regional Championships;
'National Contesting Council'	means the body made up and convened in accordance with Rule (5) below.

Basic provisions

3. The title of 'National Brass Band Championships of Great Britain' is wholly owned by Boosey & Hawkes.

4. Boosey & Hawkes reserves the right to amend or replace these rules in accordance with Rule (5*b*iii).

5. The National Contesting Council will be established as follows:
    (*a*) The Council will comprise one named representative from each of the Regional Committees, the Managing Director of Boosey & Hawkes and a chairman appointed by Boosey & Hawkes.
    (*b*) The functions of the Council will be to:
        (i) recommend persons for inclusion in the approved list of adjudicators;
        (ii) decide matters pertaining to the Regional Championships;
        (iii) consider and formulate amendments to these Rules;
        (iv) hear and decide appeals against the decisions of the Contest Management in accordance with Rule (30);
        (v) resolve any difficulties arising in connection with the Championships which are not otherwise provided for under these Rules.

Eligibility for Championships

6. (*a*) Bands will be graded into championship, second, third and fourth sections in accordance with the Grading Rules set out in Appendix I.
    (*b*) Bands must enter the section in which they are currently graded by the Regional Committee. A band which has not yet been graded will enter the fourth section or support its application to compete in the section of its choice by providing evidence of its status as required by the Regional Committee.

7. All players taking part in the Championships must be registered in accordance with the Rules of the British Brass Band Registry or an accredited registry.

8. The Championships are open to brass bands only which will be subject to the following:

    (*a*) they will, subject to Rule (10*b*) below, consist of a maximum of 25 players (plus percussionists) of recognised classification, namely: E♭ soprano cornet, B♭ cornet, B♭ flugel horn, E♭ tenor horn, B♭ baritone, B♭ euphonium, slide trombones, E♭ and EE♭ bass, B♭ and BB♭ bass (E♭ trumpets are not permitted);

    (*b*) the maximum number of percussionists allowed will be three;

    (*c*) no brass player will be allowed to play more than one brass instrument. It will be permissible for a brass player to play a brass instrument and to assist on percussion if so required;

    (*d*) a professional conductor may be engaged to conduct a band or bands at a contest. A conductor must not play an instrument in the band he/she is conducting;

    (*e*) bands must play in uniform, or in dress of a uniform nature, unless special exemption has been obtained in writing in advance from the Contest Management;

    (*f*) no band may rehearse on the day of the contest within hearing distance of the place of the contest;

    (*g*) a player in the process of transfer may not play with more than one band at the same Regional Championship.

9. Regional boundaries will be designated for the Regional Championships in accordance with the terms set out in Appendix II. Bands must take part in the Regional Championships in the region in which their bandroom is situated.

10. (*a*) No player may take part in the youth section if by the date of the Regional Championship he/she has attained the age of 18 years. Players must, if required, produce their birth certificates to the Contest Management.

      In the event of a band qualifying for the Finals, all players who competed with the band at the Regional Championships will be allowed to play with that same band at the Finals.

    (*b*) The maximum number of players in a band in the youth section shall not exceed 35, including percussionists.

11. Particular provisions for the Finals are as follows:

    (*a*) entry forms for the Regional Championships will state the number of prize-winning bands that will qualify at the Regional Championships in each section for the Finals;

    (*b*) if a band which has qualified under Rule (11*a*) above is unable to compete in the Finals, the next band in order of merit may, at the discretion of the Contest Management, be invited to compete;

    (*c*) the first prize-winning band in each section at the Regional Championships will be Regional Champions for that section for the current contesting year;

    (*d*) the winners of the Championship and Youth Sections in the Finals for any contesting year (the Champion Band of Great Britain and the Champion Youth Band of Great Britain respectively) will qualify automatically for the following year's Finals and will not compete in the Regional Championships that same following year;

(*e*) any band having won the Championship Section in the Finals for three years in succession will not compete in the Finals in the fourth successive year, but will be invited to compete in the Finals in the following year (year five).

Contest procedure

12. (*a*) In order to enter the Regional Championships a band will properly complete and return to the Contest Management the entry form together with the appropriate fee before the closing date for entries. The fee and closing date shall be as stated on the entry form. The fee is not refundable.

(*b*) Whilst every effort will be made to publish the dates of the Regional Championships and to send out entry forms, it is the responsibility of the secretary of each band to obtain the entry form from the Contest Management to allow the band to enter the Regional Championships.

13. (*a*) When the Contest Management has accepted an entry form, it will send a contest signatures form to the band secretary. The band secretary must arrange for the form to be properly completed and signed by all players who are eligible to play in the relevant contest. The secretary must return the form TOGETHER WITH THE PLAYERS' REGISTRATION CARDS on or before the date stipulated by the Contest Management.

(*b*) Any additions or amendments to the contest signatures form must be received by the Contest Management NOT LATER THAN FOUR WEEKS before the date of the contest and must be accompanied by the registration cards of the players concerned.

14. (*a*) The signatures on the registration cards will be compared by the Contest Management with the signatures appearing on the contest signatures form. Provided the Contest Management is satisfied that the signatures on the registration cards match the signatures on the contest signatures form, it will return the registration cards to the band secretary to arrive no later than one week before the contest.

(*b*) The responsibility shall rest with the band secretary to ensure that all players included in the personnel of the band on the day of the contest are registered members of that band.

15. A contest schedule will be prepared by the Contest Management and sent to all bands competing in the Championships.

16. If a substitute conductor is to be used on the day of a contest, the Contest Management should be informed of the details by the band secretary. It shall not be permissible for the original conductor to take over from the substitute conductor at any point after the band has commenced playing.

17. The order in which the bands in each section will play at a contest shall be decided by a ballot organised by the Contest Management. The ballot will take place on the day of the contest at the time and place stated by the Contest Management in the contest schedule. Bands must play in the order they are drawn.

18. (*a*) Each band shall appoint a representative to attend the ballot and act on its behalf in all matters pertaining to the Rules. The representative must properly complete and present to the Contest Controller the card supplied by the Contest Management in order to establish his/her authority as the representative appointed to attend the ballot. Any queries regarding the Rules must be raised by the representative before the ballot takes place.

(*b*) Should a representative fail to attend the ballot at the time and place stated, an official of the Contest Management will take his/her place for the purpose of the ballot, and the relevant band must accept the result.

19. (*a*) Screened adjudication will be used for the Championships.

(*b*) The representatives appointed to attend the ballot will, immediately prior to the ballot taking place, elect a supervision committee of two of their members who will escort the adjudicator/s to the adjudicators' box, inspect the box and report to the Contest Controller and the other representatives at the ballot that they are satisfied with the adequate screening of the adjudicator/s.

20. (*a*) If a player is unable to compete due to personal illness or injury, the representative may, immediately prior to the ballot taking place, apply to the Contest Controller for a deputy player and support the application by providing documentary evidence (e.g. medical certificate. Self-certification forms will not be accepted.)

Providing the Contest Controller is satisfied that the application is genuine, he/she will instruct the band drawn to play immediately before the band making the application, to supply the relevant deputy player, complete with instrument and band part. If the band making the application is drawn No. 1, the band drawn last must supply the deputy player.

(*b*) The secretary of the band supplying the deputy player, or the representative attending the ballot, shall be held responsible for ensuring that the deputy player fulfils this commitment.

A player acting as a deputy must not accept any payment for his services.

(*c*) Only one application for a deputy player per band will be considered.

21. The band drawn No. 1 must assemble at the registration table at least 15 minutes before the time stated by the Contest Management in the contest schedule for the section to commence.

22. (*a*) Each player must present his/her registration card to the officials at the registration table for scrutiny and endorsement, and must sign his/her name on the contest signatures form.

(*b*) Any discrepancy will be reported by the registration officials to the Contest Controller. In cases of doubt the Contest Controller must notify the band secretary, or the individual acting on his/her behalf, that the player concerned and the band may risk subsequent disciplinary action.

23. If any band is not ready to play within four minutes of the time stated for the section to commence, or of the preceding band leaving the platform, the band may be disqualified by the Contest Management.

24. The adjudicator/s will place the bands in order of merit for the announcement of prizes and awards. The awards will be presented at the conclusion of the contest. Cash prizes will be distributed in accordance with Rule (26) below. The decision of the adjudicator/s shall be final.

25. (a) Any objection at the time of the Championship concerning any alleged breach of the Rules must be presented in writing to the Contest Controller before the prizes and awards are announced.

    The band or individual making the objection will deposit an amount of £20, which will be returned if the objection is sustained but not otherwise. No deposit will be required when an objection is presented by an official of the Contest Management.

    (b) Any protest made after the prizes or awards have been announced concerning any alleged breach of the Rules or error in the results must be submitted in writing to the Contest Management within 14 days of the Championship.

    The protest must be accompanied by an amount of £30, which will be returned if the protest is sustained but not otherwise.

    (c) Where the Contest Management finds that there has been a breach of the Rules or an error in the results, it will revise the list of prize and award winning bands and, where appropriate, order awards to be returned.

    (d) Where either the Contest Controller or the Contest Management finds that there has been a breach of the Rules, it may take disciplinary action under Rule (29) below.

    Objection and protest forms will be available from the Contest Controller on the day of a contest or from the Contest Management.

26. If at the expiration of 14 days from the date of a contest the Contest Management is satisfied that no breach of these Rules has occurred, the cash prizes will be sent by post to the band secretaries of the prize-winning bands.

27. Challenge awards will be competed for each year unless otherwise decided by the Contest Management.

    A band winning an award must give an undertaking signed by two officials of the band to keep the award in good and safe condition and to protect and insure it against loss or any damage whatsoever, and to return the award in good condition upon instructions from the Contest Management.

Discipline and appeals

28. Disciplinary action will be taken by the Contest Management against any player who submits a false signature or who at any time improperly gives his/her signature to documents for more than one band.

    Disciplinary action will also be taken by the Contest Management against any band secretary who submits a false registration or countenances a false signature.

29. In the event of any player, official or conductor of a band being found guilty of a breach of these Rules, or failing to comply with the conditions as may be set forth in the contest signatures form and contest schedule, or who commits any act which in the opinion of the Contest Management would be prejudicial to the proper conduct or reputation of the Championships, the band may be subject to

disqualification and/or forfeiture of prizes and awards and/or suspension from entering the Championships for such time as may be decided by the Contest Management.

30. Any appeal against any decision made or disciplinary action taken by the Contest Management must be submitted in writing to the Managing Director of Boosey & Hawkes.

The National Contesting Council will hear and decide any appeal at its next meeting and the following procedure will apply:

(*a*) the individual or band making the appeal will be invited to put the case at the meeting. Where the appeal has been made by a band, its case will be put by the band secretary or other representative of the band appointed for that purpose.

(*b*) the decision of the National Contesting Council will be communicated in writing to the appellant by the Managing Director of Boosey & Hawkes within seven days, giving the reasons for that decision.

(*d*) the decision of the National Contesting Council shall be final and shall not be subject to any further appeal or any legal proceedings whatsoever.

Appendix I

Grading rules

The National Brass Band Championships of Great Britain will apply the following grading system or an accredited grading system approved by the National Contesting Council.

(*a*) Grading will be carried out annually immediately following the regional championships. New grading will become effective from 1st Jan. of the following year.

(*b*) The Regional Secretary will maintain the grading register and grading will be based only on the results of the regional championships.

(*c*) Bands affected by promotion or relegation will be notified by the Regional Secretary as soon as possible after the grading has been completed.

(*d*) Any band given exemption from competing in a regional championship under Rules (11*d*) and (11*e*) will be positioned equal first for that year.

(*e*) The Champion Band of Great Britain of the second, third and fourth sections will be promoted automatically.

(*f*) In the second, third and fourth sections, the bands with the two best aggregate placings over the previous three years will be promoted. In sections where there are ten bands or less on the grading register, only the band/s with the best aggregate placing will be promoted.

(*g*) In the Championship, second and third sections, the bands with the two poorest aggregate placings over the previous three years will be relegated. In sections where there are ten bands or less on the grading register, only the band/s with the poorest aggregate placing will be relegated.

(*h*) Any band entering a regional championship for the first time will on its first grading be given an average position for the previous two years for that section. The average position will be calculated by totalling the placings awarded and dividing by the number of bands competing in that year. The average position will be corrected to the nearest half number.

(*i*)   When two or more bands receive equal marks, each band will be given the same numerical placing. The next band will be placed the equivalent number of places below.

(*j*)   Any band failing to compete will be placed one position lower than any competing band in that section.

(*k*)   Any band failing to compete for two consecutive years will be relegated. The Regional Committee may waive this rule at its discretion. Any such relegation will be in addition to any action taken under rule (*g*).

(*l*)   Any band failing to compete for three consecutive years will be removed from the grading register before compilation of the grading tables at the end of the third year. If such a band wishes to resume contesting, it will be treated as a first time entry in accordance with Rule (6*b*).

(*m*)   Bands promoted or relegated will, for grading purposes, be given an average position for the years prior to their promotion or relegation.

(*n*)   Any band, whether or not affected by promotion or relegation, which considers it has special reasons to be regraded must, within four weeks of receiving notification of its grading, submit an appeal to the Regional Committee.

Appendix II

Regional boundaries

1. Scotland
2. North of England   Northumberland, Durham, Cleveland, Cumbria, North Yorkshire except the District of Selby
3. North West & North Wales   Lancashire, Greater Manchester, Cheshire, Merseyside, Gwynedd, Clwyd
4. Yorkshire   West Yorkshire, South Yorkshire, Humberside, the District of Selby
5. North Midlands   Salop, Staffordshire, Derbyshire, Nottinghamshire, Leicestershire, Lincolnshire
6. South Midlands & East Anglia   Hereford & Worcester, West Midlands, Warwickshire, Northamptonshire, Cambridgeshire, Suffolk, Norfolk
7. Wales   Dyfed, Powys, Gwent, West Glamorgan, Mid-Glamorgan, South Glamorgan
8. London & Southern Counties   Bedfordshire, Buckinghamshire, Essex, Hertfordshire, Oxfordshire, Berkshire, Greater London, Surrey, East Sussex, West Sussex, Kent, Hampshire
9. West of England   Devon, Cornwall, Dorset, Somerset, Wiltshire, Avon, Gloucestershire

APPENDIX 4

Enderby Jackson's Crystal Palace Contests, 1860–1863

1860   National (10 July)   Sydenham (11 July)
      1. Black Dyke Mills   Cyfarthfa
      2. Saltaire   Dewsbury
      3. Cyfarthfa   Goldshill Saxhorn

1861   National (23 July)   Sydenham (25 July)
      1. Saltaire   Marriner's, Keighley
      2. Chesterfield   Victoria
      3. Keighley   Darlington

1862   National (9 Sept.)
      1. Chesterfield Rifle Corps
      2. Black Dyke Mills
      3. Keighley

1863   National (28 July)
      1. Blandford
      2. Dewsbury Old
      3. Matlock Bath

Open and National Championship Results, 1853–1997

Contest		Conductor	Test piece
1853	Open		
	1. Mossley Temperance Saxhorn	William Taylor	Two own-choice selections
	2. Dewsbury Old	S. Greenwood	
	3. Bramley Temperance	M. Whitley	
1854	Open		
	1. Leeds Railway Foundry	Richard Smith	Two own-choice selections
	2. Dewsbury Old	John Peel	
	3. Accrington	T. Bradley	
1855	Open		
	1. Accrington	Radcliffe Barnes	Melling, *Orynthia*, & own-choice
	2. Leeds Railway Foundry	Richard Smith	
	3. Mossley Temperance Saxhorn	William Taylor	
1856	Open		
	1. Leeds Railway Foundry	Richard Smith	Flotow, *Stradella*, & own-choice
	2. Leeds (Smith's)	Richard Smith	
	3. Accrington	Radcliffe Barnes	
1857	Open		
	1. Leeds (Smith's)	Richard Smith	Verdi, *Il Trovatore*, & own-choice
	2. Dewsbury Old	John Peel	
	3. Todmorden	W. Brook	
1858	Open		
	1. Accrington	Radcliffe Barnes	Haydn, 'On Thee each living soul awaits', & 'Achieved is the glorious work', *The Creation*
	2. Dewsbury Old	S. Greenwood	
	3. Mossley Temperance Saxhorn	William Taylor	
1859	Open NO CONTEST		
1860	Open		
	1. Halifax 4th West Yorkshire Rifle Volunteers	Isaac Dewhurst	Hérold, *Zampa*, & own-choice

Contest		Conductor	Test piece
	2. Dewsbury Old	John Peel	
	3. Sherwood Rangers	W. Lilley	
1861	Open		
	1. Halifax 4th West Yorkshire Rifle Volunteers	Isaac Dewhurst	Balfe, *Satanella*, & own-choice
	2. Dewsbury Rifle Corps	John Peel	
	3. Chesterfield	T. Tallis Trimnell	
1862	Open		
	1. Black Dyke Mills	Samuel Longbottom	Auber, 'Muette de Portici', *Masaniello*, & own-choice
	2. Dewsbury Rifle Corps	John Peel	
	3. Chesterfield	T. Tallis Trimnell	
1863	Open		
	1. Black Dyke Mills	Samuel Longbottom	Gounod, *Faust*, & own-choice
	2. Bacup 4th Lancashire Rifle Volunteers	John Lord	
	3. Craven Amateur (Silsden)	G. O'Brien	
1864	Open		
	1. Bacup 4th Lancashire Rifle Volunteers	John Lord	*The Reminiscences of Auber*, & own-choice
	2. Stalybridge Old	dir. by players Cooper, Hilton, & Robinson	
	3. Leeds Model	Richard Smith	
1865	Open		
	1. Bacup 4th Lancashire Rifle Volunteers	John Lord	Verdi, *Un Ballo in Maschera*, & own-choice
	2. Dewsbury Rifle Corps	John Peel	
	3. Matlock Bath	John Naylor	
1866	Open		
	1. Dewsbury Old	John Peel	Meyerbeer (arr. Grosse), *L'Africaine*, & own-choice
	2. Matlock Bath	John Naylor	
	3. Healey Hall	J. Law	
1867	Open		
	1. Clay Cross 3rd Derbyshire Rifle Volunteers	John Naylor	Weber (arr. Winterbottom), *Der Freischütz*
	2. Bacup 4th Lancashire Rifle Volunteers	J. Ford	
	3. Compstall Bridge	Henry Tym[m]	

Contest		Conductor	Test piece
1868	Open		
	1. Burnley 17th Lancashire Rifle Volunteers	J. Ford	Meyerbeer (arr. Winterbottom), *Robert*
	2. Heckmondwike Albion	J. Brooke	*le Diable*
	3. Black Dyke Mills	Samuel Longbottom	
1869	Open		
	1. Bacup 4th Lancashire Rifle Volunteers	John Lord	Meyerbeer (arr. Winterbottom),
	2. Matlock Volunteers	John Naylor	*Le Prophète*
	3. Burnley 17th Lancashire Rifle Volunteers	W. Harrison	
1870	Open		
	1. Bacup Old	John Lord	Verdi (arr.
	2. Matlock Volunteers	John Naylor	Winterbottom), *Ernani*
	3. Dewsbury Old	John Lord	
1871	Open		
	1. Black Dyke Mills	Samuel Longbottom	Rossini (arr. Winterbottom),
	2. Bury Borough	J. Briggs	*Il Barbiere*
	3. Bacup Old	John Lord	
1872	Open		
	1. Robin Hood Rifles	H. Leverton	C. Godfrey (arr.),
	2. Saltaire	John Gladney	*Souvenir de Mozart*
	3. Meltham Mills	John Gladney	
1873	Open		
	1. Meltham Mills	John Gladney	Meyerbeer (arr. C.
	2. Robin Hood Rifles	H. Leverton	Godfrey), *Dinorah*
	3. Black Dyke Mills	Samuel Longbottom	
1874	Open		
	1. Linthwaite	Edwin Swift	Spohr (arr. C. Godfrey),
	2. Meltham Mills	John Gladney	*Faust*
	3. Besses o' th' Barn	Tom German	
1875	Open		
	1. Kingston Mills	John Gladney	Balfe (arr. C. Godfrey),
	2. Meltham Mills	John Gladney	*Il Talismano*
	3. Linthwaite	Edwin Swift	
1876	Open		
	1. Meltham Mills	John Gladney	Verdi (arr. C. Godfrey),
	2. Kingston Mills	John Gladney	*Aïda*
	3. Holm Mills	Edwin Swift	

Contest		Conductor	Test piece
1877	Open		
	1. Meltham Mills	John Gladney	Spohr (arr. C. Godfrey),
	2. Black Dyke Mills	Edwin Swift	*Jessonda*
	3. Holm Mills	Edwin Swift	
1878	Open		
	1. Meltham Mills	John Gladney	Gounod (arr. C.
	2. Kidsgrove	T. Charlesworth	Godfrey), *Romeo e*
	3. Denton Original	(?) Alexander Owen	*Giulietta*
1879	Open		
	1. Black Dyke Mills	J. Fawcett	Spohr (arr. C. Godfrey),
	2. Accrington 3rd Lancashire Rifle Volunteers	John Gladney	*The Last Judgement*
	3. Barnsley 37th West Yorkshire Rifle Volunteers	John Gladney	
1880	Open		
	1. Black Dyke Mills	Alexander Owen	Verdi (arr. C. Godfrey),
	2. Stalybridge Old	John Gladney	*I Vespri Siciliani*
	3. Nelson Old	John Gladney	
1881	Open		
	1. Black Dyke Mills	Alexander Owen	Gounod (arr. C.
	2. Meltham Mills	John Gladney	Godfrey), *Cinq Mars*
	3. Stalybridge Old	John Gladney	
1882	Open		
	1. Clayton-le-Moor	Alexander Owen	Mozart (arr. C.
	2. Linthwaite	Edwin Swift	Godfrey), *Il Seraglio*
	3. Barnsley 37th West Yorkshire Rifle Volunteers	John Gladney	
1883	Open		
	1. Littleborough Public	Edwin Swift	Mercadante (arr. C.
	2. Burslem	R. Sowerbutts	Godfrey), *Il*
	3. Honley	John Gladney	*Giuramento*
1884	Open		
	1. Honley	John Gladney	Rossini (arr. C.
	2. Oldham Rifles	Alexander Owen	Godfrey), *La Gazza*
	3. Black Dyke Mills	Alexander Owen	*Ladra*
1885	Open		
	1. Kingston Mills	John Gladney	Verdi (arr. C. Godfrey),
	2. Littleborough Public	Edwin Swift	*Nabucco*
	3. Besses o' th' Barn	Alexander Owen	

Contest		Conductor	Test piece
1886	Open		
	1. Kingston Mills	John Gladney	Donizetti (arr. C.
	2. Heywood Rifles	John Gladney	Godfrey), *La Favorita*
	3. Littleborough Public	Edwin Swift	
1887	Open		
	1. Kingston Mills	John Gladney	Meyerbeer (arr. C.
	2. Black Dyke Mills	Alexander Owen	Godfrey), *L'Étoile du*
	3. Besses o' th' Barn	Alexander Owen	*Nord*
1888	Open		
	1. Wyke Temperance	Edwin Swift	Wagner (arr. C.
	2. Black Dyke Mills	Alexander Owen	Godfrey), *Der Fliegende*
	3. Todmorden Old	Edwin Swift	*Holländer*
1889	Open		
	1. Wyke Temperance	Edwin Swift	Gounod (arr. C.
	2. Kingston Mills	John Gladney	Godfrey), *La Reine de*
	3. Leeds Forge	Edwin Swift	*Saba*
1890	Open		
	1. Batley Old	John Gladney	Weber (arr. C.
	2. Leeds Forge	Alexander Owen	Godfrey), *Euranthye*
	3. Wyke Temperance	Edwin Swift	
1891	Open		
	1. Black Dyke Mills	John Gladney	Kreutzer (arr. C.
	2. Wyke Temperance	Edwin Swift	Godfrey), *Das*
	3. Dewsbury Old	J. Sidney Jones	*Nachtlager in Granada*
1892	Open		
	1. Besses o' th' Barn	Alexander Owen	Lortzing (arr. C.
	2. Kingston Mills	John Gladney	Godfrey), *Zaar und*
	3. Lindley	Edwin Swift	*Zimmerman*
1893	Open		
	1. Kingston Mills	John Gladney	Bemberg (arr. C.
	2. Cornholme	Edwin Swift	Godfrey), *Elaine*
	3. Rochdale Old	Albert Whipp	
1894	Open		
	1. Besses o' th' Barn	Alexander Owen	Goring Thomas (arr. C.
	2. Kingston Mills	John Gladney	Godfrey), *The Golden*
	3. Black Dyke Mills	John Gladney	*Web*
1895	Open		
	1. Black Dyke Mills	John Gladney	Humperdinck (arr.
	2. Wyke Temperance	Edwin Swift	C. Godfrey), *Hänsel*
	3. Besses o' th' Barn	Alexander Owen	*und Gretel*
1896	Open		
	1. Black Dyke Mills	John Gladney	Pizzi (arr. C. Godfrey),
	2. Kingston Mills	William Rimmer	*Gabriella*
	3. Batley Old	J. Wilkinson	

Contest		Conductor	Test piece
1897	Open		
	1. Mossley	Alexander Owen	Rossini (arr. C.
	2. Kingston Mills	William Rimmer	Godfrey), *Moses in*
	3. Batley Old	J. Wilkinson	*Egypt*
1898	Open		
	1. Wyke Temperance	Edwin Swift	C. Godfrey (arr.), *Grand*
	2. Hucknall Temperance	John Gladney	*Fantasia from the Works*
	3. Lea Mills	Alexander Owen	*of Mendelssohn*
1899	Open		
	1. Black Dyke Mills	John Gladney	Verdi (arr. C. Godfrey),
	2. Hucknall Temperance	John Gladney	*Aroldo*
	3. Lee Mount	William Swingler	
1900	Open		
	1. Lindley	John Gladney	Ponchielli (arr. C.
	2. Black Dyke Mills	John Gladney	Godfrey), *La Gioconda*
	3. Pemberton Old	William Rimmer	
1900	National		
	1. Denton Original	Alexander Owen	J. Ord Hume (arr.),
	2. Black Dyke Mills	John Gladney	*Gems from Sullivan's*
	3. Wingates Temperance	William Rimmer	*Operas No. 1*
1901	Open		
	1. Kingston Mills	Alexander Owen	Gounod (arr. C.
	2. Lindley	John Gladney	Godfrey), *Mirella*
	3. Crooke	P. Fairhurst	
1901	National		
	1. Lee Mount	William Swingler	J. Ord Hume (arr.),
	2. Irwell Springs	William Rimmer	*Gems from Sullivan's*
	3. Denton Original	Alexander Owen	*Operas No. 3*
1902	Open		
	1. Black Dyke Mills	John Gladney	Appoloni (arr. C.
	2. Pemberton Old	John Gladney	Godfrey), *L'Ebreo*
	3. Besses o' th' Barn	Alexander Owen	
1902	National		
	1. Black Dyke Mills	John Gladney	Coleridge-Taylor (arr.
	2. Wyke Temperance	Edwin Swift	C. Godfrey), *Hiawatha*
	3. Luton Red Cross Silver	Angus Holden	
1903	Open		
	1. Pemberton Old	John Gladney	Elgar (arr. C. Godfrey),
	2. Black Dyke Mills	John Gladney	*Caractacus*
	3. Irwell Springs	William Rimmer	
1903	National		
	1. Besses o' th' Barn	Alexander Owen	Wagner (arr. F. C.
	2. Rushden Temperance	Alexander Owen	Shipley Douglas), *Die*
	3. Black Dyke Mills	John Gladney	*Meistersinger*

Contest		Conductor	Test piece
1904	Open		
	1. Black Dyke Mills	John Gladney	Rossini (arr. C.
	2. Pemberton Old	John Gladney	Godfrey), *Semiramide*
	3. Lindley	B. Lodge	
1904	National		
	1. Hebburn Colliery	Angus Holden	C. Godfrey (arr.), *Gems*
	2. Wingates Temperance	William Rimmer	*of Mendelssohn*
	3. Irwell Springs	William Rimmer	
1905	Open		
	1. Irwell Springs	William Rimmer	Mozart (arr. C.
	2. Black Dyke Mills	John Gladney	Godfrey), *Così fan tutte*
	3. Lindley	B. Lodge	
1905	National		
	1. Irwell Springs	William Rimmer	Mermet (arr.?) *Roland à*
	2. Wingates Temperance	William Rimmer	*Ronceveaux*
	3. Lee Mount	Alexander Owen	
1906	Open		
	1. Wingates Temperance	William Rimmer	Meyerbeer (arr. C.
	2. Goodshaw	William Halliwell	Godfrey), *Les*
	3. Rochdale Public	William Rimmer	*Huguenots*
1906	National		
	1. Wingates Temperance	William Rimmer	W. Short (arr.), *Gems of*
	2. Shaw	William Rimmer	*Chopin*
	3. Wyke Temperance (after disqualification of Linthwaite from 2nd place)	William Rimmer	
1907	Open		
	1. Wingates Temperance	William Rimmer	MacFarren (arr. C.
	2. Black Dyke Mills	John Gladney	Godfrey), *Robin Hood*
	3. Goodshaw	William Halliwell	
1907	National		
	1. Wingates Temperance	William Rimmer	W. Short (arr.), *Gems of*
	2. Goodshaw	William Halliwell	*Schumann*
	3. King Cross Subscription (Halifax)	Walter Halstead	
1908	Open		
	1. Black Dyke Mills	William Rimmer	C. Godfrey (arr.), *A*
	2. Rushden Temperance	John Gladney	*Souvenir of Grieg*
	3. Perfection Soap Works	William Halliwell	
1908	National		
	1. Irwell Springs	William Rimmer	Wagner (arr. Cope),
	2. Perfection Soap Works	William Halliwell	*Rienzi*
	3. Wingates Temperance	William Rimmer	

Contest		Conductor	Test piece
1909	Open		
	1. Foden Motor Works	William Rimmer	Marliani (arr. C.
	2. Black Dyke Mills	William Rimmer	Godfrey), *Il Bravo*
	3. Perfection Soap Works	William Halliwell	
1909	National		
	1. Shaw	William Rimmer	Wagner (arr. C.
	2. Foden Motor Works	William Rimmer	Godfrey), *Der Fliegende*
	3. Perfection Soap Works	William Halliwell	*Holländer*
1910	Open		
	1. Foden Motor Works	William Halliwell	Handel (arr. C.
	2. Shaw	William Halliwell	Godfrey), *Acis and*
	3. Perfection Soap Works	William Halliwell	*Galatea*
1910	National		
	1. Foden Motor Works	William Halliwell	W. Rimmer (arr.), *Gems*
	2. Irwell Springs	Alexander Owen	*of Schubert*
	3. Spencer's Steel Works	William Halliwell	
1911	Open		
	1. Hebden Bridge	William Halliwell	Tchaikovsky (arr. C.
	2. Foden Motor Works	William Halliwell	Godfrey), *Eugene*
	3. Perfection Soap Works	William Halliwell	*Onegin*
1911	National		
	1. Perfection Soap Works	William Halliwell	Meyerbeer (arr.
	2. Foden Motor Works	William Halliwell	Rimmer), *Les*
	3. Wingates Temperance	Alexander Owen	*Huguenots*
1912	Open		
	1. Foden Motor Works	William Halliwell	Auber (arr. C. Godfrey),
	2. St Hilda Colliery	William Halliwell	*Les Diamants de la*
	3. Shaw	William Halliwell	*Couronne*
1912	National		
	1. St Hilda Colliery	William Halliwell	Rossini (arr. W.
	2. Irwell Springs	William Halliwell	Rimmer), *William Tell*
	3. Foden Motor Works	William Halliwell	
1913	Open		
	1. Foden Motor Works	William Halliwell	C. Godfrey (arr.), *A*
	2. Shaw	William Halliwell	*Souvenir of Gounod*
	3. Irwell Springs	William Halliwell	
1913	National		
	1. Irwell Springs	William Halliwell	Percy Fletcher, *Labour*
	2. St Hilda Colliery	William Halliwell	*and Love*
	3. Black Dyke Mills	John A. Greenwood	
1914	Open		
	1. Black Dyke Mills	John A. Greenwood	Méhul (arr. C.
	2. Wingates Temperance	John A. Greenwood	Godfrey), *Joseph und*
	3. Foden Motor Works	William Halliwell	*seine Brüder*

Contest		Conductor	Test piece
1914	National		
	NO CONTEST		
1915	Open		
	1. Foden Motor Works	William Halliwell	Donizetti (arr. C.
	2. Horwich Railway Mechanics Institute (RMI)	John A. Greenwood	Godfrey), *Il Furioso*
	3. King Cross Subscription (Halifax)	John A. Greenwood	
1915	National		
	NO CONTEST		
1916	Open		
	1. Horwich RMI	John A. Greenwood	Verdi (arr. C. G.
	2. Foden Motor Works	William Halliwell	Godfrey), *La Traviata*
	3. Black Dyke Mills	John A. Greenwood	
1916	National		
	NO CONTEST		
1917	Open		
	1. Horwich RMI	John A. Greenwood	Hérold (arr. C. G.
	2. Black Dyke Mills	John A. Greenwood	Godfrey), *Le Pré aux*
	3. Woodlands Village	Alexander Owen	*Clercs*
1917	National		
	NO CONTEST		
1918	Open		
	1. Wingates Temperance	William Halliwell	Marliani (arr. C.
	2. Irwell Springs	Walter Nuttall	Godfrey), *Il Bravo*
	3. Besses o' th' Barn	Alexander Owen	
1918	National		
	NO CONTEST		
1919	Open		
	1. Harton Colliery	George Hawkins	Benedict (arr. C. G.
	2. Wingates Temperance	William Halliwell	Godfrey), *The Lily of*
	3. St Hilda Colliery	William Halliwell	*Killarney*
1919	National		
	NO CONTEST		
1920	Open		
	1. Besses o' th' Barn	William Wood	Verdi (arr. C. G.
	2. Wingates Temperance	William Halliwell	Godfrey), *I Lombardi*
	3. Yorkshire Main Colliery	John A. Greenwood	
1920	National		
	1. St Hilda Colliery	William Halliwell	Cyril Jenkins,
	2. Lincoln Malleable Iron Works	William Halliwell	*Coriolanus*
	3. Irwell Springs	John A. Greenwood	

Contest		Conductor	Test piece
1921	Open		
	1. Wingates Temperance	William Halliwell	Wallace (arr. C. G.
	2. Barrow Shipyard	John A. Greenwood	Godfrey), *Maritana*
	3. Black Dyke Mills	John A. Greenwood	
1921	National		
	1. St Hilda Colliery	William Halliwell	Cyril Jenkins, *Life*
	2. Foden Motor Works	William Halliwell	*Divine*
	3. Wingates Temperance	William Halliwell	
1922	Open		
	1. South Elmshall & Frickley Colliery	Noel Thorpe	Wagner (arr. M. Johnstone), *Lohengrin*
	2. Black Dyke Mills	William Halliwell	
	3. Besses o' th' Barn	William Wood	
1922	National		
	1. Horwich RMI	John A. Greenwood	Hubert Bath, *Freedom*
	2. Luton Red Cross Silver	William Halliwell	
	3. Hebden Bridge	William Halliwell	
1923	Open		
	1. Wingates Temperance	William Halliwell	Meyerbeer (arr. C.
	2. Creswell Colliery	John A. Greenwood	Godfrey), *Dinorah*
	3. Besses o' th' Barn	Harry Barlow	
1923	National		
	1. Luton Red Cross Silver	William Halliwell	Henry Geehl, *Oliver*
	2. Black Dyke Mills	William Halliwell	*Cromwell*
	3. Foden Motor Works	William Halliwell	
1924	Open		
	1. Newcastle Steel Works (Australia)	A. H. Bailie	T. Keighley (arr.), *Selection from the*
	2. Creswell Colliery	John A. Greenwood	*Works of Liszt*
	3. Harton Colliery	George Hawkins	
1924	National		
	1. St Hilda Colliery	William Halliwell	Henry Geehl, *On the*
	2. Black Dyke Mills	William Halliwell	*Cornish Coast*
	3. Newcastle Steel Works (Australia)	A. H. Bailie	
1925	Open		
	1. Creswell Colliery	John A. Greenwood	Thomas Keighley,
	2. Nutgrove	John A. Greenwood	*Macbeth*
	3. Foden Motor Works	William Halliwell	
1925	National		
	1. Marsden Colliery	John A. Greenwood	Denis Wright, *Joan of*
	2. Irwell Springs	William Halliwell	*Arc*
	3. South Moor Colliery	J. C. Dyson	

Contest		Conductor	Test piece
1926	Open		
	1. Foden Motor Works	William Halliwell	Thomas Keighley, *A*
	2. Wingates Temperance	William Halliwell	*Midsummer Night's*
	3. St Hilda Colliery	William Halliwell	*Dream*
1926	National		
	1. St Hilda Colliery	J. Oliver	Percy Fletcher, *An Epic*
	2. Carlisle St Stephen's	William Lowes	*Symphony*
	3. Wingates Temperance	William Halliwell	
1927	Open		
	1. Foden Motor Works	William Halliwell	Thomas Keighley,
	2. Callender's Cable	Tom Morgan	*Merry Wives of*
	Works		*Windsor*
	3. Milnrow Public	John A. Greenwood	
1927	National		
	1. Carlisle St Stephen's	William Lowes	Denis Wright, *The*
	2. Callender's Cable	Tom Morgan	*White Rider*
	Works		
	3. Carlton Main Colliery	Noel Thorpe	
1928	Open		
	1. Foden Motor Works	William Halliwell	Thomas Keighley,
	2. Callender's Cable	Tom Morgan	*Lorenzo*
	Works		
	3. Nutgrove	William Wood	
1928	National		
	1. Black Dyke Mills	William Halliwell	Gustav Holst, *A*
	2. Harton Colliery	William Halliwell	*Moorside Suite*
	3. Carlisle St Stephen's	William Lowes	
1929	Open		
	1. Brighouse & Rastrick	Fred Berry	Beethoven (arr. ?),
	2. Wingates Temperance	Harold Moss	*Pathétique*
	3. Carlisle St Stephen's	William Lowes	
1929	National		
	1. Carlisle St Stephen's	William Lowes	Cyril Jenkins, *Victory*
	2. Scottish CWS	John A. Greenwood	
	3. Luton Red Cross Silver	E. S. Carter	
1930	Open		
	1. Eccles Borough	J. Dow	Granville Bantock,
	2. Milnrow Public	John A. Greenwood	*Oriental Rhapsody*
	3. Wingates Temperance	Harold Moss	
1930	National		
	1. Foden Motor Works	Fred Mortimer	Edward Elgar, *Severn*
	2. Black Dyke Mills	William Halliwell	*Suite*
	3. Irwell Springs	William Halliwell	

Contest		Conductor	Test piece
1931	Open		
	1. Besses o' th' Barn	William Halliwell	Haydn Morris,
	2. Glazebury	John A. Greenwood	*Springtime*
	3. Milnrow Public	John A. Greenwood	
1931	National		
	1. Wingates Temperance	Harold Moss	Hubert Bath, *Honour*
	2. Horden Colliery	J. Foster	*and Glory*
	3. Rothwell Temperance	N. Sidebottom	
1932	Open		
	1. Brighouse & Rastrick	William Halliwell	Thomas Keighley, *The*
	2. Nelson Old	William Halliwell	*Crusaders*
	3. Metropolitan Works	Harry Heyes	
1932	National		
	1. Foden Motor Works	Fred Mortimer	John Ireland, *A*
	2. Black Dyke Mills	William Halliwell	*Downland Suite*
	3. Wingates Temperance	Harold Moss	
1933	Open		
	1. Brighouse & Rastrick	William Halliwell	Denis Wright, *Princess*
	2. Baxendale's Works	John A. Greenwood	*Nada*
	3. Amington	John A. Greenwood	
1933	National		
	1. Foden Motor Works	Fred Mortimer	Granville Bantock,
	2. Scottish CWS	George Hawkins	*Prometheus Unbound*
	3. Creswell Colliery	John A. Greenwood	
1934	Open		
	1. Brighouse & Rastrick	William Halliwell	Herbert Howells,
	2. Black Dyke Mills	William Halliwell	*Pageantry*
	3. Wingates Temperance	Harold Moss	
1934	National		
	1. Foden Motor Works	Fred Mortimer	John Ireland, *A Comedy*
	2. Scottish CWS	George Hawkins	*Overture*
	3. Harton Colliery	William Lowes	
1935	Open		
	1. Black Dyke Mills	William Halliwell	Thomas Keighley, *A*
	2. Wingates Temperance	Harold Moss	*Northern Rhapsody*
	3. Abram Colliery	William Haydock	
1935	National		
	1. Munn & Felton's Works	William Halliwell	Kenneth Wright, *Pride of Race*
	2. Creswell Colliery	Joe Farrington	
	3. Black Dyke Mills	William Halliwell	
1936	Open		
	1. Brighouse & Rastrick	William Halliwell	Henry Geehl, *Robin*
	2. Abram Colliery	John A. Greenwood	*Hood*
	3. Luton Red Cross Silver	Harry Mortimer	

Contest		Conductor	Test piece
1936	National		
	1. Foden Motor Works	Fred Mortimer	Arthur Bliss,
	2. Black Dyke Mills	William Halliwell	*Kenilworth*
	3. Friary Brewery (Guildford)	John A. Greenwood	
1937	Open		
	1. Besses o' th' Barn	William Wood	Brahms
	2. Slaithwaite	Noel Thorpe	(arr. D. Wright),
	3. Black Dyke Mills	William Halliwell	*Academic Festival Overture*
1937	National		
	1. Foden Motor Works	Fred Mortimer	Herbert Howells,
	2. Munn & Felton's Works	William Halliwell	*Pageantry*
	3. Black Dyke Mills	William Halliwell	
1938	Open		
	1. Slaithwaite	Noel Thorpe	Maldwyn Price, *Owain*
	2. Black Dyke Mills	William Halliwell	*Glyndwr*
	3. Luton Red Cross Silver	Fred Mortimer	
1938	National		
	1. Foden Motor Works	Fred Mortimer	Percy Fletcher, *An Epic*
	2. Bickershaw Colliery	William Haydock	*Symphony*
	3. Black Dyke Mills	William Halliwell	
1939	Open		
	1. Wingates Temperance	William Wood	John Ireland, *A*
	2. Nelson Old	C. Smith	*Downland Suite*
	3. Brighouse & Rastrick	Noel Thorpe	
1939	National		
	NO CONTEST		
1940	Open		
	1. Bickershaw Colliery	William Haydock	Joseph Holbrooke,
	2. Creswell Colliery	Harold Moss	*Clive of India*
	3. Brighouse & Rastrick	Fred Berry	
1940	National		
	NO CONTEST		
1941	Open		
	1. Fairey Aviation Works	Harry Mortimer	(*a*) Brahms (arr. D.
	2. Carlton Main Frickley Colliery	Albert Badrick	Wright), *Academic Festival Overture*; or
	3. City of Coventry	Harry Heyes	(*b*) Geehl, *Robin Hood*; or (*c*) Keighley, *The Crusaders*
1941	National		
	NO CONTEST		

Contest		Conductor	Test piece
1942	Open		
	1. Fairey Aviation Works	Harry Mortimer	(*a*) Keighley, *Lorenzo*;
	2. Bickershaw Colliery	William Haydock	or (*b*) Howells,
	3. City of Coventry	Harry Heyes	*Pageantry*
1942	National		
	NO CONTEST		
1943	Open		
	1. Bickershaw Colliery	William Haydock	Beethoven (arr. D.
	2. Fairey Aviation Works	Harry Mortimer	Wright), Themes from
	3. Creswell Colliery	Harold Moss	Symphony No. 5
1943	National		
	NO CONTEST		
1944	Open		
	1. Fairey Aviation Works	Harry Mortimer	Maurice Johnston, *The*
	2. Creswell Colliery	Harold Moss	*Tempest*
	3. Bickershaw Colliery	William Haydock	
1944	National		
	NO CONTEST		
1945	Open		
	1. Fairey Aviation Works	Harry Mortimer	Kenneth Wright, *Pride*
	2. Grimethorpe Colliery	George Thompson	*of Race*
	Institute		
	3. Bickershaw Colliery	Harry Mortimer	
1945	National		
	1. Fairey Aviation Works	Harry Mortimer	Denis Wright, *Overture*
	2. Horden Colliery	William Lowes	*for an Epic Occasion*
	3. Parc & Dare Workmen's	Haydn Bebb	
1946	Open		
	1. Bickershaw Colliery	Harry Mortimer	Eric Ball, *Salute to*
	2. Fairey Aviation Works	Harry Mortimer	*Freedom*
	3. Munn & Felton's	Stanley	
	(Footwear)	Boddington	
1946	National		
	1. Brighouse & Rastrick	Eric Ball	Henry Geehl, *Oliver*
	2. Fairey Aviation Works	Harry Mortimer	*Cromwell*
	3. Munn & Felton's	Stanley	
	(Footwear)	Boddington	
1947	Open		
	1. Fairey Aviation Works	Harry Mortimer	Maldwyn Price,
	2. Wingates Temperance	Jack Eckersley	*Henry V*
	3. Creswell Colliery	Harold Moss	
1947	National		
	1. Black Dyke Mills	Harry Mortimer	Hubert Bath, *Freedom*
	2. Fairey Aviation Works	Harry Mortimer	
	3. Foden Motor Works	Fred Mortimer	

Contest		Conductor	Test piece
1948	Open		
	1. CWS Manchester	Eric Ball	Denis Wright, *Music for*
	2. Fairey Aviation Works	Harry Mortimer	*Brass*
	3. Carlton Main Frickley Colliery	Eric Ball	
1948	National		
	1. Black Dyke Mills	Harry Mortimer	Henry Geehl, *On the*
	2. Cory Workmen's Silver	Walter Hargreaves	*Cornish Coast*
	3. Brighouse & Rastrick	Eric Ball	
1949	Open		
	1. Fairey Aviation Works	Harry Mortimer	Dean Goffin, *Rhapsody*
	2. Ransome & Marles Works	Eric Ball	*in Brass*
	3. Munn & Felton's (Footwear)	Stanley Boddington	
1949	National		
	1. Black Dyke Mills	Harry Mortimer	John Ireland, *A Comedy*
	2. Foden Motor Works	Harry Mortimer	*Overture*
	3. Munn & Felton's (Footwear)	Stanley Boddington	
1950	Open		
	1. Fairey Aviation Works	Harry Mortimer	Eric Ball, *Resurgam*
	2. Cory Workmen's Silver	Walter Hargreaves	
	3. Carlton Main Frickley Colliery	George Hespe	
1950	National		
	1. Foden Motor Works	Harry Mortimer	Herbert Howells,
	2. Hanwell Silver	George Thompson	*Pageantry*
	3. CWS Manchester	Eric Ball	
1951	Open		
	1. Ransome & Marles Works	Eric Ball	Eric Ball, *The*
	2. Prescot Cable Works	J. Capper	*Conquerors*
	3. CWS Manchester	Eric Ball	
1951	National		
	1. Black Dyke Mills	Alex Mortimer	Percy Fletcher, *An Epic*
	2. Foden Motor Works	Harry Mortimer	*Symphony*
	3. Brighouse & Rastrick	Eric Ball	
1952	Open		
	1. CWS Manchester	Eric Ball	Henry Geehl, *Scena*
	2. Foden Motor Works	Harry Mortimer	*Sinfonica*
	3. Munn & Felton's (Footwear)	Stanley Boddington	

Contest		Conductor	Test piece
1952	National		
	1. Fairey Aviation Works	Harry Mortimer	Granville Bantock (arr.
	2. Foden Motor Works	Harry Mortimer	F. Wright), *The Frogs of*
	3. Black Dyke Mills	Alex Mortimer	*Aristophanes*
1953	Open		
	1. National Band of New Zealand	K. G. L. Smith	George Hespe, *The Three Musketeers*
	2. Fairey Aviation Works	Harry Mortimer	
	3. Black Dyke Mills	Alex Mortimer	
1953	National		
	1. Foden Motor Works	Harry Mortimer	G. Bailey (arr. F.
	2. CWS Manchester	Jack Atherton	Wright), *Diadem of*
	3. Creswell Colliery	George Hespe	*Gold*
1954	Open		
	1. Munn & Felton's (Footwear)	Stanley Boddington	Eric Ball, *Tournament for Brass*
	2. Ferodo Works	George Hespe	
	3. John White Footwear	George Thompson	
1954	National		
	1. Fairey Aviation Works	Harry Mortimer	Jack Beaver (arr. F.
	2. CWS Manchester	Alex Mortimer	Wright), *Sovereign*
	3. Foden Motor Works	Harry Mortimer	*Heritage*
1955	Open		
	1. Ferodo Works	George Hespe	Erik Leidzén,
	2. John White Footwear	George Thompson	*Sinfonietta for Brass*
	3. CWS Manchester	Alex Mortimer	*Band*
1955	National		
	1. Munn & Felton's (Footwear)	Harry Mortimer	Edric Cundell (arr. F. Wright), *Blackfriars*
	2. Ransome & Marles Works	Eric Ball	
	3. CWS Manchester	Alex Mortimer	
1956	Open		
	1. Fairey Aviation Works	Harry Mortimer	Denis Wright, *Tam O' Shanter's Ride*
	2. CWS Manchester	Alex Mortimer	
	3. Carlton Main Frickley Colliery	Jack Atherton	
1956	National		
	1. Fairey Aviation Works	George Willcocks	Eric Ball, *Festival Music*
	2. CWS Manchester	Alex Mortimer	
	3. Munn & Felton's (Footwear)	Stanley Boddington	

Contest		Conductor	Test piece
1957	Open		
	1. Black Dyke Mills	George Willcocks	Helen Perkin, *Carnival*
	2. Carlton Main Frickley Colliery	Jack Atherton	
	3. Foden Motor Works	Rex Mortimer	
1957	National		
	1. Munn & Felton's (Footwear)	Stanley Boddington	R. Vaughan Williams, *Variations for Brass Band*
	2. CWS Manchester	Alex Mortimer	
	3. Carlton Main Frickley Colliery	Jack Atherton	
1958	Open		
	1. Carlton Main Frickley Colliery	Jack Atherton	Eric Ball, *Sunset Rhapsody*
	2. Besses o' th' Barn	William Wood	
	3. Black Dyke Mills	George Willcocks	
1958	National		
	1. Foden Motor Works	Rex Mortimer	Edmund Rubbra, *Variations on 'The Shining River'*
	2. Scottish CWS	William Crozier	
	3. CWS Manchester	Alex Mortimer	
1959	Open		
	1. Besses o' th' Barn	William Wood	Eric Ball, *The Undaunted*
	2. Carlton Main Frickley Colliery	Jack Atherton	
	3. Morris Motors	Stanley Boddington	
1959	National		
	1. Black Dyke Mills	George Willcocks	Lalo (arr. F. Wright), *Le Roi d'Ys*
	2. Carlton Main Frickley Colliery	Jack Atherton	
	3. Foden Motor Works	Rex Mortimer	
1960	Open		
	1. CWS Manchester	Alex Mortimer	Mozart (arr. Sargent), *Fantasia*
	2. The Fairey Band	Leonard Lamb	
	3. Grimethorpe Colliery Institute	George Thompson	
1960	National		
	1. Munn & Felton's (Footwear)	Stanley Boddington	Herbert Howells, *Three Figures*
	2. Carlton Main Frickley Colliery	Jack Atherton	
	3. Black Dyke Mills	George Willcocks	
1961	Open		
	1. The Fairey Band	Leonard Lamb	Eric Ball, *Main Street*
	2. Wingates Temperance	Hugh Parry	

Contest		Conductor	Test piece
	3. Grimethorpe Colliery Institute	George Thompson	
1961	National		
	1. Black Dyke Mills	George Willcocks	Berlioz (arr. F. Wright),
	2. CWS Manchester	Alex Mortimer	*Les Francs Juges*
	3. Crossley's Carpet Works	J. Harrison	
1962	Open		
	1. The Fairey Band	Leonard Lamb	Helen Perkin, *Island*
	2. Ransome & Marles Works	George Hespe	*Heritage*
	3. Band of Yorkshire Imperial Metals	George Hespe	
1962	National		
	1. CWS Manchester	Alex Mortimer	Verdi (arr. F. Wright),
	2. Crossley's Carpet Works	J. Harrison	*The Force of Destiny*
	3. Ransome & Marles Works	George Hespe	
1963	Open		
	1. The Fairey Band	Leonard Lamb	Cyril Jenkins, *Life*
	2. Grimethorpe Colliery Institute	George Thompson	*Divine*
	3. Black Dyke Mills	Geoffrey Witham	
1963	National		
	1. CWS Manchester	Alex Mortimer	Arthur Bliss, *The*
	2. Brighouse & Rastrick	Walter Hargreaves	*Belmont Variations*
	3. GUS (Footwear)	Stanley Boddington	
1964	Open		
	1. Foden Motor Works	Rex Mortimer	Thomas Keighley,
	2. The Lindley Band	Leonard Lamb	*Lorenzo*
	3. BMC (Morris Motors)	Clifford Edmunds	
1964	National		
	1. GUS (Footwear)	Stanley Boddington	Gilbert Vinter,
			Variations on a Ninth
	2. Black Dyke Mills	Cecil H. Jaeger	
	3. CWS Manchester	Alex Mortimer	
1965	Open		
	1. The Fairey Band	Leonard Lamb	Cyril Jenkins, *Saga of*
	2. Brighouse & Rastrick	Walter Hargreaves	*the North*
	3. BMC (Morris Motors)	Clifford Edmunds	
1965	National		
	1. The Fairey Band	Leonard Lamb	Gilbert Vinter,
	2. Cammell Laird's Works	James Scott	*Trumphant Rhapsody*
	3. GUS (Footwear)	Stanley Boddington	

Contest		Conductor	Test piece
1966	Open		
	1. CWS Manchester	Alex Mortimer	John Ireland, *A*
	2. Band of Yorkshire	Trevor Walmsley	*Downland Suite*
	Imperial Metals		
	3. BMC (Morris Motors)	Clifford Edmunds	
1966	National		
	1. GUS (Footwear)	Stanley Boddington	Berlioz (arr. F. Wright), *Le Carnaval Romain*
	2. Black Dyke Mills	Cecil H. Jaeger	
	3. The Fairey Band	Leonard Lamb	
1967	Open		
	1. Grimethorpe Colliery Institute	Stanley Boddington	John Ireland, *A Comedy Overture*
	2. The Fairey Band	Leonard Lamb	
	3. Wingates Temperance	Hugh Parry	
1967	National		
	1. John Foster & Son Ltd. Black Dyke Mills	Geoffrey Brand	Eric Ball, *Journey into Freedom*
	2. CWS Manchester	Alex Mortimer	
	3. Brighouse & Rastrick	Walter Hargreaves	
1968	Open		
	1. John Foster & Son Ltd. Black Dyke Mills	Geoffrey Brand	Gilbert Vinter, *John O' Gaunt*
	2. Wingates Temperance	Hugh Parry	
	3. Grimethorpe Colliery Institute	George Thompson	
1968	National		
	1. Brighouse & Rastrick	Walter Hargreaves	Wagner (arr. F. Wright), Prelude from *The Mastersingers*
	2. John Foster & Son Ltd. Black Dyke Mills	Geoffrey Brand	
	3. GUS (Footwear)	Stanley Boddington	
1969	Open		
	1. Grimethorpe Colliery Institute	George Thompson	Gilbert Vinter, *Spectrum*
	2. Carlton Main Frickley Colliery	Jack Atherton	
	3. The Fairey Band	Kenneth Dennison	
1969	National		
	1. Brighouse & Rastrick	Walter Hargreaves	Eric Ball, *High Peak*
	2. John Foster & Son Ltd. Black Dyke Mills	Geoffrey Brand	
	3. CWS Manchester	Alex Mortimer	

Contest		Conductor	Test piece
1970	Open		
	1. Band of Yorkshire Imperial Metals	Trevor Walmsley	Herbert Howells, *Pageantry*
	2. CWS Manchester	Alex Mortimer	
	3. Foden Motor Works	Rex Mortimer	
1970	National		
	1. Grimethorpe Colliery Institute	George Thompson	Gordon Jacob, *Pride of Youth*
	2. Ransome Hoffman Pollard	Dennis Masters	
	3. Hanwell	Eric Bravington	
1971	Open		
	1. Band of Yorkshire Imperial Metals	Trevor Walmsley	Eric Ball, *Festival Music*
	2. John Foster & Son Ltd. Black Dyke Mills	Geoffrey Brand	
	3. Grimethorpe Colliery Institute	George Thompson	
1971	National		
	1. Wingates Temperance	Dennis Smith	Lalo (arr. F. Wright), *Le Roi d'Ys*
	2. City of Coventry	Albert Chappell	
	3. The Cory Band	Arthur Kenney	
1972	Open		
	1. John Foster & Son Ltd. Black Dyke Mills	Geoffrey Brand	Jack Beever, *Sovereign Heritage*
	2. Carlton Main Frickley Colliery	Robert Oughton	
	3. The Cory Band	Arthur Kenney	
1972	National		
	1. John Foster & Son Ltd. Black Dyke Mills	Geoffrey Brand	Eric Ball, *A Kensington Concerto*
	2. GUS (Footwear)	Stanley Boddington	
	3. Grimethorpe Colliery Institute	Elgar Howarth	
1973	Open		
	1. John Foster & Son Ltd. Black Dyke Mills	Roy Newsome	César Franck (arr. Siebert), *The Accursed Huntsman*
	2. Grimethorpe Colliery Institute	Elgar Howarth	
	3. Brighouse & Rastrick	James Scott	
1973	National		
	1. Brighouse & Rastrick	James Scott	Hubert Bath, *Freedom*
	2. CWS Manchester	Derek Garside	

Contest		Conductor	Test piece
	3. John Foster & Son Ltd. Black Dyke Mills	Roy Newsome	
1974	Open		
	1. John Foster & Son Ltd. Black Dyke Mills	Roy Newsome	Gilbert Vinter, *James Cook—*
	2. Stanshawe (Bristol)	Walter Hargreaves	*Circumnavigator*
	3. GUS (Footwear)	Stanley Boddington	
1974	National		
	1. The Cory Band	Arthur Kenney	Malcolm Arnold,
	2. Grimethorpe Colliery Institute	Elgar Howarth	*Fantasy for Brass Band*
	3. John Foster & Son Ltd. Black Dyke Mills	Roy Newsome	
1975	Open		
	1. Wingates Temperance	Richard Evans	Elgar Howarth,
	2. The Fairey Band	Kenneth Denison	*Fireworks*
	3. Band of Yorkshire Imperial Metals	Trevor Walmsley	
1975	National		
	1. John Foster & Son Ltd. Black Dyke Mills	Peter Parkes	Robert Farnon, *Une vie de matelot*
	2. Stanshawe (Bristol)	Walter Hargreaves	
	3. Brighouse & Rastrick	James Scott	
1976	Open		
	1. John Foster & Son Ltd. Black Dyke Mills	Peter Parkes	Percy Fletcher, *An Epic Symphony*
	2. Stanshawe (Bristol)	Walter Hargreaves	
	3. Brighouse & Rastrick	Maurice Handford	
1976	National		
	1. John Foster & Son Ltd. Black Dyke Mills	Peter Parkes	Eric Ball, *Sinfonietta: The Wayfarer*
	2. Band of Yorkshire Imperial Metals	Trevor Walmsley	
	3. Wingates Temperance	Richard Evans	
1977	Open		
	1. John Foster & Son Ltd. Black Dyke Mills	Peter Parkes	G. Bailey (arr. F. Wright), *Diadem of Gold*
	2. Brighouse & Rastrick	Derek Broadbent	
	3. Fairey Engineering Works	Richard Evans	
1977	National		
	1. John Foster & Son Ltd. Black Dyke Mills	Peter Parkes	Edward Gregson, *Connotations for Brass Band*
	2. Grimethorpe Colliery Institute	Gerard Schwarz	

Contest		Conductor	Test piece
	3. Band of Yorkshire Imperial Metals	Dennis Carr	
1978	Open		
	1. Brighouse & Rastrick	Geoffrey Brand	Berlioz (arr. F. Wright),
	2. John Foster & Son Ltd. Black Dyke Mills	Peter Parkes	*Benvenuto Cellini*
	3. Ransome Hoffman Pollard	Stephen Shimwell	
1978	National		
	1. Band of Yorkshire Imperial Metals	Denis Carr	Bliss (arr. Ball), Four dances from *Checkmate*
	2. Besses o' th' Barn	Roy Newsome	
	3. Grimethorpe Colliery Institute	Stanley Boddington	
1979	Open		
	1. Fairey Engineering Works	Walter Hargreaves	Berlioz (arr. F. Wright), *Le Carnaval Romain*
	2. Desford Colliery	Howard Snell	
	3. Grimethorpe Colliery	Elgar Howarth	
1979	National		
	1. John Foster & Son Ltd. Black Dyke Mills	Peter Parkes	Robert Simpson, *Volcano*
	2. The Cory Band	Denzil Stephens	
	3. Birmingham School of Music	Roy Curran	
1980	Open		
	1. Band of Yorkshire Imperial Metals	John Pryce-Jones	Robert Simpson, *Energy*
	2. GUS (Footwear)	Keith Wilkinson	
	3. Desford Colliery	Howard Snell	
1980	National		
	1. Brighouse & Rastrick	Derek Broadbent	Dvořák (arr. Brand), *Carnival*
	2. John Foster & Son Ltd. Black Dyke Mills	Peter Parkes	
	3. Fairey Engineering Works	Walter Hargreaves	
1981	Open		
	1. City of Coventry	Arthur Kenney	Gilbert Vinter, *Variations on a Ninth*
	2. Leyland Vehicles	Richard Evans	
	3. Foden Motor Works	Howard Snell	
1981	National		
	1. John Foster & Son Ltd. Black Dyke Mills	Peter Parkes	Elgar (arr. Ball), *Froissart*
	2. Brighouse & Rastrick	Derek Broadbent	
	3. Whitburn Miners Welfare	Geoffrey Whitham	

Contest		Conductor	Test piece
1982	Open		
	1. Besses o' th' Barn	Roy Newsome	Herbert Howells, *Three*
	2. Fairey Engineering Works	Geoffrey Brand	*Figures*
	3. GUS (Footwear)	Keith Wilkinson	
1982	National		
	1. The Cory Band	Arthur Kenney	John McCabe, *Images*
	2. John Foster & Son Ltd. Black Dyke Mills	Peter Parkes	
	3. Brodsworth Colliery	David James	
1983	Open		
	1. John Foster & Son plc Black Dyke Mills	Peter Parkes	Edward Gregson, *Connotations*
	2. Brighouse & Rastrick	James Watson	
	3. Grimethorpe Colliery Institute	James Scott	
1983	National		
	1. The Cory Band	Arthur Kenney	Joseph Horovitz, *Ballet*
	2. John Foster & Son plc Black Dyke Mills	Peter Parkes	*for Band*
	3. GUS (Footwear)	Keith Wilkinson	
1984	Open		
	1. Grimethorpe Colliery Institute	Geoffrey Brand	John Ireland, *A Comedy Overture*
	2. John Foster & Son plc Black Dyke Mills	Peter Parkes	
	3. Fairey Engineering Works	Howard Williams	
1984	National		
	1. The Cory Band	Arthur Kenney	Edward Gregson,
	2. Sun Life	Christopher Adey	*Dances and Arias*
	3. Leyland Vehicles	Richard Evans	
1985	Open		
	1. John Foster & Son plc Black Dyke Mills	Peter Parkes	Gilbert Vinter, *Salute to Youth*
	2. British Aerospace Wingates	James Scott	
	3. Foden OTS	Howard Snell	
1985	National		
	1. John Foster & Son plc Black Dyke Mills	Peter Parkes	Stephen Bulla, *Cityscapes*
	2. Desford Colliery Dowty	Howard Snell	
	3. IMI Yorkshire Imperial	James Scott	

Contest		Conductor	Test piece
1986	Open		
	1. John Foster & Son plc Black Dyke Mills	Peter Parkes	Percy Fletcher, *An Epic Symphony* (2 movts.);
	2. Fairey Engineering Works	Roy Newsome	Howard Blake, *Fusions*
	3. GUS (Kettering)	Bramwell Tovey	
1986	National		
	1. Fairey Engineering Works	Roy Newsome	Derek Bourgeois, *Diversions*
	2. John Foster & Son plc Black Dyke Mills	Peter Parkes	
	3. Sun Life	Rob Wiffin	
1987	Open		
	1. Williams Fairey Engineering	Roy Newsome	Hubert Bath, *Freedom*
	2. Britannia Building Society Foden	Howard Snell	
	3. Grimethorpe Colliery Institute	David James	
1987	National		
	1. Desford Colliery Dowty	James Watson	Philip Sparke, *Harmony Music*
	2. John Foster & Son plc Black Dyke Mills	Peter Parkes	
	3. IMI Yorkshire Imperial	James Scott	
1988	Open		
	1. Rigid Containers Group	Bramwell Tovey	Wilfred Heaton, *Contest Music*
	2. Jaguar Cars (City of Coventry)	Ray Farr	
	3. Williams Fairey Engineering	Roy Newsome	
1988	National		
	1. Desford Colliery Dowty	James Watson	Ray Steadman-Allen, *Seascapes*
	2. Britannia Building Society Foden	Howard Snell	
	3. Jaguar Cars (City of Coventry)	Ray Farr	
1989	Open		
	1. Kennedy's Swinton Concert Brass	Garry Cutt	Derek Bourgeois, *Diversions*
	2. Hammonds Sauce Works	Geoffrey Whitham	
	3. Leyland DAF	Richard Evans	
1989	National		
	1. Desford Colliery Caterpillar	James Watson	Arthur Butterworth, *Odin*

Contest		Conductor	Test piece
	2. John Foster & Son plc Black Dyke Mills	David King	
	3. Murray International Whitburn	James Scott	
1990	Open		
	1. Sun Life	Roy Newsome	Lalo (arr. F. Wright), *Le Roi d'Ys*
	2. Leyland DAF	Richard Evans	
	3. Grimethorpe Colliery	Frank Renton	
1990	National		
	1. CWS Glasgow	John Hudson	George Lloyd, *English Heritage*
	2. Britannia Building Society	Howard Snell	
	3. Sellers Engineering	Phillip McCann	
1991	Open		
	1. Grimethorpe Colliery	Frank Renton	Philip Wilby, *Paganini Variations*
	2. Williams Fairey Engineering	Peter Parkes	
	3. Leyland DAF	Richard Evans	
1991	National		
	1. Desford Colliery Caterpillar	James Watson	Robert Simpson, *Energy*
	2. Britannia Building Society	Howard Snell	
	3. Grimethorpe Colliery	Frank Renton	
1992	Open		
	1. John Foster & Son plc Black Dyke Mills	James Watson	John McCabe, *Cloudcatcher Fells*
	2. BNFL	Richard Evans	
	3. Williams Fairey Engineering	Peter Parkes	
1992	National		
	1. Grimethorpe Colliery	Frank Renton	Philip Wilby, *The New Jerusalem*
	2. Desford Colliery Caterpillar	Stephen Roberts	
	3. Williams Fairey Engineering	Peter Parkes	
1993	Open		
	1. Williams Fairey Engineering	Peter Parkes	Philip Wilby, *Masquerade*
	2. Black Dyke Mills	James Watson	
	3. CWS Glasgow	Frans Violet	

Contest		Conductor	Test piece
1993	National		
	1. Williams Fairey Engineering	Peter Parkes	Derek Bourgeois, *The Devil and the Deep Blue Sea*
	2. Tredegar	John Hudson	
	3. Sun Life	Roy Newsome	
1994	Open		
	1. BNFL	Richard Evans	John McCabe,
	2. Black Dyke Mills	James Watson	*Salamander*
	3. Grimethorpe Colliery	Garry Cutt	
1994	National		
	1. Black Dyke Mills	James Watson	Joseph Horovitz, *Theme*
	2. Williams Fairey	Peter Parkes	*and Co-operation*
	3. Yorkshire Building Society	David King	
1995	Open		
	1. Black Dyke Mills	James Watson	Philip Wilby, *Revelation*
	2. Williams Fairey Engineering	James Gourlay	
	3. Yorkshire Building Society	David King	
1995	National		
	1. Black Dyke Mills	James Watson	Elgar Howarth, *Songs*
	2. Yorkshire Building Society	David King	*for BL*
	3. Desford Colliery	Peter Parkes	
1996	Open		
	1. Marple	Garry Cutt	Edward Elgar, *Severn*
	2. Tredegar	Nicholas Childs	*Suite*
	3. BNFL	Richard Evans	
1996	National		
	1. CWS Glasgow	Howard Snell	Robert Redhead,
	2. Grimethorpe Colliery	Peter Parkes	*Isaiah 40*
	3. Black Dyke Mills	James Watson	
1997	Open		
	1. Yorkshire Building Society	David King	Michael Ball, *Whitsun Wakes*
	2. Williams Fairey	James Gourlay	
	3. CWS Glasgow	Howard Snell	
1997	National		
	1. Brighouse & Rastrick	Allan Withington	Peter Graham, *On*
	2. Williams Fairey	James Gourlay	*Alderley Edge*
	3. Fodens (Courtois)	Nicholas Childs	

A NOTE ON DISCOGRAPHIES
AND RECORDINGS

⌘

There has always been a buoyant market for recordings of British brass bands, and almost every area of brass band repertoire has been represented on recordings, which are available either in the current catalogues or in private or public collections such as the archives of recording companies and the British Library. A comprehensive catalogue of all brass band recordings made in the non-microgroove era (before 1960) is given in Frank Andrews's *Brass Band Cylinder and Non-microgroove Disc Recordings 1903–1960* (Winchester: Piccolo Press, 1997). The existence of this volume obviates the need for further discographies of brass band recordings during this period.

More selective discographies of later recordings are given in Arthur Taylor's *Brass Bands* (St Albans and London: Granada Publishing, 1979), appendix III; in P. Gammond and R. Horricks, *Music on Record*, i. *Brass Bands* (Cambridge: Stephens, 1980); and in Mark J. Fasman, *Brass Bibliography* (Bloomington and Indianapolis: Indiana University Press, 1990).

Recordings issued on compact discs are easily found through the standard printed and on-line catalogues, such as that of the British Library National Sound Archive and the Library of Congress Recorded Sound Reference Center. There is also a web-site for the Association for Recorded Sound Collections, Inc.

The sole attempt to create the sound of a Victorian brass band is to be found on the Wallace Collection period instrument recording of a selection of the music from the Cyfarthfa Band library, *The Origin of the Species: Virtuoso Victorian Brass Music from Cyfarthfa Castle, Wales*, Nimbus NI5470. An excellent reconstruction of early rural church band (not brass band) music is given on *Under the Greenwood Tree: The Carols and Dances of Hardy's Wessex Played on Authentic Instruments by the Mellstock Band*, Saydisc CD-SDL 360. *The Voice of the People* (ed. Reg Hall, Topic Records TSCD 651–670, 1998), is an indispensable set of 20 CDs of traditional performance recordings.

The Salvation Army has released an excellent compilation of recordings of several of its best bands under the title *The Old Wells: Favourites from the 78rpm Era*, i, Salvationist Publishing & Supplies Ltd, SPS 116 CD.

Period instrument recordings of American brass bands are more plentiful. One excellent example is a recording using instruments many of which are from the Smithsonian Institution, entitled *Our Musical Past*, i, Library of Congress, OMP 101/102.

Continental brass band music has also been recorded on period instruments, one such recording being the Royal Danish Brass's *Masterpieces for Brass*, i, Rondo, RCD 8322.

Important research on vernacular brass band practices in non-Western cultures, centred at the Department of Visual Anthropology at the University of Amsterdam, has resulted in a number of recordings which are available in the *Frozen Brass Anthology of Brass Band Music* series released by PAN records. These include volumes on: *Asia* (PAN 2020CD); *Africa and Latin America* (PAN 2026CD); and *Ifi Palas: Tongan Brass* (2044CD). This series, together with the excellent contextual notes by Rob Boonzajer Flaes which accompany each recording, makes a new and important contribution to the study of brass and other vernacular bands.

SELECT BIBLIOGRAPHY

— ❧ —

The first extensive critical work to be written on brass bands was *Talks with Bandsmen* (1895) by Algernon Rose. The next book of landmark importance was not published until 1936; this was Russell and Elliot's scholarly *The Brass Band Movement*. Several volumes published since the end of the Second World War have been valuable, but the most widely quoted general works are Arthur Taylor's *Brass Bands*, and Herbert (ed.), *Bands: The Brass Band Movement in the Nineteenth and Twentieth Centuries*, the volume from which the present work derives. I should emphasize however, that there is a growing body of reliable literature which casts light on brass band histories and practices. This includes the plethora of commemorative histories of individual bands. Many such works are unpublished, or published privately, and are for limited circulation only. These include:

BALDWIN, T., *Band of the Wellington Rifle Volunteer Corps (formerly Dawley Green Brass Band)*, 55pp. (1992).

—— *Dawley Green Brass Band Becomes the Wellington R V Corps Brass Band*, 30pp. (1993).

FOWLER, E. G., 'The Bristol Victoria Band', 2pp. (handwritten, *c.*1990).

GIBB, W., *Memories of Sixty Years in the Bathgate Band*, 6pp. (1989).

HINCHLEY, L., *The History of a Brass Band 1941–94*, 1 + 8pp. (1994): describes the history of the British Aerospace (Chadderton) Band.

PICKEN, T., *The History of Minchinhampton Town Band*, 16pp. (1977).

SMYTH, C., *A Brief History of Langsett Road Salvation Army Band*, 44pp. (1989).

The two most comprehensive studies of brass instruments and their history are Anthony Baines's *Brass Instruments*, and Trevor Herbert and John Wallace (eds.), *The Cambridge Companion to Brass Instruments*. Detailed coverage of individual brass instruments is also given in *The New Grove Dictionary of Musical Instruments*. The standard reference work on wind instrument manufacturers is William Waterhouse (ed.), *The New Langwill Index*, which also has excellent prefatory essays. Latterly the Historic Brass Society has sponsored a series of books dedicated to the study of brass instruments and related subjects; this series, which is published by Pendragon Books, New York, has the series title 'Bucina'.

There are a limited number of bibliographies of writings concerning brass instruments: Mark J. Fasman's *Brass Bibliography* (Bloomington and Indianapolis: Indiana University Press, 1990) is helpful, but it is not comprehensive, and as it was published in 1990, it does not contain more recent material. Since 1990, the Historic Brass Society Journal has contained a bibliography of writings about historic brass instruments which is compiled by David Lasocki. Successive volumes of *Grove's Dictionary of Music* have included entries on brass bands, as have more general histories of music, but future researchers will not find such articles especially illuminating. Of the more general volumes on the history of popular music and its practices, none have dealt with early bands more thoroughly than Dave Russell in his *Popular Music in England 1840–1914*. Two British Ph.D. theses on brass bands are especially helpful: Jack Scott's 'The Evolution of the Brass Band and its Repertoire in Northern England', and Michael J. Lomas's 'Amateur Brass and Wind Bands in Southern England between the Late Eighteenth Century and circa 1900'. There are, of course, many other works which are relevant to the study of brass bands, especially those which come from the growing scholarship on popular music, popular culture, and the history of leisure and recreation.

The *Musical Times* and the *Proceedings of the Royal Musical Association* are among mainstream British music periodicals which have occasionally carried articles on brass bands. The leading organological journal in Britain is the *Galpin Society Journal*, which has been published annually since 1946. The most widely respected journal on historic brass instruments, their practices and music, is the *Historic Brass Society Journal*, published in New York since 1989. *Brass Bulletin*, published in Moudin, Switzerland, since 1971, has a wide circulation among contemporary brass players throughout the world. Each of these journals has, from time to time, carried articles relevant to the subject of this book.

PERIODICALS

Specialist periodicals have been devoted to brass band since the nineteenth century. A list of the main such publications is given below. The details of their first appearance, and, where possible, their final issue, are given, but not all such information is available. Several publications which had brief lives are not mentioned, because critical data about them has evaded the key bibliographical indices, especially those of the British Library. Several such publications are known to have existed. These include the *Contest Mail* (a house journal of Boosey & Co.), and *Bandsmen of the World*, which Arthur Taylor identifies as having had only two editions. Other such periodicals are the *Cornet* (which was well known to Algernon Rose), the *Cornet Annual*, and *Brass Band Review*.

Specialist brass band periodicals which survive in archives in different stages of completeness are as follows. I have tried to identify changes of titles and mergers accurately. I should stress however, that the records of such changes are not always as complete and clear as one would wish them to be.

The Bandsman and Songster, 1907–37. From Jan. 1909, *The Bandsman, Songster and Local Officer of the Salvation Army*. 1385 nos. in 92 vols.; weekly. Continued as *The Musician of the Salvation Army*.

The Bandsman's World, 1929–30, 2 vols.

The Bandmaster, 1925, 1 vol.

Brass Band Annual, 1894–1910, 17 vols.; yearly.

Brass Band News, from ?1950 continued from *Wright & Round's Brass Band News*; monthly.

British Bandsman, from 1887/8. Also variously known as (from 1891, no. 40) *British Orchestral Times and Bandsman*; incorporated the *British Musician* in 1893 (no. 64) to form the *British Musician*; from 1899 the *Bandsman and Contest Field*. But most commonly known as the *British Bandsman*. Monthly, later weekly.

British Mouthpiece: Brass and Military Band Journal, from 1958 (Shuttleworth, Lancs.); weekly.

The Conductor (National Association of Brass Band Conductors), 1955–70, 16 vols.; quarterly. Continued as *Sounding Brass and The Conductor*.

Musical Mail and Advertiser (Scottish Band Associations), Newmilns 1905–7, Glasgow 1907–12, London 1912–30, 26 vols.; monthly. Combined with *Musical Progress* to form *MPM: Musical Progress and Mail*.

Musical Progress, 1906–30, 25 vols.; monthly. Combined with *Musical Mail and Advertiser* to form *MPM: Musical Progress and Mail*.

The Musician of the Salvation Army, from 1938; weekly. Continued from *The Bandsman and Songster*.

MPM: Musical Progress and Mail, 1930–53, 24 vols. Continued from *Musical Mail and Advertiser* and *Musical Progress*.

Sounding Brass and The Conductor (National Association of Brass Band Conductors), from 1971 (Sevenoaks: Novello); quarterly. Continued from *The Conductor*.

Wright & Round's Brass Band News, 1881–1958, 1969– . From ?1950 *Brass Band News* (Liverpool, later Gloucester: Wright and Round); monthly.

BOOKS AND ARTICLES

ADKINS, H. E., *Treatise on the Military Band*, revised edn. (London: Boosey and Hawkes, 1958).

ANDREWS, F., *Brass Band Cylinder and Non-microgroove Disc Recordings 1903–1960* (Winchester: Piccolo Press, 1997).

'Annual Brass Band Contest at the Zoological Gardens, Bellevue, Manchester', *Musical World*, 50 (1872), 607–8.

ANON., *Chromatic Scale for Ophicleide* (London, n.d.).

ANON., *Life and Career of the Late Mr Edwin Swift* (Milnsbridge, 1904).

ANON., *Méthode pour ophicléide, à neuf, dix et onze clés* (Paris, n.d.).

ANZENBERGER, F., 'Method Books for Keyed Trumpet in the Nineteenth Century: An Annontated Bibliography', *Historic Brass Society Journal*, 6 (1994), 1–10.

—— 'Method Books for Trumpet and Cornet Using Stopped Notes in the Nineteenth Century: An Annotated Bibliography', *Historic Brass Society Journal*, 7 (1995), 1–11.

ARBAN, J.-B., *Grande méthode complète pour cornet à pistons et de saxhorns* (Paris, 1864).

Bacup Band, *History of the Bacup Old Band* (Bacup: L. J. Priestley, 1908).

BAILEY, P., '"A Mingled Mass of Perfectly Legitimate Pleasures": The Victorian Middle Class and the Problem of Leisure', *Victorian Studies*, 21 (1977), 7–28.

—— *Leisure and Class in Victorian England* (London: Routledge & Kegan Paul, 1978).

BAILEY, V., 'Salvation Army Riots, the "Skeleton Army" and Legal Authority in the Provincial Towns', in A. P. Donajgrodzki (ed.), *Social Control in Nineteenth Century Britain* (London: Croom Helm, 1977), 231–45.

BAINBRIDGE, C., *Brass Triumphant* (London: Muller, 1980).

BAINES, A., *Brass Instruments: Their History and Development* (London: Faber, 1976, repr. 1980; New York and London: Dover Publications, and Constable and Co., 1993).

BANKS, M. D., *Elkhart's Brass Roots* (Vermillion, SD: The Shrine to Music Museum, University of South Dakota, 1994).

BARCLAY, R., *The Art of the Trumpet-maker* (Oxford: Clarendon Press, 1992).

BATE, P., *The Trumpet and Trombone* (London and New York: Ernest Benn, 1966).

BECKETT, I. F. W., *Riflemen Form: A Study of the Rifle Volunteer Movement 1859–1908* (Aldershot: Ogilby Trusts, 1982).

BEECHFIELD CARVER, P., *How to Arrange for Brass Bands* (Keith Prowse and Co., 1939).

BEVAN, C., *The Tuba Family* (London and New York: Faber, 1978).

—— 'The Saxtuba and Organological Vituperation', *Galpin Society Journal*, 43 (Mar. 1990), 135–46.

BINNS, Lt. Col. P. L., *A Hundred Years of Military Music* (Gillingham, Dorset: The Blackmore Press, 1959).

BOON, B., *Play the Music, Play! The Story of Salvation Army Bands* (London: Salvationist Publishing and Supplies, 1966; 2nd edn. 1978).

—— *Sing the Happy Song: A History of Salvation Army Vocal Music* (London: Salvationist Publishing and Supplies, 1978).

—— *ISB: The Story of the International Staff Band of The Salvation Army and the Development of its Music* (Bristol: Record Greetings Ltd., 1985).

BOONZAJER FLAES, R., 'The Minhassa Bamboo Brass Bands', *Brass Bulletin*, 77 (1992) 38–47.

BOOTH, G. D., 'Brass Bands: Tradition, Change and the Mass Media in Indian Wedding Music', *Ethnomusicology*, 34/2 (1990), 245–62.

BOOTH, W., *All About the Salvation Army* (London, 1882).

BRADLEY, I., 'Blowing for the Lord', *History Today*, 27/3 (1977), 190–5.

BRADWELL, C. R., *Symphony of Thanksgiving: The Life and Music of Commissioner Sir Dean Goffin* (Wellington, NZ: New Zealand and Fiji Territory of The Salvation Army, 1994).

BRAND, G., and BRAND, V., *Brass Bands in the Twentieth Century* (Letchworth: Egon, 1979).

BRAND, V., 'British Brass Bands: Amateur Music with a Professional Touch', *The Instrumentalist*, 26 (Apr. 1972), 18–21.

Brass Band News, 'Brass Band Tuning' (Liverpool: Wright and Round, 1933).

BRIDGES, G. D., *Pioneers in Brass* (Detroit: Sherwood Publications, 1972).

British Bandsman, The Story of the National (Beaconsfield: British Bandsman, 1971).

BROWNLOW, Jr., J. A., *The Last Trumpet: A Survey of the History and Literature of the English Slide Trumpet* (Stuyvesant, NY: Pendragon Press, 1996).

BURGESS, D., *By Royal Command (The Story of Foden's Motor Works Band)* (Sandbach, 1977).

BYTHELL, D., 'Class, Community and Culture: The Case of the Brass Band in Newcastle', *Labour History* (Australia), 67 (1994), 149–50.

—— *Banding in the Dales: A Centenary History of Muker Silver Band* (Muker, Richmond: Muker Silver Band, 1997).

BYTHELL, D., 'Provinces versus Metropolis in the British Brass Band Movement in the Early Twentieth Century: The Case of William Rimmer and his Music', *Popular Music*, 16/2 (1997), 151–63.

CAMUS, R. F., *Military Music of the American Revolution* (Westerville, OH: Integrity Press, 1975).

CARSE, A., 'Brass bands', *Monthly Musical Record*, 58 (1928), 327.

—— *The Life of Jullien* (Cambridge: Heffer, 1951).

CATELINET, P., 'The British Concept of Brass', *The School Musician*, 29 (Feb. 1958), 10.

CIPOLLA, F. J., and HUNSBERGER, D., *The Wind Ensemble and its Repertoire* (Rochester, NY: University of Rochester Press, 1994).

COLLINS, J., 'The Early History of West African Highlife Music', *Popular Music*, 8/2 (1989), 221–30.

COOK, K. (ed. and compiler), *Oh, Listen to the Band* (London and New York: Hinrichsen Editions Ltd., 1950).

—— (compiler), *The Bandsman's Everything Within* (London and New York: Hinrichsen Editions Ltd., 1950).

—— and CAISELY, L., *Music Through the Brass Band* (London and New York: Hinrichsen Editions Ltd., 1953).

COOKE, P. M., *Eric Ball: The Man and His Music* (Baldock: Egon, 1991).

COOPER, T. L., *Brass Bands of Yorkshire* (Clapham, Yorks.: Dalesman Books, 1974).

COPLAN, D., 'Go to My Town, Cape Coast! The Social History of Ghanaian Highlife', in B. Nettl (ed.), *Eight Urban Musical Cultures: Tradition and Change* (Urbana, IL.: University of Illinois Press, 1978), 96–114.

—— *In Township Tonight! South Africa's Black City Music and Theatre* (London and New York: Longman, 1985).

COPLEY, I. A., 'Warlock on the Brass Band', *Musical Times*, 109 (Dec. 1968), 1115–16.

COUTTS, F., *The History of the Salvation Army*, vi and vii (London: Hodder and Stoughton, 1973 and 1986). See Sandall for vols. i–iii, and Wiggins for vols. iv and v.

CROFT-MURRAY, E., 'The Wind Band in England', in T. C. Mitchell (ed.), *Music and Civilization* (British Museum Yearbook, 4; London: British Museum Publications Ltd., 1980), 135–63.

CROKE, L. (ed.), *The Standard Directory of Brass and Military Bands* (London: Musical Distributors, 1939).

DEAN, F., *The Magic of Black Dyke* (no place, no publisher, 1980).

DICKENS, C. (?), 'A Musical Prize Fight', *All the Year Round* (12 Nov. 1859), 65–8.

DUDGEON, R. T., 'Keyed Bugle Method Books: Documents of Transition in Nineteenth-Century Brass Instrument Performance Practice and Aesthetics in England', *Historic Brass Society Journal*, 2 (1990), 112–22.

—— *The Keyed Bugle* (Metuchen, NJ, and London: Scarecrow Press, 1993).

DUNNIGAN, J., *Broxburn Silver Band: The First Hundred Years* (Broxburn: Broxburn Silver Band, 1992).

DUTTON, B., 'British Brass Band Championships', *TUBA Journal*, 7/4 (Spring 1980), 11–14.

EBY, W. M., *Eby's Complete Scientific Method for Cornet and Trumpet* (Buffalo, NY: Virtuoso Music School, 1926).

EHRLICH, C., *The Music Profession in England since the Eighteenth Century: A Social History* (Oxford: Clarendon Press, 1985).

ELBOURNE, R., *Music and Tradition in Early Industrial Lancashire 1780–1840* (Woodbridge: Brewer, 1980).

ELLIOT, J. H., 'The All-Brass Ensemble', *Music and Letters*, 12 (1931), 30–4.

—— 'Music for Brass', *Monthly Musical Record*, 62 (1932), 105–6.

—— 'Brass Music in Development', *Monthly Musical Record*, 67 (1937), 34–5.

ELSTOW, V., *A Century of Brass: A History of Wellingborough Salvation Army Band* (Wellingborough: Vic Elstow, 1990).

EVANS, V. (compiler), *Durham County Brass Band League: Golden Jubilee 1940–1990* ([Durham]: County Durham Books with Southgate Publishers, 1992).

FARMER, H. G., *Memoirs of the Royal Artillery Band* (London: Boosey and Co., 1904).

—— *The Rise and Development of Military Music* (London: W. M. Reeves, 1912; revised edn. 1970).

—— *History of the Royal Artillery Band, 1762–1953* (London: Royal Artillery Institution, 1954).

FASMAN M. J., *Brass Bibliography* (Bloomington and Indianapolis: Indiana University Press, 1990).

Fodens Motor Works Band, *The History of Foden's Motor Works Band* (Sandbach: Fodens Ltd., 1936).

FRIEDRICHS, H., *The Romance of the Salvation Army* (London: Cassell and Co., 1907).

GAMMON, V., '"Babylonian Performances": The Rise and Suppression of Popular Church Music, 1660–1870', in E. Yeo and S. Yeo (eds.), *Popular Culture and Class Conflict 1590–1914* (Brighton: Harvester, 1981), 62–88.

—— 'Popular Music in Rural Society: Sussex 1815–1914', D.Phil. thesis, University of Sussex, 1985.

GAMMOND, P., and HORRICKS, R., *Music on Record*, i. *Brass Bands* (Cambridge: Stephens, 1980).

GIBB, W., *Memories of Sixty Years in the Bathgate Band* (limited distribution, 1989).

GOLBY, J. M., and PURDUE, A. W., *The Civilisation of the Crowd* (London: Batsford, 1984).

GOLDMAN, R. F., *The Concert Band* (New York: Rinehart and Co. Inc., 1946).

HAILSTONE, A., *The British Bandsman Centenary Book: A Social History of Brass Bands* (Baldock: Egon, 1987).

HAMPSON, J. N., *Origin, History and Achievements of the Besses o' th' Barn Band* (Northampton: Jos. Rogers, 1893).

HARKER, D., *Fakesong: The Manufacture of British Folksong 1700 to the Present Day* (Milton Keynes: Open University Press, 1985).

HARPER, T., *Instructions for the Trumpet*, facsimile of the 1837 edn., with commentary on the life of Harper by John Webb and Scott Sorenson; foreword by John Webb (Homer, NY: Spring Tree Enterprises, 1988).

HAWEIS, H. R., *Music and Morals* (London: Strahan and Co., 1871).

HAZEN, M. H., and HAZEN, R. M., *The Music Men: An Illustrated History of Brass Bands in America, 1800–1920* (Washington, DC: Smithsonian Institution Press, 1987).

HEINS, E., 'Kroncong and Tanjidor: Two Cases of Urban Folk Music in Jakarta', *Asian Music*, 7/1 (1975), 20–32.

HERBERT, T., 'The Trombone in Britain before 1800', Ph.D. thesis, The Open University, 1984.

—— 'The Virtuosi of Merthyr', *Llafur: The Journal of Welsh Labour History* (Aug. 1988), 60–9.

—— 'The Repertory of a Victorian Provincial Brass Band', *Popular Music*, 9/1 (1990), 117–32.

—— (ed.), *Bands: The Brass Band Movement in the Nineteenth and Twentieth Centuries* (Milton Keynes: Open University Press, 1991).

—— 'A Lament for Sam Hughes: The Last Ophicleidist', *Planet: The Welsh Internationalist* (July 1991), 66–75.

—— 'Victorian Brass Bands: The Establishment of a Working-Class Musical Tradition', *Historic Brass Society Journal*, 4 (1992), 1–11.

—— 'Late Victorian Welsh Bands and Cymmrodorion Attitudes/Bandiau cymreig y cyfnod Fictoraidd diweddar: chwaeth, pencampwriaeth ac agweddau'r Cymmrodorion', *Welsh Music History*, 1 (ed. John Harper and Wyn Thomas; 1996), 92–103.

—— 'The Reconstruction of Nineteenth-Century Band Repertory: Towards a Protocol', in S. Carter (ed.), *Perspectives in Brass Scholarship: Proceedings of the International Historic Brass Symposium, Amherst, 1995* (Bucina: The Historic Brass Society Series, 2; Stuyvesant, NY: Pendragon Press, 1997), 185–213.

—— 'Victorian Brass Bands: Class, Taste and Space', in G. Reynolds *et al.* (eds.), *The Place of Music: Music, Space and the Production of Place* (New York and London: Guilford/Longman, 1998), 104–28.

—— and MYERS, A., 'Instruments of the Cyfarthfa Band', *Galpin Society Journal*, 41 (1988), 2–10.

—— and SARKISSIAN, M., 'Victorian Bands and their Dissemination in the Colonies', *Popular Music*, 16/2 (1997), 167–81.

—— and WALLACE, J. (eds.), *The Cambridge Companion to Brass Instruments* (Cambridge: Cambridge University Press, 1997).

HEYDE, H., *Das Ventilblasinstrument, seine Entwicklung im deutschsprächigen Raum von den Anfangen bis zur Gegenwart* (Leipzig: VEB Deutscher Verlag für Music, 1987).

—— 'Brass Instrument Making in Berlin from the Seventeenth to the Twentieth Century: A Survey', *Historic Brass Society Journal*, 3 (1991), 43–7.

HIND, H. C., *The Brass Band* (London: Hawkes and Son, 1934; republished 1952).

HOBSBAWM, E., and RANGER, T. (eds.), *The Invention of Tradition* (Cambridge: Cambridge University Press, 1983).

HOGARTH, G., *Musical History: Biography and Criticism* (London: John W. Parker, 1835).

—— and WILLS, W. H., 'Music in Humble Life', *Household Words* (11 May 1850), 161–4.

HOLLINSHEAD, K., *The Major and His Band: The Story of Abram/Bickershaw Colliery Band* (Bradford: Kirklees Music, 1994).

Select Bibliography

HOLST, I., *The Music of Gustav Holst*, 2nd edn. (London: Oxford University Press, 1968).

HOLZ, R. E., 'The Salvation Army's Premier Band: The International Staff Band of London, England', *The School Musician*, 28 (Apr. 1957), 24–5.

HOLZ, R. W., 'A History of the Hymn Tune Meditation and Related Forms in Salvation Army Instrumental Music in Great Britain and North America 1880–1980', Ph.D. thesis, University of Connecticut, 1981.

—— *Heralds of Victory: A History Celebrating the 100th Anniversary of The New York Staff Band and Male Chorus 1887–1987* (New York: The Salvation Army, 1986).

HOOVER, C. A., 'A Trumpet Battle at Niblo's Pleasure Garden', *Musical Quarterly*, 55/3 (1969), 384–95.

Horniman Museum, *Wind Instruments of European Art Music* (Horniman Museum: London, 1974).

HORRIDGE, G. K., *The Salvation Army, Origins and Early Days: 1865–1900* (Godalming: Ammonite Books, 1993).

HORWOOD, W., *Adolphe Sax: His Life and Legacy* (Baldock: Egon, 1983).

HOWARTH, E., and HOWARTH, P., *What a Performance: The Brass Band Plays* (London: Robson, 1988).

IHC, *The Salvation War* (London: Salvation Army Book Depot, 1883).

Irwell Springs Band, *Irwell Springs (Bacup) Band* (Bacup: Bacup Times, 1914).

JACKSON, B., *Working Class Community* (London: Routledge and Kegan Paul, 1968).

JACKSON, E., 'Origin and Promotion of Brass Band Contests', *Musical Opinion and Music Trade Review* (1896: serialized).

JOHNSON, W. V., 'The British Brass Band', *The Instrumentalist*, 34 (Nov. 1979), 25–9.

KEANE, E., *Music for a Hundred Years: The Story of the House of Paling* (Sydney: O. Ziegler, 1954).

KINNISON BOURKE, J., *The History of a Village Band 1896–1996* (Heathfield, East Sussex: Warbleton and Buxted Band, 1996).

LAFOSSE, A., *Méthode complète de trombone à coulisse*, 2 vols. (Paris: Éditions Musicales Alphonse Leduc, n.d.).

LANGEY, O., *Complete Method for Trombone* (London: Boosey and Hawkes, n.d.).

LASOCKI, D., 'A Bibliography of Writings about Historic Brass Instruments, 1988–89,' *Historic Brass Society Journal*, 2 (1990), 190–202. [First of a series which appears annually in the *HBSJ*.]

LEE, E., *Music of the People* (London: Barrie and Jenkins, 1970).

LEIDZÉN, E., 'Some Brass Tacks about Brass Bands', *The Instrumentalist*, 15 (Nov. 1960), 45–6.

LITTLEMORE, A. (ed.), *The Rakeway Brass Band Yearbook 1987* (Hollington: Rakeway Music, 1987).

LIVINGS, H., *That the Medals and the Baton be Put on View* (Newton Abbot: David and Charles, 1975).

LODGE, E. A., *The Brass Band at a Glance* (Huddersfield: Lodge, 1895).

LOMAS, M. J., 'Militia and Volunteer Wind Bands in Southern England in the Late Eighteenth and Early Nineteenth Centuries', *Journal of the Society for Army Historical Research*, 67/271 (Autumn 1989), 154–66.

—— 'Amateur Brass and Wind Bands in Southern England between the Late Eighteenth Century and circa 1900', 2 vols., Ph.D. thesis, The Open University, 1990.

—— 'Secular Civilian Amateur Wind Bands in Southern England in the Late Eighteenth and Early Nineteenth Centuries', *Galpin Society Journal*, 45 (Mar. 1992), 78–98.

LUSHER, D., *The Don Lusher Book* (Baldock: Egon, 1985).

MCDERMOTT, K. H., *Sussex Church Music in the Past* (Chichester: Moore and Wingham, 1923).

MCEWEN, J., 'The Newcastle Coalmining District of New South Wales, 1860–1900', Ph.D. thesis, University of Sydney, 1979.

MACKERNESS, E. D., *A Social History of English Music* (London: Routledge and Kegan Paul, 1964).

MACTAGGART, P., and MACTAGGART, A., *Musical Instruments in the 1851 Exhibition* (Welwyn: Mac & Me, 1986).

MAMMINGA, M. A., 'British Brass Bands', Ph.D. thesis, Florida State University, 1973.

MARR, R. A., *Music and Musicians at the Edinburgh International Exhibition 1886* (Edinburgh: T. and A. Constable, 1887).

—— *Music for the People: A Retrospect of the Glasgow International Exhibition, 1888* (Edinburgh and Glasgow: John Menzies, 1889).

MARTIN, S. H., 'Brass Bands and the Beni Phenomenon in Urban East Africa', *Africa Music*, 7/1 (1991), 72–81.

MAYER, F. N., 'Early Band Music in the United States', *Music Educators National Conference Journal* (Feb.–Mar. 1959), 40–2.

MILLER, G., *The Military Band* (London: Novello and Co., 1912).

MILLINGTON, W. H., *Sketches of Local Musicians and Musical Societies* (Pendlebury, 1884).

MONTEFIORE, C. S., *A History of the Volunteer Force: From Earliest Times to the Year 1860* (London, 1908).

MORLEY PEGGE, R., *The French Horn* (London: Ernest Benn, 1960).

MORTIMER, H., with LYNTON, A., *Harry Mortimer on Brass* (Sherborne: Alphabooks, 1981).

MUSGRAVE, M., *The Musical Life of the Crystal Palace* (Cambridge: Cambridge University Press, 1995).

Musical Times, 'The National Brass Band Festival', 77 (1936), 936–7.

MYERS, A., *The Glen Account Book 1838–1853* (Edinburgh: Edinburgh University Collection of Historic Musical Instruments, 1985).

—— (ed.), *Historic Musical Instruments in the Edinburgh University Collection: Catalogue of the Edinburgh University Collection of Historic Musical Instruments*, II, part H, fascicle i: *Horns and Bugles* (Edinburgh, 1992; 2nd edn., 1997); fascicle ii: *Cornets and Tubas* (Edinburgh, 1994); fascicle iii: *Trumpets and Trombones* (Edinburgh, 1993); fascicle iv: *Small Mouthpieces for Brass Instruments* (Edinburgh, 1995); fascicle v: *Large Mouthpieces for Brass Instruments* (Edinburgh, 1995).

—— and TOMES, F., 'PCB Cornets and Webster Trumpets: Rudall Carte's Patent Conical Bore Brasswind', *Historic Brass Society Journal*, 7 (1995), 107–22.

NETTEL, R., 'The Influence of the Industrial Revolution on English Music', *Proceedings of the RMA* (1945–6), 23–40.

NEWCOMB, S. P., *The Music of the People: The Story of the Band Movement in New Zealand 1845–1963* (Christchurch: G. R. Mowat, 1963).

—— *Challenging Brass: 100 Years of Brass Band Contests in New Zealand 1880–1980* (Takapuna: Powerbrass Music Co. Ltd, 1980).

NEWSOME, R., *Doctor Denis: The Life and Times of Dr Denis Wright* (Baldock: Egon, 1995).

—— *Brass Roots: A Hundred Years of Brass Bands and Their Music* (Aldershot: Ashgate, 1998).

ORCHARD, W. A., *Music in Australia* (Melbourne: Georgian House, 1952).

ORD HUME, J., *Chats on Amateur Bands* (London, 1900).

—— and SOUTHERN, J., *History of St. Hilda's Band* (South Shields: St. Hilda's Band, 1927; subsequent edn., 1932).

PERRINS, B., *Brass Band Digest* (Baldock: Egon, 1985).

REHRIG, W. H., *The Heritage Encyclopedia of Band Music*, 2 vols. (Westerville, OH: Integrity Press, *c.*1991).

ROSE, A., *Talks with Bandsmen: A Popular Handbook for Brass Instrumentalists* (London: William Rider, 1895; facsimile with an introduction by Arnold Myers, London: Tony Bingham, 1995).

RUSSELL, D., 'The Popular Music Societies of the Yorkshire Textile District 1850–1914', D.Phil. thesis, University of York, 1979.

—— *Popular Music in England, 1840–1914: A Social History*, 2nd edn. (Manchester: Manchester University Press, 1997).

RUSSELL, J. F., and ELLIOT, J. H., *The Brass Band Movement* (London: J. M. Dent and Sons, 1936).

SADIE, S. (ed.), *The New Grove Dictionary of Music and Musicians* (London: Macmillan, 1980).

—— *The New Grove Dictionary of Musical Instruments* (London: Macmillan, 1984).

SANDALL, R., *The History of the Salvation Army*, i–iii (London: Nelson: 1947, 1950, and 1955). See Wiggins for vols. iv and v, and Coutts for vols. vi and vii.

SATOH, T., 'Salvation Army in Japan', *Brass Bulletin*, 52 (1985), 30–4.

SCHAFER, W. J., *Brass Bands and New Orleans Jazz* (Baton Rouge: Louisiana State University Press, 1979).

SCHLITZ, *Tutor for the Ophicleide (Bass and Alto)* (Modern Tutors for Wind Instruments, 12; London: R. Cocks and Co., 1853).

SCHOLES, P., *The Mirror of Music 1844–1944* (London: Novello, 1947).

SCOTT, J. L., 'The Evolution of the Brass Band and its Repertoire in Northern England', Ph.D. thesis, University of Sheffield, 1970.

SHAW, G. B., *London Music in 1888–89 as Heard by Corno Di Bassetto* (London: Constable and Co., 1937).

SHAW, G. B., *Shaw's Music: The Complete Musical Criticism*, 3 vols., ed. D. H. Laurence (London: Max Reinhardt, The Bodley Head, 1981).

SHULL, P., *Music in the West* (Manhattan, Kan.: Sunflower University Press, 1983).

SMITH, A. M., 'Brass in Early Russia: From the Beginnings to the Birth of Victor Ewald', *Journal of the International Trumpet Guild*, 18/2 (Dec. 1993), 4–20.

—— 'Victor Vladimirovich Ewald (1860–1935): Civil Engineer and Musician', *Journal of the International Trumpet Guild*, 18/3 (Feb. 1994), 4–23.

—— 'The Brassmen Who Changed Music in America after 1900: Jewish or Russian?', *Brass Player* (Spring 1996), 18 and 20.

SORENSON, S., and WEBB, J., 'The Harpers and the Trumpet', *Galpin Society Journal*, 39 (1986), 35–57.

Stalybridge Band, *Stalybridge Old Band* (Stalybridge: Geo. Whittaker and Sons, 1914).

TARR, E. H., 'The Romantic Trumpet', *Historic Brass Society Journal*, 5 (1993), 213–61; 6 (1994), 110–215.

TAYLOR, A., *Brass Bands* (St Albans and London: Granada Publishing, 1979).

—— *Labour and Love: An Oral History of the Brass Band Movement* (London: Elm Tree, 1983).

TAYLOR, G., *Companion to the Song Book of the Salvation Army* (London: Salvationist Publishing and Supplies Ltd, 1989).

TEMPERLEY, N., *The Music of the English Parish Church* (Cambridge: Cambridge University Press, 1979).

THOMSON, M., 'The National Youth Brass Band', *Musical Times*, 93 (1952), 493–5.

VERVAET, A., *The Effective Amateur Musician* (London: Studio Music Co., 1983).

VINCENT, C., and COPE, S., *The Brass Band and How to Write for it* (London(?): Winthrop Rogers Ltd., 1908).

WADE, R., *The First 100 Years of Brighouse and Rastrick Band* (Brighouse, W. Yorks.: Brighouse Echo, 1981).

WALMSLEY, T., *You and Your Band* (Methley, Leeds: Two Ways House, 1986).

WATERHOUSE, W., *The New Langwill Index: A Dictionary of Musical Wind-Instrument Makers and Inventors* (London: Tony Bingham, 1993).

WEBB, J., 'Designs for Brass in the Public Records Office', *Galpin Society Journal*, 38 (Apr. 1985), 48–54.

WICK, D., *Trombone Technique* (London: Oxford University Press, 1971; 2nd edn. Oxford: Oxford University Press, 1984).

WIGGINS, A. R., *Richard Slater: The Father of Salvation Army Music* (London: International Headquarters, 1945).

—— *The History of the Salvation Army*, iv and v (London: Nelson, 1964 and 1966). See Sandall for vols. i–iii and Coutts for vols. vi and vii.

WINSTON, D. H., 'Boozers, Brass Bands, and Hallelujah Lassies: The Salvation Army and American Commercial Culture 1880–1914', Ph.D. thesis, Princeton University, 1996.

WRIGHT, D., *Brass Band Tuning* (Gloucester: Wright and Round, 1933).

—— *Scoring for Brass Band* (Colne: Joshua Duckworth, 1935; 2nd edn., 1942; 4th edn., enlarged, London: Baker, 1967).

—— *The Brass Band Conductor* (Colne: Joshua Duckworth, 1948).

—— *The Complete Bandmaster* (London: Pergamon Press Ltd., 1963).

WRIGHT, F. (ed.), *Brass Today* (London: Besson and Co., 1957).

WRIGHT, T., and ROUND, H., *Wright and Round's Amateur Band Teacher's Guide and Bandsman's Adviser* (Liverpool: Wright and Round, 1889).

YOUNG, P. M., *A History of British Music* (London: Ernest Benn, 1967).

ZEALLEY, A. E., 'The Great British Brass Band Movement', *Étude*, 66 (1948), 534–5.

—— and ORD HUME, J., *Famous Bands of the British Empire* (London: J. P. Hull, 1926).

INDEX

'Abide with Me' 273
Accrington Band 36
Adkins, H. E. 153
Administrative Battalion Royal Sussex Royal
    Volunteer Regiment, 2nd 43
advertising 44
Ainscoe, Raymond 171
air varié 207, 262, 288
A.L. of South Shields 107
Alcock, Revd. J. P. 147
Alexander Owen Memorial Scholarship
    83
Allen, George:
    Wizard, The 258
Allendale Saxhorn Band 173
Alpine Echoes 96
Alston, Edith 81
alt horn 162
Alwyn, William:
    Moor of Venice, The 264
Amateurs' Brass Band Quartets, The 55
Americanization:
    of British culture 112
    of popular music 102–9
Anderson, Betty 80, 81
Arararat Citizens' Band (Victoria) 237
Arban, J.-B.:
    Grande méthode complète 298
Archer, A.:
    *Arrival of William IV and Queen Adelaide
        at 'The Friars' Lewes* 141, 142
Arnold, Sir Malcolm:
    English Dances 264
    Fantasy 267
    Little Suites 267
Arts Council 113
Arundel band 43
Ashford Town Band 146
Atkins, Wulstan 255

Bach, J. S. 260, 261
    Mass in B minor 26
Bacup Band 61
Bacup Old Band 41, 42
Baglyn, Lyndon 301

Bain, Jock 106
Baker, Kenny 120
Ball, Eric 40, 257, 258–60, 261, 264, 267,
    271, 274
    Eternal Presence, The 274
    Exodus 210
    Resurgam 96, 213, 259
    Songs in the Morning 210
Ball, Michael 274
    Chaucer's Tunes 274
    Frontier! 274
    Midsummer Music 274
    Whitsun Wakes 274, 277
Bandmaster 281
Bandsmen's College of Music 83
bandsmen's registers 8, 83
Bandstand 276–7
Bantock, Sir Granville 122, 250, 259
    Festival March 95
    Frogs, The 264
    Lalla Rookh 253
    Oriental Rhapsody 253
    Prometheus Unbound 257
    Sons of Liberty 95
Barkel's band 234
Barlow, Harry 294
Barr, Willie 301
Barratts of Manchester Ltd 184
Bartók, Bela 132, 265, 267, 269
Barton Hall Works Band 271
Barton's Band 108
bass horn 157–8
bass trombone 178, 302
basses 168–9
bass-Tuba 168
Bath, Hubert 112, 249
    Freedom 111, 249
Batley Band 89
Battersea Grammar School 76
Batty's Menagerie Band 22
Bayley's Acoustic Cornet 178
BBC 85, 93, 94, 104, 116, 276–7
BBC Festival of Brass 277
BBC Military Band 276
BBC Welsh Orchestra 302

Beatles, The:
  'Penny Lane' 304
Bedford, David:
  Toccata for Tristan 277
Beecham, Sir Thomas 111, 112
Beethoven, L. van 21, 57, 245, 260, 261, 267
  Eroica Symphony 129
Ninth Symphony 272
Beevers of Huddersfield 110
Beiderbecke, Bix 103
Belle Vue contests 6, 7, 44, 50, 52, 73, 90,
  173, 246, 328–53
  1855 60
  1864 64
  1873 173
  1952 90
Bellini, Vincenzo:
  I Puritani 24
  'Suona le Tromba' 24
Bendigo (Victoria) Municipal Band 239
Benjamin, George:
  Altitude 272
Bennet, Sir Richard Rodney:
  Flowers of the Forest 277
Bentham, Percy 257
Berlin valve 166
Berlioz, Hector:
  Judges of the Secret Court 264
Bernstein, Leonard 266
Berryman, John 301
Besses o' th' Barn 21, 47, 52, 57, 93, 176,
  229, 246, 250, 270, 273, 278, 283, 284,
  291, 294
  Articles of the Stand Band 48
Besses o' th' Barn Old Band Union Limited
  48
Besson, F. 171
Besson & Co. 43, 45, 166, 176, 178, 179,
  182
Besson & Son 180
Besson prototype band instruments 45
Bickershaw 108
bicycle bands 227
Bingham, Judith:
  Four Minute Mile, Prague 277
Birkenshaw, George Fred:
  'Jenny Jones' 290
Birtwistle, Sir Harrison 272, 304
  Grimethorpe Aria 272
  Salford Toccata 272, 275
Bishop, Sir Henry 57
Black Dike, *see* Black Dyke
Black Dyke Mills Band 35–6, 47, 75, 76, 93,
  108, 176, 268, 273, 275, 278, 279, 301,
  303, 305
Black Dyke Mills band books 55
Blackett, Bill 118

Blacking, John 145
Blackman and Pace 27
Blaikley, David James 180
Bliss, Arthur 69, 111, 122, 259, 304
  Belmont Variations, The 264
  Checkmate 257, 264
  Kenilworth 95, 257
Blow, John 13
Blühmel, Friedrich 161, 165
Boddice, Jack 99
Boddington, Stanley 74
Bombarbon 168
Boosey, Charles 63
Boosey & Co. 43, 54, 171, 176, 177, 179,
  180, 182
Boosey & Hawkes 99, 176, 180, 183, 213,
  214, 215, 302
Boosey's Brass Band Journal 282
Booth, Ballington 191
Booth, Catherine 189, 196, 197
Booth, Evangeline 210
Booth, William 189, 190, 192, 193, 195,
  196, 197, 201, 202, 203, 205
  'O Boundless Salvation' 271
Booth, William Bramwell 194, 203, 205
Borland, John 76
  Musical Foundations 76
Bottomley, Owen 93
Boult, Sir Adrian 113, 222
Bourdieu, Pierre 129, 132
Bourgeois, Derek 272
  Blitz 272
  Diversions 272
  Forest of Dean, The 272
Bourne, H. 141
Bourton Band 98
Bousfield, Ian 294
Bowen, Greg 301
Bowles, George J. 134
Bradford Brass Band 44
Bradford Brass Band Contest Regulations
  1860 50
Bradford Park Band Committee 86
Brahms, Johannes 25, 269, 274
  Academic Festival Overture 263–4
  Tragic Overture 264
Brand, Geoffrey 269, 270, 276
Brandon Silver Band 99
brass and wind band 3
Brass Band Instruments Ltd. 184
Brass Band Journal 63
Brass Band Magazine 55
Brass Band News 87, 295
Brassed off 1–2, 4
Bravington, Eric 301
Brecknock Estate Silver Band 81
Brier, James 73, 82, 111

Brighouse and Rastrick 86, 93, 98
Britannia Coconut Dancers 152
British Bandsman 63, 67, 69, 70, 71, 73, 77,
    81, 83, 84, 87, 91, 94, 98, 99, 106, 108,
    111, 117, 135, 152, 246, 247, 260, 292,
    295, 303
British Open Championship, *see* Belle Vue
    contests
Britten, Benjamin:
    Young Person's Guide to the Orchestra
    271
Broadbent, Derek 303
Broadwood Piano Factory 45
Broken Hill Proprietary Company 233
Brown Brothers Iron Mill 18–19
Brown, William 171
Brownlee, John 221
bugle 25, 29
    keyed 26, 158–9
Bulch's band 234
Burney, Charles 14
Burrell, Sir Walter W. 21, 140, 147
Burstow, Henry 141, 144
Burton Constable contest:
    1844 6
    1845 169
Bury, Lord 40, 42
Bury Report 40
Butler, George 171
Butterworth, Arthur 273
    Odin 273

Callender's Cable Works Band 73, 74, 110,
    116
Calvert, Eddie 120
Cambridgeshire RVC, 2nd, Band of 39
Canal Ironworks Band 80
Canterbury Cathedral Inventory (1752) 13
Cardiff Canton (Salvation Army) Corps 202
Carleton, Commissioner John 205
Carlisle St Stephen's Band 72, 254, 294
Carnival of Venice 96, 298
Carpenter, Gary:
    Chi 277
Carpenter, General George 210
Carte, Rudall 178
Caruso, Enrico 249
Catelinet, Philip 262
    Glorious Hope, A 210
    Weber 210
Chalk Farm (Salvation Army) Corps 202
Chalk, Gordon 221
Champion Brass Band Journal 54, 61, 62
Chappell, S. A. 176
Chappell's 54, 63
Cheltenham International Festival 268
Cheshire Rifles Volunteer Band, 3rd 39

Chester, Jerome 84
Chesterfield Volunteer Band, 6th 31
Childe, William 162
Childs, Robert 277
Chisholm, George 301
Christchurch Bicycle Band 227
church bands 15–18, 125, 137, 146
cinema 102
City of Coventry band 74
City Royal Brass Band 36
civic culture function 89
Clapton corps 202
Clarke, Herbert C. 291
Clarke, Jeremiah 13
Clarke, Nigel 275, 277
    Mechanical Ballet 275
clavicor 162, 163
Clayton Aniline band 75
Clegg, John 48
Clegg's Reed Band 48
Clifton, Thomas 19
Clydebank Burgh 94
Coates, Eric 253
Cobden-Chevalier Treaty 1860 43
Cochran, C. B.:
    First Shoot, The 272
Cocks, Robert, & Company 27, 55
Code, Percy 222, 229
Code's band 234
Coldstream Guards Band 16
Cole, Grace 80
Coles, Bramwell 210
Collingwood Citizens Band 239
Compensating Pistons 180
concert bands 87
concert giving 87–9
concert-going 31
concertina 149–50
concerts, income from 46
Conn, C. G. 302
conservatoires 275
Consett (Salvation Army) Corps 191
Constable, Lady 6
Constable, Sir Clifford 6
contest rules 317–26
contesting 90–3, 249–58
    Australia 235–7
    organization of 7–8, 82–4
    origins of 5–7
    rules and regulations 7
    see also under names
contralto saxhorn 166
Cooke's Equestrian Circus 22
Cope, Sam 67, 253
Copland, Aaron 266
cornet 161, 167
cornet-à-pistons 161

cornett 13
cornopean 161, 162
Cornopean Companion of Scales, The 27
Cornophones 176
Cornsay 97
Cory Band 303
cost of musical instruments 43, 155, 306–11
Cotton, Billy 106
Courtois 166, 175, 176, 184
Couturier, Ernst Albert 44
Crawshay, Robert Thompson 20–1, 27, 32, 33, 46, 283
Crichton, James 234
Croke, Leo:
    Standard Directory of Brass and Military Bands, The 71
Crookes Band 108
Crossley Carpet Works band 75
Croydon Advertiser 116
Croydon (Salvation Army) Corps 202
Crystal Palace Company 7
Crystal Palace contest 7, 31, 50, 51, 52, 59, 64, 171, 172, 173, 327
Cundell, Edric:
    Blackfriars 264
Curwen, Frederick 221
Cyfarthfa Band 20, 57, 61, 62, 164, 176, 278, 283
Cyfarthfa Band books 58, 283–4

D'Almaine 43, 63
D'Almaine and Jordan 155
Daily Herald 83, 84, 88, 91, 110, 115
Dalby, Martin:
    Music for a Brass Band 267
dance band 86
dance band music 58, 102, 104–7
dance halls 103
Darlington Temperance Brass Band 172
Darwen Temperance Band 172
Davey, Mrs Captain Abram 197
Deptford Pier Saxhorn Band 31–2
Design Act 1843 30
designs of brass instruments 30–1
    see also Ch. 4
Dewhurst, Isaac 31
Dickens, Charles:
    'A Musical Prize Fight' 66
Dickenson, John 301
Distins 30, 54, 55, 58, 175
Distin, Henry 169, 171
Distin, John 11, 16, 43
Distin family 24, 27, 44, 168, 169
Distin family quintet 170
Distin's Brass Band Journal 282
Distin's Equisonant Pistons 177
Distin's Journal 54

Dobcross Band 38, 79
Don Pedro's Mexicans 86
Donizetti, Gaetano:
    Lucia di Lammermoor 58
Donne, John 275
Douglas, Shipley:
    Mephistopheles 258
Drummond, Sir John 277
Duke of Lancaster's Own Yeoman Cavalry Band 21
Durham Miners' Association 117

East India Brigade Band 22
East Lancashire Regiment, 30th 16
East London Christian Mission 189, 192
    see also Salvation Army
Eastbourne Council 87
Eby, Walter M. 300
Eby's Complete Scientific Method for Cornet and Trumpet 298
economics of banding 40, 43–7, 98–9, 238–9
Edgerton, Lord Francis (1st Earl of Ellesmere) 21
Edwards, Jimmy 115
Eight Hours Day Movement 241–3
electro-silverplating (ESP) 45
Eley 22
Elgar, Alice 249
Elgar, Carice 249
Elgar, Sir Edward 110, 112, 122, 249, 253, 254–6, 258, 260, 263, 264, 304
    Enigma Variations 264
    Severn Suite 95, 111, 182, 254–5
Ellerby, Martin 277
Elliot, J. H. 69, 72, 80, 104, 111, 247, 254
Ellis, George 61
Enfield (Salvation Army) Corps 202
Enharmonic Valves 180, 181
Epps, Mr 147
Esh Winning 97
Eskdale, George 294, 301
euphonium 28, 170, 181
Ezzard, Bert 301

Fairey Aviation Works Band 296
Fantasia on Scotch Airs 163
Farley, Mr 146
Farr, Ray 164–5, 264
Feldman 108
Ferodo Works Band 75
Fields, Gracie 116
Fife Artillery Volunteers, 5th, Band of 39
Fifeshire Light Horse VC, 1st 40
Finger-Slide valves 168
Firbeck Colliery Band 80

Fletcher, Percy 253
  Epic Symphony 96, 250, 257
  Heroic March 253
  Labour and Love 95, 96, 247–8
flugel horn 169, 170
Flush Mills Band 38
Foden's Motor Works Band 76, 250, 278,
  296
folk music 122–3
football, impact of 101
Forbes Municipal Band 240
Forbes Town Band 239
Formby, George 116
Foster, John 35, 75
Fox, Roy 106
French horn 157
Friary Brewery Band 73
Frichot, Louis Alexandre 158
Froggitt, W. 31
Frost & Son, J. 61
Fry, Bert 190
Fry, Charles 190
Fry, Ernest 190
Fry, Fred 190, 200
Fry family 205
Fuller, George 210

Gabrieli, Giovanni 275
Gainsborough Britannia Band 80
garrison bands, New Zealand 233–5
Garside, Derek 301
Gautrot 177
Gay, Bram 255, 264
Geehl, Henry 249, 254, 255, 259, 264
  'For you alone' 249
  Normandy 250
  Oliver Cromwell 250
  Threnody 250
Geelong Harbour Band 238
geography of banding 72–4, 100, 148
Gilbert, W. S. 95
Gilmore, Patrick 3, 44
Gisborne, James 171
Gisborne & Co. 176
Gladney, John 11, 16, 57, 61, 62, 144, 283,
  287
Glazebury bands 71
Godfrey, Charles 16, 63, 246
Godfrey, Dan 16
Godfrey, Fred 63
Godfrey family 63
Goffin, Sir Dean 210, 261
  *Rhapsodic Variations—My Strength, My
    Tower* 262
  Rhapsody in Brass 261
Goldsmith, Arthur 200, 208
  Rocksmith 208

Goose Eye band books 55
Gourlay, James 275
Graham Peter 277
Grainger, Percy 264
Granada Band of the Year Contest 276
Grange, Philip:
  Lowry Dreamscape 277
Gravesend Workers' Band 118
Great Exhibition (1851) 58
Green, John, of London 179
Greenhill 171
Greenwood, J. A. 110
Gregson, Edward 210, 261, 269, 275
  Clarinet Concerto 269
  Concertante 266
  Connotations 269
  Dances and Arias 269
  Essay 269
  Of Men and Mountains 269–70
  Plantagenets 269
  Partita 269
  Patterns 269
  Trumpet Concerto 269
Grimethorpe Colliery Band 264, 271, 272,
  277, 278, 304
Grove's Dictionary of Music and Musicians
  10–11, 110
Grund, Alfred, and Son 48
Guichard 162, 168
Guildhall School of Music and Drama 294
Guillaume, Edmé 157
Guy, John 86

Haines, Cliff 301
Halary, J. H. A. 159, 160, 161, 171
Haliday, Joseph 158
Halifax Courier 35
Hall, Ernest 300, 304
Hall, Reg 150
Hallé Orchestra 295
Halliday, Joseph 27
Hamilton Citizens Band 232, 235
Handel, G. F. 14
  See the Conquering Hero Comes 93
Hardy, Cliff 301
Harper, Thomas 22, 23
  Airs 27
  Instructions for the Trumpet 28
Harper, Thomas John 22, 23
  Harper's School for the Cornet-à-pistons
    28
Harris Departmental Committee 42
Harrison, Gerald 276
Harton Colliery Band 87, 99, 117, 118
Harty, Hamilton 295
Haweis, Reverend H. R. 32
Hawick Saxhorn Band 170

Hawker, Willie 48
Hawkes, Fred 200, 207, 208, 209, 210
  Rousseau 208
Hawkes & Son 171, 176, 180, 182
Hay, James 207
Haydn, Joseph 57
  March for the Prince of Wales 16
  Marches for the Derbyshire Cavalry Regiment 16
  Trumpet Concerto 27
Heath, Ted 120, 301
Heaton, Wilfred 261, 262, 266, 277
  Contest Music 266, 268–9
  Partita 269
  Toccata, Glory Glory 269
  Victory for Me 269
Hebburn 97
helicon 169
Helston Furry Dance 152
Hendon (Salvation Army) Corps 202
Henze, Hans Werner 304
  Ragtimes and Habaneras 272
Hepplestone and Charlesworth, Messrs 228
Herbage, Julian 257
Herd, Thomas 228, 229, 234
Hesling, William 61
Hetton band 117
Heywood, Dawn 120
Hibberd, Stuart 93
Higginbottom, Gordon 301
Higham, Joseph 30, 43, 44, 62, 165, 171, 176, 177, 179, 182
Higham's Clear Bore pistons 177
Hill, Henry 200
Hind, Harold 76, 88
  Brass Band, The 111
Hinde, Joan 120
Hindemith, Paul 267, 269, 271
Hinemoa Band 229
hire-purchase schemes 44
Hobsbawm, Eric 67
Hogarth, George 32
Holbrooke, Joseph 250
  Clive of India 253
Holgate, Mildred 80
Holgate, Percy 80
Holloway, Robin:
  From Hills and Valleys 274
  War Memorials, Men Marching 274
Holst, Gustav 110, 253–4, 258, 259, 262, 263, 264
  Moorside Suite, A 95, 122–3, 154, 254
Holst, Imogen 253

Holz, Ronald 208
horn 12, 13
  alt 162
  bass 157–8
  flugel 169, 170
  french 157
Horovitz, Joseph:
  Ballet for Band 270
  Euphonium Concerto 270
  Sinfonietta 270
  Theme and Co-operation 270
Horsham Town band 141, 144
Horwich RMI Band 118
Houghton band 117
Howard, Jack 113
Howarth, Elgar 261, 264, 271, 275, 303, 304
  Ascendit in Coeli 272
  Bandsman's Tale, The 271
  Fireworks 271
  Five Pieces for Spielberg 272
  Hymns at Heaven's Gate 272
  In Memoriam RK 271
  Songs for BL 272, 277
Howarth, Oliver 271
Howarth, Stanford 271
Howe's Great London Circus 22
Howells, Herbert 122, 253, 262, 272
  Dance before the Lord 273
  Pageantry 257
  Three Figures 264
Hughenden Town Band 237–8
Hughes, Sam 28
Hyde, John 26
Hylton, Jack 106

Idle and Thackley Band 48, 49, 99
Iles, John Henry 7, 83, 91, 92, 96, 111, 229, 236, 246, 247, 253
Imperial Guild of Trumpeters and Kettledrummers 14
Ina Ray Hutton Band 81
India, brass bands in 3
Indiana Dance Band 86
instrument making 173–82
  improvements 177–81
  mass production 175–7
  mergers 182
  supply and use 171–3
instrumentation 4, 162–4, 287–8
  before nineteenth century 12–15
  for church bands 17
  earliest brass bands 155–6
  recent changes 182–5
  standardization of 140–4
Invercargill Garrison Band 218

Ireland, John 253, 256, 258
  Comedy Overture, A 256
  Downland Suite, A 95, 256
  London Overture, A 257
  Moorside Suite, A 256
  Piano Concerto 256
Irwell Springs Band 176

Jackson, Brian 80, 120
Jackson, Enderby 5–6, 7, 18–19, 22, 27, 34,
  49, 50, 51, 59–61, 171, 173
  Bristol Waltzes 61
  'Origin and Promotion of Brass Band
    Contests' 18
  Venetian Waltzes 61
  Volunteer Quadrille 61
  Yorkshire Waltzes 60, 61
Jackson, Harold 301
James, Harry 301
James, Ifor 270, 294
jazz 103, 105–6, 109
Jenkins, Cyril 222
  Coriolanus 249
  Life Divine 249, 250
Jennison, John 6, 48
John Foster and Son Black Dyke Mills Band,
  see Black Dyke Mills Band
John White Footwear band 75
Jones, Frederick 154
Jones, Griffith Rhys (Caradog) 92
Jones, J. G. 63
Jones, Percy 229
Jones, Roland 108
journal music 47
Joy Strings, The 213
Jullien, Louis 11, 23, 24, 54, 58, 59,
  169

Kappey, J. A. 10–11
Keighley, Dr Thomas 253
  Macbeth 96
Kelly, Bryan:
  Divertimento 267
Kempe, Rudolf 271
Kenney, Arthur 303
Key & Co. 171
Kibblesworth 97
Kidson, Frank 123
Kingston Mills Band 47, 52, 176
Kippax Old Band 98
Kirkby, Edward 19
Klappentrompete 27
Know, Ralph H. 42
Koenig 55, 58, 65
Koenig Horns 175–6
Köhler 31, 166, 168, 178

La Trobe, J. A. 17, 137–8
Lafosse, André 300
Laird, Michael 304
Lalo:
  Roi d'Ys, Le 264
Lancashire Rifle Volunteer Corps, 4th 40, 41,
  42
Lander, R. C. 117
Lang, Willie 85, 110, 301, 305
Langey, Otto:
  Complete Method 300
Langford, Gordon 266
Lawther, William 117
Lear, Thomas:
  Shylock 296
learning styles 144–5
Lee, Thomas 21, 48
Leeton District Band 240
Leicester Imperial 80
Leidzén, Erik 210
Len Colvin and his Denza Players 107
Lewes Town Band 141, 142
Lewis, J. 147
Lindley Band 120
Linthwaite Band 61
Listen to the Band (BBC) 276
Liszt, Franz 249, 250, 262
Lithgow, Alexander 229
Livesey, George 62, 284
Llandudno Promenade Band 46
Llanelly Band 46
Llanelly Silver 107
Lloyd, George:
  Diversion on a Bass Theme 270
  English Heritage 270
  Royal Parks 270, 277
Lodge:
  Brass Band at a Glance, The 57
Longmire, John 256
Lostwithiel Band 116
Lumley Band 117
Lusher, Don 301
Luton Red Cross Band 72, 73, 74
Lynn Working Men's Band 36

McCabe, John 270
  Cloudcatcher Fells 270
  Images 270
McCann, Phillip 301
McDermott, K. H. 16, 17
MacDonnal, J. R. A. 42
MacFarlane 31
  Eight Popular Airs for Brass Band 27,
  54
Mackintosh, Jack 93, 102, 297–9
  'Cowboy' cadenzas 297–8

McLeavy, Johnny 301
McQuater, Tommy 301
Maelor Brass Band League 47
Mahler, Gustav 269, 271
Malvern Tramways Band 223, 229, 233, 238
Mann, Tom 241
Marriner, W. L. 21, 38
Marriner's Band, W. L. 21, 46, 48, 54, 173
Marriner's Caminado Band, W. L. 49
Marriner's Private Brass Band, W. L. 173
Marsden, Denis 80
Marsden Colliery Band 99, 117
Marsden Senior School Band 76
Marshall, George 210
Mason, David 304
Maxwell Davies, Peter 304
Mayers and Harrison, Messrs 182
Mead, Steven 277
Méhul, E. N.:
    Joseph and his Brothers 247
Melling, James 6, 31, 48, 52, 59
    Orynthia 48, 60
Melody Maker 105, 107
Meltham Mills Band 62
Mere Band 86
Metzler & Co. 171, 173, 175
Meyerbeer, Giacomo 21
Middlesex Engineer Volunteer Corps, 1st 40
Middlesex Rifles Volunteer Band, 16th 38
Middlesex RVC, 2nd 42
Mid-Sussex and Southwater Benefit
    Association 137
military bands and bandmasters 3, 15–18,
    62–4
    see also Regular Army bands
Militia Act 1852 36
militia bands 15, 17
Millington, William:
    *Sketches of Local Musicians and Musical
    Societies* 16
miners' strike (1926) 100
Morgan, Ieuan 79
Morgan, Tom 109–10
Moritz, Carl Wilhelm 166, 168
Morris Motors Band 74
Morris, Edwin Vaughan 84
Mortimer, Alex 292, 296
Mortimer, Fred 73, 112, 250, 296
Mortimer, Harry 93, 94, 106, 116, 236, 261,
    272, 273, 276, 295, 296–7, 299
    Eternal Presence 259
    Festival Music 259
    Journey into Freedom 259
    Indian Summer 259
    Mack and Mort 297
    Song of Courage, A 259
Mortimer, Rex 296

Mortimer family 169, 303
Mossley Amateur Brass Band 173
Mossley Temperance Band 169
Mount Lyell Mining Company 233
Mozart, W. A. 57, 260, 261
    Don Giovanni 33
municipal support 239–40
Munn and Felton Band 74, 108
Murphy, Maurice 120, 301, 305
Murray, Charles E. 38
Musgrave, Thea:
    Variations 267
music education 31
music teachers 31
musical literacy 130–6
Musical Times 63, 76, 95, 110, 111, 116
Musicians' Union 118
Mussorgsky, Modest:
    Pictures at an Exhibition 264

Nash, Harold 294
National Band Festival 1938 91
National Brass Band Club 83, 94
National Brass Bands Federation 83
National contests 7, 8, 91, 93, 246–9,
    328–53
    see also Crystal Palace contests
National School Brass Band Association 76
National Youth Brass Band of Great Britain
    77, 81, 260, 273
New Imperial Dance Orchestra 107
New South Wales Band Association 232
Newcastle Steelworks band 229, 233
Newcomb, Stanley 223
Newsome, Roy 273, 303
Newton, Edward 61
Nielsen, Carl 267
no (non-) pressure method 300–1
notation, musical 130–6
Novello, Ivor:
    Dancing Years 95
number of bands 69–72
Nuttall, Harry 90
Nuttall, Harvey 80
'N.V.A.' (New Valve Action) 177
Nye, James 142

Ockenden Band 140, 147
Ogden, J. T. 73
Old Philharmonic Pitch 183
Oldham band 42
Oldham Rifles 42
old-tyme dancing 103
One Thousand Guinea Trophy 91, 92
Open Championship, *see* Belle Vue contests
ophicleide 27–8, 29, 159–61, 285
Orange Grand Black Chapter 39

Orchard, W. A. 223
Ord Hume, James 57, 228, 246, 258
  Brilliant 258
Order of Druids' Brass Band Contest 1863
  173
Orwell, George 112
Overton, William 294
Owen, Alexander 11, 42, 57, 61, 62, 112,
  144, 167, 222, 229, 246, 250, 283, 284,
  287

Pace, Charles 43, 168, 170
Pace, G. H. 179
Pace, Matthew 159
Paganini 262, 274
Paley, John 301
Palings 228, 231
Parc and Dare Band 294
Parkes, Peter 303
Parkinson, Patricia 80
Parry, J.:
  Brass Band, The 54
Parry, Joseph 61
  Tydfil Overture, The 61, 95, 249
Partington family 222
Patent Level instruments 168
patronage 21–2, 34, 46, 75
Patterson, Paul:
  Cataclysm 273
Payne, Anthony:
  Fire on Whaleness 272
Payne, Jack 104
Pearce, Arthur O. 110
Peel, Jonathan 37, 39
Pendleton Brass Band 45
Penrith Volunteer Band 38
Percival 170
percussion 184–5
Perfection Soap Works band 71
Performing Right Society (PRS) 85
Périnet, Etienne François 166
Perkin, Helen 256
Perry, J. 61
Pettit, Beatrice 65, 66
Phasey, Alfred 28
Philip Jones Brass Ensemble 264, 304,
  305
Phillips, Frank 93
Pickard, John 277
Pinches, Harold 301
piston valve 25, 166–7
pitch 25, 183–4, 302
playing styles, *see* Ch. 8
Pontybederyn 19
Poole Town 86
Popowitz, Herr 22
Post Horn Gallop 23, 65

Potter, Dennis:
  Man of Brass 115
Preston United Independent Harmonic Brass
  Band 19, 20
Pridham, J.:
  *Great International Exhibition Quadrille,
  The* 58
Professional Musicians Band, Sydney 228,
  243
Professional Musicians Union 242–3
Prokofiev, Sergey 271
Prospère (Jean Prospère Guivier) 23, 28
Prout's Band 234, 241
Pryor, Arthur 291
Purcell, Henry 13, 274–5
  Three Parts on a Ground 275
Purcell, Daniel 13

Queenstown (Tasmania) Band 233
quick-step march contest 236–7

Radio Luxembourg 104
Radio Telefis Eireann 103
ragtime 106
Rankl, Karl 113
Ravel, Maurice 264
  Daphnis and Chloë 264
Rawsthorne, Alan:
  Suite 267
Redhead, Robert:
  Isaiah 213
registers of bandsmen 8, 83
Regular Army bands 15
repertoire 53–62, 94–6
  see also Ch. 7
Repertory for Cornet and Piano 54–5
Respighi, Ottorino:
  Pines of Rome, The 264
  Roman Festivals 264
Richards, Goff 266
Riedl, Joseph 165
Rifle Volunteer Corps 38
Rifle Volunteer Corps Band, 35th 38
Riley's band 234
Rimmer, William 16, 258
  Cossack, The 258
Rimsky-Korsakov 249
Rivière & Hawkes 171
Robinson, Peter 30, 177
Roderick, Stan 301
Rose, Algernon 44, 45–6, 278
  Talks with Bandsmen 45
Rossini, Gioachino 285
  Moses in Egypt 247
rotary valve 165–6
rotundas 220, 240
Round, Henry 55

Royal Academy of Music 294
Royal College of Music 129, 294
Royal Military School of Music 63
Royal Opera House 28
Rubbra, Edmund 264
    Sh*ining River, The* 263
Rudall Carte & Co. 182
Rudall, Rose, Carte & Co. 168, 171
rugby, impact of 101
Russell, J. F. 111

S.E.R. Company 146
S.P.S. Ltd., *see* Salvation Publishing and
    Supplies Ltd
sackbut 13
St Anne's Sunday School Whit Walk 89
St Augustine's Band (Geelong) 230
St George's Works Brass Band, Lancaster 46,
    49
St Hilda Band 73, 88, 93, 99, 106, 113, 117,
    118, 292, 294, 301
St Hilda Colliery Band 100
St Hilda Professional Band 299
St Vincent Boys' Band 230
Salford University Brass Band 275
Salt, Titus 35, 61
Saltaire Band 35, 61
Salvation Army 138, 152, 182, 183,
    187–216, 221, 228, 260–1, 291, 294,
    302
    abuse of 199–200
    in Australia 226
    bandmasters 316
    Bandsmaster's Correspondence Course
        209
    Bandsmen's Council 209
    Festival series 206, 210
    Gospel Meetings 206
    Holiness Meetings 206
    Household Troops Band 201, 202, 208
    instrument factory 200, 201, 214–15
    instrumentation 198
    International Headquarters Music Board
        203
    International Staff Band 183, 202, 203–4,
        206, 209–10, 260, 262
    lifeguards band 201
    Music Board 209, 213
    Order for Salvation Army bands 312
    Orders and Regulations for Field Officers
        (Salvation Army) 194–6, 203
    Praise Meetings 206
    Salvation Meetings 206
    statistics 312–14
    Triumph series 182, 210
    Unity series 182, 210
    women in 196–7

Salvation Army War Chariot 216
Salvationist Publishing & Supplies Ltd (The
    Trade Department; S.P.S. Ltd) 188, 215,
    260, 261
Samson, George 168
Samson valves 168
Sarasate, Pablo:
    Zigeunerweisen 301
Savoy Havana Band 104
Sawer, David:
    Hell-noise 277
Sax, Adolphe 11, 24, 27, 28, 31, 59, 163,
    166, 168, 169, 171
saxhorns 24, 169–70
    contralto 166
    tenor 166, 175
Scarborough Spa Band 61
Schiller:
    'Ode to Joy' 272
Schoenberg, Arnold 265, 271
school bands 76–7, 230
Schubert, Franz 260, 261, 264
Scoll, A. 32
Scoll's Operatic 32
Scott, James 303
Scottish Amateur Music Association
    267
Scout movement 102
seaside entertainment 87
sergeant trumpeter, office of 14
serpent 157–8
Shaw, George Bernard 138, 254, 255
Shaw, John 167
Shaw valves 167–8
Shepherd, James 301
Shostakovich, Dmitry 271
    Gadfly, The 264
Shugg, Harry 229, 238
Sibelius, Jean 249, 260, 267, 273
Silbron valve pistons 177
Silvani and Smith 44
silver band 45, 177
Simpson, Robert 245, 261, 267, 269
    Energy 267
Singleton Town Band (New South Wales)
    239
Skeleton Army 199, 200
Slater, Richard 200, 201, 205, 207, 208,
    291
    Jesus, Hope of Souls Repentant 208
Sloan, Major 40
Smith, Richard 55, 61, 62, 137, 255
    Bonnets of Blue 55
    Light Horseman, The 55
    Lily Bell 55
    Morning Star Polka 55
    Rock Villa Polka 55

Smith, Richard, and Company 91, 116, 171, 246, 260, 269
Smyth, James 63
Snell, Howard 264, 275, 303, 304
  Folk Festival 264
social class 32–3, 64–7, 77–80, 151
Söderström, Emil 210
Solbron valve pistons 177
sonorophones 173, 175
Sousa, John Philip 3, 210
  Salvation Army, The 210
sousaphone 169
Souster, Tim:
  Echoes 273
South Devon Militia 16
South Street contest, Ballarat, Australia 218, 222, 228, 231, 232
South Yorkshire Railway Company's Brass Band 172
Southern, Jimmy 88, 118
Southowram Band 89, 108
Southport Parks Committee 87
S.P.&S. Band 260
Sparke, Philip 266
  Between the Moon and Mexico 266
  Harmoniemusik 266
  Variations on an Enigma 266
  Year of the Dragon 266
Spohr 21
sport, impact of 101–2
Stalybridge Old Band 31, 59
Stamp, Jesse 294
Stand Band 48
Stanford, Sir Charles 249, 259
Stanley Band 80
Steadman-Allen, Ray 208, 210, 261, 262, 266, 273, 274
  Chorales and Tangents 266
  Christ is the Answer 266
  Holy War, The 273
  Hymn at Sunrise 273
  Lord is King, The 273
  On Ratcliff Highway 273, 274
Steele-Perkins, Crispian 304
Sterling Musical Instruments Ltd. 184
Stölzel, Heinrich 161, 164–5, 168
Stourton Memorial Band 98
Straughan, W. R. 117
Strauss, Richard 271
Stravinsky, Igor 265, 269, 271
  Firebird, The 264
  Rite of Spring, The 129
  Soldier's Tale, A 271
Strutt, George 35
Strutt, Joseph 35
subscription bands 34–5, 36

Sullivan, Sir Arthur 95
  'Lost Chord, The' 57
Sullivan, Bert 301
Sussex Agricultural Express 140
Sutherland, Captain Thomas 228
Swift, Edwin 11, 57, 61, 62, 138, 144, 287
Swift, George 106, 301
swivel valves 167–8

Taylor, Arthur:
  Labour and Love 85
Teddy Joyce's Girl Friends 81
Templeton, Alec:
  Sonia 301
Tenor Cor 175
tenor trombone 178
tenor tuba (tenor saxhorn) 166, 175
test pieces, 1913 246–9
Tester, Scan 150
Thompson, Lieutenant Colonel J. A. 40
Tippett, Sir Michael:
  Festal Brass with Blues 272
  Third Symphony 272
Tooth's Brewery Band, Sydney 225, 231, 233, 235, 238
Tottenham corps 202
Tournaire's Circus 22
town bands 146
Trades Hall Band 241
Tramway Trust 233
Treorchy Youth Brass Band 79
Trimnel, Thomas Tallis 31
trombone 12, 13, 14, 25, 26, 156–7
  bass 178, 302
  tenor 178
  valve 157, 165, 173
Trombone Billy 150
trumpet 12, 13–14, 157
  keyed 27
  valve 28
trumpeters, regulatory systems for 14
tuba 168, 175
  tenor (tenor saxhorn) 166, 175
Tullis Russell Mills 294
Tully:
  Tutor for Keyed Bugle 27
Turner, John Alvey 65
Turner's Cornet Journal 65
Tutton, J. R. 63

unemployment 97, 100
uniforms 89, 110, 146
United Brass Band Association 235
United States of America:
  brass bands in 3
  Salvation Army in 216

Valentine, Thomas 52
valves 27, 285
  intonation and 44
  principle of 29
Vaughan Williams, Ralph 260, 262–3, 269, 270
  Henry V 262
  Preludes on Three Welsh Hymn Tunes 210, 262
  Variations for Brass Band 185, 262
Ventil Horns 175
Verbruggen, Henri 223
Verdi, Giuseppe 285
  Falstaff 274
  Forza del Destino, La 56, 264
  Grand March from Aida 299
  Il Trovatore 56
Versatile Brass 301
Victoria, Queen 21
Victorian Band Association 232
Victorian Boot Trade Band 241
Victorian Socialist League 241
Vienna valve 167
Vinter, Gilbert 265
  James Cook—Circumnavigator 265
  Salute to Youth 265
  Spectrum 185, 265
  Triumphant Rhapsody 265
  Variations on a Ninth 265
volunteer corps bands 15, 17, 35, 36–43, 194
  see also under individual bands
Volunteer Service Gazette 38, 39, 42

Waddell, James 173
Wadsworth, George 61
Wagner, Richard 176, 245, 250, 274
  Mastersingers Overture 264
waits 12–13, 14–15
Wakefield Foresters 172
Walker, Robin:
  Miners 277
Wallace, John 294
Wallsend Band 239
Walmsley, Trevor 93
Walton, Sir William 269, 272, 304
Wanganui Garrison Band 218, 234
Ward, Cliff 107
Watkins, Derek 301
Watson, James 275, 279, 303, 304
Watson, Ron 115
Weber, Carl 21
Webster, Thomas:
  Village Choir, The 141
Wellington Garrison Band 228, 234
Welsh Choral Union 92
Wessel & Co. 54, 55, 63
West Tarring church band, Sussex 143

West York R. V. Halifax, 4th 31
West Yorkshire Volunteer Fire Brigade Guards Band, 1st 38
West Yorkshire Volunteers Band, 34th 38
Wharton, Peter 35, 36
White, John 75
Whitehaven Band 38
Whiteley, Herbert 84, 247, 249, 253, 254
Whiteman, Paul 103
Wick, Dennis 304
wide-bore instruments 185
Wieprecht, Wilhelm 166, 168
Wiggins, Bram 301
Wigglesworth 171, 178
Wilby, Frank 107
Wilby, Philip 273, 274–5
  Masquerade 274
  New Jerusalem, The 274
  Paganini Variations 274, 277
  Revelation (Symphony for Double Brass after Purcell) 274
  Shadow Songs 273
Willcocks, Major George 303
Williams, Howard 272
Williams Fairey Engineering Band 272
Wills, Mr 146
Wills, W. H. 32
Wilson, Arthur 304
Wilson, Peter 70, 72
Wilson, Thomas 268
  Refrains and Cadenzas 268, 269
  Sinfonietta 267
Wilson, W.:
  Quadrille of All Nations 58
Windsor, Basil:
  Alpine Echoes 299
Wingates Temperance 98, 176
Winterbottom, W. 63
Wombwell Town Band 186
Wombwell's Circus and Menagerie 21, 22
women players 80–2, 196–7, 230
Wood, Gareth 266
Wood, Joe 85
Woodlands 97
Woodward, Captain 200
Worcestershire AV Band, 1st 39
works bands 74–6, 147, 233
World War One 90, 96, 103, 250
Wren, John 239
Wright and Round 47, 57, 62, 69, 70, 99, 287, 294
Wright, Denis 77, 111, 250, 258–9, 260, 261, 263, 276
  Cornet Concerto 261
  Joan of Arc 250
  Overture for an Epic Occasion 261
  Tam O'Shanter's Ride 261

Wright, Frank 96, 229, 256, 263, 264
  Brass Today 113
Wright, Kenneth 256, 276
Wright, Lawrence 105
Wright, T. H.:
  'Keel Row' 289
Wright, Thomas 55
Wyatt, W. 28
Wyke Temperance 52

Yamaha 184
Yeomanry and Volunteers Consolidation Act
  (1804) 37
York Citadel Salvation Army 183
York Rifle Volunteer Corps, 35th, Band of
  173
Yorkshire Imperial Band 274
Yorkshire Imperial Metals 294
youth bands 77, 84